OUTLINE OF
MODERN EUROPEAN
GOVERNMENTS
(*Visualized*)

by J. J. Wuest

About the Author

John J. Wuest, formerly with Pacific University, the University of Maryland, and Southern Illinois University, is currently on the staff of the Department of Political Science at Western Washington State College. He has lived and travelled extensively in Europe and has a wide experience both in teaching and research in comparative government. Among his recent publications are *The Primary Sources of American Government* and the *New Source Book in Major European Governments*.

Shepherd L. Witman has taught at Yale, Omaha, and Western Reserve Universities. He pioneered in the development of college outlines and visual aids in the teaching of political science, and his original edition of *Comparative Government, Visualized* (old title) received much acclaim for its originality and conciseness.

About the Book

1. *Outline of Modern European Governments (Visualized)* provides the most up-to-date review of the basic facts of the European governments that are most frequently studied in college courses. It includes forty-five well-drawn, easy-to-remember charts.
2. The material presented is a thorough revision of the authors' 1964 edition of *Comparative Government, Visualized*. A number of obsolete charts have been dropped, new charts added, and the charts have been simplified.
3. *Outline of Modern European Governments (Visualized)* is modestly priced so that each student may enjoy the convenience of supplementing his regular textbook with a factual and visual outline in an attractive format.

OUTLINE OF

MODERN EUROPEAN GOVERNMENTS

(Visualized)

by

John J. Wuest
and
Shepherd L. Witman

1968

LITTLEFIELD, ADAMS & CO.

Totowa, New Jersey

PRINTED IN THE UNITED STATES OF AMERICA

PREFACE

This book is intended to furnish both the college student and general reader with an introductory survey of modern European governments. It presents a systematic and balanced treatment of the essential and unique features of government, today, in (1) Great Britain, (2) the French Fifth Republic, (3) the Federal Republic of Germany, (4) the Union of Soviet Socialist Republics, (5) Italy, (6) Spain, (7) Sweden, (8) Switzerland, and (9) Turkey. Included in the Appendix are also the constitutions of the (10) German Democratic Republic, (11) Portuguese Republic, and (12) Kingdom of Denmark, which represent the basic law of a communist dictatorship, a fascist dictatorship, and a democratic, constitutional monarchy. Only limitations in purpose and space precluded additional coverage of the physical and cultural frameworks of reference in which the people of these States evolved—and now maintain and operate—their particular patterns of government.

There is an extensive list of carefully selected—and rather generally accessible—readings at the end of each chapter in this book. Students and readers who wish to pursue more intensively their study of some phase or aspect of the subject-matter are encouraged to avail themselves of this additional range of experience and authority and, thereby, further enrich their knowledge and understanding. The many charts accompanying this survey are intended also to convey principal points of interest and information to the reader. All chapters have been thoroughly revised and many sections—particularly in the chapters on Great Britain, French Fifth Republic, Federal Republic of Germany, Union of Soviet Socialist Republics, and Italy—have been greatly extended in light of new developments and recent circumstances.

The comparative tables and cross-reference reading guide at the front of the book provide the student and general reader with a synoptic view of all essential data with respect to the nine European States treated in detail in the text and direction to the most important textbooks in the field, with their interpretative analyses. These additional features should prove instructive and useful.

Special acknowledgment is here made of the friendly and generous assistance of various representations in this country of the States dealt with in compiling this book. In virtually every instance, the particular embassy, information office, or consulate provided the author with an official text of the country's constitution, organic and supplementary legislation, party platforms and electoral results, and other pertinent materials. These divers representations include the British Information Services; the Press and Information Service of the Embassy of France; the Press and Information Office of the German Federal Government; the Cultural Division of the Italian Embassy; the Embassy of the Union of Soviet Socialist Republics; the Diplomatic Information Office of Spain; the Embassy of Sweden; the Embassy of Switzerland; the Turkish Information Office; the Embassy of Portugal; the Embassy of Denmark. Particular assistance was extended by the French, West German, Italian, Swedish, and Swiss consulates in Seattle. Their unstinting help is much appreciated.

Lastly, I should like to thank several persons on the staff at Western Washington State College for the indispensable part they played in the new edition: Dean Herbert C. Taylor, Jr., and the Bureau for Faculty Research, for financial assistance; Dr. Manfred C. Vernon, Chairman of the Department of Political Science, for continued interest and encouragement in this work; and Mrs. Jane Clark, who supervised the typing and editing of the entire manuscript. As always, the author enjoys a most cordial relationship with the publishers.

JOHN J. WUEST
Bellingham, Washington

CONTENTS

CHARTS

OUTLINE OF
MODERN EUROPEAN
GOVERNMENTS

COMPARATIVE TABLE

Country	Capital	Area (sq. mi.)	Population	Language	Education	Social Welfare	Religion	Resources & Industries	Defense
GREAT BRITAIN	London	94,279	54,000,000 (1964)	English	Free Primary and Secondary. Compulsory from 5-15 years.	Comprehensive plan of social security.	Predominantly Protestant	Coal, limestone, iron ore. Heavy industries, manufacturing, and trade.	Compulsory male military service between ages of 18-26, for two years
FIFTH FRENCH REPUBLIC	Paris	212,659	48,500,000 (1964)	French	Free Primary and Secondary. Compulsory from 6-14 years.	Comprehensive plan of social security.	Predominantly Catholic	Coal, iron ore, oil. Chemical textiles, and automotive industries. Wines.	Compulsory male military service at age 20, for 18 months.
FEDERAL REPUBLIC OF GERMANY	Bonn	96,114	58,000,000 (1964)	German	Free Primary and Secondary. Compulsory from 6-14 years.	Fairly comprehensive plan of social security.	Protestant Catholic	Coal, iron ore. Steel, ship-building, machine industries. Special manufactures.	Compulsory male military service for one year.
UNION OF SOVIET SOCIALIST REPUBLICS	Moscow	8,646,400	235,000,000 (1965)	Russian. Many national languages	Free and Compulsory education, from 7-14/15/16 years.	Very comprehensive plan of social security.	Russian Orthodox Many other groups.	Coal, iron ore, oil, hydro-electric power. Heavy, food, and light industries.	Compulsory military service, at age 18/19, for 2/3/4/5 year.

ITALY	Rome	116,372	52,000,000 (1965)	Italian	Free Primary and Secondary. Compulsory from 6-14 years.	Comprehensive plan of social security.	Predominantly Catholic	Natural gas, some oil. Agricultural products, fruits and derivatives. Various industries.	Conscientious objection a crime. Compulsory male military service for 18 months.
SPAIN	Madrid	194,945	31,500,000 (1965)	Spanish	Free and Compulsory Primary Education, and some religious instruction.	Comprehensive plan of social security.	Predominantly Catholic	Coal, iron ore. Hydro-electric power. Textile industries. Agricultural products. Wines. Fishing.	Compulsory male service for two years.
SWEDEN	Stockholm	173,665	8,000,000 (1965)	Swedish	Free Primary and Secondary. Compulsory for 7/8/9 years.	Very comprehensive plan of social security.	Predominantly Protestant	Forests, iron ore, water power. Agricultural and dairy products. Various industries.	Compulsory male military service between ages 18-47 for 13 months.
SWITZERLAND	Berne	15,944	6,250,000 (1965)	French Italian German Romansch	Free Primary and Secondary. Compulsory for varying terms.	Comprehensive plan of social security.	Protestant Catholic	Water power. Salt. Dairy and agricultural products. Machine industries.	Compulsory male service National Militia between ages 20-61 for varying terms.
TURKEY	Ankara	296,503	30,500,000 (1964)	Turkish	Free and Compulsory Primary Education from 7-12 years.	Fairly comprehensive plan of social security.	Predominantly Moslem	Forests, coal, iron ore, oil, chrome. Textile industries. Agricultural products. Tobacco.	Compulsory male service at age 20; two years in land and air forces, three years in navy.

COMPARATIVE TABLE

Country	Constitution	Form of Government	Suffrage	Leading Parties	Legislature	Executive	Judiciary	Local Gov't.	International Organization
GREAT BRITAIN	Unwritten (Charters, Petitions, Statutes, Conventions)	Unitary, constitutional monarchy	Universal adult suffrage, age 21 years	Labour; Conservative; Liberal	Bicameral (House of Lords; House of Commons)	Hereditary Monarch Prime Minister Cabinet	House of Lords "Supreme Ct." of Judicature" (Ct. of Appeal High Ct. of Justice).	Counties Boroughs Districts Parishes London	United Nations North Atlantic Treaty Organization, etc.
FIFTH FRENCH REPUBLIC	Written 1958	Unitary Republic	Universal adult suffrage, age 21 years	Union for New Republic; Socialists; Demo. Center; Communists; Demo. Rally Ind. Republicans	Bicameral (Senate; Nat'l. Assem.)	President Premier Council of Ministers	High Council of the Judiciary; Court of Cassation; Council of State	Departments Communes Paris (Districts, Cantons)	UN NATO etc.
FEDERAL REPUBLIC OF GERMANY	Written 1949	Federal Republic	Universal adult suffrage, age 21 years	Christian Democrat Union; Social Democrat	Bicameral (Bundesrat; Bundestag)	President Chancellor The "Government"	Federal Constitutional Court; Supreme Federal Court	States Counties Communities	UN NATO etc.
UNION OF SOVIET SOCIALIST REPUBLICS	Written 1936, as amended	Federal Republic	Universal adult suffrage, age 18 years	Communist Party of USSR	Bicameral (Council of Nationalities; Council of the Union)	President Premier Council of Ministers	All-Union Supreme Court; Union-Republic Supreme Courts	Union Republics; Autonomous Rep Territories; Regions; Areas; Districts; Cities; Villages	UN Warsaw Pact etc.

ITALY	Written 1947	Unitary Republic	Universal adult suffrage, age 21 (Lower House), 25 (Upper House) Years	Christian Demos; Communists; Socialists & Social Movement	(Bicameral (Senate; Chamber of Deputies))	President Premier Council of Ministers	Constitutional Court; Superior Council of the Magistracy; Supreme Court of Cassation; Council of State	Regions Provinces Communes	UN NATO etc.
SPAIN	Written Charter of 1945 & Acts of 1942, 1945 & 1947	Unitary (nominal) monarchy	Universal adult suffrage, age 21 years	*Falange Española Tradicionalista y de las Juntas de Offensiva Nacional Sindicalistas*	"Unicameral (Cortes)"	"Chief of State" Cabinet	"Tribunals" "Courts"	Provinces Municipalities	UN NATO etc.
SWEDEN	Unwritten (Fundamental Laws)	Unitary constitutional monarchy	Universal adult suffrage, age 21 years	Social Demos; Liberals; Center Party; Conservatives	Bicameral (Upper House; Lower House)	Hereditary monarch Prime Minister Council of State	King-in-Council; Supreme Court; Supreme Administrative Court	Counties Districts	UN Other non-political and non-military
SWITZERLAND	Written 1874	Federal Confederation	Universal male suffrage, age 21 years	Social Demos; Radical Demos; Catholic Conservatives; Farmers, Artisan Citizens; Independents	Bicameral (Council of States; Nar'l. Council)	Federal Council	Federal Tribunal; Federal Administrative Court; Cantonal High Courts	Cantons Communes (Districts)	Miscellaneous non-political and non-military
TURKEY	Written 1961	Unitary Republic	Universal adult suffrage, age 21 years	Republican Peoples; Justice Party; New Turkey; Rep. Peasants National Party	Bicameral (Senate; Grand National Assembly)	President Council of Ministers	Court of Cassation; Council of State	Provinces Communes Villages	UN NATO etc.

BIBLIOGRAPHY OF
STANDARD TEXT BOOKS

Beer, Samuel H., and Adam B. Ulam, eds., *Patterns of Government.* New York: Random House, 1962.

Carter, Gwendolen M., and John H. Herz, *Major Foreign Powers.* New York: Harcourt, Brace and World, Inc., 1962.

Cole, Taylor, ed., *European Political Systems.* New York: Alfred A. Knopf, 1960.

Dragnich, Alex N., *Major European Governments.* Homewood, Illinois: Dorsey Press, Inc., 1961.

Finer, Herman, *The Major Governments of Modern Europe.* Evanston, Illinois: Row, Peterson and Company, 1960.

Macridis, Roy C., and Ward, Robert E., eds., *Modern Political Systems.* Englewood Cliffs, New Jersey: Prentice-Hall, Inc., 1963.

Neumann, Robert G., *European and Comparative Government.* New York: McGraw-Hill Book Company, Inc., 1960.

Spiro, Herbert J., *Government by Constitution.* New York: Random House, 1959.

Stewart, Michael, *Modern Forms of Government.* New York: Rinehart and Company, Inc., 1959.

Zink, Harold, *Modern Governments.* New York: D. Van Nostrand Company, Inc., 1962.

CROSS-REFERENCE READING GUIDE

	Chapter in This Text	Beer & Ulam	Carter-Herz	Cole, ed.	Dragnich	Finer	Macridis Ward, eds.	Neu-mann	Spiro	Stewart	Zink
1.	GREAT BRITAIN	4-11	Part I	1-7	1-8	2-10	Part I	Part I	9	2-4	Part I
2.	FRENCH FIFTH REPUBLIC	12-16	Part IV	8-12	9-15	11-19	Part II	Part II	8	10	Part II
3.	FED. REPUBLIC OF GERMANY	17	Part III	13-18	16-22	20-28	Part III	Part III	7	7	Part III
4.	UNION OF SOVIET SOCIALIST REPUBLICS	22-27	Part II	23-29	23-30	29-37	Part IV	Part IV		15	Part V
5.	REPUBLIC OF ITALY			19-22					6	12	
6.	SPAIN	(See "Selected Readings" list at end of Chapter VI)									
7.	SWEDEN								4	11	Part IV
8.	SWITZERLAND								5	8	
9.	TURKEY	(See "Selected Readings" list at end of Chapter IX)									
10.	UNITED NATIONS	(See "Selected Readings" list at end of Chapter X)									

Chapter I

GREAT BRITAIN

Population: 54,000,000 (1964)
Area: 94,279 sq. miles
Capital: London

I. CHRONOLOGY

(cf. Section II below for further historical highlights)

401—Romans withdraw from Britain.

848—Alfred the Great defeats marauding Danes at Edmington.

1066—William ("the Conqueror") of Normandy wins decisive Battle of Hastings and is crowned King of England in Westminster Abbey on Christmas day.

1215—King John forced by nobles to sign Magna Carta ("the Great Charter of English liberties") at Runnymede.

1264—Simon de Montfort summons the "Model Parliament."

1338–1453—Hundred Years' War ends in loss of English territories in France, save Calais.

1509–1547—Tudor King Henry VIII strengthens the monarchy, repudiates Papal authority, and declares himself "Supreme Head of the Church of England."

1558–1603—"Virgin Queen" Elizabeth I oversees defeat of the Spanish Armada and rise of England as maritime Power.

1688–1689—"Glorious Revolution" limits for all time monarchial powers, and "Bill of Rights" is enacted by Parliament.

1714—George I of the House of Hanover attains Crown under the Act of Settlement (1701), leading to

1

emergence of the idea of responsible Cabinet government.

1760–1820—During reign of King George III the British lose American Colonies, defeat forces of Napoleon, prosper from the "Industrial Revolution," and further develop concepts of party government and Cabinet responsibility.

1837–1901—Long reign of Victoria Regina witnesses extension of the suffrage, Chartist Movement, Crimean War, Indian Mutiny, Irish Home Rule Movement, growth of Empire, and South African War.

1910–1936—George V of the House of Windsor is King during World War I, extension of suffrage to women, attainment of Irish Home Rule, rise of Labour Party, and early Hitler period.

1936—Edward VIII abdicates throne for "the woman I love" (the American divorcee, Wallis Warfield).

1936–1952—George VI reigns during World War II, return of Labour Party to power, and emergence of new Commonwealth of Nations.

1952—Accession of Elizabeth II.

1964—General Elections result in narrow victory for Labour Party; Harold Wilson (Labour) replaces Alexander Frederick Douglas-Home (Conservative) as Prime Minister.

1965—Death of Sir Winston Churchill, after 65 years' service in Parliament and Government on behalf the interests of Great Britain and the "free world"; election of Edward Heath as new leader of the Conservative Party.

1966—Labour Party, under banner of "Time for Decision," wins smashing victory over Conservatives in the General Elections.

II. BRITISH CONSTITUTION

A. THERE IS NO SINGLE, WRITTEN, CONSTITUTIONAL DOCUMENT

B. GREAT CHARTERS AND OTHER IMPORTANT ENACTMENTS

    1. *Assize of Clarendon,* 1164: provided for holding of regular courts for the settlement of disputes throughout the Realm, and established a system whereby "twelve just men" could testify as to who must suffer "trial by

ordeal" (the rudimentary beginnings of the modern grand jury).

2. *Magna Carta,* 1215: the "Great Charter" sometimes referred to as "the foundation of the British Constitution" because it acknowledged that certain customs should be accepted as "rights" (with particular respect to justice and property), and that the King must govern according to law and not according to his own will.

3. *Writ of Summons to Parliament,* 1295: convening of a "parliament" or conference (chosen by Edward I) which was more representative of the entire Nation than any predecessor and, in time, exercised various powers of decision under the King; from this, there also gradually evolved the present House of Commons and House of Lords.

4. *Petition of Right,* 1628: petition forced upon Charles I which reasserted the "ancient liberties" of the people and denounced Royal abuses of power with respect to the levy and collection of taxes and the arbitrary arrest and imprisonment of individuals.

5. *Habeas Corpus Act,* 1679: prohibited the arbitrary arrest and detention of individuals without a "right and just" explanation or trial.

6. *Bill of Rights,* 1689: established the right of the people to govern themselves and limited, for all time, the power of the King; this did not extend to the colonists in America who, nearly a century later, had to wage a separate fight against the exercise of arbitrary Royal power.

7. *Act of Settlement,* 1701: provided for the selection of a ruling House, and that only a Protestant could become the British Monarch.

8. *Acts of Union,* 1707 and 1800: formally united England and Scotland (Wales was added to the Crown in 1284) to form "Great Britain," and later, Great Britain and Ireland were joined; today, Great Britain and Northern Ireland ("Ulster") form the "United Kingdom."

9. *Abolition of the Slave Trade Act,* 1807: forbade trade in slaves; this was later (1833) supplemented by another Act to free all slaves in the British Empire, with partial compensation to the slave owners in the Colonies.

10. *Catholic Emancipation Act,* 1829: made it possible for

Roman Catholics to sit in the "Commons" or "Lords" by abolishing the former Protestant Oath for Members of Parliament; this freedom of religion was later extended to members of the Jewish religion (1858) and eventually to members of any faith (1866).

11. *Great Reform Bill,* 1832: abolished many small constituencies where the vote could be controlled by influential people and sought further to provide that each Member of Parliament should represent about the same number of votes; the Act also enfranchised a greater number of people.

12. *Electoral Reform Laws,* 1867, 1884, 1918, 1928: reduced the property qualifications for voters (1867); extended the franchise to almost all male property owners, tenants, and lodgers (1884); established adult suffrage for all male citizens over 21 years and women over 30 years (1918); and, finally, provided for universal adult suffrage for all qualified citizens at age 21 (1928).

13. *Parliament Acts,* 1911 and 1949: respectively, deprived the "Lords" of their power to veto legislation and substituted a limited power to delay certain legislation, and reduced the period of delay from two years to one year.

14. *Statute of Westminster,* 1931: among other things, reaffirmed the position (cf. Imperial Conference, 1926) that the self-governing members of the Commonwealth ". . . are autonomous communities within the British Empire, equal in status, in no way subordinate one to another in any aspect of their domestic or external affairs, though united by a common allegiance to the Crown and freely associated as members of the British Commonwealth of Nations," and that the British Monarch has a special status as the "symbol of the free association of the independent member nations and as such the Head of the Commonwealth."

15. *Representation of the People Acts,* 1948–1949: provided that a person must register and vote in only one constituency (thus eliminating "plural voting" where a person could formerly vote both in his residential or business constituency and in a university constituency), and for greater flexibility in "redistricting" through the periodic review of parliamentary constituencies by a

permanent Boundary Commission, in order to approximate an equal size for electorates.

16. *Ireland Act,* 1949: declared that Northern Ireland ("Ulster") is a part of the United Kingdom and cannot cease to be so without the consent of the Parliament of Northern Ireland, yet recognized the secession of the Republic of Ireland ("Eire") from the Commonwealth of Nations.

17. Other statutes of note.

C. JUDICIAL DECISIONS
1. Interpret the meanings and applications of the foregoing charters, documents, and statutes.

D. COMMON LAW
1. Consists of the body of rules and principles which has evolved down through the centuries of English history and, quite apart from any parliamentary action, is recognized and put into common use throughout the Queen's realm (e.g., the right to a trial by jury in criminal cases).

E. "CONVENTIONS OF THE CONSTITUTION"
1. Include the customary practices and usages in the operation of the British governmental system (e.g., the use of the Cabinet and its collective responsibility to the Parliament, the convening of the Parliament at least once a year, and the holding of General Elections at least once in every five-year period).

F. FUNDAMENTAL PRINCIPLES OF GOVERNMENT
1. Spirit of constitutionalism.
2. Limited constitutional monarchy: the sovereign Queen "reigns," but she does not "rule."
3. Legal supremacy of the Parliament, with no judicial determination of the constitutionality of legislation.
4. Individual and collective responsibility of Cabinet Ministers.
5. "Rule of law" and the protection of private rights.
6. Operation of government in accordance with "the will of the people and the Nation."
7. Unitary system of government, but respect for local autonomy and traditions.

8. Slow, gradual, evolutionary changes in the institutions and practices of government.

G. GENERAL RIGHTS OF THE PEOPLE (not enumerated in any single document).
   1. Freedom from arbitrary arrest and imprisonment.
   2. Writ of *habeas corpus.*
   3. Fair, speedy, and public judicial proceedings.
   4. Trial by jury in criminal cases.
   5. Right of petition.
   6. Freedom of speech, press, assembly, association, and religion.
   7. Protection of one's life, liberty, and property.
   8. Freedom of movement throughout the country and realm.
   9. Political rights (See Section V-D below).

III. MONARCHY, PRIVY COUNCIL, AND INSTITUTIONAL CROWN

A. MONARCH ("nominal" executive and "Head of the State")
   1. *Full title*
      a. *Royal Titles Act,* 1953: the Royal title in the United Kingdom is "Elizabeth the Second, by the Grace of God of the United Kingdom of Great Britain and Northern Ireland and of Her other Realms and Territories Queen, Head of the Commonwealth, Defender of the Faith."
   2. *Succession to the Throne*
      a. *Act of Settlement,* 1701: ". . . the Crown and regal government of the said kingdom . . . shall be, remain, and continue to the said most excellent Princess Sophia [Electress of Hanover and mother of George I, the first of the Hanoverian dynasty] and the heirs of her body being Protestants. . . . Whosoever shall hereafter come to the possession of this Crown shall join in communion with the Church of England as by law established."
         (1) Moreover, under the long-established *rule of primogeniture,* the sons of the Sovereign succeed to the Throne according to their seniority

Chart 1. STRUCTURE OF THE BRITISH GOVERNMENT

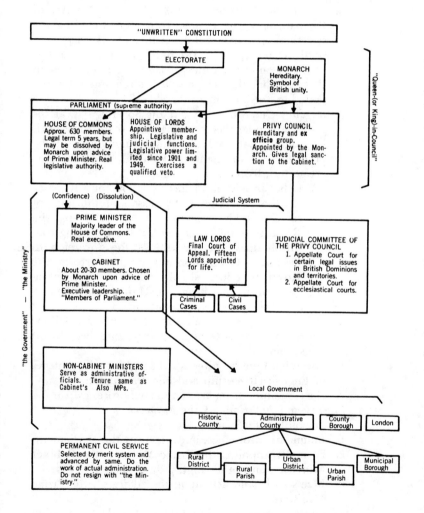

or, if there are no sons, the daughters in order of their seniority.

(2) There is never any interregnum between the death of one Sovereign and the accession of another ("Coronation" follows accession after an interval).

b. *Statute of Westminster,* 1931: ". . . 4. No Act of Parliament of the United Kingdom [including the selection of a new ruling House or dynasty] . . . shall extend . . . to a Dominion as part of the law of that Dominion, unless it is expressly declared in that Act that that Dominion has requested, or consented to, the enactment thereof. . . ."

c. *Regency Act,* 1937: ". . . If the Sovereign is, at his accession, under the age of eighteen years, then, until he attains that age, the Royal functions shall be performed in the name and on behalf of the Sovereign by a Regent. . . ."

(1) Other provisions of this Act allow for a Regency if "the Sovereign is by reason of infirmity of mind or body incapable . . . of performing the Royal functions . . .;" and, if the foregoing condition does not prevail, for the Sovereign to designate Counsellors-of-State to perform the Royal functions should the Sovereign anticipate an absence from the United Kingdom.

3. *Perquisites, privileges, and immunities*

a. "Civil List" provides an annual income and allowances for the sovereign Queen and her Royal household.

b. Sovereign Queen enjoys all the rights and privileges of English citizenship and her exalted office.

c. She is immune from arrest and civil processes.

4. *Powers and functions of the Monarch*

a. Personifies the State.

b. Summons, prorogues, and dissolves the Parliament.

c. Formally appoints the Prime Minister, the Cabinet Ministers, and other high public officials.

d. Meets with, and acts upon the advice of, the Prime Minister.

e. Confers peerages, knighthoods, and other high honors ("the fountain of honor").

    f. Formally acknowledges the jurisdiction of the courts ("the fountain of justice").

    g. Serves as nominal Head of the Church of England, the Armed Forces, etc.

    h. Appoints ambassadors and diplomatic personnel to foreign States, and accredits and receives diplomatic personnel from foreign States.

    i. Acts as Head of the Commonwealth of Nations and represents the State abroad.

    j. Symbolizes the unity and loyalty of the British Empire and Commonwealth.

    k. Performs social and ceremonial functions and other prerogative powers.

    l. *Summary statement:* ". . . the Sovereign has . . . three rights: the right to be consulted, the right to encourage, the right to warn." (Walter Bagehot, *The English Constitution,* 1867)

  5. *General evaluation of the Monarch* (Queen Elizabeth II) *today*

    a. Adds dignity, charm, and prestige to the Government.

    b. Sets the social standards and lends color to the activities of the Nation.

    c. Embodies the national political sentiment.

    d. Provides a nonpartisan "balance" between Her Majesty's Royal Government and Her Majesty's Loyal Opposition.

    e. Renders many real and valuable services, without endangering the British democracy, which seems to assure the monarchy's continued existence.

B. PRIVY COUNCIL.

  1. Although the Privy Council does not occupy nearly the important place in British affairs it formerly did, it has been the source in fairly recent years of several important Committees and Departments of government; moreover, Privy Councillors still retain the right of personal access to the Sovereign.

  2. *Membership*

    a. Consists of approximately 300 members today, including past and present Prime Ministers and Cabinet Ministers, other important State and Church officials, and distinguished persons, all of whom are appointed by the Monarch on the recommendation of the Prime Minister.

3. *Meetings*
   a. Only a very small number of its members is necessary to provide a quorum for a general meeting, where the Monarch is present, and plenary sessions are held only on very special or solemn occasions, such as when the Monarch declares the intention to marry, or upon the death of the Monarch.

4. *Organization*
   a. Includes the President of the Council, the Clerk of the Council, the committees of the Council, and the Office of the Council.

5. *Functions*
   a. Gives effect to policy decisions made elsewhere in the Government.
   b. Holds general and special meetings, where the "Queen-in-Council" issues "Orders-in-Council."
   c. Advises the "Crown" on the issuance of Royal Proclamations, such as to summon or dissolve the Parliament.
   d. Renders advice through its committees.
   e. Participates in State and ceremonial activities.

6. *Judicial Committee of the Privy Council*
   a. Includes the Lord President of the Council, the Lord Chancellor, and ex-Lord Chancellors, Lords of Appeal in Ordinary, and designated representatives of the Privy Council and "Government."
   b. Serves as a final court of appeal on certain legal issues arising in some of the Dominions and in the dependent British territories.
      (1) This function is based on the principle of the right to appeal for redress, even where the regular courts of law allegedly fail to do "justice."
      (2) Recent modifications of this power.

C. INSTITUTIONAL "CROWN"
   1. Frequently described as "the institutionalized legal repository of the Royal authority."
   2. Includes the Monarch, the Privy Council, the Prime

sents alone, or in combination with the minor parties, a "Loyal Opposition" to the "Government" party.

B. LEADING PARTIES
1. *Conservative Party:* advocates individual rights and free enterprise; encouragement to business and industry (but curb monopolistic abuses); protection for home agrarian interests; social and economic well-being for the individual and family; greater autonomy in local and colonial governments; close relations with the Commonwealth; support of the United Nations; increased cooperation with the United States; freer world trade; western European unity; assistance to the countries of Africa, the Middle East, and Southeast Asia; national, Empire, and Commonwealth defense; etc.
2. *Labour Party:* advocates individual rights and protection for the home and family; full social services and economic assistance programs; planned production for common use and full employment; higher standard of living and education for all citizens; democratic self-government for the colonies; close relations with the Commonwealth; support of the United Nations; collective security against aggression; etc.
3. *Minor parties:* include the Liberal Party, the National Liberal Party, the Ulster Unionists, the Irish Nationalists, the Independent Irish Labour Party, the "Cooperative" Party, and the Communist Party. Although the latter enjoys a full legal existence, its candidates have all been defeated in recent parliamentary elections.
4. There is also elected, from time to time, one or more "independents" to the House of Commons.

C. PARTY ORGANIZATION
1. *Main Elements.*
   a. Constituency Associations are linked together through Area Federations into a national organization.
   b. Annual Conference of the national organization provides an effective channel of communication between the party "front-benchers" (leaders) in Parliament and their supporters in the country.

Minister, the Cabinet and Ministry, the Permanent Civil Service, and the Parliament (particularly, the House of Commons).

3. Its authority rests on, and is limited by, traditions, prerogatives, statutes, etc.

4. *Principal powers*
   a. Executive: such as the appointment of officials; the supervision of administration; the conduct of foreign relations; the negotiation and ratification of treaties; the declaration of war and the conclusion of peace; the command of the Armed Forces; and the supervision of colonial governments.
   b. Legislative: such as to summon, prorogue, and dissolve the Parliament; to assent to laws; and to issue "Orders-in-Council."
   c. Judicial: such as to decide appeals from overseas areas, on the basis of recommendations by the Judicial Committee of the Privy Council; to make appointments to courts and to administer justice; and to assent to ecclesiastical laws and the hearing of appeals from the disciplinary decisions of Church courts.

IV. THE GOVERNMENT

A. PRIME MINISTER ("real" executive, First Lord of the Treasury, and "Head of the Government")

1. Leader of the majority party in the Parliament (House of Commons) and, as such, is invited by the Monarch to serve as the Prime Minister.
2. Recommends and receives from the Monarch the appointments (and sometimes the removal) of the governmental Ministers, with or without "portfolios."
3. Keeps the Monarch informed of the general business of his Government.
4. Presides over Cabinet meetings.
5. Exercises a general supervision over the various ministries and their governmental administration.
6. Addresses the Parliament on general subjects and also on important bills and matters of concern to the Government.

7. Answers, and is responsible to, the Members of Parliament for all the actions of the Government, both at home and overseas.
8. May recommend to the Monarch the formal dissolution of the Parliament.
9. Also recommends to the Monarch the appointment of other State and Church officials and the awarding of various civil honors and distinctions.
10. Assists in the preparation of Proclamations and Addresses from the Throne.
11. *Ministers of the Crown Act*, 1937: "4. (1) There shall be paid to the . . . Prime Minister and First Lord of the Treasury an annual salary of ten thousand pounds. . . . There shall be paid to the Leader of the Opposition an annual salary of two thousand pounds. . . ." [giving, incidentally, further official recognition to these two important offices]
   a. Obviously, these and other public salaries are adjusted by law, from time to time, as need requires; see VI-C-1-c below.

B. CABINET
1. Consists of 20-25 Ministers, especially recommended by the Prime Minister to form this conventional executive organ of government.
2. Includes (in the Labour Government, 1966) the Prime Minister and First Lord of the Treasury; First Secretary of State and Secretary of State for Economic Affairs; Lord President of the Council; Lord Chancellor; Chancellor of the Exchequer; Secretary of State for Foreign Affairs; Secretary of State for Defence; Secretary of State for the Home Department; Secretary of State for Commonwealth Relations; Secretary of State for Scotland; Secretary of State for Wales; Secretary of State for the Colonies; President of the Board of Trade; Lord Privy Seal; Secretary of State for Education and Science; Minister of Housing and Local Government; Chancellor of the Duchy of Lancaster; Minister of Labour; Minister of Technology; Minister of Agriculture, Fisheries and Food; Minister of Power; Minister of Transport; and Minister of Overseas Development.

3. Depending on circumstances, there exists an (a) *"inner Cabinet"* of select personal and political advisers to the Prime Minister; or a (b) *"coalition Cabinet"* of representatives of the two major parties, as in World War I and II; and, invariably, the (c) *"shadow Cabinet"* of the largest minority party or "Loyal Opposition" in the "Commons"—ready to form a new Government upon the request of the Sovereign should an incumbent Government "fall" or fail to win a majority of seats in new parliamentary elections.

4. Cabinet Ministers, and most of the non-Cabinet Ministers (See C-2 below), are also Members of Parliament ("Commoners" or "Lords"), who "stand" or "fall" together in the Government.

   a. There is both individual and collective responsibility to the Parliament for the work of individual ministries and for the general policy and actions of the Government.

   b. *Statement by Sir Robert Peel, 1841:* "If that proposition be true—if Her Majesty's Ministers do not possess the confidence of the House of Commons, then, I say, that their continuance in office is at variance with principle and spirit of the Constitution. . . . I speak . . . of that system of parliamentary government which has prevailed in this country since the accession of the House of Hanover. I speak of that system which implies that the Ministers of the Crown shall have the confidence of the House of Commons. . . . That spirit of the Constitution appears to me to be violated by the continuance in office of Ministers who have not the confidence of the House of Commons."

5. Regular and special meetings of the Cabinet are "private" in nature and their proceedings remain "confidential."

   a. A great amount of the work is done through standing and *ad hoc* committees.

6. Among the important functions of the Cabinet are the

   a. Formulation of a general policy which is submitted to, and approved by, the House of Commons;

   b. Control and coordination of the activities of the national executive authority in the implementation and execution of this policy;

c. Providing of legislative guidance by the initiation of bills in the Parliament, and also "legislation" through the "Orders-in-Council" of the Privy Council;

d. General supervision of ministerial and departmental activities;

e. Tendering of unanimous advice to the Monarch.

C. The "Ministry"

1. The sixty to seventy members of the "Ministry" include Cabinet and non-Cabinet Ministers; the heads of Government Departments and agencies; other high State officials; parliamentary undersecretaries; the Majority Party "whips"; and a few members of the Royal household.

2. Non-Cabinet Ministers include (in the Labour Government, 1966) the Minister of Health; Minister of Pensions and National Insurance; Minister of Public Building and Works; Minister of Aviation; Postmaster-General; Minister of Land and Natural Resources; Deputy Secretary of State for Defence and Minister of Defence for the Army; 2 Ministers-without-Portfolio; Paymaster-General; Chief Secretary to the Treasury; Minister of State, Department of Economic Affairs; Minister of Defence for the Royal Navy; Minister of Defence for the Royal Air Force; Minister of State, Department of Education and Science; 4 Ministers of State for Foreign Affairs; Minister of State, Home Office; Minister of State, Commonwealth Relations Office; 3 Ministers of State, Board of Trade; Minister of State, Scottish Office; Minister of State, Welsh Office; Minister of State, Department of Education and Science; Attorney-General; Solicitor-General; and Solicitor-General for Scotland.

3. The many Departments of State and Ministries vary greatly in size, number of personnel, type, and the complexity of their organization and functions.

a. They are usually grouped together according to general interest and activity, such as the agencies for finance, social and economic matters, the internal order, defense, and external relations.

b. General organization of a Ministry or Department includes the Permanent Secretary; various deputy, under, and assistant secretaries; financial and personnel offices (the "Establishments Divisions"); units for organization, management, and coordination; legal advisers; information sections; and the rank-and-file civil service employees.

4. The "Ministry" administers the Government policy as approved and implemented by legislation in the Parliament.

5. A change in "Government" may result in wide-sweeping, but not necessarily complete, changes in the overall "Ministry."

D. PERMANENT CIVIL SERVICE

1. Embraces the more than 1,000,000 persons who are employed in a civilian capacity and paid from monies voted in the Parliament.

2. It is broadly organized into the

a. *Administrative Class:* concerned with advising Ministers on policy and with the problems that arise in the administration of policy; recruited largely from University graduates.

b. *Executive Class:* concerned with the daily conduct of Government business, within the framework of established policy; its recruits usually take "in-service" training for specialized work and assignments.

c. *Clerical Class:* concerned with typical clerical work involved in the discharge of departmental business; it comprises the largest of the main classes.

d. *Typing Class:* comprised of persons who perform different categories of typing; in addition to the foregoing there are the

e. *Professional, Scientific, and Technical Classes:* concerned with carrying-out highly-specialized functions for the Government, e.g., doctors, lawyers, engineers, etc.; and such as the

f. *Inspectorate; Ancillary Technical Class; Messengerial Class;* and the *Minor and Manipulative Class.*

    g. *Foreign Service* is a separate, self-contained service of the Crown, with various classes and duties of its own; it is supplemented by numerous specialists and advisers who maintain contact with the Armed Forces, the home Government departments, and the Overseas Establishments.

3. The organization and administration of the civil service requires that special attention be given to recruitment, placement, "in-service" training, the conditions of service, employee welfare and benefits, promotions, separation, retirement, the regulation of political activities, reorganization, etc.; in regard to these matters the Civil Service Commission, the departmental "Establishments Divisions," the national and departmental "Whitley Councils" (concerned with the relationships between the "managements" and "staff"), and various staff associations all have separate responsibilities to discharge.

    a. However, the Permanent Civil Service is controlled primarily by the Treasury Department.

4. The British system compares most favorably with the civil service systems in other States.

V. POLITICAL PARTIES AND ELECTIONS

A. General Characteristics of the Party System

1. Basically, a democratic "two-party" system, with a few minor parties.

2. Parties commonly agree to maintain the free institutions and representative parliamentary government.

3. They are conceived as agents of popular government, with the two major parties representing many millions of enfranchised citizens; as such, they are pledged to carry out a definite policy and the set of principles endorsed by their supporters.

4. The party which obtains a majority of the seats in the House of Commons provides the executive authority (the Prime Minister and His Cabinet), while the party which obtains the second highest number of seats pre-

Chart 2. PATTERN OF BRITISH PARTY ORGANIZATION

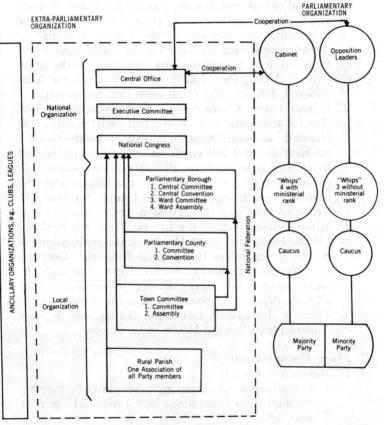

Note: The parties employ various national and local officers, e.g., Treasurer, Secretary.

sents alone, or in combination with the minor parties, a "Loyal Opposition" to the "Government" party.

B. LEADING PARTIES

1. *Conservative Party:* advocates individual rights and free enterprise; encouragement to business and industry (but curb monopolistic abuses); protection for home agrarian interests; social and economic well-being for the individual and family; greater autonomy in local and colonial governments; close relations with the Commonwealth; support of the United Nations; increased cooperation with the United States; freer world trade; western European unity; assistance to the countries of Africa, the Middle East, and Southeast Asia; national, Empire, and Commonwealth defense; etc.

2. *Labour Party:* advocates individual rights and protection for the home and family; full social services and economic assistance programs; planned production for common use and full employment; higher standard of living and education for all citizens; democratic self-government for the colonies; close relations with the Commonwealth; support of the United Nations; collective security against aggression; etc.

3. *Minor parties:* include the Liberal Party, the National Liberal Party, the Ulster Unionists, the Irish Nationalists, the Independent Irish Labour Party, the "Cooperative" Party, and the Communist Party. Although the latter enjoys a full legal existence, its candidates have all been defeated in recent parliamentary elections.

4. There is also elected, from time to time, one or more "independents" to the House of Commons.

C. PARTY ORGANIZATION

1. *Main Elements.*

   a. Constituency Associations are linked together through Area Federations into a national organization.

   b. Annual Conference of the national organization provides an effective channel of communication between the party "front-benchers" (leaders) in Parliament and their supporters in the country.

c. Each party's Central Office is staffed by professional workers.

2. *Constituency Associations*
   a. Basic party units.
   b. Vary in size, composition, structure, function, and degree of operational autonomy.
   c. Organization may include a Chairman and Vice-Chairman, Treasurer, Executive Council, various functional and "general-purpose" committees, and the Constituency Agent.
      (1) Executive Council appoints the committees, elects representatives to the regional and national organizations, raises and administers funds, conducts publicity programs and election campaigns, etc.
      (2) Constituency Agent acts as the secretary for the constituency association, and either as business manager or executive assistant to the local Member of Parliament.
   d. Labour Party's constituency associations are supported by various "affiliated" organizations (i.e., the trade unions, the "cooperatives," and the socialist societies) and have more detailed requirements and supervision for their members.
      (1) This party's constituency associations are supervised by a General Committee, which has an Executive Committee of its own.
   e. Prospective candidates to Parliament are chosen by different procedures by the constituency associations of the different parties.

3. *Area Federations*
   a. Consist of a number of party constituency associations grouped together.
   b. The Conservative Party has twelve "Provincial Areas," each of which maintains a separate organization.
   c. The Labour Party has a greater number of "County Federations" and "Regional Councils" (with both "regular" and "affiliated" members), with individual organizations of their own.
   d. Area federations crystallize political opinion over

wide spheres and prepare coordinated reports for the national organizations and party leaders.

4. *National Organization*
    a. *Conservative Party*
        (1) *National Union of Conservative and Unionist Associations* (separate Scottish Unionist Association and a separate organization for Northern Ireland), to which the constituency associations are affiliated; it has a governing
        (2) *Central Council* and *Executive Committee,* both of which report to the annual party conference; however, as the National Union does not formulate policy nor perform executive functions, its resolutions are not binding on the party leader and his associates.
        (3) *Party leader* is chosen by common consent among the leading members of the party in Parliament, the prospective parliamentary candidates, and the Executive Committee of the National Union; the outgoing leader exerts considerable influence in the choice.
        (4) *National Advisory Committees* and boards are concerned with party policy, parliamentary candidates, finance, etc.
        (5) *Central Office* or headquarters is presided over by a chairman appointed by the party leader.
        (6) Party funds come from individual donations and contributions from constituency associations on an agreed basis.
    b. *Labour Party*
        (1) *Annual Party Conference,* to which the constituency associations affiliated Trade Unions, and Socialist societies (such as the Fabian Society) send representatives to hear and consider reports from various party agencies both within and outside Parliament, discuss the party long-term goals and current program, and elect the members of the
        (2) *National Executive Committee,* which is responsible for supervising the work of the party outside Parliament.

(3) *Party leader* is elected annually by the parliamentary organization of the Labour Party in the House of Commons.

(4) *Central Office* or headquarters ("Transport House") operates under the direction of the NEC.

(5) Party funds come chiefly from contributions from the affiliated Trade Unions and the constituency associations.

c. *Liberal Party*

(1) *Assembly*, or annual conference, is attended by representatives of all constituency associations and delegates from "affiliated" bodies, together with certain *ex officio* members, such as Members of Parliament and parliamentary candidates; it hears and considers reports from, and elects new members of the

(2) *Council*, the governing body of the "Liberal Party Organization" (i.e., the Liberal Party outside Parliament), which reports at the annual conference on the work of the party and is largely responsible for determining the broad outlines of party policy.

(3) *Executive Committee* and other officers are also elected at the annual conference.

(4) *Party leader* is elected by the members of the Liberal Party in the Parliament.

(5) *Central Office* or headquarters operates under the direction of the Executive Committee.

(6) Party funds consist of contributions by individuals and affiliated associations and subscription fees from constituency associations.

5. *Auxiliary Organizations:* various clubs, leagues, societies, federations, etc.

6. *Parliamentary Organization:*

a. *General comment*

(1) Effectiveness of British parliamentary system rests largely on a basic agreement between the two major parties: the minority (Opposition) agrees that the majority (Government) must govern and, therefore, accepts its decisions, and

the majority (Government) agrees that the minority (Opposition) should criticize and, therefore, sets time aside for criticism to be heard.

(2) British Governments can ordinarily count on sufficient voting support in the "Commons" to obtain the enactment of legislation in substantially the form it is originally proposed.

(3) Party discipline both strengthens the hand of the Government and increases the importance of the Opposition.

b. *Party leaders*

(1) Prime Minister and members of his Cabinet exercise controls over the membership of the "Government" party while the "Opposition" party has a selected leadership under a single head.

c. *Party "whips"*

(1) Exercise much control over party members in Parliament, particularly in the "Commons."

(2) "Chief whip" of the "Government" party is directly answerable to the Prime Minister as the Leader of the House of Commons, and is concerned with the details of the Government's program of business, the time likely to be required for each item, the business of the individual sittings, close liaison with Ministers regarding any parliamentary business which affects their Departments and, together with the "chief whip" of the "Opposition" party, provides the "usual channels" to find time to debate some particular issue or to deal with some matter of convenience to the entire House.

(3) Duties common to "whips" of all parties are to (a) inform members about the business of the House, (b) secure the attendance of members, (c) arrange for such of their members who are unable to attend "divisions" (i.e., a vote on a Bill) to "pair" with members from the opposition side of the House so that the relative voting strength of the parties is not changed, and (d) arrange for members to serve on parliamentary committees.

d. *Party committees*

   (1) Most important committee of the Conservative Party is the *Conservative and Unionist Members' Committee* (popularly-known as the "1922 Committee"), composed of the entire "back-bench" (non-ministerial) membership of the Conservative Party in the "Commons"; this committee maintains close relations with the party leadership and provides a sounding-board for Conservative opinion and a forum to raise and reconcile party differences and disputes in the House.

   (2) Most important committee of the Labour Party (whose parliamentary party organization includes the Labour Party members in both Houses) is the *Parliamentary Committee*, a small group which acts as the "shadow Cabinet" when Labour is the "Opposition" party; it plays a much greater part in the formation of party policy than does the "1922 Committee."

   (3) In addition, both major parties maintain various committees whose interest closely parallels the special areas or functions of the principal Government Departments.

   (4) The Liberal Party has no parliamentary committee and, because of its small parliamentary membership, holds private meetings to discuss policy.

D. SUFFRAGE AND ELECTIONS

  1. British suffrage was "democratized" by a number of 19th century "electoral reform" bills and 20th century "representation of the people" acts.

  2. *Present suffrage*

   a. Based on "single-member" Districts, determined by residence or occupation.

   b. Voters must be British citizens, at least twenty-one years of age of either sex, have residence in a District, and sometimes show occupancy of property with a stipulated rental value.

   c. Nonvoters include minors, aliens, lunatics, criminals, paupers, certain high Church officials, and "peers" (members of the House of Lords).

3. *Elections* (cf. Representation of the People Act, 1949)

   a. National Elections are held at least once in every five years, unless the Parliament is dissolved by the "Crown" more frequently.

     (1) Writs of Election are issued by the Lord Chancellor on the authority of a Royal Proclamation.

   b. Nomination procedures

     (1) A candidate files a notification of his candidacy, subscribed to by at least ten registered voters; he then deposits a "bond," which is forfeited if he fails to poll one-eighth of the total votes cast in the District for which he "stands"; the candidate need not be a resident of the District in which he files; there are also certain other "extra-legal" controls by the political parties.

   c. Campaigns

     (1) Expenditures are regulated by "Corrupt Practices" Acts, which place a maximum limit upon the expenditure of money, based upon a sliding scale depending upon the nature of the constituency; there are virtually no restrictions placed upon the sources of the funds.

   d. Polling

     (1) Registered voters go to the polls on the seventeenth day after the issuance of the Election Proclamation; the secret ballot is used; then the electoral count is conducted at a Central Office, rather than in each polling place; provisions are made for "absentee" voting; a contested election is either judged by the House of Commons, if a matter of eligibility is involved, or by two judges of the "Queen's Bench," if there is an alleged violation of the laws.

   e. Other considerations

     (1) There is no system of proportional representation in the election of members of Parliament.

CHART 3. ORGANIZATION OF THE BRITISH PARLIAMENT

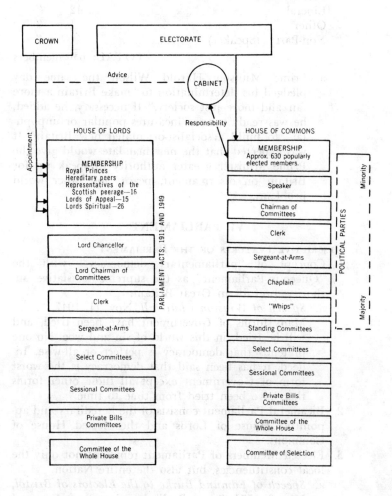

CROWN

ELECTORATE

Advice

CABINET

Responsibility

Appointment

HOUSE OF LORDS

MEMBERSHIP
Royal Princes
Hereditary peers
Representatives of the
 Scottish peerage—16
Lords of Appeal—15
Lords Spiritual—26

PARLIAMENT ACTS, 1911 AND 1949

Lord Chancellor

Lord Chairman of Committees

Clerk

Sergeant-at-Arms

Select Committees

Sessional Committees

Private Bills Committees

Committee of the Whole House

HOUSE OF COMMONS

MEMBERSHIP
Approx. 630 popularly elected members.

Speaker

Chairman of Committees

Clerk

Sergeant-at-Arms

Chaplain

"Whips"

Standing Committees

Select Committees

Sessional Committees

Private Bills Committees

Committee of the Whole House

Committee of Selection

POLITICAL PARTIES

Minority

Majority

(2) Elected Members of Parliament take their seats at once.

E. Party Representation in the Parliament ("Commons")
1. *House of Commons* (elected March 31, 1966).

Labour .... 363 members
Conservative 253   "
Liberal 12   "
Other 1   "
Non-Party (Speaker) 1   "

TOTAL: 630 members

a. Prime Minister Harold Wilson the same day pledged his determination to "make Britain a more fair and more just society." If necessary, he added, he was ready to use "measures popular or unpopular" to build a socialist-orientated new Britain. It was expected that the new mandate would give the Prime Minister greater authority to speak up for Britain on disarmament, peace, and other world problems.

VI. PARLIAMENT

A. Descriptive Features of the Parliament
1. Concept of "parliamentary democracy," with the "Queen-in-Parliament" as the supreme legislative authority, prevails in Great Britain.
   a. *Speech of Winston Churchill*, Nov. 11, 1947: ". . . . Many forms of Government have been tried, and will be tried, in this world of sin and woe. No one pretends that democracy is perfect or all-wise. Indeed, it has been said that democracy is the worst form of Government except all those other forms that have been tried from time to time."
2. Bicameral Parliament consists of the hereditary and appointive House of Lords and the elected House of Commons.
3. Elected Members of Parliament represent not only the local constituencies, but also the entire Nation.
   a. *Speech of Edmund Burke to the Electors of Bristol*, Nov. 3, 1774: ". . . . Parliament is not a *congress* of

ambassadors from different and hostile interests; which interests each must maintain, as an agent and advocate, against other agents and advocates; but Parliament is a *deliberative* assembly of *one* Nation, with *one* interest, that of the whole; where, not local purposes, not local prejudices, ought to guide, but the general good, resulting from the general reason of the whole. You choose a member indeed; but when you have chosen him, he is not a member of Bristol, but he is a member of *Parliament*. If the local constituent should have an interest, or should form an hasty opinion, evidently opposite to the real good of the rest of the community, the member for this place ought to be as far, as any other, from any endeavor to give it effect. . . ."

4. The "Commons" is divided into the "Government" party (the party which has won the majority of seats) and the "Opposition" party (the largest minority party), with the members of any other parties, or any Independents, supporting either the "Government" or the "Opposition" depending on their party's view towards a policy under debate.

5. The "Lords" have suffered a loss of power pursuant to the provisions of the *Parliament Acts of 1911* and *1949*.
   a. e.g., They may not alter a financial Bill nor delay for more than one year any Bill passed by the "Commons" in two successive sessions.

6. Parliament is formally summoned, prorogued (dismissed), and dissolved by the Queen whose "Speech from the Throne," in opening Parliament, is drafted by the Cabinet Ministers and outlines the Government's plans for the main business of the session.
   a. The Royal Assent (which is usually given by commissioners acting in her name) gives effect to legislation; the Royal veto is no longer used.

B. HOUSE OF LORDS
   1. The 950–1000 members of this House include, besides the inactive "Royal Princes," the "Lords Temporal" and the "Lords Spiritual."

    a. *"Lords Temporal"* are subdivided into (1) hereditary peers and peeresses, (2) life peers and peeresses, and up to 9 (3) Lords of Appeal in Ordinary ("Law Lords"), who perform special judicial duties; "Lords Temporal" are appointed by the Sovereign on the advice of the Prime Minister and, sometimes, after consultation with the Leader of the Opposition.

    b. *"Lords Spiritual"* include the Archbishops of Canterbury and York and 24 Bishops of the Established Church of England.

    c. About 20 office-holders in the Government, including 3–4 Cabinet Ministers, are members of the House of Lords.

2. *Important recent legislation*

    a. *Life Peerages Act,* 1958: provides that the Queen may confer "by letters patent," a life peerage on any person (man *or* woman), who shall enjoy the rank of baron and be summoned to sit and vote in the "Lords."

    b. *Peerage Act,* 1963: provides that a peer may, within a year of inheriting a peerage, disclaim his peerage for his lifetime, so that he may vote in parliamentary elections and sit in the House of Commons.

3. Usually, 140–150 peers attend the meetings of the House of Lords.

4. *Internal organization and procedures*

    a. Formal organization includes the Lord Chancellor (the "Speaker"), a limited number of committees, several clerks, an Usher, a Sergeant-at-Arms, and a Chaplain.

    b. Proceedings are kept informal and the speeches and discussions are maintained at a "high level."

    c. Lords enjoy full parliamentary privileges; they are not paid any salary, but may request an expense allowance from the "Crown."

5. *Powers and functions*

    a. Have no veto power over financial measures and exercise only a limited "suspensive veto" on nonfinancial legislation.

b. Give preconsideration to important public issues and postconsideration to some legislative measures.

c. Develop new points of view and sometimes grant advice to the Commons.

d. Occasionally suggest revisions and improvements in the form and content of bills enacted in the Commons.

e. "Law Lords" perform a judicial function, as a final Court of Appeal in law for citizens of the United Kingdom.

C. HOUSE OF COMMONS

1. The 630 members of the "Commons" are elected either at a General Election, held at least once in every 5 years, or at a "by-election" to fill a vacant seat.

a. They include 511 representatives for England, 36 for Wales, 71 for Scotland, and 12 for Northern Ireland.

b. Disqualified from membership in the "Commons" are persons under 21 years of age, judges, civil servants, members of the regular Armed Forces, sheriffs and policemen, clergymen, government contractors, English and Scottish peers (unless they have renounced their titles for life under the *Peerage Act*, 1963), lunatics, criminals, and aliens; "resignation" of membership from the "Commons" (but not from the "Lords") is possible through an appointment to the sinecure office of steward or bailiff of the "Chiltern Hundreds."

c. In 1966, the Prime Minister received 14,000 pounds (approx. $39,200); Cabinet and non-Cabinet Ministers and law officers, varying lesser amounts; the Leader of the Opposition in the "Commons" 4,500 pounds (approx. $12,600); and regular MPs 3,250 pounds (approx. $9,100) *per annum*, all with various income tax relief.

d. Leaders of the Government and of the Opposition sit on the front benches of their respective sides in the rectangular legislative chamber (as in the House of Lords), with their supporters (the "back-benchers") sitting behind them.

    e. *Standing Orders* (relative to both "public" and "private" business) distribute the House's time and regulate the conduct of legislative proceedings by its members.

    f. MPs enjoy personal inviolability and parliamentary immunity in the normal conduct of their business.

2. *Internal (non-party) organization*

    a. Consists of the Speaker and the Deputy Speaker, the committees, the Clerk, the Sergeant-at-Arms, and the Chaplain.

    b. Speaker is elected by the Commons and approved by the Queen; he is strictly nonpartisan, is regularly reelected, and performs many important duties, such as to

      (1) Preside over the meetings of the House of Commons;

      (2) Control procedure and debate, and may refuse to entertain a dilatory motion;

      (3) Recognize speakers and safeguard the rights of the minority representations;

      (4) Decide questions involving the type of bill, the chairmanships of the Standing Committees, the leadership of the Opposition, Closure Motions, etc.;

      (5) Cast the decisive vote in case of a tie vote on a legislative bill;

      (6) Issue warrants for "by-elections" to fill vacant seats in the "Commons";

      (7) Perform other miscellaneous functions.

3. *Committees of the House of Commons*

    a. Committees of the Whole House, i.e., the House itself, which are appointed to consider important bills in detail (e.g., Committee of Supply and Committee of Ways and Means).

    b. Standing Committees, which consist of 30 to 50 members each (parties represented proportionately) and consider bills and other business committed to them.

    c. Select Committees (including Joint Select Committees of both Houses), which inquire into and report to the House(s) on special matters (e.g., Select Committee on Public Accounts, Select Committee on Estimates, and Select Committee on Statutory Instruments).

    d. Parliamentary (Sessional) Committees, which deal primarily with Private Bill legislation.

    e. Various other unofficial committees, such as "study groups" and "parliamentary party committees."

    f. Cabinet is sometimes referred to as the "Chief Committee of the Commons."

4. *"Private" members* (See Section C-1 above)

    a. Represent all their constituents and the country as a whole.

    b. Perform typical parliamentary and extra-parliamentary activities.

5. *Powers and functions*

    a. Legal supremacy of Parliament, viz., the House of Commons, is absolute; it

    b. Makes or changes laws affecting the entire British community;

    c. Provides monies for the needs of this community and for the services of the State;

    d. Criticizes and controls the Government ("to make, support, and overthrow" Cabinets);

    e. Is much more stable and powerful than "the most popular branch" of the national legislature in many other countries.

6. *Bills*

    a. "Government" bills.

        (1) Initiated by the Prime Minister and his Cabinet at the behest of those Ministers or Departments which are chiefly concerned with, or responsible for, their administration when they become law.

    b. "Private Members'" bills.

        (1) Are also public bills, introduced at a designated time by individual Members of Parliament on their own initiative.

    c. "Private" bills.

        (1) Promoted by persons or organizations outside the Parliament, and have reference to some particular individual, corporate, or local interest.

CHART 4. THE BRITISH HOUSE OF COMMONS

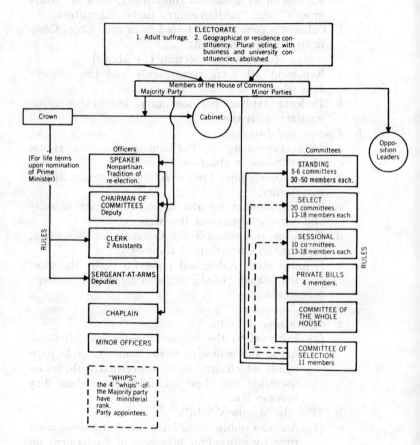

Note: There are three "whips" for the Opposition.
They hold no official positions.

7. *Steps in the enactment of law*
   a. First Reading: the formality of introducing a bill.
   b. Second Reading: the bill is read in full and debated, briefly; it is then considered in a meeting of the Committee of the Whole House or is sent to a regular Standing Committee.
   c. Committee consideration: here the bill is fully discussed and criticized, clause by clause, and finally whipped into shape in an altered form.
   d. Consideration of the bill on Report from Committee: this involves a report by the committee; further discussion; additional changes may be made by the committee or approved by the Commons.
   e. Third Reading: the reading of the bill in final form; the conclusion of debate; the taking of the vote on the bill.
      (1) "Closure" of debate may be determined by prearrangement between the parties; however, there are the *"simple closure"* (motion to the previous question and vote to end debate); *"closure by compartments"* (motion to the previous question and vote to end debate on a designated group of clauses in a Bill); *"kangaroo closure"* (arrangement to debate only the most important clauses or amendments in a Bill); and *"guillotine closure"* (arrangement to end debate on the various clauses or amendments in a Bill after a set time-limit).
      (2) Voting is either *viva voce* (verbalized "ayes" and "nays" taken in the chamber) or by a *"division"* (members voting "aye" go out the chamber on the right of the Speaker and those voting "nay" pass into the lobby on his left).
   f. Consideration, possible proposed alterations or amendments, compromise, and final approval in the House of Lords.
   g. Royal assent and promulgation: the Bill is now an Act of Parliament.

D. PARLIAMENTARY-CABINET RELATIONS
   1. *Cabinet leadership of the House of Commons*

Chart 5. LAW-MAKING PROCESS IN GREAT BRITAIN

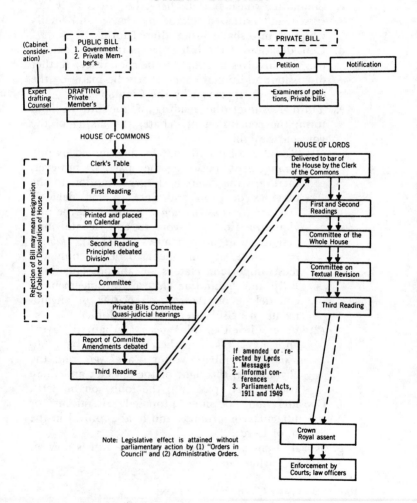

Note: Legislative effect is attained without parliamentary action by (1) "Orders in Council" and (2) Administrative Orders.

a. Prime Minister is the leader of the majority party, and Cabinet Ministers are outstanding Members of Parliament.

b. Solidarity of the Cabinet in exercising the legislative initiative and largely controlling the conduct of legislative proceedings.

c. Threat and power of *dissolution,* i.e., where the Prime Minister and Cabinet request that the Sovereign proclaim the dissolution of Parliament so that an appeal may be made to the electorate to endorse the policy of the Government.

d. Control of financial policies represented by the budget (through the Chancellor of the Exchequer) and its administration (through the Prime Minister as First Lord of the Treasury).

e. Preparation of the Queen's Annual Address from the Throne, and other Royal Proclamations.

f. Importance attributed to the Prime Minister and Cabinet as outstanding members of *"the Establishment,"* i.e., persons who currently wield the greatest degree of power and influence and are regarded, therefore, as the "right people" to do so and very much "in the know" as to what is good for other people and the country.

2. *House of Commons' checks on the Cabinet*
   a. Prevalent sense of the "spirit and content of constitutionalism" in British parliamentary government.

   b. *"Question Time,"* i.e., the devoting of parliamentary time to put questions (usually with reasonable forenotice) to the members of the Government in order to elicit information about their intentions and actions.

   (1) Material for the answers is organized in the Department of the Minister, but he is personally responsible both for his verbal and written replies.

   (2) Ministers are not bound to answer every question but as a matter of practice they do so, unless they have a strong reason (e.g., considerations of national security) for refusal.

c. *"Motion of Censure,"* i.e., a motion to censure an individual Minister or the Cabinet which, if passed (and this is not often the case), will result in the resignation of the Minister or the Cabinet.

d. *"Vote of No Confidence,"* i.e., an extreme procedure, usually moved by the Leader of the Opposition against the Government's policy in general which, if passed, will force the Government out of power.

e. Opposition to the proposed budget (through the Committee of Supply), and checks on the expenditure of State funds (through the Auditor-General and the Committee on Public Accounts).

f. Limitations placed on *"delegated legislation,"* i.e., the rules, regulations, and orders issued by the Cabinet—in the implementation of an Act of Parliament—as "Orders-in-Council" or ministerial orders which may or may not require confirmation by the Parliament to become effective or be reviewable by the courts, depending on the provisions of the Act.

g. Influence of "party, press, and public opinion."

VII. JUDICIAL SYSTEM

A. THEORY AND PRACTICE OF LAW AND JUSTICE

1. Philosophy of law and administration of justice in Great Britain compares favorably with that in other political States in Europe, the Western hemisphere, and elsewhere.

2. *Sources of the law*

   a. *Common law:* the body of legal principles and rules common to the realm and enforceable in the courts; these frequently have their origin in "immemorial antiquity."

   b. *Statutory law:* the "Acts of Parliament" and subordinate or delegated legislation; part of this represents a definition or modification of the common law, and part of it sets forth principles and rules which never existed at common law.

   c. *Equity law:* the principles and rules that developed as a means of providing equitable adjustments ("preventive" or "merciful" justice) in types of cases and juridical disputes not covered, or inadequately covered, by the common law.

d. There is no definitive body of administrative law closely analogous to that found in certain continental European States (such as the *Droit Administratif* in France), nor is there yet a separate system of administrative courts; redress from the actions of public officials must be sought in the ordinary courts (cf. *Crown Proceedings Act*, 1947).

   (1) Legal theory makes the State immune from suit, but, in practice, it may permit itself to be sued in certain kinds of actions, such as claims for the restitution of private property and also for alleged violations of contract by the Government.

3. *Branches of the law*

   a. *Civil law:* covers private claims and the redress of private wrongs.

   b. *Criminal law:* covers the punishment of offenses against the "State and society."

4. Administration of criminal justice may involve various legal rights and judicial safeguards, including

   a. The writ of *habeas corpus;*

   b. No "third degree" methods or practices;

   c. Only reasonable bail;

   d. Right to legal counsel and defense;

   e. Indictment and trial by juries;

   f. Proper court procedures;

   g. Presumption of innocence;

   h. Right of appeal against an adverse decision;

   i. No "double jeopardy."

5. Common law writs (e.g., assumpsit, trover, replevin, trespass, *quo warranto*, mandamus, injunction, etc.) are court orders necessary to the initiation of suits in civil law and equity.

B. ORGANIZATION OF COURTS

   1. *Civil courts*

      a. *County courts*

         (1) Presided over by a paid, professional judge.

Chart 6. ORGANIZATION OF THE BRITISH COURT SYSTEM

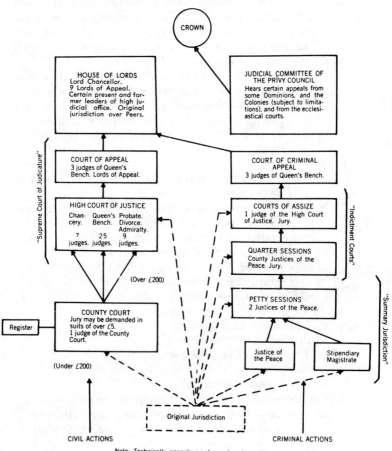

CROWN

HOUSE OF LORDS
Lord Chancellor.
9 Lords of Appeal.
Certain present and former leaders of high judicial office. Original jurisdiction over Peers.

JUDICIAL COMMITTEE OF THE PRIVY COUNCIL
Hears certain appeals from some Dominions, and the Colonies (subject to limitations), and from the ecclesiastical courts.

"Supreme Court of Judicature"

COURT OF APPEAL
3 judges of Queen's Bench. Lords of Appeal.

COURT OF CRIMINAL APPEAL
3 judges of Queen's Bench.

HIGH COURT OF JUSTICE

Chancery.	Queen's Bench.	Probate. Divorce. Admiralty.
7 judges.	25 judges.	9 judges.

COURTS OF ASSIZE
1 judge of the High Court of Justice. Jury.

QUARTER SESSIONS
County Justices of the Peace. Jury.

"Indictment Courts"

(Over £200)

PETTY SESSIONS
2 Justices of the Peace.

"Summary Jurisdiction"

Register

COUNTY COURT
Jury may be demanded in suits of over £5.
1 judge of the County Court.

Justice of the Peace

Stipendiary Magistrate

(Under £200)

Original Jurisdiction

CIVIL ACTIONS

CRIMINAL ACTIONS

Note: Technically, appeals may be made only on the basis of a question of law, although in practice they are sometimes made on a question of fact.

      (2) Exercise jurisdiction over all common law actions and civil suits where the sum of money does not exceed 400 pounds, except where otherwise provided by law.

      (3) A jury may be used in these courts.

  b. *"Mayor's and City of London" court*

      (1) Presided over by a judge appointed by the Government of the City of London.

      (2) Exercises jurisdiction primarily over civil cases and other special disputes as provided by law.

  c. *High Court of Justice* (part of the "Supreme Court of Judicature," which is not a court in fact, but a descriptive term for the High Court and the Court of Appeal together), with three Divisions.

      (1) Queen's Bench Division: staffed by the Lord Chief Justice and twenty-five other judges; it is concerned with ordinary civil actions and criminal cases "at Assizes."

      (2) Chancery (Equity) Division: staffed by the Lord Chancellor and seven other judges; it is concerned with cases in equity, such as the administration of the estates of deceased persons, certain business and financial transactions, and tax cases.

      (3) Probate, Divorce, and Admiralty Division: staffed by a number of regular judges or specially appointed "Commissioners"; they hear and decide cases involving wills, admiralty and shipping matters, and divorce proceedings.

  d. *Appellate courts,* including the

      (1) Court of Appeal (also a part of the "Supreme Court of Judicature"): headed by a judge ("the Master of the Rolls"), who is assisted by eight Lord Justices of Appeal; this court has appellate jurisdiction over appeals from the County courts, the "Mayor's and City of London" Court, and the High Court of Justice (civil cases); it may have two or three divisions, with usually three judges to a division.

      (2) House of Lords: its "court" is staffed by the Lord Chancellor and five to nine "Lords of Ap-

peal in Ordinary"; these persons are paid professional judges, with peerages for life; they serve as the Supreme Court of Appeal in civil cases throughout the United Kingdom.

2. *Summary jurisdiction and criminal courts*
   a. *Courts of summary jurisdiction*, including the
      (1) "Petty Sessional" or magistrates' courts; consist of two or more unpaid "lay" judges (or Justices of the Peace), appointed by the Lord Chancellor on the recommendation of the Lord Lieutenant in the County, or his equivalent in the Borough; they try minor offenses.
      (2) Juvenile courts: consist of two or three judges (at least one man and one woman), appointed from a panel of justices elected by the judges of the magistrates' courts from among their own number; these courts handle practically all cases (except homicide) involving children under seventeen years of age; also adoption matters; they follow special procedures and do not hold "public" hearings.
      (3) Domestic (relations) courts: consists of two or three judges (again, with one man and one woman), who are similarly appointed; these courts follow special procedures and the public is also excluded from their hearings.
   b. *Courts of quarter session*, including the
      (1) County Sessions and Borough Sessions courts; presided over by a "Chairman" (who may be paid or unpaid), sitting with a number of County or Borough judges; such courts, meeting quarterly, have jurisdiction over all but the most serious criminal cases; trial by jury may be used in their hearings.
   c. *Courts of Assize* (part of the High Court of Justice).
      (1) Convene about three times a year, in counties and large cities, to try various types of criminal cases and, sometimes, civil actions.
      (2) Presided over by a "Queen's Bench" judge or a "Commissioner of Assize" on circuit.
   d. *"Crown courts"* (in Lancastershire County).

        (1) New special courts similar to the regular assize courts.

    e. *Central criminal court.*

        (1) Exercises criminal jurisdiction for London and the "Home" counties.

        (2) Staffed by a "Queen's Bench" judge, two special "Commissioners," and two judges from the "Mayor's and City of London" Court.

    f. *Court of criminal appeal.*

        (1) Hears appeals against the convictions or sentences handed down by the lower criminal courts.

        (2) Consists of the Lord Chief Justice and several "Queen's Bench" judges.

3. *Other courts*

    a. *Coroners' Courts:* presided over by a local coroner (usually a barrister, solicitor, or medical practitioner of not less than 5 years' standing), appointed by an administrative county or county borough council, to conduct an inquest to determine the cause of a person's death, under unusual circumstances, and whether or not any particular person (or persons) are responsible and, therefore, should be committed for trial in an Assize Court.

    b. *Ecclesiastical Courts:* consist of a graduated hierarchy of courts maintained by the Established Church of England to settle matters of purely ecclesiastical concern.

    c. *Military Courts:* established under various Army and Naval Discipline Acts to conduct courts-martial in cases involving offenses committed by military personnel against the system of military law; appeals may be made to the Courts-Martial Appeal Court and, from that court, to the House of Lords if a point of law of general public importance is involved and it appears that the point should be considered by the "Law Lords."

    d. *Administrative "Courts":* may be boards, committees, councils, tribunals, etc., appointed by the Lord Chancellor to settle disputes involving (1) a Government Department or public authority, e.g., rates and taxes, (2) specialized knowledge or experience, e.g., land values and fair rents, or (3) professional discipline, e.g., doctors and solicitors.

    (1) Appeals from the "awards" of these "courts" may be made to an appropriate Minister or, on a point of law, to a higher regular court.

    (2) *Tribunal and Inquiries Act*, 1958, provides for a "Council on Tribunals," consisting of 10–15 members appointed by the Lord Chancellor and the Secretary of State, to review the actions and receive reports, periodically, from administrative tribunals, etc., performing regulatory and quasi-judicial functions; the Council prepares an annual report on its findings for the Lord Chancellor and the Secretary of State who, subsequently, submit the report with their own appropriate comments to the Parliament.

C. Judiciary and Legal Profession

1. *Judges*
   a. Appointed by the "Crown," receive an adequate annual salary, and serve a term during "good behavior."
   b. "Independent and impartial" in the conduct of "speedy, fair, and public" trials.
   c. A special Judicial Committee, consisting of the Lord Chancellor, seven judges, and four barristers, establish and regulate courtroom procedures.
   d. As there is no minister of justice, the administration of justice is largely the concern of the Lord Chancellor, the Home Secretary, the Prime Minister, and the high court judges.

2. *Barristers*
   a. Professional persons who give advice on legal problems presented to them through a solicitor, and who present cases in the higher courts.
   b. Qualifications include a university degree in law, success in the required law examinations, and membership in one of the "Inns of Court."
   c. Closely supervised by the "General Council of the Bar."

3. *Solicitors*

    a. Professional persons who handle litigation for private citizens and agencies.

    b. Qualifications include a university degree in law, proven exemplary personal conduct and behavior, a three to five-year apprenticeship with an established solicitor, and success in the required law examinations.

VIII. LOCAL GOVERNMENT

The Administrative County (62) and the County Borough (83) are the two most important divisions of English local government. By far the largest part of the total population is politically related to these units. The governmental organizations of both are essentially similar, differing only in matters of detail. Boroughs are of two types, the County Borough and the Municipal Borough. The former is distinguished from the latter not only by its possession of the same powers as the Administrative County, but also by its independent status. The Municipal Borough, although enjoying some independent functions, is, on the whole, part of the Administrative County.

A. CENTRAL CONTROLS OVER THE LOCAL AUTHORITIES

    1. Acts of Parliament and special legislation.

    2. Approval of local actions and by-laws.

    3. Departmental supervision.

    4. Inspections and inquiries.

    5. Advisory circulars.

    6. Authorization of loans.

    7. Administration of central "grants-in-aid."

    8. Studies and proposals for reform by the Boundary Commissions.

    9. The parliamentary committees, the Home Office, and the Ministry of the Exchequer all have important functions to perform with respect to the management and interests of local authorities.

   10. A Lord Lieutenant represents the "Crown" in each county.

B. PRINCIPAL TYPES OF LOCAL AUTHORITY

    1. Historic County (e.g., Middlesex, Sussex, Yorkshire).

2. Administrative County, which embraces the non-county boroughs, Urban Districts, and Rural Districts.
3. County Borough.
4. Municipal Borough.
5. Urban District.
6. Rural District.
7. Parish.
8. Special local authorities, such as the County of London, the City of London, Metropolitan Boroughs, the Port of London Authority, Harbor Boards, Water Boards, Metropolitan Asylum Boards, etc.
9. City of London is organized and governed under special legislation of Parliament.

C. ORGANS OF LOCAL AUTHORITY
1. *Council*
   a. Members are elected for a three-year term, but Aldermen, who are selected from among the Councillors, serve for six years.
   b. Qualifications of Councillors include British citizenship, a minimum age of twenty-one years, registration as a voter, and established residence or property holdings in the local area.
      (1) Almost invariably "laymen" who volunteer their public services.
      (2) Appoint the local officers and direct their activities.
   c. Council conducts full sessions, but does most of its work through various committees, subcommittees, and boards.
2. *Mayor*
   a. Usually selected by the local Councillors from among their own number, and serves a three-year term in office.
      (1) Acts as the presiding officer or Chairman of the Council.
      (2) Represents the local area and performs both social and ceremonial functions.
      (3) Sometimes issues orders to the local officers when the Council is not in session.

Chart 7. AGENCIES OF LOCAL GOVERNMENT IN GREAT BRITAIN

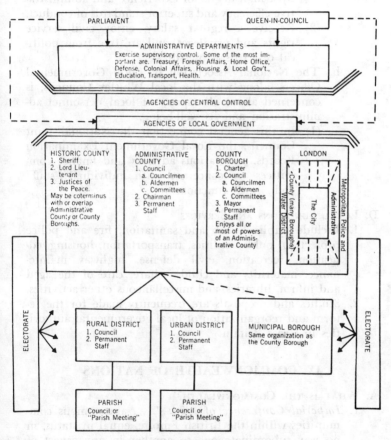

Note: The Historic County serves only as a judicial district, an area for parliamentary elections, and for the organization of the militia.

3. *Local officers*
  a. Usually appointed or approved by the Council, serve an indefinite term in office, and include the heads of the local Departments, subordinate personnel, and manual workers.
    (1) Comprise a "professional service," characterized by a high degree of experience and administrative efficiency and superior standards of conduct.
    (2) Receive a regular salary, enjoy civil service rights and privileges, and are free from political or partisan pressures.
  b. The National Association of Local Governmental Officers, along with the local Whitley Councils, is concerned about all aspects of local personnel administration and its well-being.
    (1) In this general connection the National Joint Councils, the Local Government Examination Boards, and various advisory and finance committees are concerned with individual "staff" and "line" functions.

D. LOCAL FUNCTIONS AND SERVICES
  1. Include public health and sanitation, fire and police protection, public utilities, transportation, housing, education, recreation, civil defense, highway maintenance, maternity and child welfare, care of the aged and infirm, libraries, and miscellaneous other activities.
  2. Studies and proposals are frequently made for the reform and reorganization of local governmental authorities in Great Britain.

IX. COMMONWEALTH OF NATIONS

A. WHAT IS THE COMMONWEALTH?
  1. *Imperial Conference of 1926:* ". . . autonomous communities within the British Empire, equal in status, in no way subordinate one to another in any aspect of their domestic or external affairs, though united by a common allegiance to the Crown, and freely associated as members of the British Commonwealth of Nations."
  2. *H. Duncan Hall, Historical Advisor, British Embassy:*

"The British Commonwealth of Nations is the oldest international organization of States in existence. Its uniqueness lies in its unbroken historical continuity, the loyalty of its members to each other, their solidarity on vital matters of common concern, the fluidity of their machinery for dealing with such matters, and their abhorrence of constitutional contracts within the family of the Commonwealth. These are its features so far as we can see them yet in the perspective of history."

3. *Winston Churchill:* "Some foreigners mock at the British Empire because there are no parchment bonds or hard steel shackles which compel its united action. But there are other forces far more compulsive to which the whole fabric spontaneously responds. These deep tides are flowing now. They sweep away in their flow differences of class and party. They override the vast ocean spaces which separate the Dominions of the Queen. . . . The Crown has become the mysterious link, indeed I may say the magic link, which unites our loosely-bound but strongly-interwoven Commonwealth of Nations, States and Races."

4. *Jawaharlal Nehru:* "We are members of the Commonwealth—that rather strange and odd collection of Nations which seems to prosper most in adversity. . . . This Commonwealth has grown and changed repeatedly, and while member Nations sometimes disagree, sometimes have interests conflicting with each other, sometimes pull in different directions, nevertheless, the basic fact remains that they meet as friends, try to understand each other, try to accommodate each other and try, as far as possible, to find a common way of working. That friendly approach, that sympathetic approach, that attempt to understand . . . has led . . . to the success of this rather remarkable experiment."

B. Historical Highlights
   1. *Durham Commission Report*, 1839: proposed that the people in Canada should be permitted to select their own Parliament and have a responsible Cabinet Government; moreover, the new "Governor-General"

should be acceptable to the Canadians and, in representing the British Sovereign, should take into account their interests.

2. *British North America Act,* 1867: provided a formal basic law for a federated Canada and a pattern for similar development in other British colonial territories; shortly thereafter, Australia and New Zealand followed suit.

3. *South African War,* 1899–1900: resulted in addition of Union of South Africa to the evolving Commonwealth and the exchange of "High Commissioners" between Great Britain and the Dominions of Canada, Australia, New Zealand, and South Africa; this "Old Commonwealth" was described as the product of "trial and error," not of an "inspired dialectic."

4. *Imperial Conference,* 1926: concluded that laws enacted by Dominion parliaments could be repealed by the British Parliament and that decisions of Dominion courts could be reviewed by the Judicial Committee of the British Privy Council; see also A-1 above, for description of "the Commonwealth."

5. *Statute of Westminster,* 1931: further clarified relations between Great Britain and the members of the Commonwealth by providing that
   a. Dominion constitutions could not be changed except upon the request of the Dominion Governments.
   b. British Parliament could not pass and enforce laws in the Dominions except upon the request and/or approval of the Dominion Governments.
   c. Great Britain could not invalidate laws passed by the Dominion parliaments.
   d. Limitations were placed on the power of the Judicial Committee of the Privy Council to review cases from the Dominions.
   e. No change could be made in the rule of succession to the British Throne except with the approval of the Dominion parliaments.

6. *Government of India Act,* 1935: substituted "the Federation of India" for the old central government, but did not give India full Dominion status due to the

British retention of power over defense and foreign affairs; the Act eventuated in an independent India and Pakistan twelve years later and a number of new "Independence Acts" for other British territories in Asia and Africa in the 1950's and 1960's.

7. *British Nationality Act,* 1948: described British citizenship and how it could be attained, and the citizenship of women and of the forfeiture or loss of citizenship; the British Government reported that the Act ". . . provides a new method of giving effect to the principle that the people of each of the self-governing countries within the British Commonwealth of Nations have both a particular status as citizens of their own country and a common status as members of the wider association of peoples comprising the Commonwealth."

8. *Prime Ministers' Meeting,* 1949: member countries accepted the fact that a "republican" (i.e., non-monarchical) form of government was possible within the Commonwealth; such countries as India, Pakistan, Ghana, Cyprus, Nigeria, Uganda, Tanganyika, Zanzibar, etc., have since become republics within the Commonwealth yet accept the Sovereign as "the symbol of the free association of the independent member Nations and, as such, Head of the Commonwealth."

9. Numerous Commonwealth Conferences over the last fifteen years have dealt with such a wide variety of subjects as new members, political consultation, economic cooperation, cultural exchanges, scientific and technical developments, education, medical and health services, defense and disarmament, etc.

C. MEMBERSHIP
1. *Steps which British Colonies follow in attainment of independent or Dominion status:*
    a. Control by the Government of Great Britain.
    b. Provision for an Imperial or Colonial Administration.
    c. Gradual development of a colonial Government by the local authorities.
    d. Economic development in the colony, in "cooperation and partnership" with Great Britain.

    e. People in the colony become ready, and express their desire, for political autonomy.

    f. Establishment of an advisory body to study and help develop the situation.

    g. Conferences and consultations between the British Government and the Government (or other representation of the people) in the colony.

    h. Statement of independence, as approved both by the local Assembly and the British Government.

    i. New independent or Dominion Government gets under way, etc.

2. *Recent Membership* (data provided by the British Information Services):

    a. Number of countries under British administration which have become independent since 1945 22

    b. Number which have chosen to become member nations of the Commonwealth 18

    c. Number of member countries of the Commonwealth, including the older members, Britain, Canada, Australia and New Zealand. (The Union of South Africa withdrew from the Commonwealth on May 31, 1961) 18

    d. Such other dependent territories as Northern Rhodesia, Zambia, Gambia, Malta, Basutoland, Bechuanaland, Swaziland, Federation of South Arabia, British Guiana, and Southern Rhodesia subsequently attained (or will shortly attain) full sovereignty and independence, either within or outside the Commonwealth as they might choose.

    e. Other colonies, e.g., the Bahamas, Barbados, British Honduras, and Mauritius, have enjoyed varying degrees of self-government and anticipate their independence presently or in near future.

    f. No uniform pattern has fit all the different territories: some have been strong enough to proceed to independence on their own; some have joined with others to form larger and more viable units; some have completed independence with a treaty of friendship (e.g., western Samoa with New Zealand); and some (namely, the remaining Protectorates) will probably remain, for the present, as they are.

I—COUNTRIES WHICH HAVE BECOME INDEPENDENT WITHIN THE COMMONWEALTH

Country	Area (Sq. miles)	Population (approx.)	Date of Independence
India	1,260,000	437,000,000	August 15, 1947
Pakistan	365,504	93,812,000	August 15, 1947
Ceylon	25,332	10,000,000	February 4, 1948
Ghana	91,843	6,690,741	March 6, 1957
Cyprus	3,752	577,615	August 16, 1960
Nigeria	356,669	40,000,000	October 1, 1960
Sierra Leone	27,925	2,750,000	April 27, 1961
Tanganyika*	362,688	9,237,600	December 9, 1961
Jamaica	4,400	1,639,395	August 6, 1962
Trinidad and Tobago	1,980	828,957	August 31, 1962
Uganda	93,981	6,536,616	October 9, 1962
Federation of Malaysia**	128,462	10,591,550	September 16, 1963
Zanzibar*	1,020	312,000	December 10, 1963
Kenya	224,960	8,676,000	December 12, 1963
Malawi (formerly Nyasaland)	45,747	2,921,100	July 6, 1964
Totals	2,994,263	631,553,574	

* Joined to form the United Republic of Tanganyika and Zanzibar on April 27, 1964, renamed "Tanzania" on October 29, 1964.
** The Federation of Malaysia comprises the former Federation of Malaya which became independent on August 31, 1957, the State of Singapore, North Borneo (now called Sabah) and Sarawak.

II—COUNTRIES WHICH HAVE BECOME INDEPENDENT OUTSIDE THE COMMONWEALTH

	Area	Population	Date
Burma	262,000	21,526,800	January 4, 1948
Sudan	976,750	12,109,000	January 1, 1956
Somaliland	68,000	650,000	June 26, 1960
Southern Cameroons	16,580	753,000	October 1, 1961
Totals	1,323,330	35,038,800	

D. SOME OUTSTANDING FEATURES

1. Member States vary widely in size, geographical position, race, religion, language, composition of population, history, cultural traditions, economic growth, political interests, and international importance.

2. *British Crown* is the one tangible constitutional link joining all the member States, but its constitutional position varies within the different countries.

   a. *Monarchies* (Great Britain, Canada, Australia, New Zealand, etc.): the Queen is the Head of State and the administration of public affairs is carried on in her name as the constitutional Sovereign who "reigns but does not rule"; she is represented in each of these countries by a "Governor-General," appointed by her on the recommendation of the Government concerned.

   b. *Republics* (India, Pakistan, Nigeria, etc.): the Queen is *not* the Head of State and, therefore, has no internal constitutional position in these countries.

   c. However, in both the monarchies and republics, the Queen is given the special status as the symbol of their "free association" and as "Head of the Commonwealth."

3. Commonwealth is neither a Federation (like the United States or Switzerland) nor a Contractual Alliance (like the United Nations); moreover, it has no written constitution, central government, defense forces, or rigid obligations or commitments, and no member State dictates to—or subsidizes the responsibilities of—any other member State.

4. Member States tend to have the same broad pattern of institutions: e.g., common law (except for Ceylon and the French Provinces in Canada), nationality and citizenship, rights of the individual, parliamentary authority, responsible Cabinet, independent judiciary, subdivisional governments, etc.

5. *Consultation and Cooperation* between Great Britain (or the United Kingdom) and the other members of the Commonwealth are obtained through the

   a. Commonwealth Relations Office in London;

   b. Exchange of High Commissioners among all the member States;

c. Conferences of Prime Ministers;
d. Correspondence between the United Kingdom and the other Commonwealth States;
e. Commonwealth Economic Committee in London;
f. Commonwealth Trade and Economic Conferences;
g. Commonwealth Parliamentary Association;
h. Formal and informal visitations of Prime Ministers, other members of the Commonwealth Governments, and among their diplomatic corps;
i. Scientific and cultural associations and their activities;
j. Participation of the member States in the United Nations and other international organizations;
k. Collective security arrangements, e.g., the Southeast Asia Treaty Organization;
l. Economic development programs, e.g., the Colombo Plan;
m. Commonwealth trade, involving many member States in the "sterling area" and "Commonwealth preference";

SELECTED READINGS

Adams, G. B., *Constitutional History of England.* London: Jonathan Cape, 1963.

Amery, L. S., *Thoughts on the Constitution.* London: Oxford University Press, 1953.

Bailey, Sydney D., *British Parliamentary Democracy.* Boston: Houghton-Mifflin Company, 1962.

Barker, Sir Ernest, *Britain and the British People.* New York: Oxford University Press, 1955.

Birch, A. H., *Representative and Responsible Government.* London: G. Allen, 1964.

Campion, Lord, and others, *Parliament; a Survey.* London: G. Allen, and Unwin, 1952.

Carter, Gwendolen, *The Government of the United Kingdom.* New York: Harcourt, Brace & World, Inc., 1963.

Emden, Cecil Stuart, *The People and the Constitution.* Oxford: Clarendon Press, 1956.

Gordon, Strathearn, *The British Parliament.* New York: Frederick A. Praeger, Inc., 1952.

Greaves, Harold R. G., *The British Constitution.* London: G. Allen & Unwin, 1955.

Gunn, S. E., *Crown, Parliament, and People*. London: E. Arnold and Company, 1955.

Guttsman, W. L., *The British Political Elite*. New York: Basic Books, Inc., 1964.

Harrison, Wilfred, *Conflict and Compromise*. Glencoe, Illinois: Free Press, 1965.

Harvey, James, and L. Bather, *The British Constitution*. New York: St. Martin's Press, Inc., 1964.

Jennings, William Ivor, *Cabinet Government*. London: Cambridge University Press, 1951.

————, *The British Constitution*. London: Cambridge University Press, 1958.

Mathiot, Andre, *The British Political System*. Stanford: Stanford University Press, 1958.

Michie, Allan Andrew, *God Save the Queen; a Modern Monarchy: What It Is and What It Does*. New York: William Sloane Associates, Inc., 1953.

Moodie, Graeme, *The Government of Great Britain*. New York: Thomas Y. Crowell Company, 1964.

Morrison, Herbert, *Government and Parliament, A Survey from the Inside*. London: Oxford University Press, 1959.

Muir, Ramsay, *How Britain is Governed*. London: Constable, 1940.

Pike, E. R., *Political Parties and Policies*. London: Sir Isaac Pitman & Sons, Ltd., 1949.

Rose, R., *Politics in England*. Boston: Little, Brown & Company, Inc., 1964.

Smellie, Kingsley Bryce, *The British Way of Life*. New York: Frederick A. Praeger, Inc., 1955.

Stout, Hiram Miller, *British Government*. New York: Oxford University Press, 1953.

Thomas, C. E., *The Dynamics of Nation Building*. Boston: Bruce Humphries, Inc., 1955.

Thomson, D., *England in the Twentieth Century, 1914-63*. London: Jonathan Cape, 1964.

Verney, Douglas V., *British Government and Politics*. New York: Harper & Row, 1966.

White, Leslie William, and William Douglas Hussey, *Government in Great Britain, The Empire and the Commonwealth*. Cambridge: Cambridge University Press, 1957.

Chapter II

FRENCH FIFTH REPUBLIC

POPULATION: 48,500,000 (1964)
AREA: 212,659 sq. miles
CAPITAL: Paris

I. CHRONOLOGY

486—Clovis defeats barbarians and is recognized by Catholic Church as King of the Franks.

732—Charles Martel leads Gauls in successful conflict against Mohammedan invaders and, thereby, saves Europe.

800—Charlemagne crowned "Emperor of the West" by the Pope in Rome.

987—Hugh Capet formally crowned king at Noyon and lays basis for strong monarchial power and national consciousness in France.

1214—Philip Augustus defeats English at Battle of Bouvines and reaffirms monarchial power and unity of French nation.

1338–1453—Hundred Years' War and withdrawal of English from virtually all of France.

1661–1715—"Glorious Reign" of Louis XIV witnesses a flourishing national culture and enhancement of power and prestige of France at expense of other States.

1789—"*Liberté, Egalité, Fraternité* is battle-cry of French Revolution against autocratic Bourbon dynasty.

1792—First Republic proclaimed.

1799–1804—Napoleon Bonaparte named "First Consul" and, subsequently, becomes "Emperor of all the French."

1815—Congress of Vienna marks final defeat of Napoleon and reestablishes Bourbon dynasty.

1830—"Citizen-king" Louis-Philippe becomes limited, constitutional monarch.

1848–1852—Collapse of monarchy leads to Second Republic and establishment of Second Empire under Napoleon III (Louis Napoleon, nephew of Napoleon Bonaparte).

1870–1875—Defeat in Franco-Prussian War and preparation of "Three Constitutional Laws" for the Third French Republic.

1889—"Boulanger affair" an abortive attempt to set aside Republic in favor of a "strong-man" government.

1892—"Dreyfus affair" a national scandal over false conviction of Jewish army captain for allegedly selling military secrets to Germany.

1918—France emerges triumphant in World War I and has political hegemony in western Europe.

1940—Long beset with financial corruption and political instability, France suffers humiliating military defeat by Nazi Germany.

1946—After liberation of France and conclusion of World War II, the Fourth Republic is proclaimed.

1958—Demise of Fourth Republic, recall to power of General Charles De Gaulle, and adoption of new Constitution for the French Fifth Republic.

1965—President De Gaulle is reelected by universal suffrage in the elections held on December 5 and 19 in Metropolitan France and the Overseas Departments and Territories.

1966—France withdraws from NATO, but assures Western Allies "there is no question of withdrawing from [West] Berlin."

II. FRENCH CONSTITUTION

A. *Constitutional Law of June 3, 1958*, directed the (De Gaulle) Government to draft new Constitution on five basic premises:

1. Universal suffrage is the source of power, and from which the legislative and executive powers are derived;
2. Executive and legislative powers must be separated, so that both the Government and the Parliament may properly function each within its own sphere;
3. Government (i.e., executive) must be responsible to the Parliament;
4. Judicial authority must remain independent, so that it may obtain respect for individual freedoms as defined by the "Declaration of the Rights of Man and Citizen" (1789) and by the Preamble to the Constitution of 1946;
5. Constitution should make provision for new relations between the Republic and the peoples associated with it.
6. Constitution of 1958 approved by 80% of the registered voters in Metropolitan France and the Overseas Departments and Territories in the referendum on September 28, 1958, and subsequently amended in 1960 and 1962.

B. FUNDAMENTAL PRINCIPLES OF GOVERNMENT
1. France is an "indivisible, secular, democratic, and social Republic" (Art. 2).
2. Popular sovereignty is expressed through democratic elections and representative legislative bodies.
3. Multiparty system prevails, with the representatives of several parties forming either a parliamentary "Opposition" or a coalition "Government."
4. Separation of the legislative and executive powers, with the latter divided between a President and a *Premier* who is responsible solely to the Parliament.
5. A regular judicial organization, a separate system of administrative courts, and a Constitutional Council which safeguards the interests of the Nation and the rights of the people.
6. Powers of government are centralized, but the territorial units are free to govern themselves through elected councils and other conditions of local autonomy.

Chart 8. STRUCTURE OF THE FRENCH GOVERNMENT

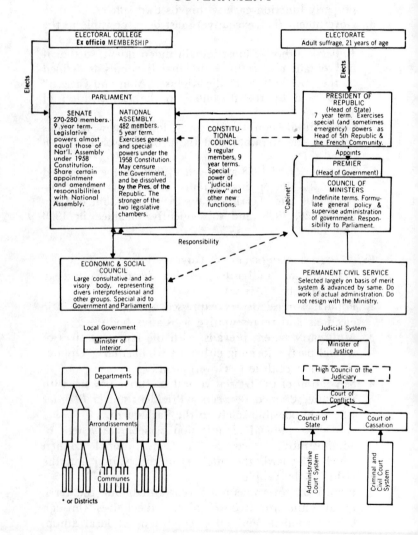

ELECTORAL COLLEGE
Ex officio MEMBERSHIP

ELECTORATE
Adult suffrage, 21 years of age

Elects

Elects

PARLIAMENT

SENATE
270-280 members. 9 year term. Legislative powers almost equal those of Nat'l. Assembly under 1958 Constitution. Share certain appointment and amendment responsibilities with National Assembly.

NATIONAL ASSEMBLY
482 members. 5 year term. Exercises general and special powers under the 1958 Constitution. May censure the Government, and be dissolved **by the Pres. of the** Republic. The stronger of the two legislative chambers.

CONSTITUTIONAL COUNCIL
9 regular members, 9 year terms. Special power of "judicial review" and other new functions.

PRESIDENT OF REPUBLIC
(Head of State)
7 year term. Exercises special (and sometimes emergency) powers as Head of 5th Republic & the French Community.

Appoints

PREMIER
(Head of Government)

"Cabinet"

COUNCIL OF MINISTERS
Indefinite terms. Formulate general policy & supervise administration of government. Responsibility to Parliament.

Responsibility

ECONOMIC & SOCIAL COUNCIL
Large consultative and advisory body, representing divers interprofessional and other groups. Special aid to Government and Parliament.

PERMANENT CIVIL SERVICE
Selected largely on basis of merit system & advanced by same. Do work of actual administration. Do not resign with the Ministry.

Local Government

Minister of Interior

Departments

Arrondissements

Communes

* or Districts

Judicial System

Minister of Justice

High Council of the Judiciary

Court of Conflicts

Council of State

Court of Cassation

Administrative Court System

Criminal and Civil Court System

7. Great emphasis is placed upon "personal dignity and freedom," based primarily on *The Declaration of the rights of Man and of the Citizen, 1789,* and the *Preamble to the French Constitution of 1946.*

C. CONSTITUTIONAL RIGHTS

1. Equal rights for all French citizens.
2. Protection for the individual and the welfare of the family.
3. Care for women and children, the aged and infirm, and those who are unable to work.
4. Right to work without any discrimination.
5. Trade union organization and voluntary affiliation.
6. Right to strike within the framework of legislation.
7. Collective bargaining and assistance in the management of stipulated enterprises.
8. Facilities used in the nationalized public services are the property of the Nation.
9. Equality of right to social security and education.
10. Equality of access to legal proceedings, public facilities, and cultural institutions.
11. Right to vote and hold public office; elections are "universal, equal, and secret" (Art. 3).
12. Right of asylum for political refugees.

D. PROCEDURE FOR AMENDMENT

1. Constitutional amendments are initiated by the President of the Republic on the proposal of the *Premier* and also by members of the Parliament.
2. Amendments must be passed by the two Chambers in identical terms.
3. Amendments become definitive after their approval by a referendum or if approved by three-fifths of the Members of Parliament convened in a joint session by the President of the Republic.
4. Two constitutional limitations.
   a. No amendment can prejudice the integrity of the French territory.
   b. The republican form of government cannot be the object of a constitutional amendment.

III. POLITICAL PARTIES

A. GENERAL CHARACTERISTICS OF THE PARTY SYSTEM
1. Multiparty system, representing many diverse political personalities, principles, policies, and opinions; traditionally
   a. "Leftist" (radical).
   b. "Moderate-Leftist" (politically liberal).
   c. "Centrist" (conciliatory).
   d. "Moderate-Rightist" (economically liberal).
   e. "Rightist" (conservative-reactionary).
2. General apprehension about political "extremism."
3. Parliamentary leadership has frequently evolved from "compromise and concessions," with party groups being "difficult to form, but easy to break."
4. Recurring wide disagreements among the parties about the policies, programs, and objectives of government.
5. Former lack of solidarity and frequent changes in the Government, largely due to the dependence of the Cabinets upon the continued support of party coalitions, partially remedied by the changed relationships of the executive and legislative authorities under the new (1958) Constitution.
6. Political parties and groups "must respect the principles of national sovereignty and of democracy" (Art. 4).

B. LEADING PARTIES AND GROUPS (See Section D below)
1. *Union for the New Republic (UNR):* the party of Charles De Gaulle, which supports the General on personal grounds, rather than for any clear-cut set of party principles; also supported at present by the *Democratic Workers Union* (UDT).
2. *Socialist Party (SFIO):* Left-wing, non-Communist party, which opposes the Government's social and economic policies and also the allegedly highly-nationalistic foreign policy of the "Gaullists."
3. *Democratic Center:* advocates some Left-wing social and economic policies, but many of its membership also associate themselves with the Catholic Church on the "Right"; favors a liberal policy towards the Atlantic Alliance and western European integration; presently

formed by a regrouping of "Moderates" (38 Popular Republicans, 1 affiliate; 6 National Independents' Center, 1 affiliate; 7 Democratic Alliance, 1 affiliate) and 1 affiliate of the "Moderates."

4. *Communist Party:* tends to play down certain basic Marxist tenets and advocates generalized policies (e.g., "peace" and "social betterment") while simultaneously supporting small landowners, business, and industries and some nationalization measures; dominates the largest labor organization (i.e., the *Confederation Generale du Travail—C.G.T.*); inclined to follow the Moscow-line in opposition to the North Atlantic Treaty Organization, German rearmament, and U.S.-supported programs in western Europe.

5. *Democratic Rally:* somewhat stronger on departmental and communal levels than in national politics, and disposed to work through parliamentary *blocs* with "Right-Center" and "Left-Center" parties and groups; defends some Right-wing economic policies, but takes a Left-wing stand in opposition to the political activities of the Catholic Church; supports greater European unity and the Atlantic Alliance; presently formed by regrouping of "Left-Center" deputies (26 Radicals, 3 Democratic Alliance, 2 Democratic and Socialist Resistance Union, 1 Republican Center, 1 Republican Alliance, 1 Socialist, 4 National Independents' Center affiliates) and 1 non-party.

6. *Independent Republicans:* normally, a conservative force which advocates individual rights and free enterprise, and a stronger position for France in international affairs; recently formed after a split in the National Independents' Center.

C. PARTY ORGANIZATION

1. Usually includes "local organizations" in the smaller rural areas, "Sections" in the municipal districts, "Federations" in the *Départements*, and the "National Council" and "Executive Committee" on the national level.

2. Each of the principal parties usually convenes an annual National Convention, Congress, or Conference.

3. Parties represented in the Parliament occasionally

maintain a parliamentary organization consisting of a Chairman, a Caucus, and several operational Committees.

4. The traditional independence of the Deputies makes their parliamentary party leadership and organization uncertain and the relationship between the parliamentary and extraparliamentary organizations, for most parties, is very loose.

5. Ancillary organizations are not usually represented directly in the Parliament, but they may have interests which exercise considerable influence upon the politics of the country; just a few examples include

   a. *Agriculture*

      (1) *General Confederation of Agriculture:* "conservative-rural"; one of the largest and most powerful interest-groups in France; strongly advocates "family agriculture" as the basis of the French economy; finds much support among the political parties, parliamentarians, and public.

   b. *Labor*

      (1) *General Confederation of Labor:* "Communist-dominated"; strongest labor union in France; dominant in the principal industries and trades.

      (2) *French Confederation of Christian Workers:* "liberal-Catholic"; essentially regional in character, but also exerts considerable influence in the textile and light industries and among railroad workers.

      (3) *General Confederation of Labor—Workers' Force:* "socialistic"; smallest labor union; tends to represent the Civil Service and the "white-collar" workers.

   c. *Business and Industry*

      (1) *National Committee of French Employers:* principal French employer's organization; very powerful in politics and in the national economy; seems able to dictate labor contracts and work conditions, due to its own strength and the disunity within the Nation's work forces.

Chart 9. PATTERN OF FRENCH PARTY ORGANIZATION

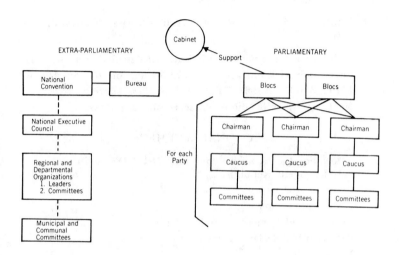

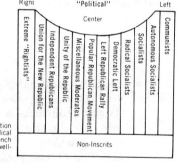

Note: The Extra-Parliamentary organization
shown here is that of the Radical
Socialists specifically. Not all French
parties have such complete and well-
regulated organizations.

d. Other interest-groups include the clerical organizations (e.g., the *National Catholic Confederation*) and military organizations (e.g., the *League of French Patriots*) and countless others, representing more specialized agricultural, cooperative, labor, trade, industrial, business, professional, educational, military, etc. groups.

D. Political Groups Represented in the National Assembly

1. Elections for a new French National Assembly were held by direct universal suffrage with two ballots on the Sunday of March 5 and 12, 1967. The results of these elections, based on final returns for 485 out of 486 seats, were as follows:

NATIONAL ASSEMBLY

Association for the Fifth Republic (UNR, UDT, and Independent Republicans	244
Communist Party	73
Democratic Center	27
Federation of Democratic and Socialist Left	116
PSU—Unified Socialist Party	5
Various Left	5
Various Moderates	15
	485

a. First Assembly (1958) dissolved by Presidential decree (October 9, 1962), following vote by National Assembly on motion of censure condemning procedure for constitutional revision undertaken by the Government.

(1) The French people were called upon to decide by referendum whether a bill to amend the Constitution of 1958, relating to the method of electing the President of the Republic should become law; they decided that it should. The bill was based on a constitutional Article which

states that: "The President of the Republic, on the proposal of the Government during [parliamentary] sessions . . . may submit to a referendum any bill dealing with the organization of the governmental authorities . . . that, without being contrary to the Constitution, might affect the functioning of [existing] institutions" (Art. 11).

b. Older parties of the "Right," "Center," and "Left," failed to regain the positions they occupied during Fourth Republic; most of them (particularly the Popular Republican Movement—MRP and the Independents) suffered big losses since 1958.

c. For first time in history of Fifth Republic the "Government" won an absolute majority in the National Assembly, if one includes the 41 Deputies from various parties elected under the aegis of the "Association for the Fifth Republic," making a total of 274 Deputies in all.

d. There were 218 new Deputies (104 UNR—UDT, 38 Socialists, 32 Communists, 44 others) in this recent National Assembly; and 8 women sat in the Assembly as opposed to 6 in the previous one (2 UNR, 2 MRP, 1 Democratic Rally, and 3 Communist members).

IV. THE GOVERNMENT

A. PRESIDENT OF THE REPUBLIC

1. *Elected by direct universal suffrage*

a. The candidate who obtains an absolute majority of the votes cast on the first ballot is elected President; if this is not obtained, there is a second ballot within eight days; only the two candidates who have received the greatest number of votes on the first ballot may present themselves, and the one who obtains a relative majority of the votes on the second ballot is elected.

b. President serves a seven-year term, receives an annual salary and expense allowances, and maintains an official residence.

2. *Constitutional and legal qualifications* include French citizenship, eligibility to vote in national elections, and such others as required under Organic Laws treating of the French Presidency.
3. *Immunities and liabilities*
   a. Immune from ordinary arrest, but may be indicted for an act of high treason.
   b. Cannot hold any incompatible public office.
   c. When the President is unable to perform his functions, or his office becomes vacant, the President of the Senate exercises his functions until a new President is elected.
4. *Functions and powers*
   Statement by President De Gaulle, January 31, 1964:
   "As far as our own Constitution is concerned, its spirit proceeds from the necessity to assure the Government the effectiveness, the stability and the responsibility which it was fundamentally lacking under the Third and Fourth Republics. . . . That is why the spirit of the new Constitution, while retaining a legislative Parliament, consists in seeing to it that the power is no longer a thing of partisans, but that it emanates directly from the people, which implies that the Head of the State [i.e., the President], elected by the Nation, is the source and holder of this power. . . . This is merely what was clarified by the last referendum [on the election of the President, 1962]. It does not seem that, since it has been applied, this concept has been misunderstood by those holding positions of responsibility, or that it has been rejected by the people, or contradicted by events.

   As for the distribution of powers, this has been observed in accordance with the provisions of our Constitution. The roles attributed respectively: to the President, guarantor of the destiny of France and the Republic, entrusted therefore with heavy duties and possessing extensive rights; to the Cabinet appointed by the Head of State, sitting around him for the determination and application of policy and directing the administration; to the Parliament exercising the legislative power and controlling the action of the Ministers—these roles have been filled as demanded by

Chart 10. FRENCH EXECUTIVE AND ADMINISTRATIVE ORGANIZATION

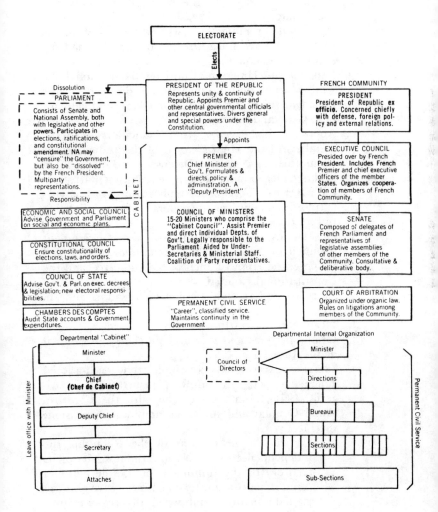

the will of the country, the conditions we are living in, the obligation to conduct affairs actively, firmly, and continuously. . . ."

a. Represents and ensures the legitimacy and continuity of the Republic.

b. Addresses messages to the National Assembly and the Senate.

c. Signs and promulgates laws, decrees, and orders ("Organic" Laws must first be validated by the Constitutional Council).

d. Issues a proclamation dissolving the National Assembly, after consultation with the *Premier* and the Presidents of the legislative Chambers, and calls for new General Elections.

e. Appoints the *Premier*, the Councillors of State, members of the High Council of the Judiciary, the committees of National Defense, the *Prefets*, high-ranking officers and Government representatives to the Overseas Territories, ambassadors and envoys extraordinary, university rectors, and other leading public officials.

f. Presides over the meetings of the Government (Council of Ministers), the committees of National Defense, the High Council of the Judiciary, and the Constitutional Council.

g. Accredits and receives foreign ambassadors and envoys.

h. Negotiates and ratifies treaties.

i. Grants pardons and reprieves (in the High Council of the Judiciary).

j. Exercises exceptional powers in time of national emergency (e.g., the military insurrection in Algeria, 1961), after consultation with the Constitutional Council and under its nominal supervision; specifically,

    (1) "When the institutions of the Republic, the independence of the Nation, the integrity of its territory or the fulfillment of its international commitments are threatened in a grave and immediate manner and when the regular functioning of the constitutional governmental authorities is interrupted, the President of the

Republic shall take the measures commanded by these circumstances, after official consultation with the Premier, the Presidents of the [parliamentary] assemblies and the Constitutional Council. He shall inform the Nation of these measures in a message. These measures must be prompted by the desire to ensure to the constitutional governmental authorities, in the shortest possible time, the means of fulfilling their assigned functions. The Constitutional Council shall be consulted with regard to such measures. Parliament shall meet by right. The National Assembly may not be dissolved during the exercise of emergency powers [by the President]" (Art. 16).

k. Serves as President of the French Community, including Metropolitan France and the Overseas Territories and their respective peoples.

l. Performs divers social and ceremonial functions of State.

B. PREMIER

1. *Appointed by the President of the Republic,* but is responsible only to the Parliament; the President may accept his resignation, but only the Parliament can remove him from office.

   a. *Premier* serves an indefinite term, receives an annual salary and expense allowances, and maintains an official headquarters.

2. *Constitutional and legal qualifications* include citizenship, eligibility as a voter, etc.

3. *Immunities and liabilities*

   a. Immune from ordinary civil arrest, but may be impeached and tried for an act of treason or other offenses as stipulated by law.

   b. Cannot hold an incompatible office, such as membership in the Parliament or a judicial organization.

   c. When the premiership is temporarily vacated, it is filled by a Minister proposed by the Government (Council of Ministers) and approved by the President of the Republic.

4. *Functions and powers*
   a. Sees to the administration of the laws and the day-to-day operations of government.
   b. Appoints governmental Ministers (with or without "portfolio") and certain other civil and military officials.
   c. Supervises the Armed Forces and coordinates measures necessary to the Nation's defense (except in a critical emergency during which the President of the Republic may assume primary responsibilities).
   d. Formulates and supervises governmental policy and its administration.
   e. Addresses the Parliament and handles executive relations with this body.
   f. Initiates legislation in the Parliament and, if necessary, can force its passage (Arts. 45–48).
   g. Countersigns the Acts of Parliament and of the President of the Republic; his own acts are countersigned by appropriate Ministers.
   h. Requests the Parliament to vote approval of the Government's policy and program; this request can only be blocked by an absolute majority vote of the National Assembly.
      (1) If the *Premier* finds an absolute majority against him on a formal "Motion of Censure," he must resign; the President of the Republic then appoints a successor or calls for new parliamentary elections.
   i. Asks the President of the Republic to issue a proclamation dissolving the National Assembly.
   j. Presides over the meetings of the Government ("Cabinet Council"), and attends meetings of other agencies on behalf of the President of the Republic *in absentia*.
   k. Performs other powers and duties as stipulated by law.

C. COUNCIL OF MINISTERS (*Cabinet*)
   1. *Terminology*
      a. "Council of Ministers" is the formal association of the *Premier* and his Ministers; its meetings are pre-

sided over by the President of the Republic; only in these sessions can the acts of the Ministers be given legal authority.

b. "Cabinet" (or "Cabinet Council") is the informal association of the *Premier* and his Ministers; its meetings are presided over by the *Premier;* it is here that the policies and actions of the Government are fully discussed and decided.

2. *Composition*

a. Each Minister is appointed by the *Premier* and is responsible to him.

b. Each Minister must resign his membership in the Parliament; this ensures the "separation of powers" between the executive and legislative branches of government and also makes it possible for the Minister to discharge his ministerial duties free from political pressures.

c. Various political parties and groups are represented in the Council, roughly in proportion to their total numbers in the Parliament.

d. Each ministry is composed of a Minister, various Secretaries and Under-Secretaries of State, and the Permanent Civil Service staff and organizational units.

e. The present ministries include Justice; Foreign Affairs; Interior; Armed Forces; Finance & Economic Affairs; Cooperation (Minister Delegate); National Education; Public Works and Transportation; Industry; Agriculture; Labor; Public Health; Construction; War Veterans & War Victims; Post Office & Telecommunications; Information; and Repatriation.

f. Important Secretaries of State include Algerian Affairs; Relations with Parliament; Foreign Affairs; and Budget.

3. *Functions and responsibility*

a. Ministers administer the policy of the "Government," and

b. Convene in regular and extraordinary meetings.

c. Introduce legislation in the Parliament and countersign parliamentary legislation and presidential actions.

d. Together, request a "vote of confidence" by the National Assembly.

e. Together, support a request by the *Premier* that the President of the Republic dissolve the National Assembly.

f. Sometimes attend and speak before the meetings of the Parliament and its committees.

g. Appoint appropriate officials to supervise the organization and administration of the important functions of the Government and of the local governmental areas.

h. Are individually responsible to the *Premier* and Parliament for their actions, and collectively responsible to the Parliament for their governmental policy and its administration.

    (1) A "Motion of Censure," taken by an absolute majority vote, results in the collective resignation of the *Premier* and his Cabinet.

i. Individually and collectively, perform other duties under the law, such as to issue a regulation to take care of some State activity promptly, or to decree a state of martial law.

    (1) They may not declare war, however, without an authorization of the Parliament.

D. PERMANENT CIVIL SERVICE

  1. *Significant factors*

a. Administrative bureaucracy has traditionally played an important role in French government and politics.

b. A "career" service based largely on the "merit" system.

c. Equality for all men and women, at least in the lower classes of the service.

d. Rights and status of civil service employees are protected by law.

e. Various laws prohibit the civil servant from engaging in outside activities incompatible with his office or which might involve a "conflict of interest" with the discharge of his public responsibility; however, he has considerable freedom to participate in political activity and can run for office and even obtain a leave of absence while holding a political office with the right to return to his civil service position.

f. Periodic reforms are usually engendered from within the service, rather than through the initiative or efforts of outside agencies.

g. Has provided continuity in administration, in spite of frequent changes in Cabinet (i.e., "Government") during the Third and Fourth Republics, and enjoys overall a record for impartiality and efficiency.

h. Alleged weaknesses have included the charge of "elitism," political favoritism in making promotional appointments to the higher classes, excessive formalism in administrative procedure, compartmentalization of individual ministries and, until the adoption of recent reforms, an undemocratic basis for entry into, and lack of uniform personnel policies within, the service.

i. Recent reforms have tended to centralize control and coordination and, largely through wider opportunities to attend the National School of Administration, the basis for recruitment is extended to more segments of the population.

2. *Personnel classifications*

a. *Civil Administrators:* comprise the administrative elite in France; apart from formal qualifications of a university degree and advanced studies in law or public administration, advancement to this class usually results from further special preparations and/or the assistance of some political executive in a position to expedite the advancement.

b. *Secretaries of Administration:* admission or promotion to this class requires a university degree and also a degree in law or advanced studies at the National School of Administration; this category is analogous to the "executive class" in the British Civil Service.

c. *Administrative Clerks:* Junior Clerks are usually re-

cruited on the basis of an open competitive examination from persons who have at least the equivalent of a high school education and can meet such
other qualifications as may be set at any given time;
Senior Clerks usually obtain their positions through
in-service promotional examinations from among
the former category; the class, as a whole, performs
typical stenographic and clerical duties.

d. *Other groups:* e.g., typists, manual workers, etc.;
fewer formal qualifications required; usually obtain
their positions either through an open competitive
examination or an equivalent specific-performance
test.

e. Advancement from a lower to a higher class may,
in addition to the in-service promotional examination, result from further education and study at the
National School of Administration, thus somewhat
equalizing opportunities based on ability rather
than (as before) on social position, wealth, or political influence.

3. *Special agencies*

a. *Civil Service Directorate:* roughly similar to the
British or American Civil Service Commission; concerned chiefly with position classification, recruitment policies, personnel standards for the administrative departments, etc.

b. *National School of Administration:* provides an
opportunity for highly-specialized advanced training for able aspirants to higher civil service positions; entry is obtained through rigorous
competitive examinations for those who meet the
prerequisite educational and other requirements;
the three-year program combines a practical intern-
ship in governmental offices with advanced studies
in specialized subject-matter (e.g., general administration, financial administration, social and economic administration, and foreign affairs); at the
end of the second year, further competitive examinations are administered with only a relatively small
number of candidates proceeding thereafter to the
completion of the third year's work; thus only the

more brilliant candidates graduate from the National School of Administration and secure positions in the higher civil service.

c. *Center for Advanced Studies:* provides an intensive three-month-long in-service training program for selected Senior Administrators, in order to broaden their experience as specialists and give them opportunities for advancement in grade within a class or to a higher class.

d. *General Confederation of Civil Servants:* one of several large-sized unions (or *syndicats*) of civil servants and, presumably, represents their interests with respect to conditions of employment, etc.; the right of civil servants to form trade unions is based primarily on the *Law on the Status of Civil Servants,* 1946; "security" personnel (e.g., prefects, public prosecutors, and police) are expressly prohibited to strike, but it is not yet clear when, and under what conditions, other civil servants may lawfully go on strike.

e. *Superior Council of the Public Service:* consists of an equal representation of staff and employers who are concerned with such matters as the general supervision of the entire civil service, the conduct of studies and preparation of reports, the proposal of reforms, and the settlement of problems affecting the civil service.

f. *Council of State* (see also Section VII-D-2 below): gives technical advice to the Cabinet Ministers on the preparation of laws and decrees, and serves as the supreme administrative tribunal in France.

g. *Court of Accounts:* audits the financial accounts of the Ministries and Departments of Government.

V. PARLIAMENT

A. Descriptive Features of the Parliament
1. Parliament is separated from the Government, so that each exercises its functions on its own responsibility.
2. Bicameral, consisting of a Senate and a National Assembly.

3. Members of Parliament are elected on the basis of universal suffrage.

   a. Their elections and conduct in office are generally adjudged by the members in the individual chamber; each member enjoys the familiar personal inviolability and parliamentary immunity, but may be expelled from his post for a gross abuse of these privileges.

   b. No person can be a member of both chambers simultaneously, or hold membership in the Economic and Social Council or in any other incompatible office.

4. Legislative responsibility resides primarily in the National Assembly, although the Senate exercises nearly equal legislative powers under the Constitution of 1958 and subsequent Organic Laws.

5. Senate and National Assembly meet in two ordinary sessions annually, and in extraordinary session at the request of the *Premier* or a majority of the members of the National Assembly.

6. Such matters as the length of the legislative sessions, the filling of vacant seats, the adjournments, and the salaries and allowances of Members of Parliament are determined by law.

NOTE: The description of the manner of electing Senators to the French Parliament is kindly provided by the Press and Information Service of the Embassy of France (New York City) and is quoted *verbatim* in Section B-1-b below.

B. THE SENATE

1. *Membership*

   a. Approximately 270–280 Senators, elected by indirect suffrage, i.e., by an Electoral College which has been elected by the people, for a nine-year term; the Electoral College consists of (1) the National Assembly, (2) the General Councils, (3) the Territorial Assemblies, and (4) representatives of the municipal councils.

   b. "The election district is the Department. The [members of the] Electoral College of each Department meets in the capital of the Department; it is

presided over by the President of the Civil Court.
. . . Each member of the Electoral College has
only one vote. . . . There are two methods of election: (1) MAJORITY VOTE WITH TWO BAL-
LOTS: this is the method used in Metropolitan
Departments that are entitled to from one to four
Senators and in the Overseas Territories [each Territory elects one Senator]. Each candidate who receives an absolute majority of the votes cast and a
number of votes equal to a quarter of the eligible
voters is elected on the first ballot. In the run-off
election a relative majority is sufficient. . . . (2)
PROPORTIONAL REPRESENTATION accord-
ing to the rule of the highest average is followed in
the Departments that are entitled to five or more
Senators. This system requires only one balloting.
It operates as follows: the number of votes cast is
divided by the number of seats to be filled in order
to obtain the electoral quotient. A list of candidates
is given one seat for each multiple it obtains of the
electoral quotient; thus if it receives a number of
votes equal to four times the electoral quotient, it
obtains four seats; if it receives a number of votes
equal to twice the electoral quotient, it wins two
seats, etc. The seats which remain undistributed
after the completion of this process are assigned to
the lists as follows: the total number of votes obtained by each list is divided by the number of seats
it has already received plus one; thus a number is
obtained for each list which constitutes an average.
The list that obtains the highest average receives an
additional seat. This process is continued until all
the remaining seats have been exhausted."

c. One-third of the Senate is elected every three years,
with original members divided into three classes
A-B-C to serve 3-6-9 years respectively, thereby providing for "staggered" terms in the future.

d. No one may be elected to the Senate who is less
than thirty-five years of age.

e. Senators ensure representation for the territorial
units of the Republic.

(1) In 1966, the Senate consisted of 273 members:

Chart 11. ORGANIZATION OF THE FRENCH PARLIAMENT

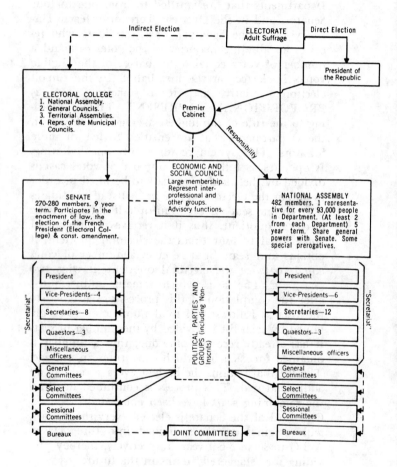

Indirect Election

ELECTORATE
Adult Suffrage

Direct Election

President of
the Republic

ELECTORAL COLLEGE
1. National Assembly.
2. General Councils.
3. Territorial Assemblies.
4. Reprs. of the Municipal Councils.

Premier
Cabinet

Responsibility

ECONOMIC AND
SOCIAL COUNCIL
Large membership.
Represent inter-
professional and
other groups.
Advisory functions.

SENATE
270-280 members. 9 year term. Participates in the enactment of law, the election of the French President (Electoral College) & const. amendment.

NATIONAL ASSEMBLY
482 members. 1 representative for every 93,000 people in Department. (At least 2 from each Department) 5 year term. Share general powers with Senate. Some special prerogatives.

"Secretariat"

President
Vice-Presidents—4
Secretaries—8
Quaestors—3
Miscellaneous officers
General Committees
Select Committees
Sessional Committees
Bureaux

POLITICAL PARTIES AND GROUPS (including Non-Inscrits)

President
Vice-Presidents—6
Secretaries—12
Quaestors—3
Miscellaneous officers
General Committees
Select Committees
Sessional Committees
Bureaux

"Secretariat"

JOINT COMMITTEES

Metropolitan France—255; Overseas Departments—7; Overseas Territories—5; and Frenchmen outside France—6.

2. *Internal Organization*

  a. Based on the Standing Orders of the Senate.

  b. Includes the Secretariat, consisting of a President, four Vice-Presidents, eight Secretaries, and three *Quaestors*; the General, Select, and Sessional Committees; and the Political Groups.

   (1) President opens, presides over, and closes the meetings; convenes the weekly Conference of Presidents; represents the Senate in its communications with the National Assembly and the Government; and maintains the security of the Senate.

   (2) Vice-Presidents assist the President and participate in the Conference of Presidents.

   (3) Secretaries control the roll call and tabulate the votes taken in the Senate.

   (4) *Quaestors*, under the direction of the President, supervise the administration of the Senate's departments.

   (5) General Committees (i.e., "Permanent Committees") maintain their own organization and procedures, with memberships determined on the basis of proportional representation among the Political Groups.

     (a) Among the more important Committees are Finance, General Economy, and Planning; National Defense and Armed Forces; and Foreign Affairs.

   (6) Political Groups consist of Senators grouped together by political affiliations and interests.

     (a) A Senator belongs to only one group at a time, although he may shift his allegiance to another group or help form a new one.

3. *Functions and powers*

  a. Participates in the investiture of the President of the Republic and the President (*Premier*) of the Council of Ministers.

  b. Introduces and passes Parliamentary bills and shares responsibility for the enactment of law.

    c. Accepts, rejects, or proposes amendments to bills passed in the National Assembly.

    d. Puts general questions to the Government.

    e. Shares with the National Assembly (and sometimes the *Premier*) the responsibility for amending the Constitution.

    f. Conducts both regular and extraordinary meetings.

    g. Provides occasional advice and assistance to the President of the Republic.

    h. Exerts a moral authority and temporizing influence on the National Assembly and the Government.

C. THE NATIONAL ASSEMBLY

1. *Membership*

    a. Deputies are elected on a territorial basis from single-member Districts, by direct popular vote with a uninominal list and two ballots for each election District, for a five-year term.

    b. One Deputy for every 93,000 people in the *Département*, and each *Département* (including Overseas) has at least two Deputies.

    c. Membership is renewable all at one time.

    d. Parliamentary elections take place within sixty days before the expiration of a legislative term and involve the

       (1) Filing of candidacies and "substitutes" with electoral officers; each candidate must deposit a guaranty of 100,000 francs, and candidates who do not obtain 5 per cent of the votes forfeit their deposit;

       (2) Conduct of campaigns, with various legal restrictions on the sources and expenditure of finances;

       (3) Compilation of voters' registration lists;

       (4) Balloting on election day (Sunday).

          (a) The people vote in the District of their legal residence, although the sick and infirm, and civilians or members of the Armed Forces serving Overseas may vote by absentee ballot.

          (b) A central Board of Elections decides ques-

tions involving the validity of election procedures and ballots, and tabulates the vote
through offices it maintains in the capital
city of each *Département.*

(c) No one is elected on the first ballot unless
he receives an absolute majority of the
votes, as well as a number of votes equal
to one-fourth of the number of registered
voters; if a second ballot is necessary, a
relative majority is sufficient; only candidates who obtained at least 5 per cent of
the votes on the first ballot may be candidates on the second ballot.

e. Deputies whose seats become vacant because of
death, the acceptance of a ministerial post, membership on a governmental council, or the extension beyond six months of a special assignment
conferred by the "Government" are replaced until
the reelection of the National Assembly by the persons (i.e., "substitutes") who were elected at the
same time as the former to serve this purpose; the
same rule applies to vacancies in the Senate.

2. *Internal organization*

a. Based on the Standing Orders of the National
Assembly.

b. Includes a Secretariat, consisting of a President, six
Vice-Presidents, twelve Secretaries, and three *Quaestors*; the General, Select, and Sessional Committees; and the Political Groups.

(1) President opens, presides over, and adjourns
meetings; convenes the Conference of Presidents; represents the National Assembly in con-
tacts with the Senate and the Government; and
maintains the security of the National Assembly.

(2) General Committees of the National Assembly
closely parallel their opposite number in the
Senate, in name, organization, procedures, etc.,
and include Constitutional Law, Legislation,
and General Administration of the Republic;
Finance, General Economy, and Planning; Pro-

duction and Trade; Cultural, Family, and Social Affairs; National Defense and Armed
Forces; and Foreign Affairs.

(3) Political Groups are established and function
in a manner similar to their counterparts in the
Senate (See Section III-D above).

3. *Functions and powers*

a. Participates in the investiture of the President of
the Republic and the President (*Premier*) of the
Council of Ministers.

b. Enacts basic legislation (but "regulations" are in
the province of the Government), new expenditures, and the national budget.

c. Regulates the accounts of the State (through the
Cour des Comptes).

d. Makes provision for the government of dependent
territories.

e. Elects some of the members of the High Court of
Justice.

f. Approves treaties negotiated and ratified by the
President of the Republic.

g. Conducts legislative investigations and hearings.

h. Puts questions to the Government.

i. May force the incumbent "Government" to resign
by adopting a "Motion of Censure" by an absolute
majority vote.

j. Impeaches the President of the Republic for an alleged act of treason and the *Premier*, Cabinet Ministers, and other high officials for criminal acts and
serious misdemeanors.

k. Grants an amnesty under conditions stipulated by
law.

l. Declares war.

m. Performs other miscellaneous duties.

4. *Lawmaking*

a. Bills: "Government" and "Parliamentary."

(1) Bills introduced by a member of the Government have priority over bills of individual
Members of Parliament.

(2) The Government may force the passage of a

bill and, under certain conditions, declare others to be inadmissible (Art. 41 ff.).

    (3) Finance bills are submitted first to the National Assembly.

b. Initial procedures.

    (1) Introduction of a bill in the parliamentary chamber.

    (2) Consideration of the bill by the appropriate General or Select Committee.

    (3) Report on the bill by the Committee to the full chamber (a "Motion of Urgency" requires a recalcitrant committee to make a report).

c. Debates

    (1) President of the legislative chamber usually permits the *Rapporteur* and other members of the Committee to speak first; then the spokesmen for the Political Groups and individual parties express themselves on the bill.

    (2) Speeches are delivered in person, from a Deputy's seat or "at the Tribune"; representatives of the Government and other non-Members of Parliament may be permitted to speak.

    (3) Three members of the reporting committee may form a group to propose taking a vote on their bill.

    (4) New organic legislation has somewhat modified the rules of procedure governing debate and closure.

d. Voting.

    (1) Except in unusual circumstances (Art. 27), Members of Parliament must vote in person; this is done by a show of hands, by a rising vote, by simple open ballot at each Deputy's seat, or "at the Tribune"; the secret ballot is also frequently used.

e. Similar treatment and passage of the bill in the other chamber.

    (1) In case of disagreement between the two chambers, the *Premier* may call for a Joint Committee, with an equal number of representatives from both chambers.

      (a) The *Premier* may request the National Assembly to rule definitively on the final text of a bill, in case of continued disagreement between the chambers.

  f. Acceptance and promulgation of the new law by the President of the Republic.

      (1) He may request the Parliament to reconsider the bill, or ask the people to express its opinion on the matter in a national referendum.

      (2) He must consult with the Constitutional Council on the constitutionality of an Organic Law (and international agreements) before he promulgates it.

      (3) The *Premier* and an appropriate Minister must countersign the law.

  g. Other considerations.

      (1) Financial legislation is primarily the work of the Ministry of Finance and the Finance Committee of each Chamber of the Parliament; an Audit Office assists the Parliament and the Government in supervising the implementation of financial legislation.

      (2) Nonparliamentary lawmaking, including the orders and regulations of the ministries, is conducted under the general surveillance of the Council of State.

VI. CONSTITUTIONAL COUNCIL; ECONOMIC AND SOCIAL COUNCIL

A. CONSTITUTIONAL COUNCIL

  1. *Membership*

    a. Consists of nine regular members, three of whom are chosen by the President of the Republic, three by the President of the Senate, and three by the President of the National Assembly, for a nine-year term; former Presidents of the Republic are *ex officio* members for life.

      (1) Originally, three members were appointed for three years, three for six years, and three for nine years; the French President and the Pres-

idents of the Senate and National Assembly appointed one member in each series.

b. Membership in the Constitutional Council is incompatible with membership in the "Government," the Parliament, and the Economic and Social Council.

c. President of the Republic administers the oath of office; the members of the Council swear to fulfill their duties faithfully, to be impartial in their application of the Constitution, to keep their deliberations and votes secret, to accept no public award, and to give no private consultation on questions within their sphere of competence.

d. Members receive a regular salary and allowances as provided by law.

e. If a member tenders his resignation to the Council, a replacement is appointed within thirty days thereafter.

(1) The replacement serves the remainder of his predecessor's term, and can be reappointed for a full term provided he has served as replacement for at least three years.

f. A decree of the Council of Ministers (presumably) guarantees the independent functioning of the Constitutional Council.

g. The President of the Council is appointed by the President of the Republic, and casts the deciding vote in case of a tie.

2. *Functions and powers*

a. Oversees the constitutionality of the election of the President of the Republic, the Members of Parliament and other officials, and the administration of national referenda and the general census.

b. Validates the text of all Organic Laws (which treat of the basic institutions of Government under the Constitution) and the rules of procedure of the various public bodies.

c. Reviews the contents of regular legislation and ministerial decrees to determine their constitutionality; if an unconstitutional provision is inseparable from the whole, the law or decree is not enforceable.

(1) A serious question may require the Parliament or the "Government" to revise the law or decree, or the Constitution itself might be amended to make the law or decree effective.

d. Expresses its opinion on the constitutionality of an international treaty or convention.

e. Consults with the President of the Republic on measures to be taken in a national emergency (Art. 16).

f. Verifies, upon the request of the "Government," a vacancy or impediment in the office of the President of the Republic, so that a new presidential election may take place.

3. *Procedures*

a. Constitutional Council is convened by its President or, in extraordinary circumstances, by the President of the Republic or the "Government."

b. Petitions to the Council must be written, and contain relevant information about the petitioner and the subject of the petition.

c. Rulings are made within thirty days, but if the "Government" declares an "urgency" the period is reduced to one week.

d. Decisions are taken by at least seven members of the Council, and "may not be appealed to any jurisdiction whatsoever. They must be recognized by the governmental authorities and by all administrative and juridical authorities" (Art. 62).

B. ECONOMIC AND SOCIAL COUNCIL

1. *Membership*

a. Represents virtually all economic and social interests in Metropolitan France and the Overseas Territories.

b. Selected by the most representative organization in each of several categories (e.g., agricultural and cooperative associations; labor and employee organizations; industrial, commercial, and trade enterprises; technical and engineering staff; civil servants; etc.), or in such other manner as prescribed by ministerial decree after consultation with the Council of State.

    c. Members serve a five-year term, with such salaries and allowances as provided by law.

    d. Maintains a *Bureau*, comprised of a President, four Vice-Presidents, and several additional members; a Secretary-General, appointed by the Government on the recommendation of the *Bureau*; and several specialized Divisions (e.g., on general economic and social problems; technical research and information; regional development; foreign economic expansion; and economic cooperation with the member States of the Community).

2. *Functions and powers*

    a. Advises the Government on proposed Government bills and decrees, and on parliamentary bills submitted to it for opinion.

    b. Consults with the Government on any economic or social matter of interest to the Republic or the Community; economic and social plans are presented to the Council for its advice.

    c. Fosters collaboration among the different interest groups in the implementation of the economic and social policies of the Government, and studies ways in which the Republic can participate in the economic and social development of the Community.

    d. Submits, on its own initiative, proposed reforms or new developments in the economic and social sectors to the Government; each year, the Premier reports to the Parliament on programs undertaken on/with the advice of the Council.

    e. Establishes temporary committees to study special problems and, later, reviews their reports and prepares recommendations for possible further assistance to the Government and the Parliament.

3. *Procedures*

    a. Meets in regular session every three months and in special sessions as convoked by the Government.

    b. President of the Economic and Social Council opens and adjourns the sessions.

    c. Members of the Government may attend the meetings of the Council and its Divisions, and be heard by them.

    d. Voting in the Council is personal, and cannot be taken by proxy.

    e. On the recommendation of the *Bureau*, the Economic and Social Council pronounces rulings which are later reviewed by the Government (with the Council of State) and confirmed in ministerial decrees.

    f. Reports and rulings of the Economic and Social Council are usually submitted to the Government within a designated time period and subsequently entered in the *Journal Officiel*.

    g. It is anticipated that additional decrees and/or laws will further clarify the role and functions of the Economic and Social Council.

VII. JUDICIAL SYSTEM

A. Theory and Practice of Law and Justice

    1. Dual system of "ordinary" and "administrative" courts.

    2. Preference for codified law (e.g., Codes Napoleon), implemented by statutory law and administrative decrees.

    3. Emphasis is placed upon the security of the Nation as well as the protection of individual rights.

    4. No grand jury indictments nor extensive use of the *petit* jury.

    5. Tradition of localized justice being altered by new attempts to centralize the courts in departmental areas.

    6. Use of the judicial collegium or panel of judges to decide important cases.

    7. Limited right of appeal, but the cost of review (in Cassation) is borne by the State.

    8. "Available, inexpensive, and equal justice" everywhere in France.

    9. Recent reform in the lower judicial structures and centralization of the regular court organization (See Section C below).

B. High Council of the Judiciary

    1. *Membership*

        a. Composed of nine members, appointed by the President of the Republic who serves as its President;

the Minister of Justice is its Vice-President *ex officio*.

(1) Three members are selected from the Court of Cassation; three members from the ordinary courts and tribunals; one member from the Council of State; and two members who are not of the judiciary, but are chosen by reason of their special competence.

b. Members of the High Council may not, during their tenure, be a Member of Parliament, or of the Government or civil service, or practice law.

c. Members serve a four-year term, and if a vacancy occurs before the end of a term, a replacement is appointed within three months; members are eligible for reappointment only once, and the appointment of new members to replace those with expiring terms takes place at least fifteen days before the expiration of the terms.

d. High Councillors cannot be promoted or transferred during their tenure, but the President of the Republic can determine that a High Councillor should be replaced by reason of inability to perform his functions; the replacement is made within three months.

e. Members of the High Council are pledged to maintain the secrecy of its deliberations; their organization (including a *Bureau* or Secretariat) and procedures are determined by ministerial decrees.

f. Salaries and allowances of members are fixed by law and the necessary funds for the functioning of the High Council are included in the budget of the Ministry of Justice.

2. *Functions and powers*

a. Submits proposals to the President of the Republic on the nomination of judges to the Court of Cassation or for First President of the Courts of Appeal and Courts of Assize.

b. Gives its opinion on proposals by the Minister of Justice for the nomination of other judges, and on the conferring of honorary distinctions to members of the judiciary.

c. Consults with the President of the Republic on all questions concerning the independence of the judiciary.

d. Advises the French President on pardons and reprieves.

e. Serves as a disciplinary council in supervising the conduct of judges.

3. *Procedures*

a. High Council convenes at the summons of its President (the President of the Republic) or Vice-President (the Minister of Justice).

b. A quorum consists of the President or Vice-Persident and at least five other members of the High Council.

c. When the High Council of the Judiciary sits as a disciplinary council, it is presided over by the First President of the Court of Cassation; the President of the Republic and the Minister of Justice do not attend the hearings, and the proceedings and applicable sanctions are determined by an Organic Law on the status of the judiciary.

d. On appeals for pardon, the High Council may delegate to one of its members the preparation of the *dossier* to be submitted to the President of the Republic before whom an appeal has been made.

e. High Council submits its opinion on a proposal by the Minister of Justice in a report prepared by one of its members for the President of the Republic.

f. Decisions are taken by simple majority vote and the President casts the deciding vote in case of a tie.

C. REGULAR COURTS

1. *Minor Courts of First Instance (Tribunaux de Premiere Instance—467)*

a. Under a single judge each and with enlarged territorial and material jurisdiction.

b. Established in each *Arrondissement* to settle small civil disputes.

2. *Major Courts of First Instance (Tribunaux de Grande Instance—178)*

Chart 12. ORGANIZATION OF THE FRENCH COURT SYSTEM

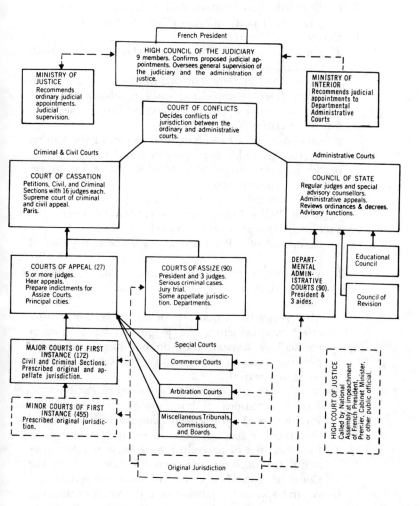

    a. Under a single judge each and with enlarged territorial and material jurisdiction.

    b. Established in each *Département* to settle larger civil disputes.

3. *Police Courts (Tribunaux de Police)*

    a. Under a single judge each *(Juge d'Instance)*.

    b. Established in Cantons and *Arrondissements* to dispose of all petty offenses *(Contraventions)*.

4. *Correctional Courts*

    a. Under a panel of three judges, who administer both criminal and civil justice.

    b. Established in *Départements* to dispose of graver offenses *(Délits)*, including cases involving terms of imprisonment up to five years; no jury is used.

5. *Courts of Assize (Cours d'Assises)*

    a. Composed of a President, two judges of the Courts of Appeal, and a *petit* jury of nine members.

    b. Sit in every *Département*, when called on to try major criminal cases.

    c. Have limited appellate jurisdiction over decisions of the Police Courts and Correctional Courts.

6. *Courts of Appeal (Cours d'Appel—30)*

    a. Composed of a President and a variable number of judges.

    b. Have jurisdiction in one or more *Départements*, and review decisions of both the regular and special courts.

    c. After reviewing a question of law or fact, or considering new evidence, the judges render a "proper verdict" on appeal; they do not merely reverse a previous decision nor remand a case back to a lower court for retrial.

7. *Court of Cassation (Cour de Cassation) in Paris*

    a. Review questions in law, not of fact; e.g., if the President and judges who comprise this court feel that the law has not been correctly interpreted, or that the rules of procedure have been violated, they annul the decision and send the case back to the Court of Appeal or Court of Assize for retrial.

    b. A final appeal for pardon or reprieve from sentence can, in an extraordinary case, be made to the President of the Republic.

D. ADMINISTRATIVE COURTS

    1. *Departmental Administrative Courts*

        a. Have replaced the former Interdepartmental Prefectural Councils, and exercise original jurisdiction in different types of cases involving the Government and public officials.

        b. Hear and decide thousands of cases annually, dealing with such matters as local tax assessments, local elections, local properties, and claims against local public officials.

        c. Decisions are not usually appealed to any higher authority.

    2. *Council of State (Conseil d'État) in Paris*

        a. Divided into specialized administrative and judicial Sections to render advisory opinions on laws and decrees and to handle cases in administrative law.

            (1) Reviews and may annul administrative decrees on the basis of an exercise of authority not legally enjoyed *(exces de pouvoir)*, or the misuse of legal authority *(détournement de pouvoir)*, or an irregularity in form.

            (2) A private citizen, professional group, or civil servant may bring an action before the Council against the arbitrary or illegal actions of a governmental agency or public official (but not against the national legislature).

            (3) A separate suit for damages from the Government may be instituted if the Council has annulled an order or decree.

        b. Councillors-of-State are exceptionally well-trained personnel, usually recruited from the National School of Administration.

        c. The *Law on the Organization of the Council of State*, 1963, describes in detail the composition and procedures of this organ performing both administrative and judicial functions.

    3. *Court of Conflicts (Tribunal des Conflits)*

        a. This adjudicative body includes the Minister of Justice, representatives from both the Court of Cassation and the Council of State, and certain other members selected by "cooptation."

        b. Its primary function is to settle conflicts of jurisdiction between the ordinary and administrative courts.

4. *Droit Administratif*
   a. Law which permits a citizen or group to seek redress (in a civil action) from either the local or national public authorities, for an alleged unlawful action by an official of the State; the question is whether or not the administrative decree or action conforms with legislation, not the "constitutionality" of legislation *per se* (cf. Constitutional Council).
   b. Liability of public officials depends on the particular kind of act they commit.
      (1) Private act: personal liability may follow in the ordinary courts.
      (2) Act of Administration: the "Government" may be held liable in its corporate capacity by the administrative courts.
      (3) Act of State: the judiciary has no jurisdiction here, so there is no liability either for a principal or agent of the State.
   c. Administrative courts provide "cheap, ready, and certain" justice in holding public officials responsible for a strict observance of the letter of the law.

E. SPECIAL COURTS
   1. *High Court of Justice*
      a. Composed of twenty-four regular members and twelve alternate members elected in equal numbers by the National Assembly and the Senate from their own memberships.
      b. Has the power to try in impeachment proceedings the President of the Republic for high treason and members of the Government for crimes and misdemeanors and, in the discharge of this responsibility, is ". . . bound by the definition of crimes and misdemeanors, as well as by the determination of penalties, as they are established by the criminal laws in force when the acts are committed" (Art. 68).
      c. The *Law on the High Court of Justice*, 1959, describes in detail the rules and procedures to be followed before the sittings of this court.

2. *State Security Court*
   a. Composed of three civilian judges and two high military judges.
   b. Has jurisdiction to deal with subversion in peacetime.
3. *Commerce Courts (Tribunaux de Commerce)*
   a. Staffed by businessmen, chosen by other businessmen, to settle disputes between commercial concerns; members serve for two years.
4. *Labor Conciliation Boards (Conseils de Prud'hommes)*
   a. Consist of an equal number of employers and employees, and deal with small trade and industrial disputes.
5. *Miscellaneous courts and commissions* (e.g., Military Tribunals, Claims Commissions, and Social Security Boards).

F. SOME OBSERVATIONS ON JUDICIAL PERSONNEL AND COURT PROCEDURES
   1. Most judges are appointed by the President of the Republic upon the recommendation of the High Council of the Judiciary, which bases its recommendations upon the results of competitive examinations.
   2. Judges and prosecutors are well-trained, highly-qualified, and experienced individuals.
   3. Members of the regular judiciary take an oath of office, ordinarily serve "during good behavior," and receive a remuneration as provided by law; they must reside in the district within their jurisdiction.
   4. Judges cannot engage in political activities, be a Member of Parliament or of the Government or a national or local Council, nor hold or practice any other incompatible office or activity.
   5. Frequently, an examining judge *(Juge d'Instruction)* will conduct a preliminary inquiry in secrecy and then decide either to dismiss a case or send it for trial before a court where a public prosecutor endeavors to prove the charge.
      a. The State's interests are represented by the *Parquets* and *Advocats-General* within the Ministry of Justice, and also by the Ministry of the Interior, which controls the national and local police authorities.

6. Judges in many of the courts have considerable control over courtroom procedures and may assume the initiative in interrogating witnesses, ascertaining facts, and deciding justice.

VIII. LOCAL GOVERNMENT

A. BASIC ELEMENTS OF LOCAL GOVERNMENT
1. The *Départements* include certain Overseas Territories; the *Arrondissements* and *Cantons* are largely judicial and military areas within the *Départements*; the *Communes* are the basic unit of local authority; and there are special arrangements for Paris and the larger cities.
2. Organization and powers of the local authorities are determined by national legislation and Organic Laws.
3. Council of Ministers appoints central authorities who supervise the coordination of activities by local governmental officials and the representation of the national interests.
4. Local authorities have a twofold function to perform, i.e., to serve as units for central administration and also as units of government on the local level.
5. Appointive civil servants (i.e., the Prefects, sub-Prefects, judges, police commissioners, educational officers, tax assessors, and tax collectors) are not eligible for election to the regional and local Councils.

B. *Département* (90 in Metropolitan France and 4 Overseas)
1. Prefect *(Prefet)*
   a. He (and his chief staff) are appointed by the Minister of the Interior and the Council of Ministers for an indefinite term of office.
   b. His general twofold function is to serve as the agent of the central Government and the representative of the *Département*; however, he also
      (1) Promulgates decrees;
      (2) Directs various public services;
      (3) Makes a large number of appointments;
      (4) Supervises mayors;
      (5) Reviews the municipal budgets;

        (6) Performs social and ceremonial duties;

        (7) Reports to the central authorities.

    c. He may be transferred or demoted, but is seldom dismissed from office.

    d. Receives a regular salary and expense allowances.

    e. In recent years, several "super-Prefects" have been established to act as general inspectors of departmental administration in France.

2. General Council *(Conseil)*

    a. Consists of a varying number of elected delegates, each of whom represents a single *Canton*.

        (1) Councillors must be French citizens, at least twenty-three years of age, and residents or taxpayers in their Districts.

        (2) They serve a six-year term of office, with one-half of their positions being filled every three years; they are unpaid for their services.

        (3) Councillors usually convene in regular sessions at least twice a year, but special or emergency meetings may be called by the Prefect or by the Council's Interim Commission on the request of two-thirds of the Councillors.

    b. Restrictions of national legislation, and the power of the Prefect and central Government to overrule its decisions, greatly limit the actions of the General Council; however, it may

        (1) Pass upon the departmental budget;

        (2) Apportion the departmental taxes;

        (3) Administer the departmental properties;

        (4) Manage the departmental (and some communal) affairs;

        (5) Perform other miscellaneous functions.

C. *Arrondissement* (more than 300)

1. Sub-Prefect

    a. He assists the Prefect in the administration of central and prefectural orders and decrees, and renders reports to the Prefect on conditions within the *Arrondissement*.

        (1) An advisory Council and administrative staff us-

Chart 13. AGENCIES OF LOCAL GOVERNMENT IN FRANCE

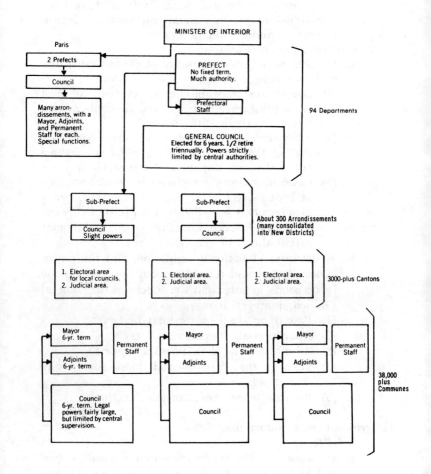

ually assist him in the performance of these duties.

2. *Arrondissements* could formerly be compared with American Congressional Districts in providing the basis for the election of members of Parliament (Fourth Republic).

D. CANTON (more than 3,000)
   1. Special area, which may have various military representatives, magistrates, police *(Gendarmerie)*, tax collectors, etc.
   2. Used as a basic election district for the departmental General Council.

E. COMMUNE (more than 38,000)
   1. Major *(Maire)*
      a. Usually selected by the Communal Council for a designated term in office.
      b. Among his many functions, he
         (1) Promulgates national and departmental decrees;
         (2) Supervises local services;
         (3) Appoints certain local officers;
         (4) Cooperates with higher authorities in the administration of national services;
         (5) Submits the budget to the Council;
         (6) Executes the resolutions of the Council;
         (7) Performs social and ceremonial duties.
      c. May be suspended or removed from office by the departmental Prefect or central Government.
      d. May hold other governmental positions and be a Member of Parliament (i.e., the Mayors' *bloc*).
      e. Receives no regular salary for his services.
   2. Communal Council
      a. Consists of a number of delegates (10 to 40) chosen by direct popular vote for a six-year term in office.
         (1) Councillors must meet the various legal requirements for office; they perform their services voluntarily.
         (2) They usually convene four general sessions a year, but may also hold special meetings called

by a higher authority or by the Council's Interim Commission.
b. Supervisory powers of the President or the departmental Council, the Prefect, and the central Government strictly limit the authority of the communal Council.
(1) It performs only functions within the framework of a Municipal Code and national legislation.
3. Other communal officers and staff
a. "Adjoints" (assistants to the Mayors).
b. Commissioner of Police.
c. Local *Bureaux*.
d. *Ad hoc* administrative units.
e. Permanent Civil Service.
f. Communal Secretary, Treasurer, etc.

F. PARIS
1. Located in the *Département* of the Seine, and has two Prefects (one for administration and one for police), a Mayor, and a Council of 90 members.
a. Seine *Département* is subdivided into 20 *Arrondissements* and 9 Districts, each of which has its own Mayor, Council, and administrative staff.
2. A recently-created Paris Area Authority *(District de la Region de Paris)* has undertaken studies to alleviate the problems of a highly-urbanized metropolitan area which comprises a fifth of the population of France; its recommendations for reorganization of the component local authorities and for reform in the administration of local services are reviewed by the Council of Ministers (in consultation with the Council of State) and, if the recommendations are accepted, they are put into effect by ministerial decrees.

IX. THE COMMUNITY

A. BASIC PRINCIPLES
1. Self-determination and autonomy of peoples.
2. Equality before the law, regardless of origin, race, or religion.

3. Representation of all members in the common institutions.
4. Consultation and participation at times of referenda.
5. Only one common citizenship.

B. COMPOSITION
1. France and the self-governing States of the former French colonial Empire which have chosen to join the Community; in 1966, this included Metropolitan France and her Overseas *Départements* and Territories, and the Republics of Central Africa, Chad, Congo, Gabon, Malagasy, and Senegal, all of which had previously concluded formal "Community Participation Agreements."
2. Other special relations or cooperation existed between France and such former colonial areas as the Cameouns, Dahomey, Guinea, Ivory Coast, Mali, Mauritania, Niger, Togoland, Upper Volta, etc.
3. Under the Constitution of 1958, as amended, member States may either leave the Community or change their status, if they wish; new member States may also be added.
   a. "A member State . . . may . . . by means of agreements, become independent without thereby ceasing to belong to the Community. An independent State not a member of the Community may, by means of agreements, join the Community without ceasing to be independent. The position of these States within the Community shall be determined by agreements concluded to this end. . . ." (Art. 86).

C. JURISDICTION
1. Community has jurisdiction over foreign policy, defense, common economic and financial policy, and policy on strategic raw materials, supervision of the courts, higher education, the organization of external transportation, and telecommunications.
2. Special agreements may create other common jurisdictions or provide for the transfer of certain jurisdictions to one of the member States.
3. Matters not enumerated above fall within the jurisdiction of the self-governing member States.

D. COMMON INSTITUTIONS
1. *President of the Community* (the President of the French Republic *ex officio*) who is represented in each member State; the President
   a. Sees that the Organic Law of the Community, Community agreements, the decisions of the Court of Arbitration (see Section 4 below), and treaties and international agreements that commit the Community are respected.
   b. Formulates and publishes the measures necessary for the management of common affairs and sees that these measures are carried out.
2. *Executive Council* (the President and *Premier* of the French Republic, the Head of the Government of each member State, and other Ministers responsible for the common affairs of the Community), which has its headquarters in Paris but may meet in the capital city of another member State to "organize the cooperation of members of the Community at Government and administrative levels" (Art. 82); the Council also
   a. Discusses questions about the general policy of the Community with respect to matters within its jurisdiction.
   b. Deliberates on the administrative budget of the Community, as well as the distribution of the expenditures resulting from common policy.
   c. Organizes its work through *ad hoc* committees, composed of a Chairman appointed by the President of the Community, of the Ministers responsible for common affairs, and of the interested Ministers of the member States of the Community, and aided by a Secretariat which is similarly appointed.
3. *Senate of the Community* (the 300 or fewer delegates from the French Parliament and the legislative assemblies of the member States) which meets semiannually in Paris to "deliberate on the common economic and financial policy before laws on these matters are voted upon by the Parliament of the Republic and . . . by the legislative assemblies of the other members of the Community" (Art. 83); the Senate also
   a. Studies the acts and international treaties which commit the Community.

    b. Makes binding decisions in the domains in which power has been delegated to it by the legislative assemblies of the member States.

4. *Court of Arbitration* (the seven judges appointed for six-year terms by the President of the Community and chosen from among the States of the Community), which settles any litigations arising between the member States arising from constitutional provisions, Organic Laws and Community agreements, and other conventions between the member States; the judges

    a. Are independent and may not be dismissed during their term of office.

    b. Review petitions presented either by a member State of the Community, or in the name of the Community.

    c. Make decisions which are binding through the whole of the territory of the Community.

E. French Government asserts the Community is more than a "Commonwealth," because it has "common affairs" over which the institutions of the Community alone have jurisdiction, but less than a "Federation," because each member State has great freedom to manage its internal affairs.

SELECTED READINGS

Aron, Raymond, *France: the New Republic.* New York: Oceana Publications, 1960.

Bauchet, P., *Economic Planning.* New York: Frederick A. Praeger, Inc., 1964.

Campbell, Peter, *French Electoral Systems and Elections, 1789–1957.* New York: Frederick A. Praeger, Inc., 1958.

Cantril, Hadley, *The Politics of Despair.* New York: Basic Books, Inc., 1958.

Charvet, Patrick Edward, *France.* New York: Frederick A. Praeger, Inc., 1955.

David, Rene, and Henry P. de Vries, *The French Legal System, An Introduction to Civil Law Systems.* New York: Oceana Publications, 1958.

Duby, G., and R. Mandrou, *A History of French Civilization.* New York: Random House, Inc., 1965.

Earle, Edward M., ed., *Modern France: Problems of the Third and Fourth Republics.* Princeton: Princeton University Press, 1951.

Furniss, Edgar, *France, Troubled Ally, De Gaulle's Heritage and Prospects*. New York: Harper and Row, 1960.

Gavin, Catherine Irvine, *Liberated France*. London: Cape, 1955.

Godfrey, E. Drexel, Jr., *The Government of France*. New York: Thomas Y. Crowell Company, 1963.

Goguel, François, *France Under the Fourth Republic*. Ithaca: Cornell University Press, 1952.

Guerard, Albert Leon, *France, A Modern History*. Ann Arbor: University of Michigan Press, 1959.

Hadrill, J. M. Wallace, and J. McManners, eds., *France: Government and Society*. London: Methuen, 1957.

Kohn, Hans, *Making of the Modern French Mind*. New York: D. Van Nostrand Company, Inc., 1955.

Laponce, J. A., *The Government of the Fifth Republic, French Political Parties and the Constitution*. Berkeley: University of California Press, 1961.

Leites, Nathan, *On the Game of Politics in France*. Stanford University Press, 1959.

Luethy, Herbert, *France Against Herself; the Past, Politics and Crises of Modern France*. New York: Meridian Books, Inc., 1960.

Macridis, Roy C., and Bernard E. Brown, *The De Gaulle Republic; Quest for Unity*. Homewood, Illinois: Dorsey Press, Inc., 1960.

Mauriac, François, *De Gaulle*. Garden City, New York: Doubleday & Doubleday, Inc., 1966.

Maurois, Andre, *A History of France*. London: Methuen, 1964.

Moraze, Charles, *The French and the Republic*. Ithaca: Cornell University Press, 1958.

Padover, Saul Kussiel, *French Institutions: Values and Politics*. Stanford: Stanford University Press, 1954.

Paul, E. H., *Understanding the French*. New York: Random House, 1955.

Pickles, Dorothy, *The Fifth Republic*. New York: Frederick A. Praeger, Inc., 1962.

Roe, Frederick Charles, *Modern France*. New York: Longmans, Green & Company, Inc., 1956.

Schoenbrun, David, *As France Goes*. New York: Harper, 1957.

Schwartz, Bernard, *French Administrative Law and the Common-Law World*. New York: New York University Press, 1954.

Tannenbaum, Edward R., *The New France*. Chicago: University of Chicago Press, 1961.

Taylor, O. R., *The Fourth Republic of France, Constitution and Political Parties*. New York: Oxford University Press, 1951.

Thomson, David, *Democracy in France: the Third and Fourth Republics*. New York: Oxford University Press, 1952.

Wahl, Nicholas, *The Fifth Republic: France's New Political System.*
New York: Random House, 1959.

Werth, Alexander, *The De Gaulle Revolution.* London: Hale, 1960.

Williams, Philip M., and Martin Harrison, *De Gaulle's Republic.*
New York: Longmans, Green & Company, Inc., 1960.

Wright, Gordon, *France in Modern Times,* Chicago: Rand McNally
& Company, 1962.

Chapter III

FEDERAL REPUBLIC
OF GERMANY

POPULATION: 58,000,000 (1964)
AREA: 96,114 sq. miles
CAPITAL: Bonn

I. CHRONOLOGY

962—Otto I crowned Holy Roman Emperor to mark beginning of First *Reich* (962–1803).

1152—Frederick Barbarossa reasserts political control of Empire over both Papacy and most of Italy.

1356—"Gold Bull" of Emperor Charles IV embodies claim of seven German princes to elect German Emperor and codifies rules and procedures for Imperial elections.

1440—Hapsburg family acquires Imperial title to establish its authority over Germany (except for two years in 18th century) until 1803.

1517—Martin Luther posts "Ninety-Five Theses" in Wittenberg and invites his colleagues to discuss Papal indulgences.

1555—Diet of Augsburg promulgates a "religious peace" by recognizing Lutheran churches and right of secular princes to determine religious status of their territories.

1618–1648—Thirty Years' War decimates much of Germany.

1756–1763—Frederick II ("the Great") wages Seven Years' War against Austria, Russia, and France, and subsequently places Prussia among the major European Powers.

Chart 14. STRUCTURE OF THE WEST GERMAN GOVERNMENT

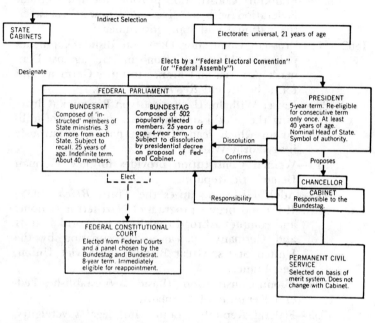

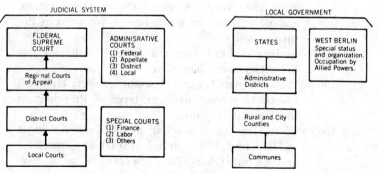

1815—Post-Napoleonic creation of loose federation of thirty-nine German States ("Germanic Confederation") "to preserve internal and external security of Germany, and independence and inviolability of individual German States."

1849—Frankfurt Constitution provides for new German Federation with a "division of powers" between the national and state governments.

1862–1871—Prussian Chancellor Otto von Bismarck pursues policy of "blood and iron" in wars against Denmark, Austria, and France to unify Germany and form the Second *Reich* (1871–1918).

1890—Kaiser Wilhelm II dismisses von Bismarck ("dropping the pilot") and embarks upon policy of militarism which leads German nation disastrously into World War I.

1919—Weimar Constitution provides for new German Democratic Republic.

1933—Adolf Hitler organizes the Third *Reich* (1933–1945) and begins program of Nazi terror at home and conquest abroad that leads to World War II and Germany's defeat and occupation by the United States, Great Britain, the Soviet Union, and France.

1949—"Bonn Constitution" (Basic Law) establishes Federal Republic of Germany.

1955—Federal Republic granted full legal sovereignty, joins the North Atlantic Treaty Organization, and participates in arrangements for western European unity.

1963—Ludwig Erhard succeeds Konrad Adenauer as West German Chancellor.

1964—West German Federal Assembly reelects Heinrich Lübke to second five-year term as President of the Federal Republic.

1966—West German *Bundestag* elects Kurt Kiesinger (CDU) and Willy Brandt (SPD) as Chancellor and Deputy-Chancellor, respectively, of a temporary "Grand Coalition" of the two major parties

II. WEST GERMAN CONSTITUTION *(GRUNDGESETZ)*

A. BASIC LAW OF 1949, WITH AMENDMENTS (the *"Bonn Constitution"*)
1. "The German People . . . conscious of its responsibility before God and Men, Animated by the resolve to preserve its national and political unity and to serve the peace of the World as an equal partner in a united Europe, Desiring to give a new order to political life . . . has enacted . . . this Basic Law of the Federal Republic of Germany. It has also acted on behalf of those Germans [in East Berlin and East Germany] to whom participation was denied. The entire German people is called on to achieve by free self-determination the unity and freedom of Germany" (Preamble).
2. Applicable to the eleven West German *Länder* (states), including West Berlin, although its application there is subject to various restrictions under "Four-Power" (i.e., the U.S.A., United Kingdom, France, and the U.S.S.R.) agreements dating from 1945.
3. Amended by a law passed by two-thirds of the members of both houses of the Federal Parliament which expressly amends or supplements it.

B. FUNDAMENTAL PRINCIPLES OF GOVERNMENT
1. West Germany is a "democratic and social federal State" (Art. 20).
2. Sovereignty is vested in the people and is expressed in free and democratic elections.
3. Multiparty system of representation in the lower house of the Federal Parliament and also in the "Government."
4. Strong "real" executive authority which is responsible to, but not completely dependent upon, the Federal Parliament.
5. Independent national judiciary which serves to ensure the rights and freedoms of individuals and groups.
6. Constitutional "division of powers" between the Federal Government *(Bundesrepublik)* and the constituent States *(Länder)*.

C. CIVIL AND POLITICAL LIBERTIES
1. Acknowledgment of the inherent dignity of the individual.
2. Legal equality of all citizens, without discrimination or preference.
3. Security for the rights of citizenship.
4. Right to a legal hearing and regular judicial process.
5. Abolition of the death sentence, and no physical or mental ill-treatments.
6. Freedom of conscience and faith, speech, press, and assembly.
7. Freedom of movement, vocation, and association.
8. Protection of the right of marriage and the inviolability of the family and home.
9. Protection of private property and the right of inheritance.
10. Right of asylum for the politically oppressed.
11. National referenda to be decided by a majority of a popular vote.
12. Right to vote and to hold public office.
    a. There are "universal, direct, free, equal, and secret elections" (Art. 38).
    b. "Anyone who has attained the age of twenty-one is entitled to vote; anyone who has attained the age of twenty-five is eligible for election" (Art. 38).
13. Other rights are guaranteed by the *Länder* Constitutions and by Federal and State legislation.

III. POLITICAL PARTIES

A. GENERAL CHARACTERISTICS OF THE PARTY SYSTEM
1. Revival of popular interest and participation in the new political life in West Germany.
2. Multiparty system, with a tendency towards a two-party system and for a few major parties to dominate in elections and government.
3. Parties individually represent broad social class and economic group interests.
4. General agreement among the leading parties on the basic principles and institutions of government.
5. Trend towards greater centralization in party authority and organizational responsibility.

6. Relatively strong and stable government on all levels by the "moderate" political parties.

7. No representation for extremist political organizations in the Federal Parliament and Government; the "Neo-Nazi" Socialist Party of the *Reich* (SRP) was outlawed as anti-constitutional by the Federal Constitutional Court in 1952, and also the Communist Party (KPD) in 1956.

   a. The Basic Law stipulates that "(1) The political parties participate in the forming of the political will of the people. They may be freely formed. Their internal organization must conform to democratic principles. . . . (2) Parties which, by reason of their aims or the behavior of their adherents, seek to impair or destroy the free democratic basic order or to endanger the existence of the Federal Republic of Germany are unconstitutional. The Federal Constitutional Court [see Section VI-D below] decides on the question of constitutionality. . . ." (Art. 21).

   b. In outlawing the KPD, the Federal Constitutional Court stated that ". . . the Basic Law has consciously, by its provision to the effect that 'the parties shall cooperate in forming the political will of the people,' taken the step to 'constitutionalize' political parties. That elevation to the rank of constitutional institutions at the same time places the parties among the 'integrating factors' in the State. From this fact, the interpretation of the constitution must make certain deductions. Oppositional parties must have political elbow room. A party intent on radical reform must have the right to criticize the existing order; that right carries with it the possibility of spreading propaganda calculated to reach the masses. This always means its political ideas being vulgarized to a certain extent, their being 'adapted' to the emotional needs of the masses; in other words, it means the use of trivial slogans and campaign mottos as a means of appealing to public sentiment. All that is harmless and, from a constitutional point of view, unobjectionable, as long as the party shows by its attitude that it is always conscious of the fact of being a political party within the framework of a free democracy. From this results the minimum duty for every political party in a free democratic State: to recognize, in its public appearances, in the form and style of its political activities, the paramount values of the Constitution as being binding on it, to cooperate in consolidating its reputation among the people; at the very least, however, to refrain from degrading, insulting, or bringing into contempt that order in any form whatsoever. Any party which consciously, continually, and systematically, undertakes a campaign of slander and mockery of these values and the order embodying them [which the KPD assertedly did], is envisaging their impairment and even their destruction. It is unthinkable that such a party could constitutionally be called upon to cooperation in the formation of the will of the State in a free democracy. . . ."

B. LEADING PARTIES

1. *Christian Democratic Union—Christian Social Union (CDU-CSU):* supports the constitutional system and individual rights, free enterprise and competition, the application of "Christian-Democratic" principles to the resolution of social and economic problems, federalist tendencies, unification of Germany, the North Atlantic Treaty Organization, western European unity, etc.; the strongest party in the *Bundestag.*

2. *Social Democratic Party (SPD):* supports the federal structure of the State with a stronger central government, equal rights and opportunities for the individual, public control of major sectors of the economy, unification of Germany, NATO, western European unity, etc.; principal opposition party in the *Bundestag.*

3. *Free Democratic Party (FDP):* supports private property and free and competitive enterprise without State interference, stronger central government, non-denominational public education, unification of Germany, etc.; has formed government coalitions with the CDU-CSU.

4. *German Reich Party (DRP):* supports Right-wing German nationalism, conservative interests and policies, unification of Germany, etc.; not recently represented in the *Bundestag.*

5. Other post-World War II parties have included the All-German *Bloc* (GB—BHE), the Center Party (ZP), and the Bavarian Party (BP).

C. Party Organization

1. Leading parties all have a party Chairman, one or more Deputy-Chairmen, an Executive Committee and Staff, as well as other national *(Bund)*, State *(Land)*, District *(Landkreis and Stadtkreis)*, and municipal *(Gemeinde)* party structures and leaders; they also have parliamentary organizations in the *Bundestag*, consisting usually of a Chairman, a Caucus, and various Committees.

2. Party finances and the conduct of campaigns and elections are regulated by Federal and state laws.

3. Non-party associations which sometimes exert influence in the political life of the country include agrarian, labor, and business organizations; professional groups; Catholic and Protestant Church organizations; veterans' organizations; refugee organizations; and various activist groups.

D. Party Representation in the Federal Parliament

1. *Bundestag* (elected September 19, 1965)

CDU—CSU	245 members
Social Democrats	190 "
Free Democrats	67 "
Total	502 members

2. West Berlin has twenty-two members in the *Bundestag*, but they do not vote.

IV. FEDERAL PARLIAMENT

A. Descriptive Features of the Federal Parliament

1. Theory of a strong national legislature, as the "guardian of the Basic Law and the interests of the *Länder*," applies to the West German Government.

2. Bicameral Federal Parliament consists of the *Bundesrat* (upper house) and the *Bundestag* (lower house).

    a. *Bundesrat* represents the *Länder* Governments, with forty-one members appointed by the *Länder* Governments for an indefinite term of office.

    b. *Bundestag* represents the people of the Federal Republic as a whole, with 502 members elected by the people for a four-year term of office.

    c. Deputies in both houses of the Federal Parliament must be German citizens, at least twenty-five years of age, and able to meet other requirements set down in Federal or State law.

    d. A Deputy in the *Bundesrat* may be simultaneously a Deputy in the *Bundestag.*

    e. Each house draws up its own rules of procedure ("Permanent Rules").

    f. Deputies enjoy the usual personal inviolability and parliamentary immunity, subject to the limitations of the house rules governing individual conduct.

    g. Both houses participate (although not equally) in the enactment of law.

  3. Convening and closing of legislative sessions, and the salaries and allowances of Deputies, are fixed by law.

NOTE: The description of the manner of electing Deputies to the West German *Bundestag* is kindly provided by the German Information Center (New York City) and is quoted *verbatim* in Section B-1-c-(1) below.

B. THE *Bundestag* (lower house)
  1. *Membership and internal organization*
    a. *Federal Election Act*, 1964, provides for 502 elected Deputies, two for each of the 251 constituencies (or electoral districts) in the Federal Republic; there are also 22 non-voting Deputies from West Berlin.

    b. West Berliners do not vote in Federal elections; their representatives in the *Bundestag* are delegated as "advisors" from the Berlin House of Representatives in proportion to the parties represented in that elected body; this situation is due to the provisions of the Four-Power Statute which still legally administers all of Berlin.

    c. In the *Bundestag* elections "each voter has two votes; the 'first vote,' which is cast for a preferred candidate in his constituency, and the 'second vote,' which is cast for a party '*Land* list.' This list consists of those candidates whom a party has selected to represent them in that particular *Land*. With the 'second vote,' the voter indicates the party of his choice and votes the straight party ticket. Votes cast for the party '*Land* lists' are counted according to the 'd'Hondt system' and result in the assignment of *Budestag* seats to the parties in direct proportion to the number of votes cast for them. Thus, if a *Land*, hypothetically, had 100 voting districts and 10 million valid votes were cast in this *Land*, of which 5 million votes were cast for party "X," then party "X" would receive 50 seats in the *Bundestag*. Since the party can only hold the number of seats to which it is entitled under proportional representation, its directly-elected 'first vote' candidates would be included in the 50 seats won in the 'second vote'. . . ."

(1) The "d'Hondt maximum number system" is a method of counting which aims at allocating the mandates [i.e., seats] for each party as fairly as possible on the basis of the votes given; specifically, "the party with the largest number of valid votes receives the first mandate to be assigned. The number of votes received by this party is then divided by 2, and the party which then has the highest number of votes receives a mandate. The votes received by the different parties are then successively divided by 2, 3, 4, etc., and after each division the party with the highest number receives a mandate. This is done until all seats have been distributed among the parties."

d. Parties must poll five per cent or more of all second votes in the country at large, or win three constituency seats by direct vote, in order to be proportionally represented in the *Bundestag*.

e. A special Review Committee of regular members passes on all disputed elections.

f. An unseated member may appeal to the Federal

Constitutional Court to set aside the adverse determination of the *Bundestag*; the Court's decision is final.

g. Internal organization includes the

   (1) President (roughly comparable to the U.S. Speaker of the House of Representatives), four Vice-Presidents; and several recording secretaries.

   (2) House Administration Committee of the *Bundestag* (consisting of the President, his four Vice-Presidents, the three parliamentary leaders of the political parties, and fifteen elected secretaries), which decides the internal affairs of the house insofar as they are not a matter for the President alone.

   (3) Functional committees (with a proportional representation of the parties).

   (4) Council of Elders (a permanent committee of fifteen Deputies, who advise the President on legislative business); it is also concerned with the nomination of the chairmen and members of the functional committees.

   (5) Chaplain, Sergeant-at-Arms, etc.

2. *Functions and powers*

   a. Holds regular "open" meetings and sometimes "closed" meetings on the request of the Government.

   b. Passes resolutions and enacts legislation.

   c. Elects the Federal Chancellor, on the proposal of the Federal President.

   d. Subpoenaes members of the Federal Government for a hearing.

   e. Conducts legislative investigations.

   f. Impeaches the Federal President.

   g. Appoints an Interim Committee to safeguard the rights of the *Bundestag* against the Federal Government between legislative terms.

   h. Exercises other miscellaneous powers provided for in the Basic Law or Federal legislation.

3. *Legislative proceedings*

   a. Proceedings are conducted in both public and pri-

Chart 15. ORGANIZATION OF THE WEST GERMAN FEDERAL PARLIAMENT

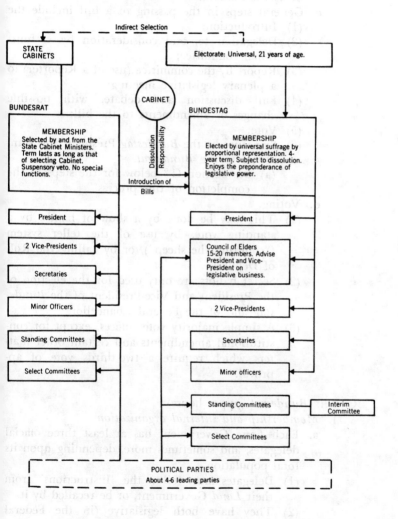

vate sessions and are usually quiet and dignified except for occasional heckling and exchange of light *repartee*.

b. Bills are introduced from the floor of the *Bundestag*, or by the *Bundesrat* through the Government, or by the Cabinet.

c. General steps in the passing of a bill include the
   (1) Introduction;
   (2) Delegation to, and consideration by, a functional committee;
   (3) Report by the committee (use of a Reporter) to a plenary legislative meeting;
   (4) Full discussion and debate, with possible changes or amendments to the bill;
   (5) Vote;
   (6) Signature by the *Bundestag* President and tranmittal to the *Bundesrat*.
      (a) See Section C-3 below for the steps in the completion of this process.

d. Voting.
   (1) This may be done by a show of hands, by a standing vote, by use of the teller system ("counting the sheep"), or by calling the Roll of Deputies.
   (2) Secret ballots are only used for the election of the President and Vice-President of the *Bundestag* and of the Federal Chancellor.
   (3) A simple majority vote suffices, except for constitutional amendments and certain other matters which require a two-thirds vote of approval.

C. THE *Bundesrat* (upper house)
   1. *Membership and internal organization*
      a. Each *Land* Government has at least three official delegates, and sometimes more, depending upon its total population.
         (1) Delegates must follow the "Instructions" from their *Land* Government, or be recalled by it.
         (2) They have both legislative (in the Federal

Bundesrat) and executive (in the *Land* Government) responsibilities.
   b. Internal organization includes the
      (1) President (which Office is held consecutively for a one-year term by each of the Ministers-President of the *Länder*) and three Vice-Presidents.
      (2) Secretarial staff and various clerks.
      (3) Functional committees.
      (4) Chaplain; etc.
2. *Functions and powers*
   a. Serves as the guardian for the *Länder* interests under the Basic Law.
   b. Holds both regular open and special closed meetings.
   c. Passes resolutions and participates in the enactment of Federal legislation.
   d. Members have access to all meetings of the *Bundestag* and its committees, and must be heard by the *Bundestag* at all times.
   e. Exercises a qualified veto power over the actions of the *Bundestag*.
   f. Participates in the election of the Federal Chancellor and some judges, the amendment of the Basic Law, and the approval of treaties with foreign States.
   g. Requests and receives information from the Federal Government on the conduct of public affairs.
   h. Exercises other powers as defined by constitutional provisions or Federal legislation.
3. *Legislative proceedings*
   a. Small membership in the *Bundesrat* makes for informal and simplified procedures and the quick dispatch of business.
   b. Bills are introduced from the floor of the *Bundesrat*; "Government" bills by the Cabinet; and "*Bundesrat*" bills through the Cabinet to the *Bundestag*.
      (1) Bills adopted in the *Bundestag* are transmitted to the *Bundesrat* in the form passed by the lower House.
      (2) Sometimes a Mediation Committee (composed

Chart 16. LAW-MAKING PROCESS IN WEST GERMANY

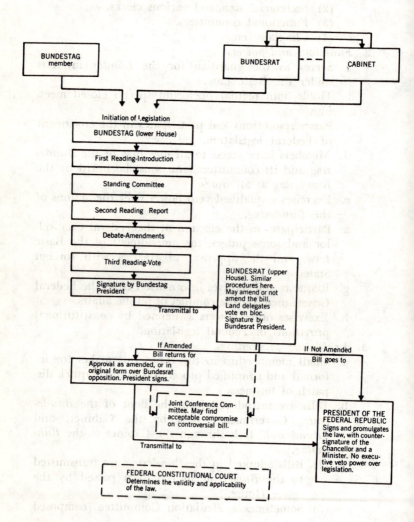

BUNDESTAG
member

BUNDESRAT

CABINET

Initiation of Legislation

BUNDESTAG (lower House)

First Reading-Introduction

Standing Committee

Second Reading   Report

Debate-Amendments

Third Reading-Vote

Signature by Bundestag President

Transmittal to

BUNDESRAT (upper House). Similar procedures here. May amend or not amend the bill. Land delegates vote en bloc. Signature by Bundesrat President.

If Amended
Bill returns for

If Not Amended
Bill goes to

Approval as amended, or in original form over Bundesrat opposition. President signs.

Joint Conference Committee. May find acceptable compromise on controversial bill.

Transmittal to

PRESIDENT OF THE FEDERAL REPUBLIC
Signs and promulgates the law, with counter-signature of the Chancellor and a Minister. No executive veto power over legislation.

FEDERAL CONSTITUTIONAL COURT
Determines the validity and applicability of the law.

of eleven members of the *Bundesrat* and eleven of the *Bundestag*) is formed to reconcile differences between the two legislative Houses on the provisions of a bill.

c. *Bundesrat* follows the normal legislative procedures in handling a bill.

d. It votes by a roll call of the *Länder* and the delegates from each *Land* vote *en bloc.*

e. Neither the Federal President nor Federal Chancellor can veto a law, although its applicability may be reviewed by the Federal Constitutional Court.

f. Finally, the Federal President signs and promulgates a law as passed by the Federal Parliament and countersigned by the Chancellor and a responsible Minister.

V. THE GOVERNMENT

A. FEDERAL PRESIDENT *(Bundespräsident)*

1. Elected, without debate, by the Federal Assembly, *(Bundesversammlung)*, which consists of the members of the *Bundestag* and an equal number of members elected by the *Länder* legislatures on the basis of the proportional representation of their political parties.

   a. Federal Assembly is convoked by the President of the *Bundestag.*

   b. If no candidate for the Federal Presidency receives a majority vote in two ballots, the candidate who receives the most votes on a third ballot is elected.

   c. President is elected for a five-year term and can be reelected only once.

   d. Granted an annual salary and expense allowances and maintains an official residence.

2. *Constitutional qualifications* for President include German citizenship, eligibility to vote in *Bundestag* elections, and a minimum age of forty years.

   a. Federal President may not be a member of the Government (Cabinet) nor of a *Bund* or *Land* legislative body, nor may he hold any other incompatible office or function.

3. Immune from ordinary civil processes, but may be

impeached by either house of the Federal Parliament and tried before the Federal Constitutional Court for a willful violation of the Basic Law or any Federal legislation.

  a. If he is found guilty on the Resolution of Impeachment, the President must forfeit his office.

  b. A vacancy in the President's office is temporarily filled by the President of the *Bundesrat* (there is no Federal Vice-President).

4. *Powers and functions*

  a. Serves as the nominal Head of State and symbol of governmental authority in West Germany; upon his reelection to a second five-year term, on July 1, 1964, President Heinrich Lübke stated that "The Federal President represents Germany, indeed, the whole of Germany in all its parts. In his office is incorporated the will of our [German] people to decide their own destiny in freedom and to restore the unity of the Nation."

  b. Represents the German Federal Republic in matters of international law.

  c. Accredits and receives diplomatic officials from foreign States.

  d. Concludes treaties with foreign States.

  e. Formally appoints Federal judges and Federal civil servants.

  f. Signs and promulgates Federal laws, orders, and decrees.

  g. Exercises the power of pardon (but not an amnesty nor a collective pardon), including the granting of commutations and reprieves.

  h. Performs social and ceremonial functions.

  i. Undertakes other powers as provided in the Basic Law or Federal legislation.

  j. In sum, the presidential powers are considerably more limited than those of the *Reich* President during the Weimar Republic between 1918 and 1933.

B. FEDERAL CHANCELLOR *(Bundeskanzler)*

  1. Elected, without debate, by the *Bundestag* on the proposal of the Federal President.

Chart 17. WEST GERMAN EXECUTIVE AND ADMINISTRATIVE ORGANIZATION

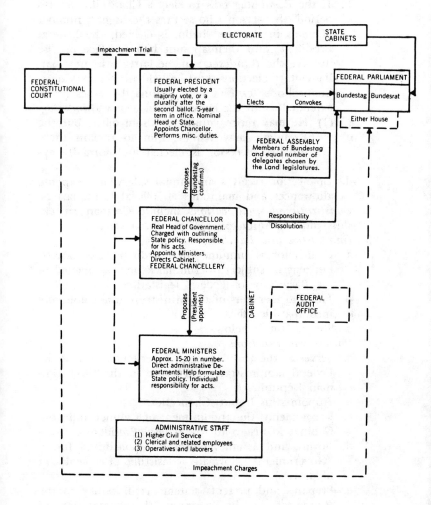

    a. Proposed candidate must secure a majority of votes in the *Bundestag* to be elected; if not, the *Bundestag* may, within fourteen days, elect another person to the Chancellorship.

    b. If the *Bundestag* fails to elect a Chancellor in this period, the person who secures the highest number of votes in the next ballot is elected; the Federal President must then appoint him to office or else dissolve the *Bundestag*; in the latter case, new parliamentary elections must be held within sixty days.

    c. Chancellor's term of office ordinarily ceases (or is extended) with the convening of a new *Bundestag*.

        (1) He may retire voluntarily from office, but the President may request him to remain there until a successor is elected and formally appointed.

    d. Chancellor receives an annual salary and expense allowances and maintains an official headquarters.

2. *Constitutional qualifications* include German citizenship and eligibility to sit in the *Bundestag*.

3. *Immunities and liabilities*

    a. Chancellor is immune from ordinary civil arrest, but may be subject to criminal actions as defined in the Basic Law or Federal legislation.

    b. He (and members of the Ministry) cannot hold any incompatible office.

    c. See Section D below.

4. *Powers and functions*

    a. Serves as the real Head of Government and of the Federal administrative structure in the West German Republic.

    b. Appoints his Deputy-Chancellor.

    c. Recommends the appointment of Cabinet and non-Cabinet Ministers to the Federal President.

    d. Forms, and assumes political responsibility for, a "Government" (normally consisting of a coalition of parties).

    e. Prepares and presents statements of policy to the *Bundestag*; i.e., he determines the general lines of policy for his Administration and sees that they are carried out.

    f. Signs the laws passed by the Federal Parliament and the orders and decrees of the Federal President.

    g. Negotiates agreements with foreign States.

    h. Performs other functions as provided in the Basic Law and Federal legislation.

  5. *Federal Chancellery (Bundeskanzleramt)*

    a. This is the immediate Office of the Chancellor, headed by the State Secretary for Internal Affairs, a permanent official.

    b. Primarily coordinates the administrative and routine work of the Ministers, each of whom has direct access to the Chancellor and his Deputy in the Chancellery.

    c. There is also an adjunct Press and Information Section which, as its title suggests, serves as a public relations agency and issues, from time to time, various reports on the Government and its activities.

C. FEDERAL CABINET

  1. Consists of approximately twenty Ministers (usually *Bundestag* members) who are proposed by the Chancellor and appointed by the Federal President.

    a. They normally serve a four-year term, receive a regular salary and allowances, and are responsible to both the Chancellor and the *Bundestag*.

    b. They take care of the day-to-day administrative operations of the Government.

  2. Important Cabinet ministries today are: Vice-Chancellor and Economic Affairs; Foreign Affairs; Interior; Justice; Finance; Food, Agriculture, and Forestry; Labor and Social Affairs; Defense; Transport; Posts and Telecommunications; Housing; Refugee Affairs and War Victims; Federal Council (*Bundesrat*) Affairs; All-German Affairs; Family and Youth Affairs; Atomic Energy; Federal Property; Economic Cooperation; Health; and Special Tasks.

  3. *Cabinet Meetings*

    a. Regular and special meetings, presided over by the Chancellor or his Deputy, in "closed" executive session, to discuss governmental policy.

    b. Participation is limited to Cabinet Ministers, other

outstanding non-Cabinet Ministers, and administrative and technical experts.

c. Intra-Cabinet disagreements are settled by normal procedures or, in an extreme case, by the resignation of a Minister.

D. CABINET-PARLIAMENTARY RELATIONS
1. Chancellor and Cabinet-Ministers are usually Members of Parliament.
   a. They may address the *Bundestag* at any time.
   b. They may also be called by the *Bundestag* or *Bundesrat* for a hearing.
2. *Bundestag* elects the Federal Chancellor.
3. Cabinet and Federal Parliament participate together in the enactment of law.
   a. Most bills are introduced and enacted through the initiative of the Government.
   b. *Bundestag* may ask the Government to draft a bill on a designated subject.
   c. Failure of the *Bundestag* to pass a "Government" bill may lead the Chancellor to request a "vote of confidence" by the *Bundestag*; if this is not forthcoming, a "legislative emergency" may be proclaimed by the Federal President at the request of the Chancellor, not to exceed six months (Art. 81).
   d. The Government has only a limited and indirect veto over Federal legislation under the Basic Law.
4. At the time of voting "no confidence" in the Chancellor, the *Bundestag* must elect a successor by a majority vote and also request the Federal President to dismiss the incumbent Chancellor.
   a. This provision of electing a successor before dismissing the Chancellor is designed to prevent recurrent political crises; its success is evident in the fact that West German Governments since 1949 have been able to function uninterruptedly during their entire term of office.
   b. If the *Bundestag* fails to sustain a motion of no confidence, or is unable to elect a new Chancellor, the Government may ask the Federal President to dissolve the *Bundestag*, and new elections will be held,

on the basis of which a new *Bundestag* and Government will be formed.

5. Federal Parliament undertakes legislative "motions," "questions," "interpellations," investigations, and a general review of the governmental policy.

6. It also confirms treaties and other executive actions.

E. PERMANENT CIVIL SERVICE
1. *Significant factors*
   a. Traditionally, the higher administrative bureaucracy has enjoyed an important and privileged position in German Government.
   b. Directly, or indirectly, the administrative bureaucracy exerts influence on the determination and execution of governmental policy on all levels.
   c. Professional civil servants must meet rigid qualifications for admission into the Service and maintain high standards in the performance of their duties.
   d. There is a prevailing sense of "duty to the State" that requires the individual civil servant to be exemplary in his personal conduct and willing to accept limitations in his individual rights (e.g., freedom of speech and freedom of political activity) and to make personal sacrifices (e.g., frequent changes in residence and considerable non-paid overtime work).
   e. Some question remains as to the extensiveness and effectiveness of post-World War II measures both to "denazify" and "democratize" the West German Civil Service.
      (1) It is interesting to note that the average civil servant tends not to commit himself, politically, but merely to carry out the orders of his superiors.
      (2) Sporadic interest is shown in broadening the opportunities for entry into the career service for those who do not have the traditional legal training or a long period of service in the lower administrative bureaucracy.
   f. The fundamental character of the Civil Service has

remained the same, in spite of changes in the system of government and political leadership.

2. *Personnel classifications*

a. Based on the *Reich Civil Service Code of 1873*, the *National Socialist Civil Service Law of 1937*, and the *Federal Officials Law of 1953*, as amended.

b. *Angestellten:* include all temporary public employees who perform unskilled or lowly tasks and are usually entitled only to limited Civil Service benefits under the law.

c. *Beamten:* include the permanent professional civil servants, classified into "regular," "middle," "superior," and "higher" grades.

   (1) Entrance into the "regular" grade requires the completion of an elementary school or equivalent education and some preparatory training; mostly clerical positions.

   (2) Entrance into the "middle" and "superior" grades requires a training period of from one to three years followed by a State examination; typical positions are those of secretary or inspector.

   (3) Entrance into the "higher" grade requires a university degree (usually in Law), a first State examination, three years' additional training, and a second State examination; includes higher administrators, specialists, etc.

d. *Federal Officials Law* (1953), as amended, further treats in detail of the conditions of employment, the legal status, and the administration of the West German Civil Service.

3. *Specialized agencies*

a. *Civil Service Commission:* consists of seven regular and seven alternate members, the former including the President of the Federal Audit Office, the Director of the Legal Division in the Personnel Office of the Ministry of the Interior, the Director of the Personnel Office in some other Federal ministry and four other governmental officials

   (1) Concerned mainly with the implementation of general rules related to Civil Service employ-

ment, the administration of Civil Service examinations, problems of personnel administration, and recommendations to improve or reform the Civil Service.

(2) The Commissioners determine their own rules of procedure and order of business for their regular meetings; they enjoy an independent status and are not liable, nor incur any penalty or disadvantage, for the lawful performance of their duties.

b. *National Personnel Committee:* consists of the President of the Government Accounting Office, the Personnel Directors of the Ministry of Finance and the Ministry of the Interior, representatives from the leading Civil Service organizations, and an appointee of the Federal President.

(1) Concerned mainly with reviewing the qualifications for civil servants and the settlement of complaints by civil servants.

(2) Corresponding Personnel Committees have been established on the lower levels of administration.

VI. JUDICIAL SYSTEM

A. THEORY AND PRACTICE OF LAW AND JUSTICE
1. Dual system of ordinary and administrative courts.
2. Preference for codified law, implemented by statutory law and administrative decrees.
3. Uniformity in law and integration of courts are generally accepted as the right of the State, not only to secure its own interests, but also to provide "fair and equal" justice for all citizens.
4. Legal processes and judicial actions are uniformly recognized and applied throughout the country.
5. Recent development of a "rule of precedent," as applied by judges in deciding cases under the German law.
6. General use of the collegial jury or panel of judges, both in the ordinary and administrative courts, with

professional and lay judges sitting together in the local and district civil courts.

7. Exercise of judicial review by the Federal Constitutional Court.

8. Federal legislation supersedes *Land* legislation; hence, there is no conflict of laws.

9. "Judges are independent and subject only to the law" (Art. 97).

10. Full complement of legal rights and judicial safeguards for the individual, with designated prohibitions against the State:

   a. No *ex post facto* legislation, denial of *habeas corpus*, mental or physical ill-treatment, extraordinary courts, "double-jeopardy," etc.

   b. However, in 1962, the (Adenauer) Government was seriously embarrassed, and almost forced to resign, over *der Spiegel* (the "Mirror") affair; this involved a severe criticism of the Government's defense program in a liberal weekly news magazine and the subsequent arrest—under the orders of the Defense Minister—of important members of the magazine's editorial staff, the occupation of their offices, and seizure of their personal properties; the affair almost provided a *cause celebre*, as it was hotly discussed, both at home and abroad, with the severest critics of the Government indicting it for "neo-fascistic" actions; after much pressure had been brought to bear by Opposition political forces, the Defense Minister submitted his resignation and the Government profusely expressed its "keen regrets" over the incident.

B. ORDINARY CIVIL AND CRIMINAL COURTS

   1. *Local courts (Amtsgerichte)*

      a. Composed of one or several judges, depending on the size of the local area.

      b. Settle both minor civil and criminal cases as provided by law.

   2. *District courts (Landsgerichte)*

      a. Composed of many judges, who are sometimes grouped together into Sections to try particular types of cases.

Chart 18. ORGANIZATION OF THE WEST GERMAN COURT SYSTEM

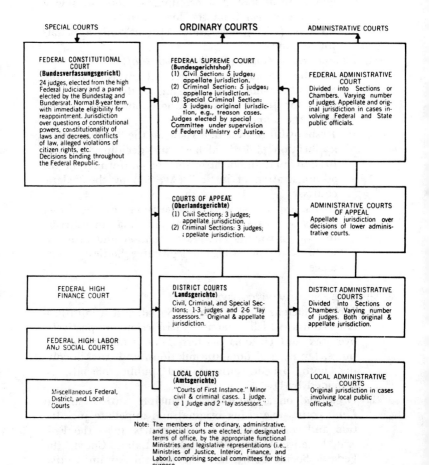

SPECIAL COURTS   **ORDINARY COURTS**   ADMINISTRATIVE COURTS

FEDERAL CONSTITUTIONAL COURT (Bundesverfassungsgericht)
24 judges, elected from the high Federal judiciary and a panel elected by the Bundestag and Bundesrat. Normal 8-year term, with immediate eligibility for reappointment. Jurisdiction over questions of constitutional powers, constitutionality of laws and decrees, conflicts of law, alleged violations of citizen rights, etc. Decisions binding throughout the Federal Republic.

FEDERAL SUPREME COURT (Bundesgerichtshof)
(1) Civil Section: 5 judges; appellate jurisdiction.
(2) Criminal Section: 5 judges; appellate jurisdiction.
(3) Special Criminal Section: 5 judges; original jurisdiction, e.g., treason cases.
Judges elected by special Committee under supervision of Federal Ministry of Justice.

FEDERAL ADMINISTRATIVE COURT
Divided into Sections or Chambers. Varying number of judges. Appellate and original jurisdiction in cases involving Federal and State public officials.

COURTS OF APPEAL (Oberlandsgerichte)
(1) Civil Sections: 3 judges; appellate jurisdiction.
(2) Criminal Sections: 3 judges; appellate jurisdiction.

ADMINISTRATIVE COURTS OF APPEAL
Appellate jurisdiction over decisions of lower administrative courts.

FEDERAL HIGH FINANCE COURT

DISTRICT COURTS (Landgerichte)
Civil, Criminal, and Special Sections; 1-3 judges and 2-6 "lay assessors." Original & appellate jurisdiction.

DISTRICT ADMINISTRATIVE COURTS
Divided into Sections or Chambers. Varying number of judges. Both original & appellate jurisdiction.

FEDERAL HIGH LABOR AND SOCIAL COURTS

LOCAL COURTS (Amtsgerichte)
"Courts of First Instance." Minor civil & criminal cases. 1 judge, or 1 Judge and 2 "lay assessors."

Miscellaneous Federal, District, and Local Courts

LOCAL ADMINISTRATIVE COURTS
Original jurisdiction in cases involving local public officals.

Note: The members of the ordinary, administrative, and special courts are elected, for designated terms of office, by the appropriate functional Ministries and legislative representations (i.e., Ministries of Justice, Interior, Finance, and Labor), comprising special committees for this purpose.

    b. Exercise both original and appellate jurisdiction in civil and criminal cases.

3. *Courts of appeal (Oberlandsgerichte)*

    a. Consist only of professional judges, grouped together into civil and criminal sections to review cases on appeal from the lower courts.

    b. Exercise (with a few rare exceptions) only appellate jurisdiction.

4. *Federal High Court (Bundesgerichtshof)*

    a. Members elected by the Federal Minister for Justice and a committee, consisting of the *Länder* Ministers for Justice and an equal number of persons from the *Bundestag*.

    b. Responsibilities include securing the "uniformity of application of Federal law" and deciding cases "of fundamental importance for the uniformity of the administration of justice" (Art. 95) by the Federal courts.

    c. Hears appeals against the decisions of the lower courts and exercises original and final jurisdiction in cases involving charges of treason and attempts to break up meetings of legislative bodies by violence.

C. SPECIAL AND ADMINISTRATIVE COURTS

1. Include such as Finance, Labor, Social, and Administrative courts which exercise jurisdiction, respectively, over tax and customs matters, labor-management disputes, family and domestic relations, and cases involving both private citizens and public officials, as provided by law.

2. Organized on a hierarchical principle, with local and *Land* courts exercising original and appellate jurisdiction and corresponding Federal courts (e.g., the Federal Finance Court, the Federal Labor Court, the Federal Social Court, and the Federal Administrative Tribunal) exercising final jurisdiction.

3. Presided over by judges with specialized legal training and/or administrative experience, who are elected in the same manner as the Federal High Court, with the participation of the appropriate Federal and *Land* Ministers.

4. Various Federal and *Land* disciplinary courts arc established, as needed, to conduct disciplinary proceedings against Federal and *Land* civil servants.

D. FEDERAL CONSTITUTIONAL COURT *(Bundesverfassungsgericht)*

1. Frequently called the highest and most distinguished court in the West German Republic.
2. *Membership* "consists of Federal judges and other members" (Art. 94).
   a. Judges of this court cannot be members of the Federal Parliament, the Federal Government, nor of the corresponding legislative and executive organs in the *Länder*.
3. *Organization* (under revised law) includes the
   a. President and Deputy-President, alternately elected by the *Bundestag* and *Bundesrat*;
   b. Two panels *(Senate)* with eight judges in each panel *(Senat)*; one-half of the judges are elected by the *Bundestag* and one-half by the *Bundesrat*; however, six of these judges (i.e., three in each panel) are chosen from the judges of the high Federal courts and serve a life tenure; the remainder serve for eight years and can be reelected.
4. *Jurisdiction* covers
   a. Disputes concerning the rights and duties of high Federal agencies "or of other parties" under the Basic Law;
   b. Disputes concerning the compatibility of Federal or *Land* law with the Basic Law, or of *Land* law with Federal law;
   c. Disputes concerning the rights and duties of the *Bund* Government and the *Länder*, with regard to the execution of Federal law by the *Länder* and the exercise of Federal supervision;
   d. Disputes between the *Bund* and the *Länder*, between different *Länder*, or within a *Land*;
   e. Other disputes, such as the
      (1) Alleged deprivation of an individual's basic or civic rights (a "constitutional complaint");
      (2) Legality of political parties;
      (3) Federal impeachments;

        (4) Appeals against the Federal Parliament;

        (5) Constitutionality of *Bund* and *Land* legislation;

        (6) Applicability of international law.

    f. Court may issue a temporary order to avert the inflicting of damage or disadvantage upon the public interest.

  5. *General procedures*

    a. President or his Deputy presides over the judicial sessions.

    b. Nine judges comprise a quorum, to enable a panel of the court to pronounce a judgment.

    c. Anonymous and formalistic administration of justice.

    d. A simple majority decision suffices in ordinary cases; in other cases, a two-thirds majority decision is required.

    e. Decisions of the Federal Constitutional Court are binding throughout the Federal Republic.

E. STATUES OF JUDGES

  1. Determined by the Basic Law and special Federal legislation.

  2. Normally serve a life tenure, but they may be removed from office or suspended (for cause), transferred to another position, or retired under the law.

  3. Receive a regular salary and stipulated allowances.

  4. Judges (and the Federation's prosecutors) are generally supervised by the *Bund* and *Land* Ministries of Justice.

VII. FEDERATION AND STATES *(Bund* and *Länder)*

A. SIGNIFICANT FACTORS

  1. A division of competence between the Federation and the States on legislative powers.

    a. States may legislate where the Basic Law does not grant legislative powers to the Federation.

    b. States may legislate, on matters within the scope of the exclusive legislative powers of the Federation, only where they are explicitly authorized to do so by a Federal law.

    c. States may legislate, within the scope of the concurrent legislative powers, only to the extent the Federation has not there used its legislative power.

2. A dual assumption of authority by the Federation and the States for the execution of the Federal laws and administration.

    a. States may, under certain conditions, administer Federal laws as matters of their own concern or as agents of the Federation.

        (1) States may establish the necessary authorities and procedures for administration.

        (2) Federal Government may issue general administrative rules to guide the States.

        (3) Federal Government (with the approval of the *Länder* or the *Bundesrat*) may appoint Commissioners to supervise the lawful administration of Federal laws by the States.

        (4) *Bundesrat*, in a dispute between the Federal and *Land* Governments over the State administration of Federal law, determines whether the State has acted unlawfully; the decision of the *Bundesrat* may be reviewed by the Federal Constitutional Court.

        (5) Federal Government may issue "individual instructions for particular cases" (Art. 84) in the administration of Federal legislation.

        (6) Federal Government itself may provide the necessary authorities for the Federal administration.

3. Federal Government's authority covers those fields of activity where the implementation of Federal legislation by the State Governments would be impracticable.

4. *Länder* generally are permitted to regulate their own affairs (e.g., local government, public health and welfare, police, education), in conformity with the Basic Law and applicable Federal legislation.

    a. Federal Government may take reasonable action to secure the full compliance of the *Länder* with their legal obligations.

5. *Länder* interests are fully represented by their delegates to the *Bundesrat*.

B. EXCLUSIVE LEGISLATIVE POWERS OF THE FEDERATION

1. Important examples include foreign affairs; Federal citizenship; immigration and emigration; currency and coinage; inter-*Länder* and foreign commerce; transportation and telecommunications; postal services; border control; Federal civil service; and the Federal courts and legal system.

2. Federal Government may also enact general rules concerning the legal status of the *Länder* civil services; the regulation of the press and motion pictures; the conservation of certain natural resources; land distribution; regional planning; and matters relating to registration and personal identification.

C. CONCURRENT LEGISLATIVE POWERS OF THE FEDERATION AND THE STATES

1. Important examples include the organization and administration of *Land* courts and justice; registry and census; associations and assemblies; aliens, refugees, and expellees; *Länder* citizenship; war veterans and their surviving dependents; labor law and management-labor relations; social insurance; public welfare; prevention of the abuse of economic power; commercial and financial transactions; public finance and tax administration; expropriation of property; medicines, drugs, and narcotics; road traffic and railways other than Federal railways; protection of German cultural works; scientific research.

D. BUND AND LÄNDER RELATIONS

1. *Statement by the Federal Government*, 1964:
". . . . The Federal Government includes a special Ministry for *Bundesrat* and *Länder* Affairs. This has the task of instructing the *Bundesrat* and the *Länder* on the work and intentions of the Federal Government and, *vice versa*, of conveying the wishes and ideas of the *Bundesrat* and *Länder* to the Federal Cabinet. In this manner, conflicts of interest between the State as a whole and the member-states can be recognized in good time and smoothed out within the bounds of possibilities. It is of decisive importance that the general rela-

tionship between *Bund* and *Länder* should remain attuned to the principle of loyalty to the Federal whole binding both sides equally. According to the Federal Constitutional Court's jurisdictional views, the constitutional principle of loyalty to the Federal whole is inherent in the rules of conduct laid down in the Basic Law in regard to the relationship between *Bund* and *Länder*. For both *Bund* and *Länder* this duty to adopt an attitude of friendly alliance signifies a limitation when they make use of their competencies. In point of fact, in spite of many a clash in individual questions, both have cooperated without serious conflict in the difficult period of the build-up of State arrangements since 1949."

VIII. LOCAL GOVERNMENT

A. BASIC ELEMENTS OF LOCAL GOVERNMENT

1. Units of regional and local government are the State (*Land*), the District (*Regierungsbezirke*), the Rural or City County (*Landkreis* or *Stadtkreis*), and the Village (*Gemeinde*).

2. Many recent changes in the number, organization, functions, and responsibilities of the State and lesser governments.

3. State governments are organized on constitutional principles, including basic civil and political liberties, unicameral or bicameral legislative assemblies, responsible Cabinet governments, direct legislation (the initiative and referendum), etc.

4. They are constituent components in the Federal system of government, and serve occasionally as agents of the Federation in the administration of Federal law, as well as principals in their own right in assuming responsibility for State and local affairs.

5. Counter-tendencies of centralization and federalization in the relations between the State and Federal governments and centralization *vs.* decentralization in the relations between the State and local governments.

B. STATE GOVERNMENT
1. *Constitution*
   a. Must conform to the principles of government stated in the Basic Law of 1949.
   b. May be reviewed by the Federal Constitutional Court for the determination of the validity of its provisions and amendments, and any *Land* action taken thereunder.
2. *Legislature (Landtag)*
   a. Unicameral, except in Bavaria.
   b. Members must be twenty-five years of age; they are elected by the qualified voters for a four-year term of office.
   c. Provides its own organization (President, secretaries, clerks, committees, etc.) and rules of procedure.
3. *Executive authority*
   a. Cabinet-type, coalition Government, with the parties represented according to their strength in the *Landtag*.
   b. Composed of a Minister-President and from 5 to 20 Ministers.
      (1) Ministers aid the Minister-President in formulating policy and making decisions.
      (2) They individually head and supervise the administrative Departments.
      (3) They are also collectively responsible to the *Landtag*.
4. *Judiciary*
   a. Varying systems of regular (district, county, appellate, Supreme), administrative, special (admiralty, finance, labor, social, etc.), and Constitutional courts.

C. DISTRICTS
1. These are administrative (nonpolitical) subdivisions of the larger States.
2. Each has a District President (but no legislative body) appointed by, and responsible to, the State Government.
3. They have supervisorial powers over the lesser governmental units and other special functions designated by the State Government.

CHART 19. AGENCIES OF LOCAL GOVERNMENT IN THE WEST GERMAN REPUBLIC

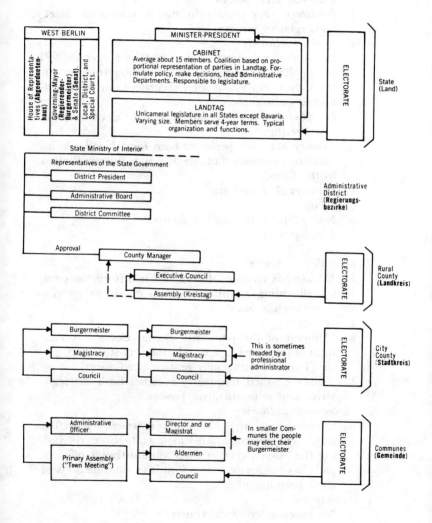

D. County Governments

1. These are created by the States and vary greatly between States.
2. *Legislature (Kreistag)*
   a. Members are elected by the qualified voters for a four-year term of office.
   b. *Kreistage* vary greatly in size, frequency of meetings, relative powers, etc.
3. *Executive authority*
   a. Consists of a County Manager *(Oberbürgermeister)* in the Rural County or Mayor *(Bürgermeister)* in the City County and an Executive Council *(Landrat)* or Committee.
      (1) County Manager and Mayor are elected by the *Kreistag*.
   b. County Manager performs both formal and administrative functions, but the Mayor is usually limited to the former.
   c. Local civil service staff.
4. *Judiciary*
   a. No independent County courts.
   b. *Landsgerichte*.

E. Village Government

1. Each State has its own Municipal Code *(Gemeindeordnung)*, providing a uniform system of village government within the State.
2. *Legislature*
   a. Members of the popularly elected Council serve a term of two years or more; in the very small villages, the Town Meeting may replace the Council.
   b. Village Council frequently exercises both the legislative and administrative powers.
3. *Executive authority*
   a. Composed of the Mayor *(Bürgermeister)* in the larger villages and, sometimes, a *Magistrat* (including the Mayor, certain chief administrative officials, and "lay" delegates) to administer the functions of local government.
4. *Judiciary*
   a. No independent local courts.
   b. *Amtsgerichte*.

IX. WEST BERLIN

A. LEGAL AND POLITICAL BASES OF ALLIED OCCUPATION

1. Protocol on Zones of Occupation and Administration of the "Greater Berlin" Area, September 12, 1944.
2. Amending Agreements on Zones of Occupation and Administration of the "Greater Berlin" Area, November 14, 1944, and July 26, 1945.
3. Statement of Principles for Berlin, by the Allied (Western) *Kommandatura*, May 14, 1949.
4. Statement by the Western Foreign Ministers, on Allied Rights in Berlin, May 13, 1950.
5. Declaration by the Allied (Western) *Kommandatura*, on Berlin, May 26, 1952.
6. Declaration by the Western Foreign Ministers, on Berlin, October 22, 1954.
7. Four-Power (United States, Great Britain, France, Federal Republic of Germany) Communique on Berlin, December 14, 1958.
8. NATO Declaration on Berlin, December 16, 1958.
9. Subsequent declarations and statements.

B. EMERGENCE OF WEST BERLIN GOVERNMENT

1. Establishment of the *Kommandatura* Administration, July 7, 1945.
2. Uniform court system for all of Berlin put into effect, October 15, 1945.
3. "Temporary Constitution" approved by the Four Powers (United States, Great Britain, France, Soviet Russia), September 20, 1946.
   a. It provided that the activities of each of the Borough Administrations *(Bezirksverwaltungen)* was subject to the approval of the Military Government of the respective Sectors.
   b. It also provided that amendments of the Constitution, the resignation of the City Government *(Magistrat)* or any of its members, and the appointment and discharge of senior members of the City Administration could be effected only with the concurrence of the *Kommandatura*.
4. Compromise decision of *Kommandatura* gives Occupa-

tion Powers control in their respective Sectors through special Sector sub-chiefs of police, October 4, 1946.

5. Defeat of Communists in city-wide election, October 20, 1946, leads to Soviet obstruction of work of Allied *Kommandatura*, and the withdrawal of the Soviet Union from the Allied Control Council, March, 1948.
   a. The results of the election were as follows:

Social Democratic Party	48.7%
Socialist Unity (Communist) Party	19.7%
Christian Democratic Party	22.2%
Liberal Democratic Party	9.4%

6. Currency reform initiated by three Western Allies in West Berlin is followed by Soviet blockade of the city and the Allied "airlift" to provide for its people, 1948.
7. First Statement of Principles for Berlin grants limited authority to the West Berlin city government, May 14, 1949.
   a. ". . . . 1. (a) Greater Berlin shall have . . . full legislative and executive and judicial powers in accordance with the Temporary Constitution of 1946 or with any subsequent Constitution adopted by the City Assembly and approved by the Allied *Kommandatura*. . . . 4. Greater Berlin shall have the power, after due notification to the Allied *Kommandatura*, to legislate and act in the fields reserved to the Allied *Kommandatura*, except as the Allied *Kommandatura* itself otherwise specifically directs, or as such legislation or action would be inconsistent with decisions or actions taken by the Occupation Authorities themselves. 5. Any amendment to the Temporary Constitution, any new Constitution approved by the City Assembly designed to replace the Temporary Constitution, any amendment to such new Constitution, or legislation in the fields reserved above will require the express approval of the Allied *Kommandatura* before becoming effective. All other legislation will become effective twenty-one days after official receipt by the Allied Kommandatura unless previously disap-

proved by them provisionally or finally. . . ." *(Principles Governing the Relationship Between the Allied (Western) Kommandatura and Greater Berlin,* 1949).

8. Allied (Western) *Kommandatura* revises the Statement of Principles for Berlin and gives West Berlin government, formally established under the *Berlin Constitution of 1950,* additional authority to regulate its own affairs, March 13, 1951; this authority was further extended by another supplementary Statement, May 26, 1952.
   a. ". . . . I. Berlin shall exercise all its rights, powers and responsibilities, set forth in its Constitution as adopted in 1950. . . . IV. The Allied *Kommandatura* will not . . . raise any objection to the adoption by Berlin under an appropriate procedure authorized by the Allied *Kommandatura* of the same legislation as that of the Federal Republic. . . . VII. Berlin legislation shall come into force in accordance with the provisions of the Berlin Constitution. . . . In cases of inconsistency with . . . the rights of the Allied authorities under this declaration, Berlin legislation will be subject to repeal or annulment by the Allied *Kommandatura.* . . ." *(Declaration by the Allied (Western) Kommandatura, on Berlin,* 1952).

9. Declaration of the *Kommandatura* clarifies relationships between government of West Berlin and military quasi-governments in the separate American, British, and French Sectors of the city, and reaffirms the *de jure* authority and ultimate control by the Allies; this Declaration, as amended, is still in effect today.
   a. ". . . the security and welfare of Berlin and the maintenance of the position of the Three Powers there are regarded by the Three Powers as essential elements of the peace of the free world in the present international situation. Accordingly they will maintain armed forces within the territory of Berlin as long as their responsibilities require it. They therefore reaffirm that they will treat any attack against Berlin from any quarter as an attack upon

their forces and themselves." (*Final Act of the Nine-Power Conference at London*, October 3, 1954).

C. GOVERNMENT OF WEST BERLIN

1. *Constitution of 1950*

    a. "In the resolve to protect the freedoms and rights of all individuals, to regulate the community and the economy on a democratic basis, to serve the spirit of social progress and peace and in the desire to remain the capital of a new united Germany, Berlin has adopted this Constitution (Preamble). . . . Berlin is a German *Land* and at the same time a City. Berlin is a *Land* of the Federal Republic of Germany. The Basic Law and the Laws of the Federal Republic of Germany are binding on Berlin." (Art. 1)

2. Democratic suffrage and free elections

    a. ". . . . All German citizens who on the day of the election have passed their twentieth birthday and have had their domicile in Berlin for a minimum period of six months shall have the right to vote" (Art. 3, *Electoral Law of West Berlin*, 1950).

3. Leading political parties include the Social Democratic Party (SPD), Christian Democratic Union (CDU), Free Democratic Party (FDP), and others.

4. *Results of elections* for West Berlin's city legislature (*Abgeordnetenhaus*), February 17, 1963, were as follows:

Party	Votes	Percentage	Seats
Social Democrats	961,943	61.9	89
Christian Democrats	448,389	28.9	41
Free Democrats	123,318	7.9	10
Socialist Unity Party (Communist)	20,887	1.3	—
Total			140

    a. Total of more than 1.5 million votes cast for these parties represented approximately 93 per cent of all eligible voters.

    b. Communists and other parties are not currently represented in the *Abgeordnetenhaus* because electoral laws require that a political party must poll a minimum of 5 per cent of the total vote in order to gain representation.

c. High percentage of free voter participation was a good indication of the "democratic process" at work, and the results of the election were a crushing defeat for the Communists.

5. *Legislature:* unicameral House of Representatives *(Abgeordnetenhaus)*, with 200 members elected by a system of proportional representation.

6. *Executive:* includes a Governing-Mayor *(Regierender-Bürgermeister)*, a Deputy-Mayor, and a Senate *(Senat)*, elected by, and responsible to, the legislature; the Senate consists of not more than sixteen Senators.

a. Recently, it has been divided into twelve Departments (or Ministries): Interior, Justice, Public Education, Labor and Welfare, Youth and Sport, Health, Building and Housing, Economy and Credit, Finance, Traffic and Services, Federal Affairs, and Post and Telecommunications.

b. For administrative purposes, West Berlin itself is divided into twelve Districts each of whose District Office is headed by a District Mayor who is elected together with up to seven District Councillors from the forty-five members of the District Deputies Assembly; a number of Committees (consisting of members of the District Office, the District Deputies Assembly and citizens) are appointed for the various administrative tasks, and these Committees take part in the Administration with decisive powers.

7. *Judiciary:* composed of nine District courts *(Amtsgerichte)*, one *Land* court *(Landsgericht)*, and one Supreme Court *(Kammergericht)*.

a. Special courts, exercising both original and appellate jurisdiction, include the labor, social, and administrative courts on the District and *Land* levels.

b. The Federal Constitutional Court has no right of jurisdiction in Berlin.

(1) ". . . . Due to the reservations of the Military Governors in approving the Basic Law, it is out of the question that the Federal agencies

exercise any direct authority in the broadest sense, including judicial power in Berlin, except where the Three (Western) Powers have in the meantime granted such rights in individual Districts. Since no such exceptions have hitherto been made for the Federal Constitutional Court, the Constitutional Court has at present no jurisdiction to decide on a submission of a court concerning the compatability of Berlin laws with the Basic Law. . . ." (*decision of the Federal Constitutional Court, 1957, on the application of the Basic Law to Berlin*)

    c. At least four penal institutions and a juvenile institute are also concerned with the administration of justice in Berlin.

D. RELATIONSHIPS WITH THE FEDERAL REPUBLIC
    1. Sometimes called a "common-law marriage" between West Berlin and the Federal Republic (cf. Basic Law, 1949; Constitution of Berlin, 1950; and the *Drittes Uberleitungsgesetz,* 1952).
    2. *Summary*
        a. Application of various Articles of the Basic Law and Federal legislation to West Berlin.
        b. Maintenance of an effective "lobby" in Bonn by the delegates (22) from West Berlin to the Federal Parliament.
        c. Major political parties (i.e., the CDU, SPD, and FDP) maintain party organizations in West Berlin.
        d. West Berlin is integrated into the general system of tax administration and uses the currency of the Federal Republic.
        e. Bonn Government extends other financial, economic, and administrative assistance to West Berlin.
        f. Psychological affinity between West Berlin and the Federal Republic.
        g. In short, West Berlin is autonomous in her normal daily functions; the Bonn Government has a qualified form of "sovereignty" over her internal and external affairs; and the United States, Great Britain, and France continue to wield primary rights as Occupation Powers in West Berlin.

3. Special difficulties continue, due largely to Berlin's isolated position in Communist East Germany and recurrent tensions between the Western Powers and Communist governments of East Berlin, the German Democratic Republic, and the Soviet Union.

SELECTED READINGS

Alexander, Edgar, *Adenauer and the New Germany*. London: Farrar, Straus, 1957.

Almond, Gabriel A., ed., *The Struggle for Democracy in Germany*. Chapel Hill: University of North Carolina Press, 1949.

Barraclough, G., *The Origins of Modern Germany*. New York: G. P. Putnam's Sons, 1963.

Bithell, J., ed., *Germany*. London: Methuen, 1955.

Bölling, K., *Republic in Suspense*. New York: Frederick A. Praeger, Inc., 1964.

Conlan, W. H., *Berlin: Beset and Dedevilled*. New York: Fountainhead Publishers, Inc., 1963.

Flenley, R., *Modern German History*. New York: E. P. Dutton & Company, Inc., 1964.

Golay, John F., *Founding of the Federal Republic of Germany*. Chicago: University of Chicago Press, 1958.

Grosser, A., *The Federal Republic of Germany*. New York: Frederick A. Praeger, Inc., 1964.

Heidenheimer, Arnold J., *The Governments of Germany*. New York: Thomas Y. Crowell Company, 1966.

Hiscocks, Richard, *Democracy in Western Germany*. London: Oxford University Press, 1957.

Holborn, H. A., *A History of Modern Germany*. New York: Alfred A. Knopf, 1964.

Keller, J. W., *Germany, the Wall and Berlin; Internal Politics During An International Crisis*. New York: Vantage Press, Inc., 1964.

Kohn, Hans, *German History, Some New German Views*. Boston: Beacon Press, 1954.

Lane, J. C., and J. K. Pollock, *Source Materials on the Government and Politics of Germany*. New York: George Wahr Publishing Company, 1965.

Litchfield, E. H., *Governing Postwar Germany*. New York: Oxford University Press, 1954.

McInnis, Edgar, Richard Hiscocks, and Robert Spencer, *The Shaping of Postwar Germany*. New York: Frederick A. Praeger, Inc., 1961.

Merkl, Peter H., *The Origin of the West German Republic*. New York: Oxford University Press, 1963.

Meyer, Ernst Wilhelm, *Political Parties in Western Germany*. Washington: Library of Congress, European Affairs Division, 1951.

Pinson, Koppel Shub, *Modern Germany: Its History and Civilization*. New York: Macmillan Company, 1954.

Plischke, Elmer, *Contemporary Government of Germany*. Boston: Houghton Mifflin Company, 1961.

Pollock, James K., et al., *Germany Democracy at Work: A Selective Study*. Ann Arbor: University of Michigan Press, 1955.

Prittie, Terence, *Germany Divided, The Legacy of the Nazi Era*. Boston: Little, Brown & Company, Inc., 1960.

Riess, Curt, *The Berlin Story*. New York: Dial Press, Inc., 1952.

Robson, Charles B., ed., *Berlin, Pivot of German Destiny*. Chapel Hill: University of North Carolina Press, 1960.

Rodes, J. E., *Germany: a History*. New York: Holt, Rinehart & Winston, Inc., 1964.

Smith, J. E., *The Defense of Berlin*. Baltimore: Johns Hopkins Press, 1964.

Speier, Hans, *Divided Berlin, the Anatomy of Soviet Political Blackmail*. New York: Frederick A. Praeger, Inc., 1961.

Wallich, Henry Christopher, *Mainsprings of the German Revival*. New Haven: Yale University Press, 1955.

Wiking, P., *Changing Germans*. London: Lincoln-Prager, 1956.

Zink, Harold, *The United States in Germany, 1944–1955*. New York: D. Van Nostrand Company, Inc., 1957.

Zurcher, Arnold J., *Constitutions and Constitutional Trends Since World War II*. New York: New York University Press, 1951.

Chapter IV

UNION OF SOVIET SOCIALIST REPUBLICS

POPULATION: 235,000,000 (1965)
AREA: 8,646,400 sq. miles
CAPITAL: MOSCOW

I. CHRONOLOGY

860—Varangian chieftain, Rurik, lays basis for dynasty that lasts until 1598.

988—Christianity, in form practiced by Byzantine Church, introduced into Russia from Constantinople.

1380—Grand Prince Dimitri Donskoi of Moscow begins struggle for Russian independence by defeating Tatars at Battle of Kulikovo.

1492—Ivan III ("the Great") expels the Mongols and establishes Moscow as center of government for all Russia.

1547–1584—Ivan IV ("the Terrible") strengthens the Czardom by eliminating hereditary aristocracy through use of dreaded *Oprichniki*, forerunner of today's secret police.

1613—After short "Time of Troubles" involving disputes to the succession to the throne, Michael Romanov is elected Czar by a national assembly and begins dynasty that lasts until 1917.

1682–1725—Peter the Great introduces Western reforms in the State administration and economic system, adds new lands to his realm, and makes Russia a European Power.

1762–1796—During "Golden Age" of Catherine the Great, the Russians triumph over the Prussians, Swedes, and

149

Turks, and extend their Empire at expense of Poles and Turks.

1801–1825—Alexander I confirms Russia's position as major military Power in struggle against Napoleon and plays important role in settlement of Europe at Congress of Vienna.

1855–1881—Alexander II ("the Czar-Liberator") introduces liberal reforms, frees the serfs, institutes local self-government (the *Zemstvos*)—and is assassinated.

1894—Nicholas II begins unhappy reign as ill-fated 13th and last of the Romanov Czars.

1917—Vladimir Lenin ("the Founder of the Soviet State") directs the Bolshevik Revolution and subsequently proclaims "the dictatorship of the proletariat" in Russia.

1924–1945—Joseph Stalin defeats opponents in brief struggle for power, introduces Five-Year Plans, purges Communist Party, adopts new Constitution, negotiates Nazi-Soviet Non-Aggression Pact, and leads the USSR to victory in World War II.

1953—New Premier Georgi Malenkov adopts policy of "peaceful co-existence" between capitalism and Communism.

1956—Nikita Khrushchev becomes undisputed leader of Communist Party and Soviet Government, denounces "Stalinism," and modifies policy of "peaceful co-existence."

1961—Adoption of New Program and Statute (Rules) of the C.P.S.U. at 22nd Party Congress in Moscow.

1964—Political *coup* results in ouster of Nikita Khrushchev from power and his replacement by Leonid I. Brezhnev as First Secretary of the C.P.S.U. and Aleksei N. Kosygin as Chairman of the All-Union Council of Ministers; the ideological split between the Soviet Union and Communist China widens, as other Communist countries and parties assert increasing independence of both of them.

1965—Further major shifts in Kremlin as Soviet President Anastas Mikoyan resigns and is replaced by Nikolai Podgorny, whose position as Deputy-

Secretary in the Presidium of the C.P.S.U. is given to Alexander Shclcpin, former Deputy Premier and Chairman of the Party-State Control Committee; this committee is renamed the Committee of People's Control (headed by Pavel Kovanov) and continues to ensure that party orders are carried out on all levels of Government.

1966—Twenty-third Congress of the C.P.S.U. convenes in Moscow to discuss the report of the Central Committee and the Five-year economic development plan for 1966–1970 and to elect the leading Party bodies.

II. SOVIET CONSTITUTION

Although the Constitution asserts that each of the fifteen Union-Republics (SSRs) is equal to every other, the fact of the matter is that the Russian Soviet Federated Socialist Republic (RSFSR) dominates all the rest. The whole governmental structure is permeated by the Communist party, in which is located the actual ruling authority.

A. CONSTITUTION (Fundamental Law) of the Union of Soviet Socialist Republics, 1936, as Amended to 1966.

   1. Previously, a Constitution (Fundamental Law) for the Russian Federation was adopted on July 10, 1918; it formally proclaimed a new social and State system in which power was [theoretically] put into the hands of the Soviets [Councils] of Working People's Deputies, elected by the people and subject to recall by them; this Constitution also legalized the people's ownership of the means and instruments of production and abolished private capitalist and landlord ownership; many of the nationalities living in Russia were given the right to form their own autonomous Republics or regions within the Russian Federation.

   2. The name of the country was changed to the Union of Soviet Socialist Republics in 1922 and the first Constitution (Fundamental Law) of the U.S.S.R. was adopted in 1924; this remained in force until the adop-

Chart 20. STRUCTURE OF THE SOVIET GOVERNMENT

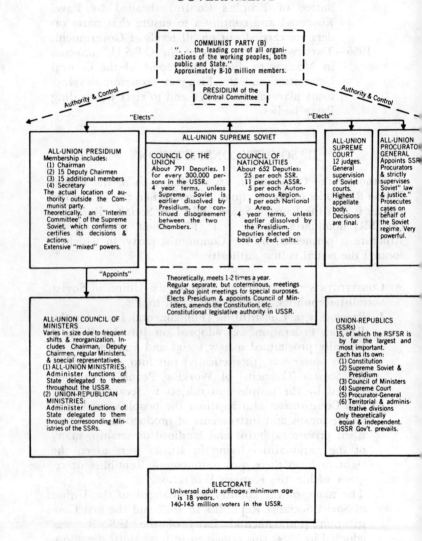

COMMUNIST PARTY (B)
". . . the leading core of all organizations of the working peoples, both public and State."
Approximately 8-10 million members.

PRESIDIUM of the Central Committee

Authority & Control

Authority & Control

"Elects"

"Elects"

ALL-UNION SUPREME SOVIET

ALL-UNION PRESIDIUM
Membership includes:
(1) Chairman
(2) 15 Deputy Chairmen
(3) 15 additional members
(4) Secretary
The actual location of authority outside the Communist party.
Theoretically, an "Interim Committee" of the Supreme Soviet, which confirms or certifies its decisions & actions.
Extensive "mixed" powers.

COUNCIL OF THE UNION
About 791 Deputies. 1 for every 300,000 persons in the USSR.
4 year terms, unless Supreme Soviet is earlier dissolved by Presidium, for continued disagreement between the two Chambers.

COUNCIL OF NATIONALITIES
About 652 Deputies:
25 per each SSR.
11 per each ASSR.
5 per each Autonomous Region.
1 per each National Area.
4 year terms, unless earlier dissolved by the Presidium.
Deputies elected on basis of Fed. units.

ALL-UNION SUPREME COURT
12 judges.
General supervision of Soviet courts.
Highest appellate body.
Decisions are final.

ALL-UNION PROCURATOR GENERAL
Appoints SSR Procurators & strictly supervises Soviet" law & justice."
Prosecutes cases on behalf of the Soviet regime. Very powerful.

"Appoints"

Theoretically, meets 1-2 times a year.
Regular separate, but coterminous, meetings and also joint meetings for special purposes.
Elects Presidium & appoints Council of Ministers, amends the Constitution, etc.
Constitutional legislative authority in USSR.

ALL-UNION COUNCIL OF MINISTERS
Varies in size due to frequent shifts & reorganization. Includes Chairman, Deputy Chairmen, regular Ministers, & special representatives.
(1) ALL-UNION MINISTRIES: Administer functions of State delegated to them throughout the USSR.
(2) UNION-REPUBLIC MINISTRIES: Administer functions of State delegated to them through corresponding Ministries of the SSRs.

UNION-REPUBLICS (SSRs)
15, of which the RSFSR is by far the largest and most important.
Each has its own:
(1) Constitution
(2) Supreme Soviet & Presidium
(3) Council of Ministers
(4) Supreme Court
(5) Procurator-General
(6) Territorial & administrative divisions
Only theoretically equal & independent.
USSR Gov't. prevails.

ELECTORATE
Universal adult suffrage; minimum age is 18 years.
140-145 million voters in the USSR.

tion of the "Stalin Constitution" in 1936, (i.e., *Constitution of the U.S.S.R.*).

3. "Amendments to the Constitution of the U.S.S.R. shall be adopted by a majority of not less than two-thirds of the votes in each of the Chambers of the Supreme Soviet of the U.S.S.R." (Art. 146).

B. FUNDAMENTAL PRINCIPLES OF GOVERNMENT

1. "The Union of Soviet Socialist Republics is a socialist State of workers and peasants" (Art. 1).
2. Sovereignty is vested in the people, as represented by their Soviets (Councils).
3. One party (totalitarian) system of representation in the bicameral national legislature, the unicameral territorial legislatures, and in the Government on all levels of State authority.
4. Economic structure of the State is based upon the planned "socialization" of property and use of the "instruments and means of production," with all land and resources belonging "to the whole people."
5. A theoretically strong and democratic executive authority, with responsibility to the people's representatives in the legislature, but, in fact, wholly dependent on an "infallible" and dictatorial ruling elite of the Communist party.
6. Justice is nominally administered by an independent judiciary (with respect for the rights of the individual under the Constitution), but is really determined by the present requirements of State policy (in the implementation of the Communist party line).
7. Constitutional division of powers (federalism) between the All-Union Government (USSR) and the theoretically sovereign and equal Union-Republic Governments (SSRs).
8. In practice, there is an integration of Party and State, with the former determining the governmental policy throughout the USSR; "freedom" and "democracy" are enjoyed only by those who support the political regime.

C. FUNDAMENTAL RIGHTS AND DUTIES OF CITIZENS

These are theoretically broad, yet many of them have never been made effective in practice. It is particularly important, therefore, in considering the Government and society of the USSR, to distinguish between the constitutional theory and the political reality. For example, Art. 125 of the Soviet Constitution states that "In conformity with the interests of the working people, and in order to strengthen the socialist system, the citizens of the U.S.S.R. are guaranteed by law: (a) freedom of speech; (b) freedom of the press; (c) freedom of assembly, including the holding of mass meetings; (d) freedom of street processions and demonstrations. These civil rights are ensured by placing at the disposal of the working people and their organizations printing presses, stocks of paper, public buildings, the streets, communications facilities and other material requisites for the exercise of these rights." Yet the ruling elite, i.e., the leaders of the Communist Party of the Soviet Union (C.P.S.U.), reserve to themselves the power to say what is in "the interests of the working people" and when and what "material requisites" shall be made available for the exercise of these rights. In fact, all Soviet leaders, from Vladimir Lenin to Leonid Brezhnev, have emphasized that freedom of speech, press, etc., cannot be permitted "the foes of socialism" and any attempt on their part to utilize to the detriment of the State (i.e., to all the workers) these freedoms granted to the workers must be classified as "a counter-revolutionary crime." Withal, here follows a summary of the "Fundamental Rights and Duties of Citizens" as recited in the Soviet Constitution.

1. Equal rights for all citizens under the law, irrespective of nationality or race.
2. Equal rights for men and women in all spheres of social economic, political, and cultural life, and special care for the mother and child.
3. Inviolability of the individual person, his residence, and his correspondence.
4. Freedom from arbitrary arrest.
5. Freedom of speech, press, assembly, street processions, and demonstrations.
6. Right to form public organizations (i.e., trade unions, cooperative associations, youth organizations, and scientific and cultural societies).
7. Separation of Church from the State, and school from the Church, with freedom of conscience and religious worship and of anti-religious propaganda. (i.e., ". . .

freedom of anti-religious propaganda is recognized for all citizens," Art. 124).

8. Right to free elementary and higher education.
9. Right to work and to receive compensation for one's work.
10. Right to rest and leisure, annual vacations with full pay, and the use of sanitoria, rest homes, and clubs, etc.
11. Right to maintenance in old age, and care for the sick and infirm.
12. Right to own and inherit personal property.
13. Right of asylum to foreign citizens persecuted for their economic, political, or scientific beliefs.
14. Duty to support the Constitution and to observe the laws of the USSR.
15. Duty to maintain "labor discipline" and to fulfill public duties.
16. Duty to safeguard the public socialist property.
17. Duty to perform military service in the Armed Forces of the USSR.
18. Duty to defend the Motherland.
19. Duty and honor to work according to the principles (Art. 12):
    a. "He who does not work, neither shall he eat."
    b. "From each according to his ability, to each according to his work."

D. SUFFRAGE AND ELECTIONS

1. Elections to Soviets [Councils] at all levels—from the local Soviets to the Supreme Soviet of the U.S.S.R.—are based on "universal, equal and direct suffrage by secret ballot" (Art. 134).
2. ". . . all citizens . . . who have reached the age of eighteen, irrespective of race or nationality, sex, religion, education, domicile, social origin, property status or past activities, have the right to vote in the election of Deputies, with the exception of persons who have been legally certified insane [or are convicted criminals]" (Art. 135).
3. Soviet women have the right to elect or be elected on equal terms with men; servicemen also enjoy these rights on equal terms with all other citizens.
4. Special provision is made for voters who may be travel-

ing or are confined in hospitals, maternity homes, etc., and ballot boxes are brought to the homes of the aged and disabled persons who cannot go to the polls; in case of change of residence a voter may go to the polls in his new constituency on presentation of a special certificate.

5. Candidates for election are nominated from electoral areas by the public organizations and societies of the working people (i.e., the Communist party, trade unions, cooperatives, youth organizations, and scientific and cultural societies).

6. Lists of voters containing the names of all the citizens enjoying electoral rights and permanently or temporarily domiciled in a given constituency at the time these lists are compiled are made public twenty days before the elections.

   a. Should a citizen find an error in the list, he can report it to the local Electoral Commission or directly to the Electoral Commission of the local Soviet which must investigate the complaint within three days and communicate its decision to the appellant; if the latter is not satisfied, he may appeal to a People's Court whose decision is final.

7. Electoral bulletins, ballots, and results are printed in the language of the given constituency, due to the multi-national character of the Soviet people.

8. An elected Deputy who does not justify the trust placed in him can be recalled and his office filled at a by-election (cf. *Law on Procedure for the Recall of a Deputy of the All-Union Supreme Soviet*, 1959).

9. It is important to note the special role of the Communist party in determining who can vote, what candidates shall be nominated, and how the elections are administered, in contrast to the electoral systems in the Western democracies. In this connection, one might draw some interesting inferences from the data kindly provided by the Soviet Embassy (Washington, D.C.) with respect to election returns in the R.S.F.S.R. (Russian Soviet Federated Socialist Republic) in March, 1961, and for the Supreme Soviet of the U.S.S.R. in March, 1962. The examples are typical of elections in the Soviet Union:

a. ". . . . Deputies were elected to 6 territorial Soviets, 49 regional Soviets, 10 national area Soviets, 1,947 district Soviets, 860 city Soviets, 203 urban district Soviets, 2,731 rural Soviets and 1,597 township Soviets. The poll in the elections was as follows:

Type of Soviet	Total Number of Voters	Voters Who Went to the Polls	
		Number	Per cent
Territorial	8,967,707	8,961,434	99.93
Regional	52,124,721	52,084,623	99.92
Area	463,011	462,648	99.92
District	42,184,112	42,155,044	99.93
City	41,021,268	40,978,970	99.90
Urban District	18,351,574	18,332,215	99.89
Rural	32,931,316	32,908,729	99.93
Township	6,587,643	6,581,804	99.91

"Thus with insignificant exceptions, all the voters went to the polls. . . . The following table shows the number of electors that cast their ballots for the candidates run on the *joint Communist and non-Party slate* (italics, the author's):

Type of Soviet	Number of ballots cast for candidates	Proportion (in per cent to voters who went to the polls)
Territorial	8,914,673	99.48
Regional	51,742,665	99.34
Area	458,685	99.14
District	41,858,570	99.30
City	40,634,542	99.16
Urban District	18,190,917	99.23
Rural	32,616,672	99.11
Township	6,505,258	98.84

"The number of ballots on which the names of the candidates were crossed out (the number of votes cast against the candidates) comprised 46,553, or 0.52 per cent of the total, for the territorial Soviets; 341,472, or 0.66 per cent of the total, for the regional Soviets; 3,962 or 0.86 per cent of the total, for the area Soviets; 297,137, or 0.70 per cent of the total, for the district Soviets; 343,915, or 0.84 per cent, for the city Soviets; 141,191, or 0.77 per cent of the total, for the urban district Soviets; 291,576, or 0.89 per cent of the total, for the rural Soviets; and 76,468, or 1.16 per cent of the total, for the township Soviets. The number of ballots declared invalid . . . was 2,211. Thus the election returns demonstrate a unanimous vote for the candidates running on the Communist and non-Party slate."

b. ". . . According to the data of the Electoral District Commissions, the number of voters registered for the U.S.S.R. as a whole is 140,022,359. Of this number 139,957,809—or 99.95 per cent—went to the polls. . . .

"The number of electoral districts created for elections to the Soviet of the Union was 791. Elections were held in all of them. The candidates nominated for Deputy of the Soviet of the Union polled a total of 139,210,431 votes, which is 99.47 per cent of the total number of ballots cast. The total number of ballots cast against was 746,563. . . . 815 ballots were found invalid. All the candidates nominated [*on the joint Communist and non-Party slate*] polled an absolute majority and were returned as Deputies. The following table shows the results of the elections to the Soviet of the Union for each Union Republic: . . .

"The number of electoral districts created for elections to the Soviet of Nationalities was 652 including 375 for the Union Republics, 220 for the Autonomous Republics, 40 for the Autonomous Regions, and 10 for the National Areas. Elections were held in all of them. The candidates nominated for Deputy to the Soviet of Nationalities polled 139,391,455 votes, which is 99.60 per cent of the total number of ballots cast. . . . The number of ballots cast against totalled 564,155. . . . 706 ballots were found invalid. All the candidates nominated (*on the joint Communist and non-Party slate*) polled an absolute majority and were returned as

Union Republic	Total of Votes Polled by Candidates	
	In Figures	In Per Cent
Russian Federation	78,105,309	99.26
Ukraine	29,413,239	99.77
Byelorussia	5,332,600	99.78
Uzbekistan	4,754,004	99.69
Kazakhastan	6,229,802	99.46
Georgia	2,640,588	99.91
Azerbaijan	2,189,614	99.78
Lithuania	1,853,451	99.90
Moldavia	1,859,318	99.82
Latvia	1,585,562	99.68
Kirghizia	1,239,990	99.47
Tajikistan	1,155,318	99.73
Armenia	1,061,883	99.87
Turkmenistan	910,187	99.48
Estonia	879,566	99.17

Deputies. The following table shows the results of the elections to the Soviet of Nationalities for each Union Republic: . . .

Union Republic	Total of Votes Polled by Candidates	
	In Figures	In Per Cent
Russian Federation	78,279.687	99.49
Ukraine	29,419,223	99.79
Byelorussia	5,335,346	99.85
Uzbekistan	4,752,605	99.66
Kazakhstan	6,227,005	99.42
Georgia	2,641,118	99.93
Azerbaijan	2,189,283	99.78
Lithuania	1,853,301	99.90
Moldavia	1,860,915	99.83
Latvia	1,587,675	99.80
Kirghizia	1,238,443	99.36
Tajikistan	1,151,795	99.45
Armenia	1,061,663	99.85
Turkmenistan	911,491	99.62
Estonia	881,905	99.36

In the Autonomous Republics, Autonomous Regions and National Areas, the total number of registered voters from these administrative divisions for elections to the Soviet of Nationalities was 12,057,479. Of this number 12,052,744—or 99.96 per cent—went to the polls and of this number, in turn, 11,968,855—or 99.30 per cent—cast their ballots for the candidates nominated for Deputy. The number of ballots cast against was 83,848. . . . 41 ballots were found invalid. . . . A total of 1,443 Deputies have been elected. This includes 791 Deputies to the Soviet of the Union and 652 Deputies to the Soviet of Nationalities. *All the elected Deputies are candidates of the people's Communist and non-Party bloc* (italics, the author's)."

III. COMMUNIST PARTY (C.P.S.U.)

In the hierarchical organization of the Communist Party of the Soviet Union each party unit is limited by the next higher unit until the All-Union Party Congress is reached where authority is, theoretically, supreme. However, the facts must be distinguished from the theory. Real power lies in a group selected by the Party's Central Committee, namely, the Party Presidium headed by the First Secretary. It is this small body which wields the actual governing authority in Russia, both Party and State. Moreover, one should note the interlocking membership of the various units of the Party and the government organizations, which fact contributes so much to making the concentration of power in the hands of a small group of Party leaders possible. The ramifications of the Party throughout all parts of the country, and the dominant position its members hold in local government, permit it to exercise a very powerful influence upon the masses even before the structure reaches national proportions. The Communist youth organizations maintain close relations with the primary party units and in this way, provide the potential membership of the Party. To quote from the *"New Program of the C.P.S.U."* (1961): ". . . . The Party holds that *the moral code of the builder of Communism* should comprise the following principles: devotion to the Communist cause; love of the Socialist Motherland and of the other Socialist countries; conscientious labor for the good of society—he who does not work, neither shall he eat; concern on the part of everyone for the preservation and growth of public wealth; a high sense of public duty; intolerance of actions harmful to the public interest; collectivism and comradely mutual assistance: one for all and all for one; humane relations and mutual respect between individuals—man is to man a friend, comrade and brother; honesty and truthfulness, moral purity, modesty, and unpretentiousness in social and private life; mutual respect in the family and concern for the upbringing of children; an uncompromising attitude to injustice, parasitism, dishonesty, self-seeking ambition and money-grubbing; friendship and brotherhood among all peoples of the U.S.S.R.; intolerance of national and racial hatred; an uncompromising attitude to the enemies of Communism, peace and the freedom of Nations; fraternal solidarity with the working people of all countries, and with all peoples." (See especially Section E below)

A. MARXIST PROGRAM OF "REVOLUTIONARY SOCIALISM": THEORETICAL TENETS (*Communist Manifesto*, 1848)

1. *"Historical materialism":* Marxian view of history which espouses the idea that our opinions and moral outlook are determined by the society in which we live, which itself is dependent on economic factors.

2. *"Class struggle":* the idea that history is a study of classes (rather than nation-States), and that the human society consists of a ruling class of capitalists (*bourgeoise*) and a class of workers (*proletariat*) which it oppresses or "exploits"; by "class" is meant a group of people with common economic interests.

3. *"Proletarian (or Socialist) revolution":* this involves the use of direct force by the exploited workers against the ruling capitalists (the latter will use every means, fair or foul, to retain their position), and anticipates the eventual emergence of a state of socialism from a state of capitalism; this violent overthrow of the capitalists is accelerated by two conditions:

   a. The capitalists, who are the owners of the *"means of production"* (raw materials, factories, etc.), use their power to increase their wealth while cheating the workers of their fair share, i.e., the capitalists pay the workers a mere subsistence level wage and retain for themselves profits in the form of *"surplus value"* (the difference between the cost of producing a good and the price for which it is sold on the open market); and

b. The increasing disparity between the wealthy (the *bourgeoisie*) and the impoverished (the *proletariat*) cannot last for long, as the workers are too poor to buy their employer's products (which inevitably leads the latter to compete for foreign markets and is one of the causes of wars) and the constant exploitation leads to a sense of grievance among the workers who eventually arise and overthrow their masters.

4. *"Dictatorship of the proletariat":* refers to the leadership [of the Communists] on behalf of the proletariat during the transitional stage of "socialization" between the proletarian revolution and the realization of the classless society.

5. *"Withering-away of the State":* an expression used by Friedrich Engels (collaborator with Karl Marx) to connote the elimination of the coercive institutions of the former capitalist State and the beginning of the utopian Communist society.

B. A Few Criticisms of the Marxist Program
  1. The type of society is not necessarily determined by its material background, but rather men can (and do) plan their activities to result in desired material conditions.

  2. History is not solely a struggle between classes, but has also involved religious, racial, and political struggles.

  3. The advancement of capitalism has not resulted in lower wages, longer hours, more adverse conditions of work, and extremes in poverty for the working class.

  4. There has been no example of a revolution along the lines predicted by Marx-Engels, i.e., in a highly-industrialized society such as Great Britain, West Germany, Japan or the United States.

5. Many modifications have been made (in contradiction to Marx) in "revolutionary socialism" in the U.S.S.R. since the "October Revolution" of 1917, e.g., the "New Economic Policy" in the 1920's and the "capitalistic tendencies" of the 1960's.

6. There has been a continued increase, rather than a "withering-away," of the institutions of the State; etc.

C. STATUS AND MEMBERSHIP OF THE COMMUNIST PARTY

1. *Constitution, Art. 126:* ". . . the most active and politically-conscious citizens in the ranks of the working class, working peasants and working intelligentsia voluntarily unite in the Communist Party of the Soviet Union, which is the vanguard of the working people in their struggle to build communist society and is *the leading core of all organizations of the working people, both public and State"* [italics, the author's].

2. *"New Program of the C.P.S.U."* (1961): "As a result of the victory of socialism in the U.S.S.R. and the consolidation of the unity of Soviet society, the Communist Party of the working class has become the vanguard of the Soviet people, a Party of the entire people, and has extended *its guiding influence over all spheres of social life"* (italics, the author's); moreover, this is asserted to be not a slogan projected for the future, but a declaration of the actual state of present Soviet affairs.

3. *Statement by Leonid Brezhnev,* First Secretary of the C.P.S.U., 1964: ". . . . The bigger the tasks to be solved in the course of Communist construction, the greater is the role and importance of the Communist Party as a leading and guiding force of Soviet society. We are convinced of this in practice. That is why the further improvement of *Party guidance in all fields of Communist construction* (italics, the author's), and the consistent implementation of Leninist principles and standards in the life of the Party and the State, acquire special importance. . . . The tasks of building a new society demand a considerable improvement in the Party's entire ideological work. The education of the new man and the inculcating of a scientific Marxist-

Chart 21. PATTERN OF SOVIET PARTY ORGANIZATION

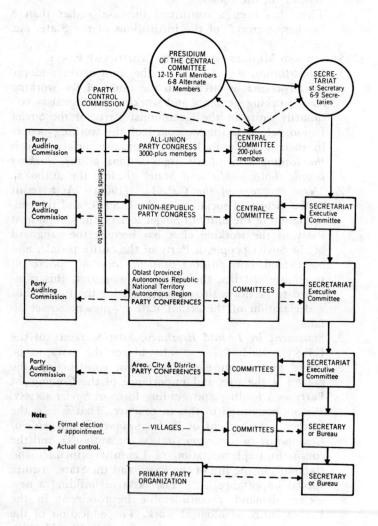

Leninist world outlook in the Soviet people are the main features of this work. . . . All Communists should clearly understand the tasks confronting the Party and the country and should be prepared to fight for the fulfillment of these tasks as for vital and personal matters. An irreconcilable attitude towards hostile bourgeois ideology should be an inherent quality of every Communist. . . . Under the guidance of the Party, under the banner of Marxism-Leninism, the Soviet people will build a Communist society. . . . Long live the glorious Communist Party of the Soviet Union, set up by Lenin! . . ."

4. *Procedures for membership*

   a. Applicant is recommended by three party members, with three years' standing in the party, who have known the applicant (professionally and socially) for at least one year.

   b. Application is discussed and a decision taken at a general meeting of the primary party organization.

   c. Decision of the primary party organization takes effect after an endorsement by the district party committee, or by the city party committee in cities with no district divisions.

   d. An applicant is a "candidate member" on probation for at least one year prior to obtaining full membership; it is assumed that he will display knowledge of current "Marxist-Leninist" principles and will steadfastly follow the party line and discipline.

5. *Some obligations of membership*

   a. Rigid adherence to the party rules and discipline.

   b. Active participation in the activities of State and society (See Section C-3 above)

   c. Serve as a model of exemplary personal conduct and provide ideological instruction for others to follow.

   d. Show little or no concern for personal social or economic gains.

   e. Renounce all religious affiliations and support antireligious propaganda.

   f. If a party member fails to fulfill his duties or commits certain other offenses, he may be admonished, severely reprimanded, or even expelled from the party.

    (1) The decision to expel a member from the party is taken by a two-thirds majority vote at a general meeting of the primary party organization; the decision takes effect after its endorsement by a higher party structure.

    (2) The decision to expel a high-ranking member of the party (e.g., a member of the Central Committee of the C.P.S.U.) is made, and endorsed, by the appropriate higher party organs.

    (3) An appeal against expulsion from the party (or the imposition of a penalty) must be made within two months and the appeal is examined within one month thereafter.

6. *Some rights and privileges of membership*

    a. Enjoy considerable prestige and usually have a good job or other "rewarding" work.

    b. May elect and be elected to party office.

    c. Theoretical right to help form the party policy ("intraparty democracy").

    d. Theoretical right to a fair hearing when one's personal conduct or party activity is being investigated.

    e. May request information from, or make representations to, party agencies.

D. Bases of Communist Party Strength

    1. Only party permitted a legal existence in the USSR.

    2. Limited, dedicated, and militant party membership (which is approximately 3 per cent of the qualified electorate in Russia).

    3. Complete domination of State and society through parallel party structures, and a membership which permeates and controls all of the important agencies and activities, including,

        a. Nomination and election of party and State officials;

        b. Use of propaganda media in the formation and direction of public opinion;

        c. Economic, cultural (including the educational system), and scientific institutions;

        d. Military organization and national defense.

4. Vigorous suppression of opposition by recurrent party and Government purges, involving
   a. Extra-legal use of Soviet law and the judicial system;
   b. Activities of the Committee on State Security;
   c. Correctional camps;
   d. Other devices and techniques of control.
5. Philosophic and pragmatic ramifications of the Communist Party (B) as "the vanguard of the working peoples," the calculated policy of "perpetual crisis," the maintenance of the "Iron Curtain," etc.
6. Perpetuation of the authoritarian political tradition in contemporary Russian history.

E. HIERARCHY OF PARTY ORGANIZATION

Some of the important features of party organization and function on virtually all levels of authority are: (1) the Party Secretary or Secretariat, Bureau, Committees, and Administrative Staff; (2) the strict and faithful observance by party members of the party rules, discipline, and policy; (3) the conduct of self-criticism by party members and their agitation and enlightenment of the masses; (4) the convoking of periodic meetings or conferences to hold party elections, submit and discuss reports, arrive at tentative resolutions, endorse party actions, distribute various materials, etc.; (5) the supervision and direction of party units from the next higher unit downward (i.e., the "guiding principle" of "democratic centralism").

1. *Primary party organizations:* formed "at the places of work of party members—in factories, on State farms and at other enterprises, collective farms, units of the Soviet Army, offices, educational establishments, etc., wherever there are not less than three party members. Primary party organizations may also be organized . . . in villages and at house administrations. . . ." (Art. 53, *"Revised Rules of the C.P.S.U."* 1961); among other things they
   a. Admit new members to the C.P.S.U.
   b. Educate Communists in a spirit of loyalty to the party cause.
   c. Organize the study by Communists of current Marxist-Leninist theory.

    d. Ensure the "vanguard role" of Communists in all areas of State and social activity.

    e. Organize the working people for the performance of the tasks of Communist construction.

    f. Conduct propaganda work among the masses.

    g. Engage in extensive criticism and self-criticism, to prevent errors and violations of State discipline.

    h. Assist the area, city and district committees in their activities and are accountable to them.

2. *Area, City and District party organizations:* meet in a conference or general meeting, convened by their respective committees, at least once in every two years; and the committees meet at least once in every three months; these party organizations

    a. Elect members to their committees.

    b. Discuss various questions of interest to them.

    c. Elect representatives to party conferences.

    d. Prepare reports for higher party organs.

    e. Receive and review reports from other party organs, e.g., the appropriate Auditing Commission.

    f. Oversee the activities and work of lower party organs.

3. *Republican, Territorial and Regional party organizations:* meet in a conference or congress, convened by their respective committees, at least once in every two years; and the committees meet at least once in every four months; these party organizations

    a. Elect members to their committees.

    b. Discuss various questions of interest to them.

    c. Elect representatives to party conferences or congresses.

    d. Prepare reports for higher party organs.

    e. Receive and review reports from other party organs, e.g., the Central Committee of the Communist Party of the Union Republic and the appropriate Auditing Commission.

    f. Oversee the activities and work of lower party organs.

4. *Higher party organizations:* include the *Party Congress* (convened in regular meeting at least once in every four years and sometimes in extraordinary meeting

Chart 22. INTERRELATIONSHIP OF THE COMMUNIST PARTY AND THE SOVIET GOVERNMENT

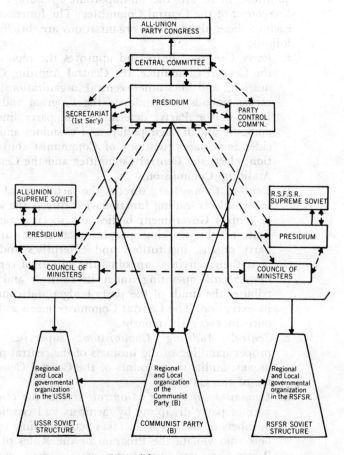

Note: ──────▶ Indicates control; ─ ─ ─ ─▶ indicates interlocking membership.

Theoretically, power runs from the governmental Soviets through their Deputies and the people's representatives in the Presidiums to the Councils of Ministers; actually, the power runs from the party Presidium through its membership and control in the governmental Presidium to the Council of Ministers on all levels of State authority in the U.S.S.R.

called by the Central Committee), the *Central Committee* and *Central Auditing Commission* (elected by the Congress), and the *Committee of People's Control,* formerly called the Party Control or Party-State Control Committee (organized by the Central Committee). In addition, there are the all-important *Presidium* and *Secretariat* of the Central Committee. The functions of each of these higher party organizations are, briefly, as follows:

a. *Party Congress:* hears and approves the reports of the Central Committee, the Central Auditing Commission, and the other central organizations; reviews, amends and endorses the Program and the Rules of the Party; determines the party line in domestic and foreign policy, and examines and decides important questions of Communist construction; elects the Central Committee and the Central Auditing Commission.

b. *Central Committee:* directs the activities of the party; selects leading functionaries; directs the work of central Government bodies and social organizations of the working people; establishes various party organs, institutions and enterprises and directs their activities; appoints the editors of central news media operating under its control; and distributes the funds of the party budget and controls its execution. The Central Committee meets at least once in every six months.

c. *Central Auditing Commission:* supervises the proper handling of the business of the central party organs; audits the accounts of the Central Committee of the C.P.S.U.

d. *Committee of People's Control:* verifies the observance of party discipline by members and candidate members of the C.P.S.U.; takes action against members who violate the Program or the Rules of the Party; considers appeals against decisions of the Central Committees of the Communist Party in the Union Republics or of territorial and regional party committees to discipline or expel members of the party.

e. *Presidium and Secretariat of the Central Committee*

(the real and final authority in the U.S.S.R.): elected by the Central Committee of the C.P.S.U.; directs the work of the Central Committee between its meetings; oversees the fulfillment of party decisions; establishes a Bureau (or Secretariat) for the Central Committee of the C.P.S.U. for the Russian Soviet Federated Socialist Republic (RSFSR).

5. *Party organizations in the Soviet Army*
   a. Organized and function in accordance with the "New Program" and "Revised Rules" of the C.P.S.U., and on the basis of instructions issued by the Central Committee.
   b. Maintain close contact with local party committees and coordinate political work with them.
   c. Principle functions are to carry out party policy in the Armed Forces, indoctrinate servicemen in the spirit of "Marxism-Leninism," and rally them around the C.P.S.U.

6. *Party groups in non-party organizations*
   a. Organized to function in the elected Soviets (councils), trade unions, cooperatives, and other mass organizations of the people.
   b. Chief function is to carry out party policy among the non-party people.

7. *YCL—Young Communist League ("Komsomol")*
   a. A "voluntary social organization of young people" (15–28 years of age) which serves as the "active helper and reserve" of the C.P.S.U.
   b. Maintains its own organization, rules, elected bodies, clubs, cultural and leisure activities, publications (e.g., *Komsomolskaya Pravda*), etc. on all levels of the State.
   c. More than 400,000 members have been elected to local, regional and republic Soviets, and more than 200 members are deputies in the Supreme Soviet of the U.S.S.R.
   d. Discuss and submit to the appropriate party organizations questions related to the activities and work in which they are engaged, and implement party directives "in all spheres of Communist construction."
   e. Lower YCL organizations are directed and con-

trolled by the appropriate (i.e., district, city, area, regional, and republican) higher party organizations.

8. *Other Communist youth organizations* include the "Little Octobrists" (8–11 years of age) and the "Young Pioneers" (10–16 years of age), who engage in various activities for young people of these ages, largely under the guidance of the *"Komsomol."*

9. *International Communist organizations and meetings:* briefly, these have included such as the *Communist International,* or "Comintern" (1919–1943), for the proselytizing of international Communism; the *Communist Information Bureau,* or "Cominform" (1947–1956), for the creation of a united Communist *bloc* in Eastern Europe after World War II and the control of the policies of the satellite Communist States by the U.S.S.R.; the *Warsaw Treaty Organization* (1955-date), or the Soviet equivalent of the North Atlantic Treaty Organization; and periodic Congresses of Communist parties convoked at Moscow

F. "NEW PROGRAM OF THE C.P.S.U. (1961)"

1. *Preeminent role of the C.P.S.U.,* with emphasis on "collective leadership" described (*Tass* News Agency) as follows:

"The party rules point out that the highest principle of party leadership is collectivism—which is an indispensable condition of the normal functioning of party organizations, the correct education of the personnel, the development of the Communist's activity and initiative. The personality cult [i.e., "Stalinism"] and the violations of intra-party democracy connected with it cannot be tolerated in the party. They are incompatible with the Leninist principles of party life. . . . The collective leadership does not exempt them. . . . Discussion on debatable or insufficiently clear issues are possible within the framework of individual organizations or the party as a whole. A party-wide discussion is necessary if

a. The need for it is recognized by several regional or Republic party organizations;

      b. There is no firm majority within the Central Committee on important questions of party policy; and

      c. The Central Committee finds it necessary to consult the entire party on some question of party policy. . . ."

2. Members of the party Central Committee and Presidium ostensibly can serve no more than three successive terms in office and can be expelled by a two-thirds majority in secret voting, for action resulting in their loss of "honor or dignity."

3. However, any threat to the position of top party officials is eliminated by the statement that such leaders "because of their acknowledged authority, high political organization, and other qualities," can remain at their posts.

4. *Summary of main points*

      a. Communism is based on "scientific laws of social development" which "inevitably" will bring about the fall of capitalism.

      b. Capitalism, in its present final decline, is still viewed as a challenge to further Communist advances.

      c. "Peaceful co-existence" rather than "inevitable war" is possible between the forces of capitalism and communism, and constitutes a specific form of the "class struggle."

      d. Communists will acquire new power by "peaceful competition," "parliamentary means," and the "buying-out" of the capitalists.

      e. International conflict of any kind poses a danger and this necessitates the continued build-up of the Soviet armed forces.

      f. New Program promises to include the common people of Russia more in the processes of their government.

      g. Under the leadership of the C.P.S.U., the people of the Soviet Union will experience the fuller development of "socialism" and a transition to a "true" Communist society stated as follows:

      "Communism is a classless social system with one form of public ownership of the means of production and full social equality of all members of society; under it, the all-round development of people will be accompanied by the growth of the productive forces through continuous progress in science and technology; all the springs of cooperative wealth will flow more abundantly, and the great principle 'From each according to his ability, to each according to his needs' will be implemented. Communism is a highly organized society of free, socially-conscious working people in which public self-government will be established, a society in which labor for the good of society will become the prime vital requirement of everyone, a necessity recognized by one and all, and the ability of each person will be employed to the greatest benefit of the people" ("*New Program of the C.P.S.U.*," 1961).

h. Other points, such as emergent "natural developments," attacks against "revisionism" and "dogmatism," and steadfast support of "anti-imperialist wars of liberation," are repeatedly stressed in the extensive 55,000 word "New Program of the C.P.S.U."

5. *Some tentative conclusions*

a. Further modifications in the theoretical principles of "Marxism-Leninism."

b. "State" does not "wither away" but continues to be "the most important instrument for the transformation of society according to Communist principles," which, in effect, preserves the totalitarian system created by Stalin.

c. Soviet system allegedly serves as the center of the world struggle, as the "New Program" lays down the course of action for the C.P.S.U. in forthcoming decades and also the future for all Communist parties (cf. struggle for ideological leadership within the Communist world between the USSR and the People's Democracy of China; also "national communism" in Yugoslavia and other States).

d. Difficult to reconcile the contents of Soviet promises with the facts of surrounding reality in the USSR.

IV. ALL-UNION SUPREME SOVIET;
ALL-UNION PRESIDIUM

A. ALL-UNION SUPREME SOVIET (Supreme Soviet of the U.S.S.R.)
  1. *Constitution* (Art. 30) stipulates that the All-Union Supreme Soviet is the highest State authority in the USSR, and exercises exclusively (Art. 32) the legislative power; however, it must be remembered that the members of this bicameral national legislature
      a. Secure election primarily as a reward for their loyalty and productivity in the Soviet system;
      b. Do not perform an independent representative function, as do the members of Western parliaments;
      c. Merely certify or endorse decisions made elsewhere in the Government and by the Communist Party;
      d. Lack an organized and effective "Opposition" (to the Communist Party delegates) and have no opportunity seriously to question or reject party policy or decisions made by leading party members in other agencies of the Government;
      e. Conduct meetings which really provide a sounding-board for party propaganda; in fact, the Deputies themselves are "educated" and "inspired," and subsequently "explain" the Government's (party) policies and decisions to their "constituents."
  2. *Composition and membership*
      a. The 791 members of the Council of the Union are elected directly by the Soviet citizens, for a four-year term, with one Deputy for every 300,000 inhabitants of the USSR.
      b. The 652 members of the Council of Nationalities are also elected directly by the Soviet citizens, for a four-year term, with 25 Deputies from each Union-Republic (15 SSRs), 11 Deputies from each Autonomous Republic (ASSR), 5 Deputies from each Autonomous Region, and 1 Deputy from each National Area.
      c. "Every citizen of the U.S.S.R. who has reached the age of twenty-three is eligible for election to the

Supreme Soviet of the U.S.S.R., irrespective of race or nationality, sex, religion, education, domicile, social origin, property status or past activities" (Art. 135).

d. Members of both Councils enjoy equal rights and have an equal power to propose laws, which are passed by a simple majority vote in both Councils.

e. Members of both Councils are also free from arrest and prosecution, unless otherwise consented to by the Supreme Soviet or the Presidium when the Supreme Soviet is not in session.

3. *Internal organization*

a. Each Council of the Supreme Soviet has its own, but similar, internal organization which includes the Chairman and Deputy Chairmen; Secretariat and staff; regular commissions (Credentials, Budget, Legislative Proposals, and Foreign Affairs) and special commissions (Investigation and Audit); the chief functions of each of the regular commissions are as follows:

(1) *Credentials Commission* (21 members): verifies the results of the election and the credentials of Deputies.

(2) *Budget Commission* (39 members): prepares the draft of the State Budget and checks on receipts and expenditures.

(3) *Legislative Proposals Commission* (31 members): drafts bills and studies the changes recommended by citizens (actually the Communist Party) when a bill is published for nationwide discussion.

(4) *Foreign Affairs Commission* (23 members): concerns itself with the international relations of the Soviet Union.

(5) *Economic Commission* (in the Soviet of Nationalities): sees to it that long-term economic plans and budgets (subject to approval by the Supreme Soviet) take sufficient account of the special needs and interests of each of the national Republics, Territories, and Regions.

4. *Functions and powers*

a. Each Council simultaneously holds semi-annual regular meetings and also special meetings called by the Presidium of the Supreme Soviet or on the demand of a Union-Republic.

b. The two Councils sit together to appoint (or "certify") the Presidium of the Supreme Soviet, the Council of Ministers, the members of the Supreme Court and of special courts, and the Procurator-General of the USSR; joint sessions are presided over alternately by the Chairman of each Council.

c. Pass resolutions and enact legislation.

d. Perform other functions as permitted by law (party policy and decisions).

5. *Legislative procedure*

a. A bill is introduced by a party-designated Deputy or by the All-Union Council of Ministers.

b. Consideration and report on the bill by a commission.

c. Limited discussion and debate in the legislative Council.

d. Acceptance of the bill by an open vote.

e. Transmittal of the bill to the other legislative Council, which then follows the same general procedures.

   (1) A Conciliation Commission may, theoretically, be established to attempt to settle any differences between the two Councils on the bill; if the Commission fails to reach an agreement, or its agreement is disapproved by one of the Councils, the question is again considered by the Councils; failing agreement between the Councils, the Presidium dissolves the Supreme Soviet and orders new elections.

      (a) Presidium retains its powers after the dissolution of the Supreme Soviet, or on the expiration of the latter's term of office), until a new Presidium is chosen by a newly elected Supreme Soviet.

      (b) New elections to the Supreme Soviet are held within two months after the dissolution (or expiration of the term of office).

      (c) A newly elected Supreme Soviet is convened by the outgoing Presidium within thirty days after the elections.

     f. Ratification of the law and its promulgation by the Chairman of the Presidium of the Supreme Soviet.

     g. As there is never a "lack of confidence" in the Government, the Presidium, the Council of Ministers, and the Communist Party are, in actual practice, the real legislative power in the USSR.

B. All-Union Presidium (Presidium of the Supreme Soviet of the U.S.S.R.)

  1. *Constitution* (Art. 48) stipulates that the All-Union Presidium is elected at a joint sitting of the two Councils of the All-Union Supreme Soviet, and is accountable to it for all its activities.

     a. Presidium is composed of a Chairman (or President), 16 Deputy-Chairmen, a Secretary, and 15 additional members, all of whom are members of the Supreme Soviet; the Chairman (or President) is the nominal Head of State.

  2. *Functions and powers*

     a. Convenes the sessions of the All-Union Supreme Soviet.

     b. Issues decrees.

     c. Interprets laws.

     d. Dissolves the Supreme Soviet and calls new elections.

     e. Conducts nationwide referenda on its own initiative or on the demand of a Union Republic.

     f. Annuls decisions and orders of the All-Union and Union-Republic Councils of Ministers if they do not conform to law.

     g. Appoints and removes All-Union Ministers (when the All-Union Supreme Soviet is not in session) on the recommendation of the Chairman of the All-Union Council of Ministers.

     h. Awards decorations and confers titles of honor.

     i. Grants pardons.

     j. Creates diplomatic ranks, military titles, etc.

     k. Appoints and removes high-ranking officers in the Armed Forces.

     l. Orders general or partial mobilization and proclaims a state of war (when the All-Union Supreme Soviet is not in session).

m. Ratifies and denounces international treaties of the USSR.

n. Appoints and recalls Soviet diplomatic representatives to foreign States.

o. Accredits and receives diplomatic representatives from foreign States (and may also request their recall).

p. Proclaims martial law in separate localities or throughout the USSR to defend the national interests and ensure the public order and security.

q. Serves as an "interim body" which meets when the All-Union Supreme Soviet is not in session and, in this situation, performs legislative, executive, and judicial functions.

3. *Relationship to the All-Union Supreme Soviet*
   a. See Sections A-4 and A-5 above.

4. *Relationship to the Communist Party Presidium*
   a. Some interlocking membership.
   b. Party Presidium gives directives to the All-Union Presidium which, in turn, gives legal effect to the party policy and decisions.
   c. All-Union Presidium is an official governmental agency; the Party Presidium is non-official.
   d. Party Presidium (particularly its Secretariat and "First Secretary") remains the most powerful single force in the USSR.

V. ALL-UNION COUNCIL OF MINISTERS

A. CONSTITUTIONAL POSITION

1. "The highest executive and administrative organ of the State power of the USSR" (Art. 64).

2. Appointed by, and responsible to, the All-Union Supreme Soviet or its Presidium when the Supreme Soviet is not in session.
   a. Actually, the Party Presidium directs the appointments, which are made by the All-Union Presidium and subsequently certified by the Supreme Soviet.

3. Consists of:
   a. Chairman of the Council of Ministers of the USSR.
   b. First Deputy Chairmen of the Council of Ministers of the USSR.

   c. Deputy Chairmen of the Council of Ministers of the USSR.

   d. Ministers of the USSR, including the Ministers of Foreign Trade; Merchant Marine; Railways; Medium Machine-Building Industry; Construction of Electric Power Stations; Transport Construction; Higher and Specialized Secondary Education; Geological Survey and Conservation of Mineral Resources; Public Health; Foreign Affairs; Culture; Defense; Communications; Agriculture; and Finance. A number of Ministers included in the Government fulfill their leading functions not in the Ministries but in other State administrations (committees, commissions, etc.). In accordance with the Constitution, as amended, the executives of the following administrations are included in the Council of Ministers:

   e. Chairman of the State Planning Committee; Commission of Soviet Control; State Labor and Wages Committee; State Committee on Professional and Technical Training; State Scientific and Technical Committee; State Committee on Automation and Machine-Building; State Committee on Aircraft Technology; State Committee on Defense Technology; State Committee on Radio-Electronics; State Committee on Shipbuilding; State Committee on Chemistry; State Committee on Construction; State Grain and Cereal Committee; State Committee on Foreign Economic Relations; State Security Committee; Administrative Board of the State Bank of the USSR; Central Statistical Board; State Council of Economic Research; State Committee for Cultural Relations with Foreign Countries; State Committee for the Utilization of Atomic Energy.

   f. All-Union Council of Ministers also includes the Chairmen of the Council of Ministers of all the fifteen Union Republics by virtue of their office.

B. DIFFERENTIATION IN TYPES OF MINISTRIES

   1. *All-Union ministries*

      a. Administer designated branches of the State administration throughout the territory of the Soviet Union, either directly or through bodies appointed by them.

2. *Union-Republic ministries*

   a. Administer other designated branches of the State administration through the corresponding Ministries in the Union-Republics, and only administer directly a small number of enterprises confirmed by the All-Union Presidium.

3. Each of the ministries has a Minister at the head who works with a collegium or (ministerial Presidium) of leading officials, and the ministries operate on the principle of collegiate management with the final decision and personal responsibility resting with the Minister.

4. Constant revision and reorganization of ministries makes it difficult to give, for any length of time, a definitive list of both All-Union and Union-Republic ministries.

C. FUNCTIONS AND POWERS

1. Direct the various branches of State administration within the U.S.S.R.

2. Coordinate and direct the work of the All-Union and Union-Republic Ministries, and the economic and cultural institutions under their jurisdiction.

3. Supervise the organization and administration of the national economic plan and the State budget.

4. Maintain the public order, protect the interests of the State, and safeguard the rights of citizens.

5. Provide general guidance in the conduct of foreign relations.

6. Direct the general organization and development of the nation's Armed Forces.

7. Establish the special committees and central administrations necessary to the development and organization of economic, cultural, and defense activities.

8. Issue and administer binding orders and instructions (including the power to suspend those of a Union-Republic Council of Ministers) and make decisions in the implementation of the governmental programs.

9. Note, again, that actual power is always retained by the "First Secretary" and other members of the Party Presidium who may be (and usually are) members of the All-Union Council of Ministers.
   a. Thus, all important decisions of national scope are made by the Council of Ministers jointly with the Presidium and, theoretically, the Central Committee of the C.P.S.U.
   b. This is the so-called "duality of purpose and function" in the permeation and direction of the governmental structures by the outstanding figures in the Communist Party.

VI. NATIONAL ADMINISTRATION

The All-Union and Union-Republic ministries assume the primary responsibility for the administration of the various phases of the planned economy, but are assisted in this task by a host of regional and local subsidiaries and special "staff" and "control" agencies. Various Planning Commissions, Economic Councils, Consultative Committees, and units of the Ministry of Party-State Control have particularly important functions to perform in this regard.

A. BACKGROUND AND DEVELOPMENT OF THE PLANNED ECONOMY
   1. Diversity of economic problems in the early Bolshevik period of civil war and "war Communism" (1918–1920).
   2. Adoption of the *New Economic Policy* (N.E.P.) and the temporary "compromise with capitalism" (1921–1927).
      a. Stalin's emphasis on *"Socialism in one country"*: ". . . . What does the *possibility* of the victory of socialism in a single country mean? It means the possibility of solving the contradictions between the workers and the peasants with the aid of the internal forces of our country; it means the possibility of the proletariat's seizing power and using that power for the construction of complete socialist society in our country, with the sympathy and the support of the workers of other countries, but without the preliminary victory of the proletarian revolution in other countries. In the absence of such a

possibility, the building of socialism is building without prospects, building without the assurance that socialism can be completely constructed. It is no use building socialism without the assurance that we will be able to complete it, without the conviction that the technical backwardness of our country is not an *insuperable* obstacle to the construction of complete socialist society. To deny such a possibility is to display lack of faith in the task of building socialism, is to abandon Leninism. . . ." (from *Problems of Leninism*).

    b. Further revision of economic plans and reorganization of the national administration at the 15th Party Congress in Moscow, 1927.

3. *General goals of the early Five-Year Plans* (1928 *et seq.*)
    a. Construction of basic heavy industries.
    b. "Collectivization" and increased productivity in agriculture.
    c. Economic development of the remote areas of the country.
    d. Organization of the national defense.
    e. Technological and scientific accomplishments.
    f. Subserviency of individual needs and consumer interests to the accomplishment of the foregoing goals.

4. *Aftermath of World War II* (1946 *et seq.*)
    a. Postwar physical rehabilitation and economic reconstruction throughout the country.
    b. Determination and pursuit of "New Tasks" in agriculture and industry.
    c. Emphasis on national security and defense.
    d. Organizing an emergent new "Soviet society."

5. Completion of the Seven-Year Plan (1959–1965) and projection of the new Five-Year Plan (1966–1970).

NOTE: Portions of the following section are prepared from materials kindly provided by the Embassy of the U.S.S.R. (Washington, D.C.).

B. ORGANIZATION AND MANAGEMENT OF THE PLANNED ECONOMY (1966)
    1. *"Socialist" and "public" property*
       a. Property owned by all the people, primarily the in-

struments and means of production, in the creation of "material values" (i.e., goods).

b. No class is deprived of the means of production, nor is there any one class which owns them exclusively; the accumulated "material values" belong to the whole society.

c. The fact that the country's natural and technological resources belong to the entire people allegedly rules out the possibility of one man exploiting other men.

d. There are two forms of "public" property in the "socialist" society: that property which belongs to the entire population and that which is "cooperative" and collective farm property.

   (1) "Public" (or State) property includes the means of production on a country-wide scale.

   (2) "Cooperative" or collective farm property includes the means of production owned by the members of the "cooperative" or collective farms.

   (3) "Public" property is administered on behalf of the people by the State, which represents the interests of all sections of the population; all the people, including members of "cooperatives" and collective farms, make use of this property.

   (4) "Cooperative" and collective farm property is managed only by the groups of individuals belonging to the "cooperative" and collective farms; theoretically, they dispose of this jointly-owned property as they see fit.

e. In addition to the two forms of "socialist" or "public" property, the people of the U.S.S.R. are permitted to own personal property.

   (1) ". . . the law permits the small private undertakings of individual peasants and handicraftsmen based on their own labor and precluding the exploitation of the labor of others. . . . The right of citizens to own, as their personal property, income and savings derived from work, to own a dwelling-house and a supple-

mentary husbandry, articles of household and . . . personal use and convenience, is protected by law, as is also the right of citizens to inherit personal property" (Arts. 9–10).

2. *Rationale for Economic Planning*

   a. Since the property of the entire people includes the country's basic means of production, the Soviet economy is organized according to a single national plan, which means that most of the activities of the people are guided by the country's "interests" as determined by the incumbent political leaders.

   b. The economic plan is a sketch of the economic structure and functioning of the Soviet society in the accomplishment of designated economic tasks and objectives over a given period of time.

   c. The principle of the *"socialist distribution of productive forces"* refers to the endeavor to bring industry closer to the raw material and power sources and to consumer areas for the planned and most efficient use of natural and manpower resources throughout the country for the good of all the people.

      (1) It predicates a "division of labor" based on economic specialization in the various regions, and

      (2) Its goal is the speediest development of the country by developing each of the Union-Republics.

   d. Similarly, the prevailing system of "economic areas" (as distinguished from "administrative districts") provides for the territorial organization of agriculture, industry, etc. along lines planned to obtain the best distribution and use of the country's productive forces and the speedier development of the national economy.

      (1) *"Economics Areas"* (47): the determining criteria for this division include the climatic conditions, the natural and manpower resources, the composition and distribution of the population, the transport and communications facilities, the present development and specialization of the area, etc.; 24 of the 47 "economic areas"

CHART 23. SOVIET EXECUTIVE AND ADMINISTRATIVE ORGANIZATION

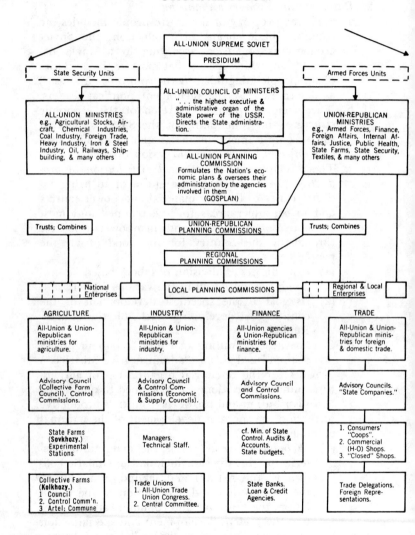

ALL-UNION SUPREME SOVIET

PRESIDIUM

State Security Units

Armed Forces Units

ALL-UNION COUNCIL OF MINISTERS
". . . the highest executive & administrative organ of the State power of the USSR. Directs the State administration.

ALL-UNION MINISTRIES
e.g., Agricultural Stocks, Aircraft, Chemical Industries, Coal Industry, Foreign Trade, Heavy Industry, Iron & Steel Industry, Oil, Railways, Shipbuilding, & many others

UNION-REPUBLICAN MINISTRIES
e.g., Armed Forces, Finance, Foreign Affairs, Internal Affairs, Justice, Public Health, State Farms, State Security, Textiles, & many others

ALL-UNION PLANNING COMMISSION
Formulates the Nation's economic plans & oversees their administration by the agencies involved in them
(GOSPLAN)

Trusts; Combines

UNION-REPUBLICAN PLANNING COMMISSIONS

Trusts; Combines

REGIONAL PLANNING COMMISSIONS

National Enterprises

LOCAL PLANNING COMMISSIONS

Regional & Local Enterprises

AGRICULTURE	INDUSTRY	FINANCE	TRADE
All-Union & Union-Republican ministries for agriculture.	All-Union & Union-Republican ministries for industry.	All-Union agencies & Union-Republican ministries for finance.	All-Union & Union-Republican ministries for foreign & domestic trade.
Advisory Council (Collective Farm Council). Control Commissions.	Advisory Council & Control Commissions (Economic & Supply Councils).	Advisory Council and Control Commissions.	Advisory Councils. "State Companies."
State Farms (**Sovkhozy.**) Experimental Stations	Managers. Technical Staff.	cf. Min. of State Control. Audits & Accounts. State budgets.	1. Consumers' "Coops". 2. Commercial (H-O) Shops. 3. "Closed" Shops.
Collective Farms (**Kolkhozy.**) 1 Council 2. Control Comm'n. 3 Artel; Commune	Trade Unions 1. All-Union Trade Union Congress. 2. Central Committee.	State Banks. Loan & Credit Agencies.	Trade Delegations. Foreign Representations.

are located in the Russian Federation, 7 in the Ukraine, and 7 in Kazakhstan.

(2) *"Large Economic Areas"* (18): the determining criterion for the merger of "economic areas" into a "large economic area" is specialization on either a republican (i.e., Union-Republic) or national scale; planning commissions and co-ordinating technical and economic councils have been established for the large areas to improve planning and guidance.

e. The part of labor in the production process is planned on both the national and local scale, the objective being to distribute available manpower most efficiently in the many sectors of the country's economy and make the most economical use of its working time; the *"labor plan"* provides for the training of skilled personnel and a rise in real income (i.e., wages and profits) based on the planned increase in productivity.

f. Various agencies, i.e., the *State Planning Commission of the All-Union Council of Ministers (Gosplan)*, the Union-Republic Planning Commissions, the planning commissions of the large and other economic areas, the All-Union and Union-Republic ministries and departments, the Supreme Economic Council and the Union-Republic Economic Councils, the trade unions and other public organizations all take part in drawing-up and/or administering the national economic plan.

3. *Planning Commissions and Economic Councils*

a. The planning commissions of the "large economic areas" are responsible for improving the distribution of the productive forces, in order to plan more efficiently both by industry (or whatever) and by territory.

(1) *State Planning Commission of the All-Union Council of Ministers (Gosplan)*, the Union-Republic Planning Commissions, and the planning commissions of the large areas plan the development of the smaller economic areas; the Union-Republic Planning Commissions and of

the large areas provide a link between the central and local planning bodies.

(2) Planning Commissions study the resources and potentials of the economic areas, collate proposals for their development, and oversee the administration of the different phases of the national economic plan by the agencies involved in them.

b. The economic councils are responsible for the production activities of the industries (or whatever) in their area of jurisdiction.

(1) *Supreme Economic Council of the U.S.S.R.* provides guidance for the Economics Councils of the Russian Federation, the Ukraine, Kazakhstan, and the Central Asian Economic Area, as well as for the other economic councils indirectly; it is also concerned with the implementation of the national economic plan, the adoption of new techniques in economic management, and the solution of unforeseen problems in production.

(2) Periodic conferences of representatives of the Economic Councils of the "large economic areas" and the Union-Republics are called by the Supreme Economic Council to further coordinate and facilitate the fulfillment of planned assignments and also to determine and meet new requirements arising in the course of plan fulfillment.

(3) *Economic Councils* are concerned with the needs of the individual enterprises under their supervision, as they relate to the needs of the country, and draw-up and implement plans for production, specialization, cooperation, and materiél supply; the Economic Councils usually consist of a Chairman, three or four assistants, and the top executives and representative workers of the individual enterprises.

(4) *Technical and Economic Councils* are concerned with solving technical and economic problems and the adoption of new technologi-

cal methods and approaches for enterprises supervised by the Economic Councils; the Technical and Economic Councils usually consist of agricultural and industrial experts, scientists, production innovators, and representatives of the trade unions and other public organizations.

4. *Control Commissions and Inspection Groups*

a. A most important aspect of the Soviet socialist system, involving the extensive use of joint control organs for the Communist Party and the Government.

b. Includes approximately 3,300 *Party-State Control Commissions* (or *People's Control Committees*) in the districts, cities, areas, regions and Republics, supplemented by an extensive network of approximately 4,300,000 *"Public Inspection" Groups.*

   (1) Work of the local commissions is coordinated by a national commission in Moscow.

   (2) "Public Inspection" Groups operate at industrial enterprises, construction projects, on the collective and State farms, in offices, educational establishments, research institutes, and in places of residence.

   (3) Members of Control Commissions are appointed (or approved) by the party or party-dominated organs, whereas members of Inspection Groups are elected and include both party and non-party workers, farmers, professionals, office employees, artists, students, pensioners, housewives, etc.

c. Control system is rationalized on the basis of the size and complexity of the task of assisting the Communist Party and Government improve the "guidance and management" of State policies and programs.

   (1) It largely involves organized check-ups and inspection of both individual enterprises and whole branches of the national economy by the volunteer inspectors.

   (2) The Control Commissions presumably adopt

the recommendations made by the Inspection Groups to correct any shortcomings and perhaps also demote or penalize persons at fault.

d. People's participation in inspection groups allegedly gives them the administrative experience necessary to run the country; in fact, more than 130,000 volunteer inspectors have been selected to help manage more than 16,000 departments and committees of the Control Commissions.

5. *Banking and Finance*

a. Largely under the control of the *All-Union Ministry of Finance*, which supervises the State banks and assists in the administration of the State budgets, and the *All-Union Ministry of State Control*, which conducts current and post-audits and enforces anti-inflationary measures.

b. The *State Bank of the U.S.S.R.*, the *Bank of Foreign Trade (Vneshtorgbank)* and the *Bank for Financing Capital Investments (Stroibank)* comprise the Soviet Union's banking system.

c. The State Bank has approximately 240,000 people on its staff, with 4,000 offices and branches, and more than 72,000 savings banks.

d. Centralized management of the State Bank includes a Board of Directors, appointed by the All-Union Council of Ministers, and a Chairman (a member of the Government) appointed (i.e., "certified") by the All-Union Supreme Soviet.

e. State Bank serves as a credit agency; a settlement, collection, and disbursement center; and a bank of issue; it also exercises direct control over the financial and business operations of all the agricultural, industrial, commercial, and other enterprises and organizations throughout the country.

f. Banking resources derive from the temporary surplus funds of enterprises and organizations held on deposit; the settlement and current accounts; the deposits of private individuals; State Budget surpluses; the State Bank's own funds; various State taxes; and money in circulation.

g. Accounts are settled by the transfer of funds from

one account to another, so that no handling of cash is involved; and cash receipts of all enterprises and organizations are deposited with the State Bank's branch offices.

h. Funds owned by private individuals are deposited in the savings banks of the State Bank, and obtain two per cent interest *per annum* on demand deposits and three per cent on time deposits; as in other banking systems, the State uses the temporarily idle funds of private depositors for various investment and credit purposes.

i. Short-term and long-term credits provide financial aid to collective farms, industrial enterprises, other organizations, (and even to private individuals for such purpose as to build a home for themselves), etc., for current needs (e.g., raw materials and supplies), expansion and modernization, and new construction.

   (1) In fact, the State Bank invests its funds in every sector of the economy.

   (2) Loans are made according to plans approved by the All-Union Ministry of Finance and the State Planning Commission *(Gosplan)*, at designated interest rates *per annum*.

j. Wages and prices are set by the Government according to plan, in order to regulate cash in circulation and to curb inflation.

k. State Bank has a monopoly on foreign exchange operations, i.e., all financial transactions with foreign countries, export and import arrangements, and credit from abroad.

   (1) The Bank of Foreign Trade *(Vneshtorgbank)* discharges most of these responsibilities (subject always to the control of the State Bank) through more than 1,000 institutions in more than 80 countries.

   (2) The Government monopoly on foreign exchange and foreign trade allegedly creates a stable foundation for planning foreign exchange operations and enables the State Bank to ensure adherence to the details of plans

Chart 24. STRUCTURE OF THE STATE BANK OF THE USSR

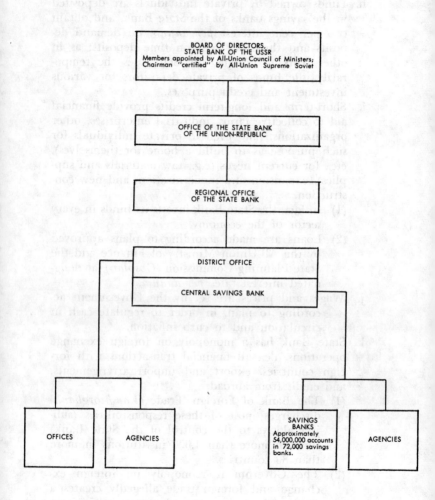

dealing with this important phase of the Soviet economic system.

C. MAJOR SECTORS OF THE PLANNED ECONOMY (1966)

1. *Agriculture*

a. There are two basic types of farms in the U.S.S.R.: (1) *collective farms (Kolkhozy)*, which are "voluntary associations for the cultivation of land," and (2) *State farms (Sovkhozy)*, which are owned and operated by the State.

b. Theoretically, the collective farms are run by the people, but actually their managerial staff (including a General Council, a Chairman, and an Executive Committee) is selected and supervised by the State.

c. Properties on collective farms are both personal (e.g., a plot of land for an individual household) and community (i.e., the land of the collective is secured for the permanent use of the people).

d. System of payment on the collective farms is determined in various ways, but is essentially cash payments (rather than payment in cash and kind) to individual workers.

e. State procurements of produce from the collective farms are made in the form of State purchases according to a sliding scale of prices determined by the State.

f. Former system of "tractor stations" has been modified, so that they are now repair and technical service stations and most collectives have their own tractors, combines, and other farm machinery.

g. Increasingly, smaller collective farms are merged into fewer large ones ("farm giantism") or with State farms which trend suggests that the State will soon directly control or supervise production on most farm lands ("etatization").

h. Various new measures, e.g., the wider use of machinery, adoption of scientific methods of farming, development of virgin and long-fallow lands, have been introduced to increase agricultural output; similarly, new efforts have been made in animal husbandry to increase the production of livestock and meat and dairy products, etc.

i. *Council on Collective Farm Affairs* works closely with the All-Union Ministry of Agriculture and various planning and control agencies to plan and coordinate production on the collective farms.

2. *Industry: Production*

a. Based on the "territorial-productive" principle of organization (see also Section B-2 above), involving local, regional, and national enterprises and regional and national trusts and combines.

b. Planning Commissions and Economic Councils consult, as required, with the appropriate All-Union and Union-Republic ministries to plan and supervise the distribution and use of manpower and natural resources.

c. Managerial and technical staffs have particularly important functions in connection with industrial or plant supervision and research and consultative services.

d. Heavy industries continue to account for more than two-thirds of industrial activity within the U.S.S.R.

e. Under the Seven-Year Plan (1959–1965) and the new Five-Year Plan (1966–1970) special emphasis is given to increased production in iron and steel, non-ferrous metals, fuel, electrical power, atomic energy, engineering products, chemicals, paper and woodworking industries, building materials, textiles, food industry, etc.

f. Widespread use of incentives and penalties to increase and control the productive efforts of industrial workers (and also agricultural workers on the State and collective farms).

g. Part of the profits (i.e., the income left after all production expenses are deducted) of industries and factories (or whatever) are used to expand production, improve the working and living conditions of their personnel, and pay for bonuses and other benefits and services; the other part, in the form of a "profits tax," goes to the State and is used for general budgetary needs.

    h. Labor Codes prescribe rules of conduct for industrial workers and Arbitration Courts settle disputes involving industrial enterprises.

    i. Ultimately, the Ministry of Party-State Control, the republican State Control Commissions, and various party organs are responsible for the implementation of State policies and the realization of desired goals thereunder.

3. *Industry: Trade Unions*

    a. Theoretically, a free and voluntary representative organization for workers and other employees, but actually an arm of the State and Communist Party.

        (1) ". . . . The Soviet trade unions conduct all their activities under the guidance of the Communist Party of the Soviet Union, the organizing and directing force of Soviet society. The trade unions of the U.S.S.R. rally the masses of workers and other employees around the Party and mobilize them for the struggle to build a Communist society. . . ." (*Rules of the Trade Unions of the U.S.S.R.*, 1959).

    b. Virtually all factory and office employees belong to one of the 20–25 trade unions (each of which consists of one or several branches of industry), with more than 450,000 affiliates and a total membership in excess of 67,000,000.

    c. *Functions of trade unions* are to

        (1) Participate actively in State and economic matters.

        (2) Help draft legislation concerning production, working and living conditions, and cultural facilities.

        (3) See to the observance of labor laws and participate in deciding labor quotas and wages.

        (4) Promote the "socialist emulation" movement of workers and other employees for the maximum fulfillment of State plans at every factory and office.

        (5) Support innovators and model workers in production, and publicize their methods and accomplishments.

(6) Administer State insurance funds from which pensions and temporary disability benefits are paid.

(7) Organize health and holiday facilities, including sanatorium treatment, and safeguard the health of women and children.

(8) Supervise the fulfillment of plans for housing construction and participate in the distribution of housing accommodations.

(9) Promote physical culture, sports, and tourism.

(10) Perform many other functions under their laws and Rules.

d. *Rights and Duties of Trade-Union members*

(1) Elect and be elected to trade union organizations, conferences, and congresses.

(2) Participate in discussions at trade-union meetings.

(3) Submit questions and suggestions relative to trade-union activities and work.

(4) Approach and appeal to any trade-union body to protect one's rights as a trade-union member.

(5) Be present in all cases where trade-union bodies pass an opinion on one's work or conduct.

(6) Share in the trade-union mutual-aid fund.

(7) Work unremmitingly for the development of the Communist State.

(8) Safeguard and strengthen "public socialist" property.

(9) Observe State and labor discipline.

(10) Expose shortcomings in production and work to eliminate them.

(11) Attend all trade-union meetings and fulfill all "social assignments."

(12) Follow the *Rules of the Trade Unions of the U.S.S.R.*, etc.

(13) *Privileges of members* include greater State social insurance benefits, priority home and holiday accommodations, free legal advice and assistance from trade-union bodies, grants from trade-union funds, various inducements and awards, etc.

e. *Membership* is obtained by personal application which is approved by the shop, factory, or office committee of the trade-union; for failure to pay dues, for lack of discipline, and for unseemly conduct in private life, a member may be "cautioned, reproved, publicly reprimanded, censured" or even expelled from the trade-union.

f. *Organizational Structure of the Trade Unions* includes the

  (1) *U.S.S.R. Congress of Trade Unions,* which meets every four years, and its interim *All-Union Central Council of Trade Unions,* which hear and approve reports of the highest trade-union bodies and the Auditing Commissions; adopt the *Rules of the Trade Unions of the U.S.S.R.*; specify the tasks of the trade unions generally and in the international trade-union movement; participate in drafting national economic plans; direct the socialist emulation movement; receive reports by Economic Councils, Government ministries and departments, etc.; approve the budget of the trade unions and the State social insurance budget; arrange various mass undertakings; issues trade-union magazines and bulletins; etc.

  (2) A.U.C.C.T.U. convenes at least once in every six months, and elects a *Presidium* and a *Secretariat* to direct the current work of the trade-unions.

  (3) *Republican, Territorial, Regional, City and District Trade-Union bodies* parallel in their organizational structures and functions the trade-union bodies on the next highest level, and are directly accountable to them; inter-union conferences or congresses of the trade unions convene at least once in every two years and their trade-union councils (which also elect corresponding Presidiums and Secretariats) convene at least once in every six months.

  (4) *Primary Trade-Union organizations* are composed of trade-union members in the various

local enterprises and convene at regular intervals in committee or general meetings; among many other functions, they negotiate "collective agreements" and participate with management in the Permanent Production Conference.

g. *"Collective agreements"* are negotiated between management and the trade-union local committee at every Soviet enterprise once a year.

(1) The agreement lists in detail the commitments of both labor and management with regard to production and working conditions.

(2) As Soviet labor laws contain detailed provisions on every aspect of work and production—and are rigorously applied in every place of work—there is no struggle between management and the trade unions for the rights of their members.

h. *Permanent Production Conference* (PPC) convenes at least once in every three months at most enterprises with one-hundred or more workers and employees, and consists of elected trade-union members and representatives of management.

(1) The Conference elects a permanent Presidium of five-fifteen members which prepares agendas for the regular meetings and is responsible for carrying out the Conference decisions.

(2) The management helps the Conference plan and implement its recommendations, while the local trade-union commmitte presumably supervises the work of the PPC.

i. *"Union Activists"* are trade-union members who give a considerable portion of their free time to work on (or for) the local trade-union committee; actually, the 23,000,000 or more "union activists" do most of the trade-union work, as paid union staffs are small in number at all levels.

j. *Union funds* are derived from entrance fees, monthly membership dues, proceeds from cultural, educational and sports institutions, auxiliary establishments, etc., and are expended to defray the costs of maintaining the trade-unions and their activities.

h. *Auditing Commissions,* elected by the appropriate general meeting, trade-union committee, or conference of union members, check on the fulfillment of trade-union budgets and the proper expenditure of trade-union funds, and report on their activities to congresses, conferences, and general meetings simultaneously with the trade-union bodies.

4. *Trade*

a. All-Union Government maintains a virtual monopoly on domestic and foreign trade; it oversees the activities of the *Central Union of Consumer's Cooperatives of the U.S.S.R.* (which operates commission shops to sell foodstuffs to the urban population) and of the State trading establishments in rural communities and consumers' cooperatives on collective farms.

b. Under the direction of the Ministry for Foreign Trade, "State companies" and "trade delegations" export specified products and goods and negotiate and implement trade agreements with foreign States.

D. THE SEVEN-YEAR PLAN (1959–1965)

1. *Statement by Nikita Khrushchev,* 1959:

"By fulfilling the Seven-Year Plan, we shall take a decisive step toward accomplishing the basic economic task of the U.S.S.R.—to overtake and outstrip the most advanced capitalist countries in output per head of population in the briefest possible period of history. . . . In this stage of the competition, the Soviet Union intends to surpass the United States economically. The U.S. production level is the ceiling which capitalist economy has been able to achieve. . . . The very fact that we now set ourselves this task shows how much our strength, our resources have grown. . . . With its present productive forces, its enhanced productivity of social labor, its modern technology, its planned Socialist economy, and the creative energies of its people, the Soviet Union has every chance of winning this competition of peaceful endeavor. . . . It should be stressed that although the level of production in a capitalist and a Socialist country—the United States and the U.S.S.R., for example—may be the same, the social effects of this will be poles apart. This is precisely where the superiority of Socialism reveals itself, for under it production is subordinated not to profit-making but to the maximum satisfaction of the requirements of all members of society."

   a. Countless similar statements have been made, almost *ad infinitum*, by other Soviet spokesmen in spite of considerable evidence to disprove their claims and contentions.

2. Fundamental reorganization of the system of management in industry and construction, including the

   a. Abolishment of scores of All-Union, Union-Republic, and Republican ministries;

   b. Reorganization of the central and Republican planning agencies;

   c. Increase in planning powers of the Union-Republics;

   d. Widening of authority of Union-Republic Supreme Soviets and Economic Councils under their jurisdiction;

   e. All-Union Council of Ministers continues to give "general guidance" to work of Economic Councils in the economic areas in the Union-Republics.

3. *General goals of the Seven-Year Plan*

   a. Catch up in peaceful economic competition with the most highly-developed capitalist countries, and surpass them.

   b. Substantial improvements in all sectors of the Soviet economy, with particular priority to heavy industry.

   c. Bigger increase in output of agricultural commodities.

   d. Attainment of "proper distribution of productive forces" and further economic development in the Eastern regions (i.e., the Urals, Siberia, the Far East, Kazakhstan, Central Asia, the Transcaucasus, etc.) of the country.

   e. Considerable increase in the productivity of "social labor," in construction industries, railway transport, the State farms, collective farms, etc., with decreases in production costs.

f. New advances in public education, science, art, the press, radio, television, and other cultural fields.

g. Continued rise in the people's standard of living.

4. *New Trend toward Capitalism?*

a. Increased use of the profit motive (e.g., bonuses) as a basic incentive for plant managers and workers.

b. Further decentralization of State administration of planned activities and more autonomy for directors of local enterprises.

c. Some relaxation of price controls over agricultural produce.

d. Private plots of ground increasing in number and supply food far out of proportion to their size.

e. Extension of consumer credit (i.e., installment buying) to the individual for the purchase of such items as cameras, radios, TV sets, etc.

NOTE: Late in 1965, Premier Alexei Kosygin outlined a new economic program, designed to strengthen Socialism and "speed up our progress toward Communism." He emphasized the need to increase both the role of incentive in the Soviet economy and centralized planning. The program would abolish the network of regional planning commissions (also variously called "committees" or "councils") in favor of 28 central planning bodies, each to govern a branch of industry on a national basis. Moreover, "the role of party leadership in management" would increase. Soviet industrial enterprises would be judged by the central planners on the basis of efficiency and sales rather than on "over-fulfillment" of production plans. As an incentive to efficiency, enterprises would keep more of their "profits" to reinvest in better equipment and as incentive bonuses to workers. The term "profits" was understood to mean "value produced beyond cost" and not private gains resulting from private investments. Wages and prices would get their investment funds in the form of long-term credits instead of grants. Repayment would be at a fixed rate so that by being "thrifty" an enterprise could increase its annual "profits." It remained to be seen how successful the Soviet leaders would be in implementing the new economic program.

E. THE FIVE-YEAR PLAN (1966–1970)
  1. *Statement by Leonid Brezhnev,* Twenty-third Communist Party Congress, 1966: "The Congress has outlined the main directions of our domestic policy and economic activity for the next five-year period. The essence of this policy is to ensure that we reach new targets in building Communism in our country, that we achieve a sharp increase in the efficiency of the entire sphere of social production, a steady growth in the material welfare of the working people and a further strengthening of our country's defense potential. In this five-year period we are to attain stable growth in agricultural production and a high pace of industrial development. All this will raise our planned economy to a new level. . . . We are looking forward to the future with confidence and optimism. It is well-founded optimism. It is based on a realistic evaluation of our huge potentialities, on the inexhaustible strength of our Party, of all the people. . . . We have trained excellent personnel in all branches of production, science and culture. The Soviet working class, collective farm peasantry and people's intelligentsia heartily support the policy of the Party, regarding its plans as their own vital cause. . . . Mobilizing all our strength and energy, we shall confidently advance to new victories of our great Communist cause."
  2. Adoption of new and improved methods of planning and economic management, with emphasis upon the
     a. "Principle of profitability" in all branches and links of the economy;
     b. "Forward surge" in the economy and culture of all the Union-Republics;
     c. "Socialist emulation" by all Soviet citizens in their common participation in the building of Communism.
  3. *"New targets"* of the Five-Year Plan
     a. Achieve a rapid rise in (the national and) real incomes.

b. Narrow the gap between the rate of consumer goods and producer goods production.

c. Raise the economic and cultural level of the rural population, bringing it closer to the urban living standard.

d. Increase the rate of development of agriculture to bring it closer to the rate of industrial development.

e. Boost the agricultural and industrial production in the underdeveloped areas East of the Urals.

f. Further strengthen the country's defense capacity and maintain the Armed Forces at a high level.

g. *Statement by Alexei Kosygin*, Twenty-third Communist Party Congress, 1966: "The cardinal economic-political task is to set into motion, and give leadership to, the creative energies of the people, to enliven activity and develop the initiative, the craving for the new, the high sense of responsibility of every Communist, every worker in all the sectors of the economy."

VII. SOVIET JUDICIAL SYSTEM

It is of interest to note that the members of the Supreme Court of the U.S.S.R., of the Union-Republic and Autonomous Republic Supreme Courts, and of other high courts are elected by the Supreme Soviets on their respective levels, and are (theoretically) accountable to them. The members of the People's Courts on lower levels and of the "Comrade's Courts" are elected by the qualified citizens of the particular area or enterprise, and may be recalled by them. All of the members of the Supreme Court of the U.S.S.R., and most of the members of the other regular courts, are members of the C.P.S.U. and the remainder obtain their nominations for election on the behest or approval of the Party structures on the corresponding levels of "State authority." Although judges are (also theoretically) independent, they are "subject to the law" and, therefore, equate the legal rights and judicial safeguards of Soviet citizens in accordance with the current party line, or the so-called "will of the proletariat" as determined by the Presidium of the Central Committee of the C.P.S.U. *Fundamental Laws of Criminal and Civil Legislation* and

Codes of Criminal and Civil Procedure for the U.S.S.R. and the Union-Republics are basic "socialist law" and emphasize the construction of the Communist State, the protection of the "socialist economic system" and the strict observance and enforcement of prescribed rules of conduct for all citizens. Nor should one overlook the fact that individual rights are exercised with respect always for "the rules of socialist society" and that cases are tried in public "unless otherwise provided by law." There are so many other constitutional and legal reservations that it is difficult to discern clearly how much fair and impartial "law and justice"—at least in the Western sense—is consistently obtained by the individual in the Soviet Union. Moreover, it should be reemphasized that the C.P.S.U. continues to be *the leading core of all organizations of the working people,*" including the courts of law. With these observations in mind, there follows a somewhat detailed description of the "Soviet Judicial System."

A. THEORY AND PRACTICE OF "LAW AND JUSTICE"

1. Legal and judicial systems are instruments of the Communist party in the regulation of all human activity and the maintenance of the socialist regime in the USSR.

2. Protection of individual rights and interests is uncertain, principally because there are no well-established principles of common or equity law, binding judicial precedents, guaranteed impartial judicial proceedings, or uniform application of the Soviet law.

3. No rule of law (as in democratic States) to protect the individual against an *ultra vires* action or provide him with redress for a wrong committed by a public official.

4. Administration of the criminal law is often severe, owing to the party's primary concern for safeguarding the "public interest," but leniency is shown in the administration of the civil law, involving a lesser "private interest."

5. Extraordinary means are sometimes used to administer "justice" in the USSR, such as *ad hoc* "courts," the important Committee on State Security (KGB), "Correctional Camps," "Volunteer Labor Brigades," and (in the recent past) purges of the Government and party.

Chart 25. ORGANIZATION OF THE SOVIET COURT SYSTEM

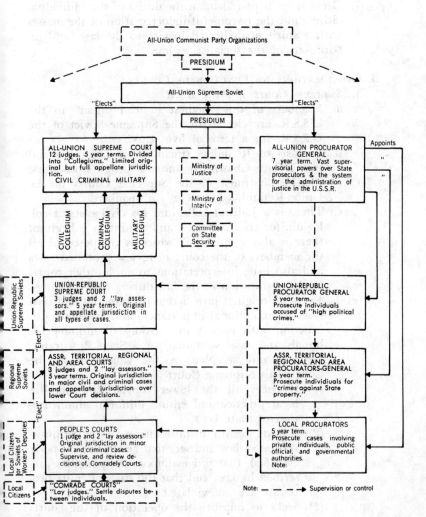

All-Union Communist Party Organizations

PRESIDIUM

All-Union Supreme Soviet

"Elects"   "Elects"

PRESIDIUM

ALL-UNION SUPREME COURT
12 judges. 5 year terms. Divided into "Collegiums." Limited original but full appellate jurisdiction.
CIVIL CRIMINAL MILITARY

CIVIL COLLEGIUM

CRIMINAL COLLEGIUM

MILITARY COLLEGIUM

Ministry of Justice

Ministry of Interior

Committee on State Security

ALL-UNION PROCURATOR GENERAL
7 year term. Vast supervisorial powers over State prosecutors & the system for the administration of justice in the U.S.S.R.

Appoints

"

"

UNION-REPUBLIC SUPREME COURT
3 judges and 2 "lay assessors." 5 year terms. Original and appellate jurisdiction in all types of cases.

Union-Republic Supreme Soviets

"Elect"

UNION-REPUBLIC PROCURATOR GENERAL
5 year term.
Prosecute individuals accused of "high political crimes."

ASSR, TERRITORIAL, REGIONAL AND AREA COURTS
3 judges and 2 "lay assessors." 5 year terms. Original jurisdiction in major civil and criminal cases and appellate jurisdiction over lower Court decisions.

Regional Supreme Soviets

"Elect"

ASSR, TERRITORIAL, REGIONAL AND AREA PROCURATORS-GENERAL
5 year term.
Prosecute individuals for "crimes against State property."

PEOPLE'S COURTS
1 judge and 2 "lay assessors" Original jurisdiction in minor civil and criminal cases. Supervise, and review decisions of, Comradely Courts.

Local Citizens or Soviets of Workers' Deputies

"Elect"

LOCAL PROCURATORS
5 year term.
Prosecute cases involving private individuals, public official, and governmental authorities.
Note:

"COMRADE COURTS"
"Lay judges." Settle disputes between individuals.

Local Citizens

Note: ─ ─ ─ → Supervision or control

6. Widespread use of the judicial collegium, consisting of appointed professional judges or popularly elected judges and "people's assessors," all of whom are "politically-reliable."

7. Great stress is placed upon the duties of the individual citizen and the purposeful indoctrination of the masses with a spirit of dedicated loyalty to the laws and institutions of the socialist regime.

B. ORGANIZATION AND FUNCTION OF COURTS
   1. *Supreme Court of the U.S.S.R.*
      a. Members of this "highest judicial organ" in the U.S.S.R. are elected by the Supreme Soviet of the U.S.S.R. for a term of five years.
      b. Consists of 16 judges (including a Chairman and two Deputy-Chairmen) and 45 people's assessors; the 15 Chairmen of the Supreme Courts of the Union-Republics are *ex officio* members.
      c. There is a judicial collegium for civil cases, a collegium for criminal cases, and a military collegium; there is also a "plenum" which is composed of all the members of the court to review protested cases and also issue interpretations to guide other courts in the application of the law during their hearings.
      d. Exercises original jurisdiction (in criminal and civil cases of exceptional importance) and appellate jurisdiction with respect to decisions of military tribunals and cases submitted by a State Procurator-General and accepted by the Chairman of the Court; this Supreme Court also
         (1) Oversees all the lower courts, to generalize legal practice and ensure uniform administration of State laws.
         (2) Guards against inconsistencies in the administration of law and sees that crimes are properly classified, that judges impose the penalties prescribed by law, and that the rules of court procedure are not violated.
         (3) Seeks to improve the operation of the courts and other legal agencies, so that they will be more effective guardians of "socialist law" and the rights of the citizen.

(4) Submits to the Chairman (or President) of the Supreme Soviet of the U.S.S.R. and to the Presidiums of the Union-Republic Supreme Soviets recommendations for repealing or amending laws.

2. *Supreme Courts of the Union-Republics*
   a. Members of these highest judicial organs of the Union-Republics are elected by the Union-Republic Supreme Soviets for a term of five years.
   b. There is a collegium for civil cases, a collegium for criminal cases, and a "plenum" (similar in composition and function to the "plenum" of the Supreme Court of the U.S.S.R.).
   c. These courts have original jurisdiction (with three judges and two people's assessors) in the most important civil and criminal cases and appellate jurisdiction (with one judge and two people's assessors normally) over the decisions and rulings of the lower courts and certain other matters under the law.
   d. Union-Republic Supreme Courts also prepare and revise codes of laws and supervise their administration and all judicial activities in their republics.
   e. Verdicts are usually final, except when the Chairman of the Supreme Court of the U.S.S.R. accepts an appeal by a Union-Republic Procurator-General to review them.

3. *Supreme Courts of the Autonomous Republics; Territorial, Regional, and Area Courts*
   a. Members of these courts are elected by their respective Supreme Soviets for a term of five years.
   b. There are collegiums and "plenums" for these courts similar in composition and function to their counterparts on the higher court levels.
   c. Principal function of these courts is to supervise the activity of the People's Courts and to correct errors committed by the latter in hearing criminal and civil cases.
   d. Exercise original jurisdiction (with three judges and two people's assessors) in complicated criminal cases (e.g., crimes against the State, premeditated murder, and gangsterism) and important civil cases

which they decide to try themselves; they also exercise appellate jurisdiction (with one judge and two people's assessors) over the decisions and rulings of the People's Courts which have not come into legal force.

4. *People's (District and City) Courts*
    a. Lowest courts in the regular judicial hierarchy, consisting of a Chairman, a Deputy-Chairman, and several court members.
    b. People's judges are elected by the citizens of the District or City on the basis of "universal, equal, and direct suffrage by secret ballot" (Art. 109), for a term of five years.
    c. People's assessors (who must be at least 25 years of age) are elected at general meetings of workers and peasants, in their places of work or residence, for a term of two years; actually, people's assessors only serve 10–20 days in each year.
        (1) They receive their regular wages or salary while discharging their duties in court; those who do not work in factories or offices or on farms are reimbursed for the expenses incurred in connection with their service in court.

5. *"Comrades' Courts"; "Commissions on the Affairs of Minors"; and "Voluntary Public Order Squads"*
    a. *"Comrades' Courts": ad hoc* quasi-judicial elective public bodies located in virtually every locale and enterprise; their principal tasks are to prevent law-breaking and acts harmful to the society, to educate people through persuasion and public influence, to create a climate of intolerance towards anti-social acts; they also settle minor disputes between individuals; they may impose comradely warnings, reprimands, and fines (up to ten rubles) on individuals found guilty of misconduct, or none of these measures if the individual has sincerely repented, publicly apoligized, and voluntarily made recompense to the injured party for damages inflicted; so-called "parasitic" individuals (i.e., chronic idlers) can be sentenced to 2–5 years exile by a majority vote of 100 or more people at a public meet-

ing, with the approval of the Executive Committee of the local Soviet.

b. *"Commissions on the Affairs of Minors"*: function under the Executive Committee of the District, City, Regional and Territorial Soviets, to prevent law-breaking by minors, to implement measures to combat neglect of minors, and to bring pressure to bear on parents or guardians to give proper attention to their children; the Commissions also examine cases of minors under 16 years of age who have committed "socially-dangerous" acts, and may ask a court not to impose a penalty or to impose a milder penalty or take some other course of action.

c. *"Voluntary Public Order Squads"*: composed of very socially-conscious workers in various enterprises who conduct educational activity and seek by persuasion to prevent breaches in the public order; similar work is carried on by the Standing Commissions (i.e., committees) of local Soviets, local trade-union groups, local "parent-teacher" associations, etc.

C. JUDICIAL PROCEDURE

In addition to the preeminent role of the C.P.S.U. Party-State Control Commissions, ministerial agencies, etc., throughout the Soviet State and society, certain other organs discharge responsibilities which cause one to have reservations about the impersonality and impartiality of "judicial procedure" in the Soviet judicial system. For example, each of the higher courts has a Presidium whose chief functions are to supervise its own personnel and oversee the functions of those in the next lower court as well as to review the decisions, etc. of the lower court and make presentations to the next higher court; further, the Constitution of the U.S.S.R. (Art. 113) states that the "Supreme supervisory power to ensure the strict observance of the law . . . by people in office and citizens of the U.S.S.R., generally, is vested in the Procurator-General of the U.S.S.R." It is not a mere coincidence that this person has always been a member of the C.P.S.U. (as are the members of Presidiums of courts) and is empowered to appoint and supervise the activities of all Procurators-General and staff below himself in the law-enforcement machinery. These facts should be kept in mind reading this section.

1. All citizens are equal before the law and have equal access to the courts of law.

2. No person may be arrested and detained except upon a proper judicial or legal order.

3. A person must be informed of the charges against him, and cannot be forced to confess under duress.

4. Defense counsel is either retained by the accused or is appointed by the court upon his request.

5. Sufficient opportunity must be given the defendant to prepare his defense before the trial begins.

6. Cases are heard in public, *except where they involve* such exceptional circumstances as *State secrets and security* (italics, the author's), persons under 16 years of age, sex crimes, etc.

7. Judicial proceedings are conducted in the language of the defendant or, if this is not possible, an interpreter is provided to acquaint him fully with all the materials in the case.

8. Defendant has the right to participate directly, or indirectly through his counsel and supporting witnesses, in all phases of his trial.

9. No one may order or recommend that a court hand down a particular decision in a specific criminal or civil case.

   a. however, in some exceptional cases, e.g., the gross misappropriation of State property or illegal deal in foreign exchange, the courts have applied laws retroactively (in terms of decisions and punishments) under the direction of the Presidium (i.e., supervisory group) of the Supreme Court of the U.S.S.R.

10. Decisions are taken by majority vote of the court (i.e., the judges and assessors), and must be pronounced in public.

11. A defendant has a reasonable period of time in which to appeal to a higher court against an adverse decision before it takes effect; however, a procurator may also make an appeal to a higher court if he feels the deci-

sion is contrary to law or is not warranted by the facts.

12. An appellate court may confirm or modify the decision of a lower court, order a new trial in another lower court, or protest the decision to a higher court; in this connection, the Chairman of the U.S.S.R. Supreme Court or the Procurator-General of the U.S.S.R. may file a protest with one of the collegiums of the U.S.S.R. Supreme Court or with its "plenum."

NOTE: Recently, a few Soviet jurists have sought to criticize public prosecutors and police officials for whipping-up public opinion against defendants before their cases have been heard in court, and to press for "an unchallenged integrity of law and independence of the courts"; the public prosecutors and police officials, in turn, contend that denunciations of defendants by "indignant citizens" are helpful in obtaining convictions and, furthermore, any ban against public pressure on judges would "isolate the courts from the people" and thereby violate "socialist democracy". The reader can draw his own conclusions.

C. PROSECUTION AND SECURITY ORGANS

1. *All-Union Procurator-General*

   a. Elected by the All-Union Supreme Soviet for a term of seven years; he is the chief prosecutor, and a most important official of the State.

   b. Supervises the execution of laws by all ministries, officials, and citizens; prosecutes serious crimes and actions against the State security; and reviews the functions of judges and courts.

   c. Enforces the sentences, judgments, and rulings of courts, in defense of the socialist regime and the security of the State.

   d. Appoints the Union-Republic Procurators for a five-year term; they, in turn, appoint the Procurators on the lower levels for terms of five years.

2. *Union-Republic, Autonomous Republic, Territorial, Regional and Area Procurators-General* perform similar duties on their corresponding levels of State authority.

3. Among the possible types of punishment for criminal offenses are: public censure, fines, corrective labor without deprivation of liberty, deprivation of the right to occupy certain posts or engage in certain activities, deprivation of liberty, banishment or exile, and death.

   a. Frequent use of the suspended sentence or probationary period (in minor cases), under which the individual seeks to amend his ways or endeavors are made by appropriate State and local agencies or enterprises to reform him.

   b. Deprivation of liberty may, in no instance, exceed 15 years; the individual is sent to a "corrective labor colony" where he is put to productive work or learns a trade and is required to take educational courses to improve his character; upon release from the colony, the individual may be assisted by a local Soviet or economic body to find a job.

   c. A sentence of death by shooting may be imposed for such grave crimes as high treason, espionage, sabotage, large misappropriations of State or other public property, premeditated murder or rape under aggravating circumstances, counterfeiting or violating regulations covering foreign exchange operations involving large sums, and certain others.

     (1) Death sentences may not be imposed on persons under 18 years at the time the crime was committed, or on women who were pregnant when they committed the crime or at the time the sentence is passed.

     (2) Each death sentence is reviewed by the Supreme Court of the Union-Republic concerned, and an appeal to the President of the All-Union Supreme Soviet for clemency can be made by the convicted person, his lawyer, or relatives.

4. *Ministries for the maintenance of law and order* in the 15 Union-Republics supervise the police forces which

   a. Help administer State laws and local ordinances.

   b. Protect State and public property and the safety of citizens.

   c. Investigate crimes and make arrests.

   d. Perform miscellaneous other duties.

5. *People's Control Committees* (or *Party-State Control Committees*) exist on all levels of State authority throughout the U.S.S.R.; the principal one, on the national level, is the Committee of People's Control of the Central Committee of the C.P.S.U. and the Council of Ministers of the U.S.S.R.

6. Significantly, party and prosecution officials of the State check not only the citizenry, but also the judicial and other law-enforcement personnel, rather than *vice versa* as in Western democracies; thus "law and justice" is largely relative and subjective; and protection of individual rights and actions is still subject to vague and ambiguous concepts of "popular" and "social" justice.

7. Lastly, foreigners committing a criminal offense in the U.S.S.R. are answerable under Soviet law; in such cases, foreign embassies may inquire through the All-Union Ministry for Foreign Affairs or other proper channels about their detained citizen and set into motion procedures available for the protection of his rights, etc.

VIII. "FEDERALISM" IN THE USSR

A. ALL-UNION CONSTITUTION declares the USSR is "a Federal State, formed on the basis of the voluntary union of equal Soviet Socialist Republics" (Art. 13); however,

1. RSFSR (Russian Soviet Federated Socialist Republic) dominates the other Union-Republics and provides for the central Government.

   a. It has approximately three-fifths of the total population and three-fourths of the total land area of the USSR.

   b. Its people (the Great Russians) have unified the 150 to 200 ethnic groups into a uniform Soviet citizenry, but some cultural autonomy is permitted, however.

2. All-Union Government controls every important aspect of the country's life and possesses an unlimited opportunity to interfere with the Union-Republics and all other organs or levels of governmental authority.

   a. Never any disagreement between the All-Union and Union-Republic Governments, not only because of this centralization of power in the former, but also because of the political activities of the Communist Party throughout the USSR.

b. All-Union Government proclaims the basic policies and plans, and the Union-Republic Governments and peoples accept them.

c. Soviet "federalism" is not an actual division of powers, but rather a form of administrative organization and control.

B. JURISDICTION OF THE ALL-UNION GOVERNMENT

1. Conduct the international relations of the USSR and determine the relations of the Union-Republics with foreign States.

2. Determine questions of war and peace.

3. Approve the admission of new Union-Republics (SSRs) into the USSR.

4. Control the observance of the All-Union Constitution and secure the conformity of Union-Republic Constitutions with it.

5. Confirm any alterations in Union-Republic boundaries and also the formation of new Autonomous Republics (ASSRs), Territories, and Regions within Union-Republics.

6. Organize the national defense and direct the Armed Forces of the USSR.

7. Maintain and manage the State monopoly on foreign trade.

8. Safeguard the security of the State.

9. Establish the national economic plans and maintain the national economic statistics.

10. Approve the State budget and the taxes and revenues which go to the All-Union, Union-Republic, and local budgets; also raise and grant loans.

11. Administer the agricultural, industrial, trading, and banking institutions and enterprises of national importance.

12. Organize, administer, and direct such activities as State insurance, the monetary and credit system, and transport and communications.

13. Establish the basic principles for the use of the land and natural resources.

14. Provide the educational and public health plans.
15. Determine the principles of labor legislation.
16. Organize the judicial system and judicial procedures; also the criminal and civil codes.
17. Determine the laws of citizenship and the rights of foreigners.
18. Issue All-Union acts of amnesty.

C. STATUS AND FUNCTIONS OF THE
UNION-REPUBLIC GOVERNMENTS
1. Each Union-Republic is located on the border of the USSR, and must possess a nationality which forms a compact majority within the area, with a total population of at least one million people.
2. Territory of a Union-Republic cannot be altered without its consent.
3. Sovereignty of the Union-Republics is limited by the jurisdiction of the All-Union Government, but is protected by the USSR.
4. Union-Republics maintain their own constitutions, in conformity with the All-Union Constitution.
5. They administer educational, health, and economic plans on their level of authority.
6. Each Union-Republic is encouraged to use and develop its local languages and cultural activities (the policy of "cultural autonomy" or "cultural pluralism").
7. All-Union laws apply equally within the territories of the Union-Republics and are always superior to Union-Republic laws.
8. Union-Republics theoretically have the power to maintain their own police and military forces, conduct foreign relations independently, and secede from the USSR, but these powers are of questionable practical significance because they can never be exercised or, at most, can be exercised only under the closest supervision of the All-Union authorities.
9. The head of the Government of each Union-Republic is a permanent member of the All-Union Council of Ministers.
10. In sum, the Union-Republics are always politically and economically subordinated to the Government of the U.S.S.R.

IX. REGIONAL AND "LOCAL ORGANS OF STATE POWER"

The organization of regional and local government in the USSR is a complicated affair, including a great number and variety of units and considerable difference among them in size of territory, number and diversity of people, economic resources and activity, and political importance.

A. DIVISIONS OF AUTHORITY IN THE USSR
  1. 15 *Soviet Socialist Republics* (SSRs): Russian, Ukrainian, Byelorussian, Uzbek, Kazakh, Georgian, Azerbaijan, Lithuanian, Moldavian, Latvian, Kirghiz, Tajik, Armenian, Turkmen, and Estonian.
  2. 20 Autonomous Soviet Socialist Republics (ASSRs): 16 in the Russian Federation—Bashkirian, Buryat, Daghestan, Kabardinian-Balkar, Kalmyk, Karelian, Komi, Mari, Mordovian, North Ossetian, Tatar, Tuva, Udmurt, Checheno-Ingush, Chuvash, and Yakut; two in Georgia; and one each in Azerbaijan and Uzbekistan.
  3. 8 *Autonomous Regions:* in the Russian Federation—Gorny Altai, Adygei, Khakass, Karachai-Cherkess and Jewish; in Georgia—South Ossetian; in Azerbaijan—Nagorny Karabakh; and in Tajikistan—Gorny Badakhshan.
  4. 10 *National Areas*, all of which are located in the Russian Federation: Taimyr, Evenki, Nenets, Ust-Ordynsky-Buryat, Koryak, Chukot, Komi-Permyak, Khanty-Mansi, Yamal-Nenets, and Aginsky-Buryat.
  5. 1000-plus large *Cities*, with special governments of their own.
  6. 2000-plus *Districts* (both urban and rural), which are both administrative and economic units.
  7. 500,000 or more *Villages*.

B. GENERAL PRINCIPLES OF ADMINISTRATION
  1. Theoretically, the division of authority between the USSR and the SSRs is formally set out in the All-Union Constitution, but in fact, the SSRs are subordinate to the USSR in every important field of endeavor.
  2. Union-Republic Constitutions are closely patterned after the All-Union Constitution and their provisions

and the agencies established by them must conform with the All-Union Constitution and the laws of the USSR.

3. The typical governmental organization consists of a Soviet (legislative Council), its Presidium or Executive Committees (or Sections), a Council of Ministers, and a Supreme Court or other judicial organs.

4. Agencies of Government on one level are directly or indirectly accountable and responsible to corresponding or other agencies of Government on the next highest level of authority.

5. Periodically, there are new attempts to reorganize and regroup the regional and local governments ("organs of State power") and also to establish plans for the further development of the remoter areas and the larger cities in the U.S.S.R.

C. ORGANIZATION AND POWERS OF THE UNION-REPUBLICS
   1. *Constitution*
      a. Amendments to the Constitution of a Union-Republic require a two-thirds vote by the members of its Supreme Soviet for adoption.
   2. *Supreme Soviet*
      a. "The highest organ of State power in a Union-Republic" (Art. 57).
      b. The basis of representation is established in the Union-Republic's Constitution.
      c. Large-sized unicameral legislative body whose members are popularly elected for a term of four years; they have a Chairman (or President), one or more Deputy Chairmen, various Permanent Commissions, etc., and meet four times a year to discharge such constitutional responsibilities as to
         (1) Adopt and amend the Union-Republic Constitution;
         (2) Confirm the constitution of each of the Autonomous-Republics and define their boundaries;
         (3) Draft its own economic plan and budget, and enact laws;
         (4) Issue an amnesty or pardon for citizens sentenced by the Union-Republic judicial organs;

(5) Decide questions involving the military defense and foreign relations of the Union-Republic;

(6) Elect its Presidium, consisting of a Chairman (or President), and Deputy-Chairmen, a Secretary, and regular members;

(7) Appoint the Union-Republic Council of Ministers.

d. Supreme Soviet sessions are attended by Ministers (without a right to vote) who are not Deputies, members of the Supreme Court and the Procurator-General of the Union-Republic; decisions are taken by a simple majority, voting by a show of hands.

e. In actual practice, however, the Union-Republic Supreme Soviet merely certifies or endorses decisions and actions already taken elsewhere in the Government (and by the Communist Party), but does have utility in serving as a forum for general discussion, criticizing the nonpolitical aspects of the local administration, and unifying the people in support of the socialist regime.

3. *Presidium*

a. Similar in manner of selection, organization, functions, and powers to the All-Union Presidium.

b. Its actual duties are usually determined by the party organs in the Union-Republic.

4. *Council of Ministers*

a. "The highest executive and administrative organ of the State power of a Union-Republic" (Art. 79).

b. Similar in manner of selection, organization, general powers, and responsibility to the All-Union Council of Ministers.

(1) Union-Republic ministries are subordinate both to the Union-Republic Council of Ministers and to the corresponding Union-Republic ministries of the USSR, whereas the "Republican" ministries are directly subordinate to the Union-Republic Council of Ministers.

(2) Ministers direct designated branches of the State administration, issue decisions and orders and supervise their execution, suspend the de-

cisions and orders of the Autonomous-Republic Councils of Ministers, and annul the actions of the Executive Committees of the Soviets of Working People's Deputies on the lower levels of authority.

(3) Theoretically, responsibility and accountability is to the Union-Republic Supreme Soviet or to its Presidium when the Supreme Soviet is not in session.

c. Some of the important ministries are: Internal Affairs, Justice, Armed Forces, Finance, Education, Culture, Public Health, Light Industry, Agriculture, and Foreign Affairs.

5. The national language of the people who live in the Union-Republic is the official language of all its governmental bodies and agencies.

D. ORGANIZATION AND POWERS OF THE AUTONOMOUS REPUBLICS

1. *Constitution*
   a. Usually copied from that of the Union-Republic (of which it is a part), taking into account the national features of the given autonomous unit.

2. *Supreme Soviet*
   a. "The highest organ of State power in an Autonomous Soviet Socialist Republic" (Art. 89).
   b. Similar in manner of election, tenure in office, meetings, internal organization, general functions and powers, etc., to the Union-Republic Supreme Soviet.
   (1) The Supreme Soviet passes laws and issues decrees valid on the territory of the Autonomous Republic, appoints the Council of Ministers of the Autonomous Republic (to which are responsible the local industries, construction, the health services, education, the social welfare agencies, etc.) and the Supreme Court of the Autonomous Republic.

3. *Presidium*
   a. Similar in manner of selection, organization, functions, and powers to the Union-Republic Presidium.
   b. The Chairman (or President) of the Presidium of

CHART 26. AGENCIES OF REGIONAL AND LOCAL GOVERNMENT IN SOVIET RUSSIA

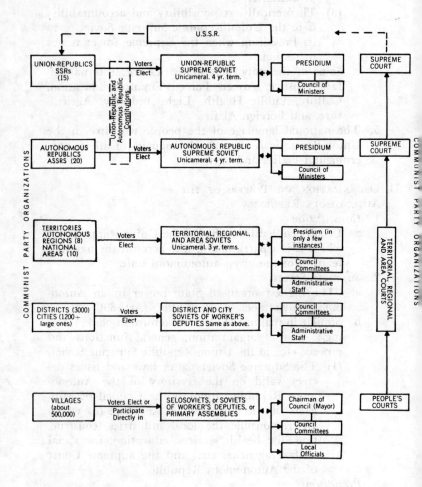

the Supreme Soviet of an Autonomous Republic is a Deputy-Chairman of the Union-Republic's Presidium.

4. *Council of Ministers*
   a. Similar in manner of selection, organization, general powers, and responsibility to the Union-Republic Council of Ministers.

E. ORGANIZATION AND POWERS OF THE AUTONOMOUS REGIONS, NATIONAL AREAS, CITIES, DISTRICTS AND VILLAGES

1. Each of the Autonomous Regions and National Areas has its own governing bodies and administrative agencies; the language of the national group is used in every sphere of activity within the territory of the given autonomous unit.
   a. Neither the Autonomous Region nor the National Area has a constitution of its own, but the rights required by its specific national character are expressly provided for in the Constitution of the Union-Republic of which it is a part.

2. The "organs of State power" for these divisions are either Supreme Soviets or Soviets of Working People's Deputies, popularly elected for a term of two or three years, depending on the division; they
   a. Receive and follow instructions from local groups of workers and can be recalled by the voters.
   b. Maintain their own internal organization, consisting of a Chairman, Deputy-Chairmen, Secretary, functional committees or sections (e.g., Agriculture, Education, Finance, Public Health, Local Industry, and Culture), and volunteer "Activists."
      (1) "Activists" assist in the local administration and help to unify the workers behind the political regime; their work may be a stepping-stone to a supervisorial position in a local enterprise or membership in the local organs of the Communist Party.
   c. Perform such responsibilities as the direction of the organs of local administration, the maintenance of the public order, the securing of the observance of

the law, the protection of the rights of citizens, the supervision of the local economic and cultural affairs, the drawing-up of the local budgets, and the adoption of decisions and issuance of orders.
  2. The "executive and administrative organ" of a City, District, or Village is usually an Executive Committee (Chairman, Deputy-Chairmen, Secretary and members) elected by and responsible to the Soviet.

F. The City of Moscow
  1. Metropolis of more than 6,000,000 people, with a special government of its own.
  2. Chief governmental functionaries include the Moscow City Soviet (*Mossevet*) and Mayor, an Executive Committee and Presidium, approximately thirty administrative Departments, and a permanent staff of several thousand people.
  3. *Mossevet*
    a. For elections to the Moscow Soviet the capital is divided into 1,084 Election Districts, each of which elects one Deputy.
    b. Approximately one-half of the Deputies are members of the Communist Party; other Deputies include industrial workers, engineers, heads of industrial plants, scientists and artists, doctors, teachers, etc.
    c. First session of a new *Mossevet* is called from seven to ten days after the elections, and the first order of business is to verify the credentials of the Deputies.
    d. Term of office of the Deputies and Mayor is two years, but they can be removed earlier, by a majority vote at a *Mossevet* session, if their work is not satisfactory.
    e. The Mayor is also a Deputy to the Supreme Soviet of the U.S.S.R. and frequently serves as a Deputy Chairman of the Council of Ministers of the Russian Federation (RSFSR).
  4. *Executive Committee*
    a. Elected by *Mossevet* and includes the Chairman, eight Deputy Chairmen, a Secretary and fifteen members.

b. A permanent body that acts between *Mossovet* sessions.

c. Once a week there is a three-hour meeting of the Presidium of the Executive Committee to consider such matters as the selection of administrative personnel, pensions and retirement benefits, development of local enterprises, budgetary questions, etc.

SELECTED READINGS

Armstrong, John A., *The Politics of Totalitarianism*. New York: Random House, 1961.

Bauer, Raymond Augustine, and others, *How the Soviet System Works: Cultural, Psychological and Social Themes*. Cambridge: Harvard University Press, 1956.

Bergson, A., *The Economics of Soviet Planning*. New Haven: Yale University Press, 1964.

Clarkson, Jesse D., *A History of Russia*. New York: Random House, 1961.

Conquest, Robert, *Power and Policy in the U.S.S.R., the Study of Soviet Dynastics*. New York: St. Martin's Press, Inc., 1961.

Crankshaw, Edward, *Khrushchev's Russia*. Baltimore: Penguin Books, Inc., 1960.

Dallin, David J., *The Changing World of Soviet Russia*. New Haven: Yale University Press, 1956.

Daniels, R. V., *Russia*. Englewood Cliffs, New Jersey: Prentice-Hall, Inc., 1965.

DeHuszar, George B., and Associates, *Soviet Power and Policy*. New York: Thomas Y. Crowell Company, 1955.

Deutscher, Isaac, *Russia in Transition*. New York: Grove Press, Inc., 1960.

Ellison, H. J., *History of Russia*. New York: Holt, Rinehart & Winston, Inc., 1964.

Fainsod, Merle, *How Russia Is Ruled*. Cambridge: Harvard University Press, 1963.

Florinsky, Michael T., *Russia: a Short History*. New York: Macmillan Company, 1964.

Gunther, John, *Inside Russia Today*. Baltimore: Penguin Books, Inc., 1964.

Harcave, S. S., *Russia: a History*. Philadelphia: J. B. Lippincott Company, 1964.

Hazard, John N., *The Soviet System of Government*. Chicago: University of Chicago Press, 1964.

Hendel, Samuel, ed., *The Soviet Crucible, Soviet Government in Theory and Practice*. New York: D. Van Nostrand Company, Inc., 1963.

Holt, Robert T., and John E. Turner, eds., *Soviet Union Paradox and Change*. New York: Holt, Rinehart & Winston, Inc., 1962.

Inkeles, Alex, and Kent Geiger, eds., *Soviet Society, A Book of Readings*. Boston: Houghton Mifflin Company, 1961.

Kassof, A. H., *The Soviet Youth Program*. Cambridge: Harvard University Press, 1965.

Kulski, Whadyshaw W., *The Soviet Regime; Communism in Practice*. Syracuse: Syracuse University Press, 1959.

McClosky, Herbert, and John E. Turner, *The Soviet Dictatorship*. New York: McGraw-Hill Book Company, Inc., 1960.

Mehnert, Klaus, *Soviet Man and His World*. New York: Frederick A. Praeger, Inc., 1961.

Meyer, Alfred G., *The Soviet Political System*. New York: Random House, 1965.

Miller, W. W., *The U.S.S.R.* London: Oxford University Press, 1963.

Nove, Alec, *The Soviet Economy*. New York: Frederick A. Praeger, Inc., 1963.

Paszkiewicz, H., *The Making of the Russian Nation*. Chicago: Henry Regnery Company, 1965.

Richman, B. M., *Soviet Management*. Englewood Cliffs, New Jersey: Prentice-Hall, Inc., 1965.

Rieber, A. J., and R. C. Nelson, *A Study of the U.S.S.R. and Communism*. New York: G. P. Putnam's Sons, 1964.

Riha, T., ed., *Readings in Russian Civilization*. Chicago: University of Chicago Press, 1964.

Rush, M., *Political Succession in the U.S.S.R.* New York: Columbia University Press, 1965.

Schapiro, Leonard, *The Communist Party of the Soviet Union*. New York: Random House, 1960.

Schuman, Frederick L., *Government in the Soviet Union*. New York: Thomas Y. Crowell Company, 1961.

Schwartz, Harry, *The Soviet Economy Since Stalin*. Philadelphia: J. B. Lippincott Company, 1965.

Scott, Derek J. R., *Russian Political Institutions*. New York: Rinehart & Company, Inc., 1957.

Shaffer, H. G., ed., *The Soviet System in Theory and Practice*. New York: Appleton-Century-Crofts, Inc., 1965.

Spector, Ivan, *An Introduction to Russian History and Culture*. New York: D. Van Nostrand Company, Inc., 1963.

Stipp, John L., ed., *Soviet Russia Today, Patterns and Prospects*. New York: Harper & Brothers, 1957.

Swearer, H. R., and M. Rush, *The Politics of Succession in the U.S.S.R.* Boston: Little, Brown & Company, Inc., 1964.

Treadgold, D. W., *The Development of the U.S.S.R.* Seattle: University of Washington Press, 1964.

Tucker, R. C., *The Soviet Political Mind.* New York: Frederick A. Praeger, Inc., 1963.

Whiting, Kenneth R., *The Soviet Union Today, A Concise Handbook.* New York: Frederick A. Praeger, Inc., 1962.

Wolfe, Bertram D., *Communist Totalitarianism, Keys to the Soviet System.* Boston: Beacon Press, 1961.

Chapter V

ITALY

POPULATION: 52,000,000 (1965)
AREA: 116,372 sq. miles
CAPITAL: Rome

I. CHRONOLOGY

476—Final disintegration of Western Roman Empire.

774—Charlemagne confirms the "Donation of Pepin" and extends Frankish rule over the "kingdom of Italy."

962—Otto I, king of Germany, crowned both king of Italy and Holy Roman Emperor in Rome.

1183—Council of Constance affirms right of Italian communes to local autonomy while preserving the sovereignty of the Holy Roman Empire.

1469–1492—Unstable equilibrium maintained among the five Italian city-States under the patronage of Lorenzo de' Medici; Italian social and cultural life continues to advance during the Renaissance.

1748—Treaty of Aix-la-Chapelle, concluding the War of the Austrian Succession, extends the territory of the House of Savoy and kingdom of Sardinia.

1815–1848—Fall of Napoleonic Empire and the Congress of Vienna followed by restoration of independent Italian States and rebirth (*Risorgimento*) of Italian national sentiment.

1849–1871—Proclamation of a republic in Rome leads to successful efforts by Mazzini, di Cavour, and Garibaldi to unify Italy.

1871–1918—Post-*Risorgimento* period and era of liberal monarchy.

1922—Benito Mussolini's "March on Rome" and advent of Fascist regime.

1929—Lateran Treaty and Concordat between Roman Catholic Church and the Government of Italy.

1936—Formation of Rome-Berlin Axis by Fascist Italy and Nazi Germany.

1940—Italy declares war on France and Great Britain.

1943—Dismissal of Mussolini by King Victor Emmanuel III.

1943–1947—Liberation of Italy by Western Allies and establishment, by a popular referendum, of the new Italian Republic.

1949—North Atlantic Treaty Organization includes Italy as a signatory member.

1957—Italy and five other Western European States sign treaties creating the European Economic Community ("Common Market") and European Community of Atomic Energy ("Euratom").

1964—Reform of broad coalition of "Center" and "Left" parties under Prime Minister Aldo Moro; Giuseppe Saragat, Right-wing Socialist, elected new President with Communist support.

II. ITALIAN CONSTITUTION

A. FUNDAMENTAL PRINCIPLES OF GOVERNMENT

1. Italy is a "democratic Republic based on labor" (Art. 1).
2. Sovereignty belongs to the citizens, all of whom are equal before the law.
3. Free democratic elections and multiparty representations in the Parliament.
4. Cabinet system of responsible Government.
5. Judicial organization includes both ordinary and administrative courts.
6. Unitary form of Government, but with legal protection for the local autonomies.
7. Constitutional and statutory separation of Church and State:
   a. "The State and the Catholic Church are, each within its own sphere, independent and sovereign. Their relations are regulated by the Lateran Pacts

[see Sec. VIII below]. Such amendments to these Pacts as are accepted by both parties do not require any procedure of constitutional revision" (Art. 7).

   b. This Article may appear to accept the principle that the Catholic religion is the official religion of the Italian State, but all religious creeds are equally 'free, and freedom of organization is recognized to each of them provided its tenets do not contradict the Italian constitutional and legal system.

8. Renunciation of aggression in foreign affairs and expressed support of international law.

B. RIGHTS AND DUTIES OF CITIZENS
   1. Right of legal status and of citizenship.
   2. Protection of the dignity of the individual and the inviolability of human rights.
   3. Freedom of speech, press, assembly, religious confession and faith, movement, correspondence and communication, and residence.
   4. Right to petition the Parliament.
   5. Inviolability of the home and protection of matrimony and the family.
   6. Protection against arbitrary arrests and unreasonable searches and seizures.
   7. Protection of personal property and private economic enterprises, except where restricted by law to protect or advance the general welfare.
   8. Obligation to pay only legal personal and property taxes.
   9. Protection of the citizens' health and special care for women and children.
   10. Right of parents to support and to instruct their children.
   11. Compulsory and free primary education.
   12. Right to work and protection for labor (conditions of work, wages, rest, annual vacations with pay, maintenance, social assistance, some participation in management, trade unionism, right to strike, etc.).
   13. State encouragement of economic cooperatives.
   14. Universal and compulsory suffrage for all adult citizens (21 years), with free, equal, and secret voting.

Chart 27. STRUCTURE OF THE ITALIAN GOVERNMENT

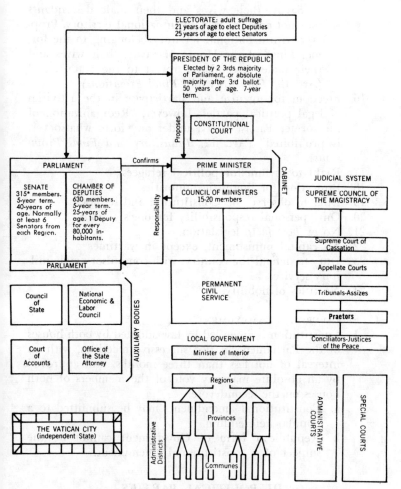

* In actual fact, Senators total 321, of which 315 are elected, 5 have life appointments, and 1 sits by right (Giovanni Gronchi, former President of the Republic).

15. Right to hold public office (except members of the House of Savoy).
   a. "The members and descendants of the House of Savoy are not electors and may not hold any public office or elective position. Former kings of the House of Savoy, their wives and their male descendants may not enter or remain in national territory. Property within national territory belonging to the former kings of the House of Savoy, their wives and their male descendants, revert to the State. . . ." (Art. 13, *Transitory and Final Provisions*)

16. Freedom to organize and participate in the activities of legal political parties; however, "Reorganization of the former Fascist Party, under any form whatsoever, is prohibited" (Art. 12, *Transitory and Final Provisions*).

17. Right to asylum for political refugees.

18. Protection for linguistic minorities.

19. Duty to observe the Constitution and its laws.

20. Only personal responsibility for one's actions.

21. No *ex post facto* legislation.

22. No capital punishment, except in wartime.

23. Duty to defend the country, with compulsory male military service.

24. No titles of nobility.

C. PROCEDURE FOR AMENDMENT
   1. Constitution is amended by law adopted by both houses of the Parliament in two successive meetings, with an interval of not less than three months, and approved by an absolute majority vote of the members of both houses on the second vote.
      a. Constitutional amendments may be submitted to a popular referendum.
      b. Republican form of Government cannot be the subject of a constitutional amendment.

III. POLITICAL PARTIES

A. GENERAL CHARACTERISTICS OF THE PARTY SYSTEM
   1. Multiparty system, with the strong right-wing (Catholic) and left-wing (Communist) influences checked and

often dominated in the Government by a Centrist Coalition, representing the Nation as a whole.

2. All parties traditionally insist upon the rigid adherence of their memberships to party principles, frequently resulting in internal disagreement among the leaders, party splits, and the rise of new political groups.

3. Only a few of the innumerable minor parties ever achieve success in the National Elections, and then only through bargain and compromise with other parties or by the formation of a temporary party group.

4. Larger parties individually represent broad social class and economic group interests and find most of their support in the Regional areas.

5. There are wide disagreements among the political parties on the basic policies and programs of government.

6. Trend toward stronger leadership and the centralization of authority in the national organization of several political parties.

7. Although there is almost complete freedom to form political associations (except for the former Fascist party), membership in some parties is not always easy to attain, due to their requirements and rigorous intraparty discipline.

B. LEADING PARTIES

1. *Christian Democratic Party (DC):* seeks to maintain its dominant position in government and parliament by reconciling different and conflicting interests and protecting the constitutional and political system against both extreme Leftist and Rightist factions; supports concepts of order and stability and some of the social doctrines of the Catholic Church; gives higher priority to austerity measures deemed necessary both to check inflation and retain their conservative supporters than to the measures of social reform demanded by the Socialists.

2. *Communist Party (PCI):* follows the Moscow "party line" very closely in foreign affairs, but is more autonomous than most Communist parties in domestic affairs; inclined to be violently anti-Western (i.e., anti-United States) and advocates the nationalization of industries, wide-sweeping labor and social reforms, and the redis-

tribution of land; has expressed bitterness over the ouster of Nikita Khrushchev, without a full public explanation as to the reasons, as head of the C.P.S.U. and, among other things, proposes that

a. World Communism must undergo basic democratic reforms to make it palatable to more people;

b. Each Communist Party should determine independently its own paths towards the realization of "socialism"; and

c. If Italian Communists ever gain control of the Government, they will not change the present parliamentary system which provides full rights to all political parties.

3. *Italian Socialist Party (PSI):* possesses rather poorly defined policies and objectives, but tends to support the prevailing parliamentary system and individual rights, works towards tax revision, the nationalization of some industries and commercial enterprises, and land reform; seems to have abandoned "Marxism" somewhat in favor of bourgeois goals; in foreign affairs, it tends to be "neutralist" or "anti-Western" in its sentiments.

4. *Italian Democratic Party (PDI):* no longer a strong advocate for the restoration of the monarchy, but is a reactionary defender of vested interests, democratic republicanism, and of the Catholic Church; in foreign affairs, it favors a stronger Italian position than that maintained under the present political administration.

5. *Italian Social Movement (MSI):* this small party supports the conservative traditions of Italian Fascism, yet defends the Republic; it advocates and defends the Catholic Church and its institutions and vigorously opposes the Communists.

6. *Social Democratic Party (PSDI):* works primarily through other parties in seeking revision in the prevailing political system and moderate social and economic reforms, and claims to be independent of the Italian Communist Party; in fact, it has vigorously protested Socialist Party ties, in the past, with the Communists; "neutralist" or "pro-Western" in foreign affairs.

7. *Liberal Party (PLI):* conservative supporter of the Catholic Church, big industrialists, and big landown-

ers, and advocates protection for individual rights and private initiative, freedom from governmental regulation and competition by State-owned enterprises, and parliamentary government.

8. Various other "Left-wing," "democratic-center," and "Right-wing" groups.

C. PARTY ORGANIZATION

1. Each of the parties listed above has a national organization (including the party secretary, executive committee, advisory councils, and party congress) and various regional, provincial, and communal party units.

   a. Extreme "Rightist" and "Leftist" parties are well organized and disciplined, while many of the other parties are characterized by inner struggles for leadership, disputes over policies and implementary actions, and not infrequent schisms among the memberships.

2. Larger parties in the national Parliament also maintain a parliamentary party organization which, except for the Communist and Catholic parties, usually has only loose ties with the extra-parliamentary units.

3. Legal control over the sources and uses of party finances and the organization and conduct of elections is not as effective in Italy as in other Western European States.

D. PARTY REPRESENTATION IN THE PARLIAMENT

1. *Senate* (elected April 28–29, 1963)

Christian Democrats	133	members
Communists	85	"
Italian Socialists	44	"
Liberals	19	"
Italian Social Movement	15	"
Social Democrats	14	"
Monarchists	2	"
Other Groups	3	"
Total:	315	members

2. *Chamber of Deputies* (elected April 28–29, 1963)

Christian Democrats	260	members
Communists	166	"

Italian Socialists	87	ʺ
Liberals	39	ʺ
Social Democrats	33	ʺ
Italian Social Movement	27	ʺ
Monarchists	8	ʺ
Republican Party	6	ʺ
Other Groups	4	ʺ

Total: 630   members

3. An Amendment enacted on February 9, 1963, provides for a fixed number of 315 elected (and 5 lifetime) members in the Senate and 630 elected members in the Chamber of Deputies.

E. NON-PARTY ASSOCIATIONS, such as
   1. *Labor:*
      a. *Italian General Confederation of Labor (CGIL):* Communist-dominated, but has an effective Socialist minority; the largest labor organization, with about 4,000,000 members.
      b. *Italian Confederation of Free Syndicates (CISL):* associated with the Christian Democrats, and has about 2,500,000 members.
      c. *Italian Labor Unions (UIL):* usually support the Social Democrats and Republican elements, and has about 1,500,000 members.
      d. These—and other—labor organizations are highly-centralized, with an oligarchical leadership in their organizational structures throughout the country; important labor leaders also occupy key positions in party structures and frequently serve as Members of Parliament or in important Regional and Provincial Councils; however, the endless schisms and political maneuvers within the Italian labor movement have prevented the realization of many desired objectives and contributed to the apathy and discouragement of many Italian workers (cf. strong sense of class and trade union solidarity in Great Britain).
   2. *Business and Industry:*
      a. *Confederation of Industry (Confidustria):* composed of representations from many divers business and

industrial enterprises; high-concentration of wealth and power in the hands of a few large-scale firms; control most of the informational media and contribute heavily to the "Center" and "Right-Center" political parties and their election campaigns.

3. *Agriculture:*

   a. *National Confederation of Direct Cultivators (Coltivatori Diretti):* most influential agricultural organization in Italy today, and represents the very large number of small independent and tenant farmers; frequently linked with the Christian Democrats.

   b. *Confederation of Agriculture (Confagricoltura):* represents the interests of the large landowners, who tend to support the "Center" and "Right-Center" political parties and their candidates.

4. *Church:*

   a. *Italian Catholic Action Society (Azione Cattolica):* represents the Catholic Church, which is the most powerful nonparty organization in Italy; its "Civic Committees" are very active in political affairs and many of their members occupy important positions in the administrative bureaucracy throughout the country; the Church has a strong press, and tends to recommend or endorse approved political candidates and policies and to instruct the citizenry how it should vote.

5. Many other ideological, professional, commercial, etc., organizations and groups.

IV. PARLIAMENT

A. Descriptive Features of the Parliament

1. Parliament serves as "the organ of popular sovereignty" and is also the supreme governmental authority in the Italian Republic.

2. Bicameral Parliament consisting of a Senate (upper house) and a Chamber of Deputies (lower house), both of which have approximately the same political composition and enjoy complete equality under the Constitution.

   a. Both houses are elected by direct and universal suffrage; all citizens who have reached the age provided for by law (i.e., 21 for the election of the Chamber of Deputies and 25 for the Senate) may vote, except those legally incapacitated, condemned criminals and a few others morally unfit according to the law; absentee ballots are not permitted, so Italians abroad must repatriate if they wish to vote.

3. Deputies in the Parliament represent not only their own constituencies and Regions, but also the entire Italian people.

4. No person may be simultaneously a member of both houses of Parliament.

5. Several political parties send delegates to the Parliament and each party is represented in the legislative commissions and committees roughly in proportion to its total strength in the particular house.

6. The two houses meet in joint session (presided over by the President of the Chamber of Deputies) for special purposes, such as the election of the President of the Republic.

7. Most, but not all, actions by the individual house (or both) are taken by a majority vote.

NOTE: The description of the manner of electing Senators and Deputies to the Italian Parliament is kindly provided by the Embassy of the Republic of Italy (Washington, D.C.) and is quoted *verbatim* in Section B-1-c and C-1-c below.

B. SENATE *(Senato)*
   1. *Membership*
      a. Electors of Senators must be twenty-five years of age.
      b. Qualifications of Senators include Italian citizenship, status as an elector, and a minimum age of forty years.
      c. Senators are elected on a Regional basis, with one Senator for every 160,000 inhabitants; no Region has less than six Senators, except the Vale d'Aosta which has only one.
         (1) They serve a five-year term of office.
         (2) Though a term of six years was originally established for the Senate, it was dissolved simul-

taneously with the Chamber of Deputies in 1948, 1953, and 1958; this constitutional tradition was subsequently written into the Constitution itself by an Amendment enacted on February 9, 1963, stipulating that both the Chamber and the Senate shall henceforth be elected for a five-year term.

   (3)   "Election of the Senators follows a pattern which is different from the one adopted for the election of the [other] house. The Regions are divided into uninominal districts (as many as the seats to be filled). Therefore, the parties do not run with a list, but with a single candidate in each district. However, the seat is not won . . . by the candidate receiving a simply plurality. A majority of 65% of the votes cast in the district is required. When no candidate receives such a majority—as actually happens in most of the districts—then the seats are assigned on a regional and party basis through the d'Hondt system of proportional representation [See also p. 115 above]. The seats won by each party are allotted to the party candidates having obtained the highest percentages of votes in their district or districts (each candidate may run in two or three districts within the same Region)."

  d. President of the Republic may appoint five outstanding Italian citizens as Senators for life; ex-Presidents are life members *de jure* of the Senate.

2. *Organization*
  a. Includes the President and regular staff, and a number of Permanent Commissions (Finance, Foreign Affairs, etc.) and Special Committees (Elections, Rules, etc.).
  b. Adopts its own rules and regulations.
  c. Eligibility and fitness of Senators are determined by the Senate itself.

3. *Meetings*
  a. Meets in regular session early in February and also in October of each year; a session may be prolonged under extraordinary circumstances.

b. Extraordinary sessions may be called by the President of the Senate or the President of the Republic, on the request of one-third of the Senators.

c. Convenes in both open and closed meetings.

4. *Perquisites and privileges*

a. Senators receive a regular salary as fixed by law and enjoy both personal inviolability and parliamentary immunity.

C. CHAMBER OF DEPUTIES *(Camera dei Deputai)*

1. *Membership*

a. Electors of Deputies to the Chamber of Deputies must be twenty-one years of age.

b. Qualifications of Deputies include Italian citizenship, status as an elector, and a minimum age of twenty-five years.

c. Deputies are elected by universal and direct suffrage (from party lists and by preferential voting), with one Deputy for every 80,000 inhabitants; they serve for a term of five years.

(1) "The territory of the Republic is divided into 32 electoral districts each including one or more of the country's 92 Provinces. . . . With the exception of Valle d'Aosta (a small area . . . electing a single Deputy by the majority system), all electoral districts use a list system of proportional representation of the parties running in the district. Each party presents a list of candidates (who may not be more than the number of seats to be filled in the district) and selects a party symbol. . . . The ballot includes all symbols of the parties running in the district and a blank space. The voter makes his choice by marking one of the symbols and may express his preference for some of the candidates (from one to four, according to the district's size) included in the same party's list, by writing their names or numbers on the ballot. The total votes cast in each district are divided by the number of seats alloted to the district *plus two* to determine the 'electoral quotient,'

Chart 28. ORGANIZATION OF PARLIAMENT AND THE LAW-MAKING PROCESS IN ITALY

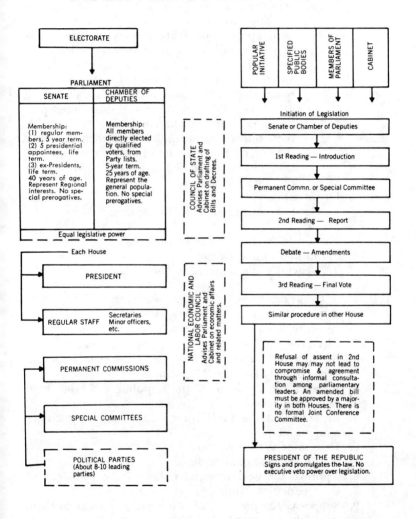

and each party is granted a proportional share of seats according to the votes cast for its symbol (a seat for each quotient). Within the list, the seats won by the party are then assigned according to the preferences obtained by the running candidates. Through this system a certain number of seats usually remain unassigned, while parties not achieving at least one quotient in the district or totalling more than an entire number of quotients score unutilized remainders. The unassigned seats are pooled by a National Election Office and distributed proportionally among the competing parties with their respective remainders (provided that they have elected at least one candidate in one district and have totalled at least 300,000 votes in the whole country)."

2. *Organization*
   a. Generally the same as in the Senate.
3. *Meetings*
   a. Generally the same as in the Senate.
4. *Perquisites and privileges*
   a. Generally the same as in the Senate.

D. PARLIAMENTARY FUNCTIONS AND POWERS
   1. Pass resolutions and enact legislation.
   2. Approve budgets and audit the State accounts.
   3. Elect the President of the Republic and one-third of the members of the Constitutional Court and the Supreme Council of the Magistracy.
   4. Impeach the President of the Republic and other high public officials.
   5. Propose that the President of the Republic grant an amnesty or pardon.
   6. Determine a state of war.
   7. Ratify international treaties.
   8. Approve the governmental policy of the President of the Council of Ministers.
   9. Subpoena the presence of Ministers and grant to them the right to attend all legislative meetings and to be heard.

10. Take votes of confidence and pass motions of censure.
11. Initiate public investigations (use of quasi-judicial special investigating committees).
12. Invest the "Government" with emergency decree powers, but only for a limited time and under detailed instructions.
13. Receive and consider annual reports from the "Government."
14. Act upon a "Petition of Initiative" and submit bills to a popular referendum.
15. Oversee the administration of Regional and local governments.
16. Amend the Constitution.
17. Perform other functions as specified by the Constitution and laws.

E. LEGISLATIVE PROCEDURES
1. Legislative function is exercised by both the Chamber of Deputies and the Senate.
2. Legislative measures are initiated by the "Government," the Members of Parliament, certain public bodies, and through the "initiative" as supported by at least 50,000 voters; the majority of these are "Government" bills.
3. Assignment to, and consideration by, a Permanent Commission or Special Committee.
4. Report by the commission or committee (a Bill of Urgency may force a report, if necessary), followed by general discussion and debate.
5. Approval of the bill, section by section and then in its entirety, by a majority vote of the members of the legislative house; voting is by roll call or by secret ballot.
6. Similar steps and approval in the other house.
   a. As there is no conference committee, any disagreement between the two houses on the provisions of a bill must be worked out by informal consultations among their memberships.
7. Transmittal of the bill to the President of the Republic; he may invite the Parliament to reconsider its action, but if the Parliament approves the bill once again, it is considered a law.

8. A popular referendum may be conducted on a bill, at the request of at least 500,000 voters or five Regional Councils acting together; a majority vote of the participating voters decides the issue.

9. Promulgation of the law by the President of the Republic.

10. The legislative function cannot be delegated to the "Government," except under detailed directions and for only a limited time as provided by legislative resolution or instructions.

   a. There is no government by decree without the express authorization and approval of the Parliament.

   b. "Government" decrees must be converted into law within sixty days of their publication, or become ineffective as originally dated.

V. THE GOVERNMENT

A. PRESIDENT OF THE REPUBLIC *(Presidente della Repubblica)*

1. He is nominated and elected by the Parliament in a joint session of its members, by a two-thirds majority vote (or an absolute majority vote after the third ballot), on a secret ballot.

   a. The election is participated in by three delegates from each Region.

   b. President is elected for a seven-year term and receives a salary and allowances as provided by law.

   c. He must be an Italian citizen, enjoying full civil, and political rights, and at least fifty years of age.

   d. He cannot accept any incompatible appointment, and takes an oath of fidelity to the Republic and its Constitution.

   e. Should the President, for reasons of a temporary nature, be unable to exercise his functions, his office is assumed by the President of the Senate; should the disability be of a permanent nature, or through death or resignation, the President of the Chamber of Deputies orders the election of a new President within fifteen days, e.g. the election of President Giuseppe Saragat, on December 28, 1964, following the resignation of former President Antonio Segni, on December 6, for reasons of sickness and poor health.

f. He is only held responsible for acts of treason and violations of the Constitution; he may be impeached by an absolute majority of the Members of Parliament, sitting in a joint session, and tried by the Constitutional Court.

g. Within thirty days of the expiration of his term, the Parliament is called together in joint session (along with the Regional delegates) to elect the new President of the Republic.

2. *Functions and powers*
   a. Symbolizes the unity of the Italian Nation.
   b. Sends messages to the Parliament.
   c. Calls the election of a new Parliament and sets the date for its first meeting.
   d. Authorizes the transmittal of "Government" bills to the Parliament.
   e. Promulgates laws and issues regulations and decrees with the force of law.
   f. Proclaims a popular referendum.
   g. Dissolves either one or both Houses of the Parliament, after consultation with their Presidents, but not within six months of the end of his term of office.
   h. Appoints State officials.
   i. Accredits and receives diplomatic representatives.
   j. Ratifies international treaties, with the authority and approval of the Parliament.
   k. Commands the Armed Forces, presides over the Supreme Defense Council, and declares a state of war as determined by the Parliament.
   l. Presides over the Supreme Council of the Magistracy.
   m. Confers the honors of the Republic.
   n. Presidential actions must be countersigned by the appropriate Ministers.

B. PRESIDENT OF THE COUNCIL OF MINISTERS *(Presidente del Consiglio dei Ministri)* AND THE MINISTERS
   1. President of the Council of Ministers and the Ministers

are appointed by, and take an oath of office before, the President of the Republic.

a. The "Government" must maintain the confidence of the Parliament.

(1) This is first secured within ten days after the formation of the "Government."

(2) Either one or both houses grants or revokes confidence.

(3) A contrary vote by one or both houses on a "Government" bill does not force the resignation of the "Government."

(4) A motion of no confidence must be signed by at least 10 per cent of the members of the house and passed by an absolute majority.

(5) If the "Government" is refused the confidence of either house it must resign, unless the President of the Republic decides to put the question to the people and hold new elections, dissolving the house which refused the confidence, or both houses.

b. Organization of the Presidency of the Council of Ministers and the number, structure, and functions of the ministries are determined by law.

(1) Among the important ministries, today, are Deputy Prime Minister, Foreign Affairs, Defense, Finance, Treasury, Education, Public Works, Interior, Justice, Budget, Transport, Posts, Labor and Social Security, Foreign Trade, Merchant Navy, State Participation, Health, Tourism and Recreation, Agriculture and Forestry, Industry and Commerce, Government-Parliament Relations, Administrative Reform, and Southern Development.

(2) Each Department in the ministry has a number of under-secretaries (the Minister's Cabinet), a permanent Director-General, and various administrative Divisions and Sections; the administrative units are staffed by classified civil service personnel.

c. Ministers are individually responsible for their ministries (or Departments) and collectively responsible for the actions of the Council of Ministers.

Chart 29. ITALIAN EXECUTIVE AND ADMINISTRATIVE ORGANIZATION

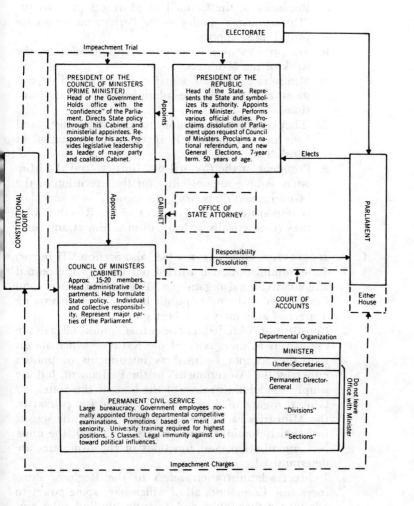

ELECTORATE

Impeachment Trial

PRESIDENT OF THE COUNCIL OF MINISTERS (PRIME MINISTER)
Head of the Government. Holds office with the "confidence" of the Parliament. Directs State policy through his Cabinet and ministerial appointees. Responsible for his acts. Provides legislative leadership as leader of major party and coalition Cabinet.

PRESIDENT OF THE REPUBLIC
Head of the State. Represents the State and symbolizes its authority. Appoints Prime Minister. Performs various official duties. Proclaims dissolution of Parliament upon request of Council of Ministers. Proclaims a national referendum, and new General Elections. 7-year term. 50 years of age.

Appoints

Elects

CABINET

Appoints

OFFICE OF STATE ATTORNEY

CONSTITUTIONAL COURT

PARLIAMENT

Responsibility

Dissolution

COUNCIL OF MINISTERS (CABINET)
Approx. 15-20 members. Head administrative Departments. Help formulate State policy. Individual and collective responsibility. Represent major parties of the Parliament.

COURT OF ACCOUNTS

Either House

Departmental Organization

| MINISTER |
| Under-Secretaries |
| Permanent Director-General |
| "Divisions" |
| "Sections" |

Do not leave Office with Minister

PERMANENT CIVIL SERVICE
Large bureaucracy. Government employees normally appointed through departmental competitive examinations. Promotions based on merit and seniority. University training required for highest positions. 5 Classes. Legal immunity against untoward political influences.

Impeachment Charges

      d. President of the Council of Ministers and the Ministers can be impeached by the Parliament and tried by the Constitutional Court for offenses committed in the exercise of their functions.

  2. *General functions*

      a. President of the Council of Ministers presents the "Government's" policy to the Parliament for its approval and support.

      b. He presides over its meetings and coordinates the work of the Ministers.

      c. Ministers each head a major governmental department and oversee the administration of its functions.

      d. They propose legislation to the Parliament and issue decrees and orders in the implementation of legislation.

      e. President of the Council of Ministers and the Ministers assume responsibility for the execution of the "Government's" policy; the former, in particular, is responsible to the President of the Republic who may (theoretically at least) dismiss him at any time.

C. ADMINISTRATIVE ORGANIZATION (See also Section VII below)

  1. State administration is carried out through the central and subdivisional organs (i.e., Regions, Provinces, and Communes) or by other public bodies to which varying degrees of autonomy have been granted.

  2. Constitution (Art. 98), provides that "public officials are exclusively at the service of the Nation," which means that they cannot be used as instruments of politics either by the "Government" or the Parliament, but are simply the administrators of the laws of the State.

  3. Central organs of direct administration are, primarily, the Ministries each of which directs one of the sectors into which administrative activity is divided; the number, organization, and functions of the Ministries are determined by law.

  4. Indirect administration refers to the Regions, Provinces, and Communes all of which have some power to administer themselves and to issue binding rules and regulations within the limits of the law and their own competency.

5. The Government Commissioner in the Regional capital, and the Prefect in the Provincial capital, represent the national authority and generally supervise administrative functions within their respective jurisdictions.
6. Various non-territorial public organizations, dealing with the general interests of the public, are classified according to their specialized functions, e.g., the different economic organizations, and are known as "para-State" organizations.

D. AUXILIARY BODIES (See also Section VI-D below)
1. *National Economic and Labor Council (Consiglio Nazionale del l'Economia e del Lavoro).*
   a. Approximately sixty experts and representatives from various commercial, industrial, and labor organizations who consult with the "Government" and the Parliament on economic affairs and other matters assigned to the Council by law.
   b. Has advised, or consulted with, the "Government" and the Parliament on draft bills and measures treating of trade union regulations, collective labor agreements, vocational training, the organization of technical instruction, social security, health insurance, and responsibilities and activities of professional groups, etc.
   c. Maintains its own budget and financial procedures, internal organization, and operational rules and regulations.
   d. Its internal organization (drawn largely from the permanent Civil Service) consists of a President, two-Vice-Presidents, various Permanent Commissions and Special Committees, a Secretariat and the Staff; and for discussion and action on important matters the Council meets in Plenary Assembly.
      (1) Whereas the Special Committees are called upon to look into particular matters and then refer to the Plenary Assembly, the Permanent Commissions are responsible for the division of all the activities for which the National Council is responsible; there are five such Commissions, each with competence in a specific field, i.e., general economic affairs and development

planning; industrial production, trade and tourism; agriculture; public works and communications; and labor, social security and cooperation.

2. *Council of State (Consiglio dello Stato)*
   a. Approximately seventy-five persons who consult with the "Government" on the drafting of laws and decrees, and serve as an appellate body in administrative law cases.
3. *Court of Accounts (Corte dei Conti)*
   a. Agency which approves administrative decrees, exercises budgetary control over the expenditures of public offices, and audits the financial accounts of the State.
4. *Office of the State Attorney*
   a. Agency which gives legal advice to the "Government" and represents the State in civil cases.

VI. JUDICIAL SYSTEM

A. THEORY AND PRACTICE OF LAW AND JUSTICE
   1. Justice is administered in the name of the entire Italian people.
   2. Every citizen has an equal right to legal proceedings and the protection of his legal rights and interests under the Constitution.
   3. Protection for the individual citizen against any arbitrary action by a public official.
   4. Judges are highly qualified, nonpartisan, and independent of any other power; they are subject solely to the Constitution and its laws.
   5. There are both ordinary and administrative courts, but no extraordinary or unconstitutional judicial bodies.
   6. Widespread use of the plural bench to decide cases at law.
   7. Preference for codified law (civil and criminal), with very little use of judicial precedents.
   8. Exercise of the power of judicial review by the Constitutional Court.

CHART 30. ORGANIZATION OF THE ITALIAN COURT SYSTEM

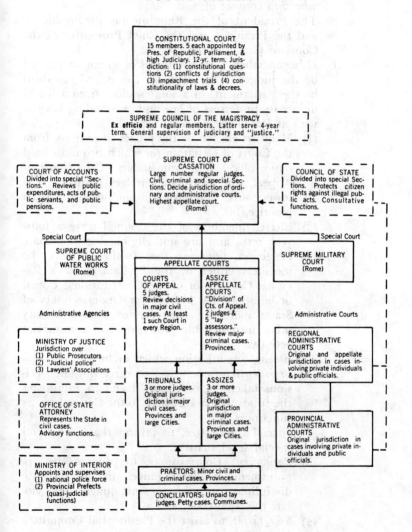

CONSTITUTIONAL COURT
15 members. 5 each appointed by Pres. of Republic, Parliament, & high Judiciary. 12-yr. term. Jurisdiction: (1) constitutional questions (2) conflicts of jurisdiction (3) impeachment trials (4) constitutionality of laws & decrees.

SUPREME COUNCIL OF THE MAGISTRACY
Ex officio and regular members. Latter serve 4-year term. General supervision of judiciary and "justice."

COURT OF ACCOUNTS
Divided into special "Sections." Reviews public expenditures, acts of public servants, and public pensions.

SUPREME COURT OF CASSATION
Large number regular judges. Civil, criminal and special Sections. Decide jurisdiction of ordinary and administrative courts. Highest appellate court. (Rome)

COUNCIL OF STATE
Divided into special Sections. Protects citizen rights against illegal public acts. Consultative functions.

Special Court — **SUPREME COURT OF PUBLIC WATER WORKS (Rome)**

Special Court — **SUPREME MILITARY COURT (Rome)**

APPELLATE COURTS

COURTS OF APPEAL
5 judges. Review decisions in major civil cases. At least 1 such Court in every Region.

ASSIZE APPELLATE COURTS
"Division" of Cts. of Appeal. 2 judges & 5 "lay assessors." Review major criminal cases. Provinces.

Administrative Agencies

Administrative Courts

MINISTRY OF JUSTICE
Jurisdiction over
(1) Public Prosecutors
(2) "Judicial police"
(3) Lawyers' Associations

REGIONAL ADMINISTRATIVE COURTS
Original and appellate jurisdiction in cases involving private individuals & public officials.

TRIBUNALS
3 or more judges. Original jurisdiction in major civil cases. Provinces and large Cities.

ASSIZES
3 or more judges. Original jurisdiction in major criminal cases. Provinces and large Cities.

OFFICE OF STATE ATTORNEY
Represents the State in civil cases. Advisory functions.

PROVINCIAL ADMINISTRATIVE COURTS
Original jurisdiction in cases involving private individuals and public officials.

MINISTRY OF INTERIOR
Appoints and supervises
(1) national police force
(2) Provincial Prefects (quasi-judicial functions)

PRAETORS: Minor civil and criminal cases. Provinces.

CONCILIATORS: Unpaid lay judges. Petty cases. Communes.

B. Supreme Council of the Magistracy
1. Generally, it is concerned with the protection of judges from untoward political influences and their competence in discharging their judicial duties.
2. *Membership* consists of
   a. The President of the Republic (as its President), and the President and the Chief Prosecutor of the Court of Cassation, *ex officio*.
   b. Other members (21), two-thirds of whom are elected by the judges of the ordinary courts and one-third by the Parliament, in a joint session, from a list of university professors of law and outstanding lawyers with at least fifteen years practice.
      (1) Members elected by the judges include six from the Court of Cassation (of which two must hold senior office), four from judges of the Court of Appeal, and four from judges sitting in the lower courts who have a minimum of four years practice.
      (2) Elected members of the Council serve a four-year term and are not eligible for immediate reelection, nor may they (while in office) be members either of the Parliament or a Regional Council, or of the Constitutional Court, or be appointed Minister or Undersecretary of State; moreover, they cannot engage in any other incompatible professional or commercial activity.
   c. An internal organization which includes a
      (1) *Presidential Committee*, to carry out the decisions taken by the Council and to administer the funds which are voted to the Council for its functions;
      (2) *Special Committee*, to inform the Council on special legal matters;
      (3) *Permanent Commissions,* to propose the appointment of senior judges and to institute disciplinary measures against judges who violate the legal code; and a
      (4) *Secretariat,* to assist the Presidential Committee in general administrative work.

    d. A Vice-President of the Council is chosen from the members elected by the Parliament.

3. *Functions and powers*

    a. Regulates its own internal affairs.

    b. Supervises the recruitment, assignments, promotions, transfers, etc. of the regular judiciary and also the general administration of justice in the Italian courts.

    c. Applies disciplinary sanctions, and is generally responsible for all questions which the law considers to be within its competence.

    d. Proposes to the Ministry of Justice modifications in the organization and functioning of the courts and legal services.

    e. Advises the Ministry of Justice on legislative bills dealing with the structure of the judiciary, the administration of justice, and other related subjects.

    f.   Takes decisions on matters within its competency.

        (1) These are usually included in decrees issued by the President of the Republic (or in ministerial decrees when the law so permits) and countersigned by the Minister of Justice.

        (2) Appeals against the decisions of the Supreme Council can only be made on the basis of law.

        (3) Disciplinary action, which results in suspension from office, may be appealed against in a plenary meeting of the Court of Cassation.

4. *Procedures*

    a. Supreme Council is convoked and presided over by its own President or, in the event of his absence or inability to attend, by its Vice-President.

    b. Minister of Justice is usually informed of the agenda of a Council meeting and may present his views before it.

    c. Decisions of the Council are valid only if taken in the presence of at least fifteen members, with at least ten members concurring in the decisions.

    d. The Council may call upon the Ministry of Justice for such assistance as the Council requires; it may also ask the Ministry for permission to inspect the personal file of any judge.

e. Elections for the Council are held three months prior to the termination of office of current members, who remain in power until the new Council is sworn in.

f. Supreme Council may in unusual circumstances, e.g., the inability of the Council to function properly due to the continued absence of members or of continued disagreement among the members, be dissolved under a decree issued by the President of the Republic after opinions have been received from the Presidents of the Senate and the Chamber of Deputies and the Presidential Committee of the Supreme Council.

   (1) In this case, the election of a new Council is held within one month after the date of dissolution.

C. ORDINARY COURTS

1. *Conciliators*
   a. Highly regarded citizens who are selected from the local community to sit in judgment of petty civil cases; their decisions may be appealed to the next highest judicial authority.

2. *Praetors*
   a. Lowest of the paid judges who sit in every Province and, singly, exercise jurisdiction in minor civil disputes and criminal cases.

3. *Tribunals*
   a. At least one Tribunal in every Provincial capital and major city.
   b. Plural bench of three judges hears appeals against the decisions of the Praetors and also exercises original jurisdiction in important civil and criminal cases.

4. *Courts of Appeal*
   a. At least one appellate court in every Region and major city.
   b. Plural bench of five judges hears appeals against the decisions of the lower courts.

5. *Courts of Assize*
   a. These courts (i.e., special Sections of the appellate

courts) are periodically established in every Province.

b. Plural bench consists of two regular judges and five lay assessors, who have original jurisdiction in the most serious criminal cases.

6. *Supreme Court of Cassation*

a. Highest court divided into special Sections to exercise appellate jurisdiction in civil and criminal cases; it may sustain or reverse the judgment of a lower court or order a new trial.

b. Also decides jurisdictional disputes between the ordinary and administrative courts.

D. ADMINISTRATIVE COURTS

1. *Council of State*

a. This court (consisting of six special Sections) has power to review cases involving the protection of the individual against illegal ordinances and actions by public officials, and then only if the individual has exhausted all other legal remedies.

(1) Only the ordinances and actions are invalidated; the individual must seek redress for actual damages in the ordinary courts of law.

2. *Court of Accounts*

a. This court (also divided into special Sections) gives legal effect to governmental decrees, approves public expenditures, reviews governmental contracts, and sits as a court of claims in pension cases.

(1) Appeals in Cassation against the decisions of this court (or the Council of State) can be based only on a jurisdictional question.

3. *Regional and Provincial administrative courts*

a. Special courts maintained in the Regions and Provinces to decide conflicts between individuals and public organizations on various questions.

E. SPECIAL COURTS

1. *Military courts*

a. Have jurisdiction in criminal cases involving military personnel; in peacetime, their decisions may be appealed to a higher military court (in Rome) or to the Supreme Court of Cassation.

2. *Public water courts*
   a. Settle conflicts over the use of public water; their decisions may be appealed to a higher public water court (in Rome).

F. CONSTITUTIONAL COURT
1. The Constitution (Arts. 134–137) confers great prestige upon this supreme State organ and assures it the maximum independence; the Court represents the guarantee that the fundamental laws of the Italian State are observed for the benefit and protection of the individual citizen and that the various State organs do not exceed the powers granted to them by the Constitution.
2. Any question of the constitutionality of a law, or any act that has the force of law, may be brought before the Constitutional Court by the interested organs of State or the Regions, and may also be appealed to by one of the parties in a trial as long as the judge (or judges) has not ruled that such referral is unfounded in law.
3. *Membership*
   a. Consists of fifteen judges: five judges appointed by the President of the Republic, five judges elected by the Parliament in a joint session, and five judges appointed by the courts (three by the Supreme Court of Cassation, one by the Council of State, and one by the Court of Accounts).
   b. Includes top-ranking active or retired judges, university professors of law, and practicing lawyers with at least twenty years experience.
   c. Serve a twelve-year term of office and are not eligible for immediate reelection.
   d. Cannot be members of the Parliament or a Regional Council, or practice or hold any incompatible profession or office.
   e. Elect a President from among their own numbers.
   f. Are not subject to censure, nor liable for opinions expressed or ballots cast in the exercise of their functions.

g. May not be removed or suspended from office for physical or civil incapacities or for serious deficiencies in the exercise of their functions, unless the Court itself so decides.

4. *Functions and powers*

   a. Determine the constitutionality of laws and of decrees having the force of law, as enacted by the Republic and the Regions; if the Court declares a law or decree unconstitutional, that law or decree automatically ceases to be valid.

   b. Interpret the meaning and applications of the constitutional powers of government.

   c. Settle conflicts of jurisdiction between the State organs of the Republic, and conflicts between the Republic and a Region, or between Regions.

   d. Try the President of the Republic (for treason or activities against the Constitution) and the President of the Council of Ministers or a Minister (for misdemeanors committed in the exercise of their functions) with the assistance of sixteen lay members elected by the Parliament in joint session from citizens who meet the qualifications necessary to hold a seat in the Senate.

   e. Virtually no area of interest between private citizens and the State, and between the Republic and the Regions, has not been reviewed by the Constitutional Court including such matters, for example, as individual freedoms, procedural due process of law, rights of labor and industry, social assistance, economic planning, tax and financial measures, national referenda, relations of central and local authorities, etc.

5. *Procedures*

   a. Eleven judges are necessary to comprise a quorum.

   b. Decisions are taken by a two-thirds majority vote.

   c. Decisions must be made public and also be formally transmitted to the National Parliament and the Regional Councils.

   d. There is no appeal against the decisions of this court, on either a constitutional question or an impeachment.

G. OTHER AGENCIES IN THE ADMINISTRATION OF JUSTICE

1. *Minister of Justice*
   a. Assumes responsibility for the organization and management of all services connected with the administration of justice outside the jurisdiction of the Supreme Council of the Magistracy (i.e., the Public Prosecutors, whose status and functions are protected by law, and the Judicial Police, who are placed at the disposition of the State authorities to secure the enforcement of court decisions).
   b. Supervises various professional associations, such as those to which the members of the legal profession belong.
2. *Minister of the Interior*
   a. Assumes responsibility for the National Police Forces *(Carabinieri)*, which work closely with the local police personnel to maintain the State order and security.
   b. Appoints and dismisses the Prefects, who have both quasi-judicial and administration functions in the Provinces.

VII. LOCAL GOVERNMENT

A. BASIC ELEMENTS OF LOCAL GOVERNMENT

1. Italy is constitutionally divided into Regions, Provinces, and Communes, and also has a number of special administrative Districts *(Circondari)*.
2. A unified and uniform system of local government, with opposing tendencies of centralization and decentralization in administration.
3. Post-World War II re-formation of Regions, and the reestablishment of democratic institutions, has allegedly resulted in an increased popular interest in government on the part of local citizens.
4. Republic controls the local government in a number and variety of ways, viz., constitutional legislation; financial assistance and control; decrees, orders, and regulations; the preparation of the Regional constitutions; the appointment of the Provincial Prefects; joint administration of public services; expert consultation and

advice; inspections; approval of local actions; reports; etc.

5. Special forms and conditions of autonomy for Sicily, Sardinia, Trent-Alto Adige, and the Vale d'Aosta (Art. 116), but not yet for Friuli, Venezia-Giulia (See Section B below).

6. Local governments are territorial units for the administration of national services and units for governmental activities on the local level.

B. REGIONS (4): Nineteen autonomous regions were provided for in Arts. 114, 115, and 131 of the Constitution, but the present regions are only geographical entities of the central government; however, five special autonomous regions have been established under Art. 116, namely, Sicily, Sardinia, Aosta, Trentino-Alto Adige, and Friuli-Venezia Giulia.

1. *Constitution:* prepared and enacted by the national Parliament.

2. *Legislature:* popularly-elected, unicameral Regional Council; the Deputies serve a four-year term.

   a. Enacts legislation on local boundaries, local police, public roads, markets, vocational training, hunting and fishing, etc.

   b. Exercises the tax power, but may also accept financial aid from the Republic to defray the costs of Regional administration.

   c. May, in an exceptional case, be dissolved by the parliamentary Committee on Regional Affairs, to maintain the public security.

   d. Delegates administrative functions to the Provinces and Communes.

   e. Prohibited from action with regard to foreign affairs, the Military Service, inter-Regional commerce, the rights of Italian citizens, etc.

   f. Proposes laws to the national Parliament and implements national legislation.

   g. May use the initiative and the referendum in the legislative process.

   h. May establish a special commission to protect the interests of the Council between legislative sessions.

CHART 31. AGENCIES OF LOCAL GOVERNMENT IN ITALY

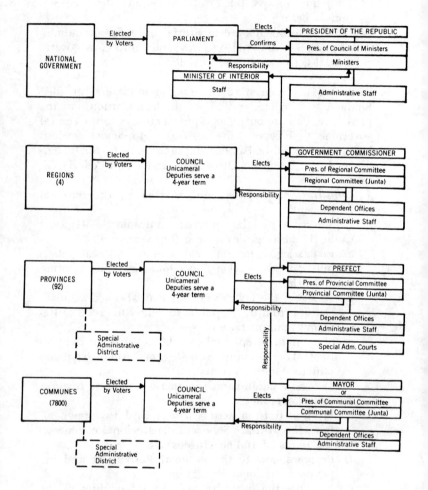

      i. Provides its own organization, including a President, a regular staff, and legislative commissions.

      j. Qualifications, elections, prohibitions, immunities, etc., of Regional Councillors are determined by Regional constitutions and legislation.

3. *Executive:* Regional Committee (*Giunta*) and President, elected by and from the Regional Council.

      a. The President is the formal Head of the Regional Government.

      b. Each member of the Regional Committee supervises the administration of a designated governmental function or service.

      c. Executive authority is assisted by various dependent offices and the civil service staff.

      d. A "Commissioner of the Government" (Art. 124) coordinates the activities of the Regional authorities in the administration of the Republic's laws and functions.

      e. General status and powers of the President and Regional Committee are defined by constitutional legislation.

C. PROVINCES (92)

1. *Prefects:* represent the interests of the Republic in the Provinces.

2. *Legislature:* popularly-elected, unicameral Provincial Council; the Deputies serve a four-year term.

      a. Enacts legislation on Provincial properties, roads, schools, public health, hospitals, charities, and other matters.

      b. Establishes the Provincial Deputation to represent the interests of the Council when it is not in session.

      c. Maintains its own rules and organization, including a President, a regular staff, and legislative commissions.

      d. Qualifications, elections, prohibitions, immunities, etc., of Provincial Councillors are determined by general legislation.

3. *Executive:* Provincial Committee (*Giunta*) and President, elected by and from the Provincial Council.

      a. The President represents the Province and generally supervises the Provincial administration.

      b. Each member of the Provincial Committee is responsible for a designated service or function of government.

      c. Various dependent offices and the local civil service staff assist the Provincial Committee and the President.

      d. Prefect (appointed by the Minister of the Interior) has authority to safeguard the national order and security in the Province; in doing so, he may issue orders and decrees, with the force of law, to both the Provincial and Communal authorities.

      e. Powers and restraints relating to the Provincial Executive are also determined by law.

4. *Judiciary:* the Republic sometimes establishes administrative courts in the Provinces to perform special judicial functions.

5. *Circondari* are Districts within the Provinces and Communes for designated administrative purposes.

D. *Communes* (More than 8000)

  1. *Prefects and Regional authorities:* exercise varying degrees of authority and control over the Communes.

  2. *Legislature:* popularly-elected, unicameral Communal Council; its members serve a four-year term.

      a. Enacts ordinances on Communal properties, police, transport, public utilities, public health, sanitation, charities, schools, commercial activities, and other matters.

      b. Provides its own organization and rules of procedure.

      c. Status and powers of Communal Councillors are set by law.

  3. *Executive:* Communal Committee *(Guinta)* and Mayor, elected by and from the Communal Council.

      a. The Mayor represents the Commune, promulgates laws and regulations, and directs the administrative functions of the Commune.

      b. Members of the Communal Committee have individual administrative responsibilities.

    c. Dependent offices and Communal civil service, including the Secretary of the Commune, legal advisers, etc., assist the Mayor and Communal Committee.

    d. Powers and limitations of the Communal executive are delimited by law.

VIII. VATICAN CITY

A. BRIEF DESCRIPTION

1. Vatican City is a small part of Rome, but not Italian territory.

2. Belongs to the Pope, in order to show his independence from the Italian Republic and every other political State.

3. Contains the Basilica of St. Peter, the Vatican Palace (where the Pope lives), the offices of the Papal Government, the barracks of the Swiss Guard, and the Vatican communications center.

4. On the second day of voting (June 21, 1963) in the Sistine Chapel, the eighty Cardinals of the Sacred College named Giovanni Battista Cardinal Montini, Archbishop of Milan, as successor to Pope John XXIII.

    a. The new Pope took the name of Paul VI and is the 262nd. Pontiff of the Roman Catholic Church.

    b. He was crowned on June 30, 1963, on the threshold of St. Peter's in a ceremony attended by ninety-six official delegations and a crowd of 300,000 persons from every part of the world.

B. LEGAL AND CONSTITUTIONAL BASES OF GOVERNMENT

1. *Lateran Treaty* (February 11, 1929) (major provisions)

    a. Pope has sovereign jurisdiction over the Vatican City within Rome; he serves as the Temporal Sovereign and is equal, in international law, to the Head of State in all independent countries.

    b. Papacy has sovereign jurisdiction over all Catholic Church properties within Rome.

    c. Pope (as Head of the Roman Catholic Church) is personally inviolable and has complete freedom of communication abroad.

        d. Holy See receives financial indemnities from the Italian Government for the loss of Papal sovereignty outside the Vatican City and certain property losses incurred by the Catholic Church when Italy annexed the Papal States.

  2. *Concordat between the Holy See and Italy* (February 11, 1929)

        a. Contains a number of religious provisions and agreements between the Papacy and Italy relative to the status and functions of the Catholic Church within Italy.

           (1) Roman Catholicism as the official State religion.

           (2) Appointments to ecclesiastical positions and the legal rights of Church officers.

           (3) Financial support by Italy to maintain the Church and the Church's exemption from taxation.

           (4) Regulation of marriages.

           (5) Religious instruction in Italian schools and the State's subsidization of Church schools.

  3. *Constitutional Laws* (June 7, 1929) (major provisions)

        a. Pope as source of sovereign power in the Vatican City.

        b. Rights of citizenship and sojourn in the Vatican City.

        c. Organization of the Holy See (Government) in the Vatican City.

        d. Regulation of commercial, economic, and professional organizations in the Vatican City.

        e. Maintenance of the public security in the Vatican City.

C. ORGANIZATION OF GOVERNMENT

  1. Pope is sovereign.

  2. Legislative power is vested in the Pope (or the Holy College of Cardinals); he may delegate this power to his appointed State Governor.

  3. Executive power is vested in the Pope; he may delegate this power to the State Governor.

  4. Judicial power is vested in the Pope; he may delegate this power to single judges (appointed by him), the

Sacred Roman Rota (Court of First Instance), and to the Supreme Tribunal of the Signature.

SELECTED READINGS

Adams, John Clarke, and Paolo Barile, *The Government of Republican Italy.* Boston: Houghton Mifflin Company, 1961.

Almond, G. A., *The Appeals of Communism.* Princeton: Princeton University Press, 1954.

Banco di Roma, *Ten Years of Italian Economy, 1947–1956.* Rome: 1957.

Calamandrei, Piero, *Procedure and Democracy.* New York: New York University Press, 1956.

Cecchelli, C., *The Vatican City.* Rome: L. Morpurgo, 1933.

Falco, M., *Legal Position of the Holy See Before and After the Lateran Agreement.* London: Oxford University Press, 1935.

Gardini, T. L., *Towards the New Italy.* London: Drummond, 1944.

Grew, R., *A Sterner Plan for Italian Unity.* Princeton: Princeton University Press, 1963.

Grindrod, Muriel, *New Italy.* London: Royal Institute of International Affairs, 1947.

———, *The Rebuilding of Italy: Politics and Economics, 1945–1955.* London: Royal Institute of International Affairs, 1956.

Hilton Young, Wayland, *The Italian Left: a Short History of Political Socialism in Italy.* New York: Longmans, Green & Company, Inc., 1949.

Holisher, D., *The Eternal City.* Toronto: Oxford University Press, 1943.

Kogan, Norman, *The Government of Italy.* New York: Thomas Y. Crowell Company, 1962.

Kornhauser, W., *The Politics of Mass Society.* Glencoe, Illinois: Free Press, 1959.

La Palombara, J. G., *Interest Groups in Italian Politics.* Princeton: Princeton University Press, 1964.

Neufeld, M. F., *Italy: School for Awakening Countries.* Ithaca: Cornell University Press, 1961.

Presidency of the Council of Ministers, *Ten Years of Italian Democracy, 1946–1956.* Rome: Information Office, Documentation Center, 1956.

Salvadori, Massimo, *Italy.* New York: Foreign Policy Association, 1951.

Seldes, G., *Vatican: Yesterday—Today—Tomorrow.* New York: Harper & Brothers, 1941.

Sforza, Carlo, *Italy and Italians*, New York: E. P. Dutton and Company, 1949.

Smith, Denis Mack, *Italy: a Modern History*. Ann Arbor: University of Michigan Press, 1959.

Steel, R., ed., *Italy*. New York: H. W. Wilson Company, 1963.

Trease, G., *The Italian Story*. New York: Vanguard Press, 1965.

Wall, B., *Report on the Vatican*. London: Weidenfeld, 1956.

Whelpton, E., *A Concise History of Italy*. London: R. Hale, 1964.

Wiskemann, Elizabeth, *Italy*. Toronto: Oxford University Press, 1947.

Chapter VI

SPAIN

POPULATION: 31,500,000 (1965)
AREA: 194,945 sq. miles
CAPITAL: Madrid

I. CHRONOLOGY

711—End of Visogothic domination of Spain.

1137—Christian kingdoms of Leon, Castile, Navarre, Aragon-Barcelona continue their fight against the Moors.

1217–1252—Ferdinand III of Castile adds Córdoba and Seville to his kingdom and reduces the Moslems to the kingdom of Granada.

1391—End of policy of tolerance among the Christians, Jews, and Moors.

1469—Political unity achieved through marriage of Isabella I of Castile and Ferdinand II of Aragon.

1492—Capture of Granada completes Catholic reconquest of the Iberian peninsula and ends Moslem power in Spain; discovery of America by Columbus opens up a new "Golden Age."

1516–1556—Charles I introduces Hapsburg rule in Spain; series of wars with France and Holland during the Protestant Reformation.

1588—Defeat of the "Invincible Armada" by the English.

1659—Treaty of the Pyrenees, and marriage of Marie Thérèse to Louis XIV, ends war with France.

1701–1714—"War of the Spanish Succession" and extension of Bourbon rule to Spain.

1759–1788—Internal improvements in public works and administration during the "Enlightened Despotism" of Charles III.

1808—Napoleon designates Joseph Bonaparte military dictator and king in Spain.

1810–1825—Spain loses her colonies in North and South America.

1868–1902—Extended "Period of Troubles" marked by extraordinary political confusion, national decline, and foreign wars.

1823—*Coup d'état* results in establishment, with Royal consent, of a military directorate.

1931—Proclamation of the new Republic.

1936–1939—Spanish Civil War and establishment of the Falangist regime under General Francisco Franco.

1947—Law of Succession declares the "Chief of the State" (Franco) may, at any time, name a Royal successor.

1953—Defense agreement signed between the United States and Spain.

1966—General Franco proposes new Fundamental Laws to bring modified democracy to Spain after twenty-seven years' dictatorship. The changes—obtained by decision of Parliament (*Cortes*) and a national referendum—include a separate Head of the State, a Premier, and a larger, more representative Parliament.

II. SPANISH CONSTITUTION

A. There is no Single, Written Constitutional Document

B. The Fundamental Laws
1. Law for the Government of the Nation, 1938.
2. Labor Charter (*Fuero del Trabajo*), 1938.
3. Constitutive Law of the *Cortes*, 1942.
4. Charter of the Spanish People (*Fuero de los Españoles*), 1945.
5. National Referendum Act, 1945.
6. Law of Succession to the Chief of the State, 1947.

C. Supplementary "Constitutional" Laws
1. Bills on Association and Public Meetings, 1938.
2. Code of Standing Rules, 1943.
3. Law on the Bases of Local Government, 1945.

4. Provisions in the "Law of Succession" for the future promulgation of other laws of constitutional rank.

D. FUNDAMENTAL PRINCIPLES OF GOVERNMENT
   1. Spain is "a Catholic, social, representative State . . . a Kingdom" (Law of Succession, Art. 1).
   2. No universally accepted belief in the workability of traditional democratic government, with its free political expression and opposition, party politics, and parliamentary supremacy.
   3. Emphasis placed upon (a) unity, under law and centralized controls; (b) order, under schematic politico-administrative organization; and (c) progress, under syndicalized economic activity.
   4. Faith also maintained in the stabilizing influence of the Catholic Church upon the Spanish State and society.
   5. Constitutional and political ideals of the National Movement personified in *el Caudillo* as the leader and Chief of the State.
   6. Popular representation manifested through pluralized familial, local or provincial, and syndical institutions.
   7. The *Cortes,* the national Congress, is theoretically the "superior organ of participation of the Spanish people in the tasks of the State" (Constitutive Law of the *Cortes,* Art. 1).
   8. No independent judiciary in the traditional Western sense.
   9. *Note:* Although one must surely distinguish between the constitutional theory and the socio-political facts, in assessing the fascist-type dictatorship in Spain, one might also observe that the individual Spanish citizen has learned to evaluate "Government" from a different point of view, and on different premises, than does the individual American or Englishman. "Paternalistic authoritarianism" is almost traditionally acceptable to the average Spanish citizen and he is taught to believe the State exists for the benefit of society and not society for the State. This point, the Spanish Government contends, is in sharp contrast to the political theory of former Italian Fascism and German National Socialism. Moreover, Spaniards are indoctrinated with the idea

Chart 32. STRUCTURE OF THE SPANISH GOVERNMENT

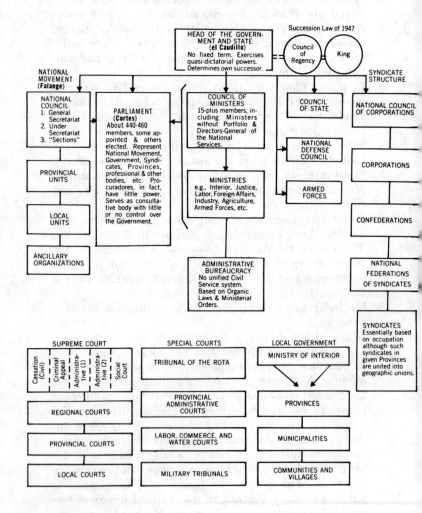

that an attack against *el Caudillo* is an attack against the State and, therefore, is against the interests of the Spanish society.

Nonetheless, late in 1966, a kind of "creeping liberalism" seemed to alter the "paternalism of society" and, along with the new "economic revolution" (i.e., rapid industrialization and increased urbanization) at least affected the social mores, if not the political structure, of the Spanish people. A new "Press Law" abolished direct censorship and afforded new freedoms and responsibilities for newspaper and magazine writers. In addition, numerous student groups—in part supported by the "liberal wing" of the Catholic Church—demonstrated widely throughout the country in behalf of still more freedoms. The emergent question was: "Would the 'liberalization' prove to be illusory or real, promise or performance?" Obviously, only future events could provide an answer.

E. CIVIL RIGHTS AND DUTIES (Charter of the Spanish People, 1945)
"The Spanish State proclaims as a guiding principle of its acts, respect for the dignity, integrity and liberty of the human being, recognizing Man as the bearer of eternal values and member of the national community, to be holder of . . . duties and rights, the exercise of which it guarantees for the common good." (First Clause)
1. Faithful service and obedience to the country and the Chief of the State.
2. Equality of all citizens under the law.
3. Respect for personal and family honor.
4. Protection of the family and the institution of marriage.
5. Parents must provide for, and instruct, their children.
6. Freedom of residence and the security of the home.
7. Recognition and protection of private property.
8. No arbitrary confiscation of property, although its use may be subordinated to the necessities of the Nation and the common good.
9. Right to receive education at public expense.
10. Official protection for the precepts and practices of the

Roman Catholic religion and the private exercise of religious beliefs.

11. Freedom of lawful expression of ideas, personal correspondence, association, and petition.

12. Right of legal security, including prohibitions against arbitrary action and arrest and the denial of fair judicial hearings.

13. No denial of citizenship, except for treason or for military or public service in a foreign State.

14. Exercise of personal services on behalf of the national and public interest.

15. Individual contributions to the maintenance of public expenditures.

16. Compulsory male military service.

17. Right (and duty) to work and to receive a "just and sufficient return" in order to provide one's family with a "dignified existence."

18. Protection and fostering of "institutions of assistance."

19. Exercise of rights should not prejudice "the spiritual and social unity" of the national community.

   a. Significantly, the Thirty-fifth Clause of the Charter provides that "The enforcement of clauses twelve [freedom of expression], thirteen [inviolability of correspondence], fourteen [freedom of residence], fifteen [protection of the home against illegal searches], sixteen [freedom of association], and eighteen [no unlawful arrests or detentions] may temporarily be suspended in part or in whole by the Government by means of a Decree which must define and limit the scope and duration of this measure."

F. POLITICAL RIGHTS AND OBLIGATIONS (Charter of the Spanish People, 1945)

   1. Obedience to the laws and service to the Nation.

   2. Right to vote (based on the Electoral Act of 1907, as amended).

      a. In fact, in national referenda, casting the ballot on one side or another is a political responsibility to be assumed by all citizens and is as compulsory— the Spanish spokesmen say—as taxes and military service are in other countries; in fairness, it should be added that the discharge of this responsibility does not mean that balloting is not secret nor freely exercised.

3. Equal right of all citizens to hold public office and participate in public functions "of a representative character" according to individual merit and capacity.

4. Also, constitutional amendments agreed upon in the *Cortes,* and assented to by the Chief of the State, may be submitted to popular approval in a national referendum.

III. NATIONAL MOVEMENT
(Falange Española Tradicionalista y las Juntas de Ofensiva Nacional-Sindicalista)

A. GENERAL CHARACTERISTICS AND STATUS OF THE
F.E.T.—J.O.N.S.
The Falange:

1. Was originally an organization of young intellectuals who were dedicated to the restoration of political unity and order in Spain.

2. Was only one of several different groups which supported the rise of the Franco regime.

3. Was elevated to power and prestige by *el Caudillo,* not *vice versa.*

4. Has been supported in recent years by the State and is not an indispensable prop for the State regime.

5. Has not been supported by all prominent Spaniards nor is membership in it a necessary condition to personal advancement or influence in Spain.

6. Is not a political party, but rather a National Movement, and although it has lost some of its former influence and prestige, continues to provide membership in important operational agencies of the Franco regime (e.g., the Cabinet and Ministry, the *Cortes,* the National Syndicates, the Provincial and local governments, the Military Forces, etc.).

7. Is still the only organized political group permitted in Spain; it maintains rather close relations with the Catholic Church and is described as "the representative of the national ideals and social justice."

    a. This latter position is roughly analogous to that of the Church-Army coalition (Catholic Action), which generally supports (and sometimes criticizes) the Franco regime.

B. GENERAL OBJECTIVES OF THE F.E.T.—J.O.N.S.

The following is a general condensation of the Falangist "Twenty-Seven Points" (1934), which provided the theoretical basis for the subsequent development of the "Movement" and "National Syndicalism" in modern Spain. Note the contributions of this program to the present "Constitution" and the political and economic organization of the Spanish society under the Franco regime:

1. To restore Spain to greatness.
2. To reorganize the State as a "totalitarian instrument" in the service of the national interest, and to form "family, municipal, and syndical" units in the conduct of State activities.
3. To abolish political parties.
4. To encourage the expression of individual initiative and talent in the advancement of the public interest.
5. To reorganize economic activities along corporate lines and establish a system of vertical syndicates.
6. To repudiate both capitalism and communism, as detrimental to the interests of the individual and society.
7. To condemn class warfare and the domination of one class over another.
8. To improve the conditions of life and the standard of living of the Spanish people.
9. To recognize private property, but to confiscate it where it is unlawfully acquired or used against the public interest.
10. To nationalize designated institutions and also provide a corporate organization of the public services.
11. To protect the right, and enforce the duty, to work.
12. To reorganize and improve agricultural activity, the production of livestock, reforestation, etc.
13. To establish a program of training in the national defense.
14. To incorporate the "Catholic spirit" in the national reconstruction and re-define Church-State jurisdictions and relations.

15. To use direct methods in attaining these aims and infuse a spirit of "sacrifice and service" in the Spanish people.

C. GENERAL ORGANIZATION OF THE F.E.T.—J.O.N.S.
1. National Leader (*el Caudillo*): all-powerful Chief of the State.
2. National Council: consists of *ex officio* and elected members; representatives of all phases of Spanish life who perform advisory functions and serve in the *Cortes;* special committees.
3. General Secretariat and Under-Secretariat: administer the National Movement; special sections and delegations.
4. Other dependent national units: e.g., the hierarchical structure of youth organizations.
5. Provincial and local units.

D. GENERAL EVALUATION OF THE F.E.T.—J.O.N.S.
1. Important organization during the Spanish Civil War (1936–1939) and the rise of the Franco regime.
2. Assisted the reestablishment of unity and order among the Spanish people.
3. Provided some personnel for governmental and economic structures.
4. Postwar (World War II) decrease in the importance of the *Falange* in the State (but an increase in the position and influence of the Catholic Church).
5. Incomplete success in the realization of the "Twenty-Seven Points."
6. Unsuccessful attempts have been made by former political parties (e.g., the Socialists, Social Democrats, and Christian Democrats) and new pseudo-political groups (e.g., the "Spanish Union") to form an opposition to the National Movement.
Hugh Trevor-Roper, Professor of Modern History at Oxford University: ". . . the Government of Spain does not really fit into any familiar twentieth century pattern. It may be described as 'Fascist' or 'anti-Communist' but in fact it is neither. It is an ancient Bourbon monarchy, with no parallel in the world, and Franco is not really a dictator in the modern sense: he is a Regent." However, ". . . he has prevented any

rival from approaching his Throne. The *Cortes* or Parliament is completely packed and managed by him. Though it can legally reject a Government measure, it has never done so. The *Falange* is ultimately under his control. He is Generalissimo of the Army. And in these positions he has known how to prevent the emergence of any threat to his own supremacy. He manipulates, balances, cajoles, pensions, in such a way that he alone rules and no one in Spain can . . . see any alternative to him. . . . Since political parties are forbidden in Spain, [opposition] cannot be expressed in parties at all. It is expressed in 'movements,' in 'tendencies' which seek not to overthrow the regime—that would open the door to civil war—but to transform it from within. . . . If he [Franco] can close his own reign by placing upon the throne a real Spanish prince brought up in the old pre-constitutional tradition, then he will die happy with a *Nunc Dimittis*." [in effect, "Lord now lettest thou thy servant depart in peace"]

IV. NATIONAL GOVERNMENT

A. CHIEF OF THE STATE AND HEAD OF THE GOVERNMENT (*El Caudillo, General Francisco Franco y Bahamonde*)
1. *Selection and succession*
   a. Franco confirmed as *el Caudillo* by the Spanish people in a National Referendum, 1947.
   b. Law of Succession, 1947, makes provision for the reestablishment of the traditional Monarchy and the creation of a special council to determine the Royal succession.
      (1) "In the event of a vacancy in the Chief of the State, a Council of Regency will assume the supreme authority, to be formed by the President of the *Cortes*, the prelate of highest rank, and the Captain-General of the Armed Forces" (Art. 3).
      (2) The Council of Regency will convoke the Royal Council, within three days after the vacancy oc-

curs, to propose a successor to the Chief of the State before the *Cortes*.

    (a) Royal Council consists of the President of the *Cortes*, the Captain-General of the Armed Forces, the Chief of the General Staff, the President of the Council of State, the Chief Justice of the Supreme Court, the President of the Spanish Institute, representatives for the various sections in the *Cortes*, and three additional members appointed by Franco.

    (b) New Chief of the State (either king or temporary regent) must be a Spanish citizen, at least thirty years of age, a Catholic, and dedicated to uphold the principles of the National Movement (*Falange*); in future, the kingship will be hereditary and restricted only to males (the Salic Law).

  (3) Franco was empowered, at any time he might desire, to propose before the *Cortes* the person who would succeed him as king or regent.

2. *Position and powers*

  a. *El Caudillo* is the Chief of the State and Head of the Government, Commander in Chief of the Armed Forces, Head of the National Movement, *ex officio* Head of the National Congress (*Cortes*) and of the court system; other than this, he is

  b. "Responsible only to God and history."

  c. Provides concentrated political leadership and exercises the executive power through his appointive Cabinet and Ministry.

  d. Directs and implements foreign affairs.

  e. Sanctions and promulgates the laws passed by the *Cortes*.

  f. Issues emergency or extraordinary decree-laws.

  g. Directs all national advisory bodies and heads the civil and military orders.

  h. Awards national honors and grants peerages and titles of nobility.

  i. Enjoys an indefinite term in office, maintains an official residence, and receives an annual budget for necessary State expenses.

B. COUNCIL OF MINISTERS

The Ministers:

1. Are appointed (and removed) by the Chief of the State and are responsible only to him.

2. Are members of the *Cortes*, which body can petition or question them; however, there is no Cabinet responsibility to the legislature.

3. Convene as a Cabinet in closed weekly meetings to discuss matters of concern to several or all ministries; the meetings are presided over by the Chief of the State and no formal minutes or records are kept.

4. Initiate legislation in the *Cortes* and countersign acts enacted there and approved by the Chief of the State.

5. Direct the various Departments of government and issue binding orders and regulations with the consent of the Chief of the State.

6. Ministries include the Chief of the State, the Under-Secretary of the Presidency, Foreign Affairs, Justice, Army, Navy, Air, Finance, Interior, Public Works, Education, Labor, Industry, Agriculture, National Movement, Commerce and Food, Information and Tourism, and Housing.

7. There are also various Ministers without Portfolio, Directors General of the National Services, and such advisory bodies as the Council of State and the National Defense Council.

C. ADMINISTRATIVE BUREAUCRACY

1. No unified civil service system nor a common organization and standardized procedures among the various administrative structures.

2. Numerous Organic Laws, decrees, regulations, and ministerial orders regulate the bureaucracy.

3. University graduates are given preference in securing public positions, with in-service promotions, etc., determined by tenure or by special circumstances as decided by a supervisorial staff.

4. State controls the organization of the economic (syndicalist) units.

V. NATIONAL CONGRESS (*Cortes*)

A. DESCRIPTIVE FEATURES OF THE CORTES
1. Theoretically, the people's "superior body" for participation in the tasks of the State.
2. Unicameral national legislature, composed of *ex officio* and elective members who serve different terms in office.
3. Legislative officers and committees are appointed or approved by the Chief of the State.
4. No free interplay of party politics, as in other Western parliaments.
5. Legislative powers are strictly limited and may be abrogated or superseded in favor of extraordinary or emergency decrees, with the force of law, issued by the Chief of the State.
6. Factually, a consultative body, with virtually no control over the "Government."

B. MEMBERSHIP
1. Members (*Procuradores*) must be Spanish citizens, at least twenty-one years of age, in full enjoyment of civic rights, and not otherwise disqualified by law.
2. The 443 members (1965) include the
   a. Ministers of State (18);
   b. National Councillors (103);
   c. Presidents of the Council of State, the Supreme Court of Justice, and of the High Court of Military Justice (3);
   d. Representatives of the National Syndicates (guilds and labor unions) (142);
   e. Mayors of the fifty Provincial capitals and other Provincial and Municipal representatives (102);
   f. Heads of the Spanish universities (12);
   g. Presidents of the Spanish Institute (*Instituto de España*) and of its Royal Academies, and the President of the High Council for Scientific Research (6);
   h. Presidents and representatives of the Institute of Civil Engineers, the Bar Associations, the Medical Associations, and other professional, commercial, and cultural associations (7);

       i. Various outstanding persons from ecclesiastical, administrative, military, and social life (50).

          (1) Terms in office vary according to the type of *Procurador*; some terms end when the members lose their regular Government posts; others, when the members are recalled by the Chief of the State; still others, at the end of the three-year legislative period, unless the members are reelected to office.

          (2) Vacant seats are filled by new appointments and elections.

  3. Privileges and immunities of the *Procuradores* theoretically include

     a. Freedom of speech on the floor of the *Cortes* without fear of reprisals;

     b. Freedom from arrest and trial without the specific authorization of the *Cortes*; a trial, on the authorization of the *Cortes*, is conducted only by the Supreme Court.

  4. Perquisites of the *Procuradores* include a monthly allowance and rebates for travel and ordinary expenses.

C. ORGANIZATION

  1. The Bureau consists of the President, two Vice-Presidents, and four Secretaries, all nominated by the Chief of the State.

  2. Also a number of regular committees and commissions (approved by the Chief of the State), each of which has its own President, Secretariat, staff assistants, etc.

     a. One commission serves as a liaison body between the *Cortes* and the "Government."

     b. Other commissions help determine the jurisdiction of the *Cortes*, draft legislation, and regulate the internal administration of the legislature.

     c. Regular functional committees include: Agriculture, Appropriations, Constitutional Laws, Finance, Home Affairs, Industry and Commerce, Justice, Labor, National Defense, National Education, Public Works, and Treaties.

  3. Rules of procedure and by-laws of the *Cortes* are established with the approval of the "Government."

D. LEGISLATIVE PROCEEDINGS
1. Time and length of legislative meetings is indeterminate.
2. *Procuradores* must attend all plenary sessions of the *Cortes* and vote on legislation at these times.
3. *Enactment of law*
   a. Opening of the legislative meeting.
   b. Introduction and reading of bills ("Government" and "Committee" bills).
   c. Consideration of the bills and reports by committees or sub-committees.
   d. Discussion and limited debate.
   e. Voting: simple ayes and nays (*viva voce*), the standing vote, and vote by roll call of the *Procuradores*.
   f. Approval and promulgation of law by the Chief of the State.
      (1) He may return bills to the *Cortes* for further study or veto them, but this is seldom done.

E. FUNCTIONS AND POWERS (always subject to approval by the Chief of the State)
1. Conduct plenary and committee meetings.
2. Levy taxes, appropriate monies, regulate currency and banking, and perform the legislative audit.
3. Legislate on matters related to constitutional affairs, citizenship, and civil rights, the organization of the administrative and judicial systems, Provincial and local governments, national education, social and economic problems, and the public order.
4. Participate in the amendment of constitutional laws and the ratification of international treaties.
5. Submit questions and requests to Ministers on matters within the competence of the *Cortes* (without ministerial parliamentary responsibility).
6. "Study special subjects, carry out investigations, and draft petitions or suggestions" through committees especially established for these purposes (Constitutive Law, Art. 15).
7. Maintain a special commission to report to the "Government" on the business and actions of the *Cortes*.

8. Receive and endorse the decree-laws of the Chief of the State.
9. Accept petitions from Spanish citizens (theoretical) and provide for national referenda.

VI. NATIONAL SYNDICALISM

The ultimate goal of the Falangist syndicate program is to carry into effect, in the economic realm, the "paternalistic-authoritarianism" of the State. All economic activity, from both the employers' and employees' standpoints, is collated into one great national structure under central direction. At the same time, a certain amount of autonomy (in theory at least) remains with each individual organization, whether local or national in scope. Although employers and employees maintain *quasi*-independent organizations (e.g., cooperative unions), they are finally brought together in the National Council of Corporations. Thus do the Falangists repudiate class-conflict dogma.

A. SIGNIFICANT FACTORS
1. Desire for "social and economic justice" for all people.
2. Reorganization of the private economic system so that power to operate and control particular enterprises is vested in the hands of groups (syndicates) of workers and producers.
3. Production is kept in line with demand, and the alleged superfluous middle-men eliminated, so that producers may secure a reasonable profit while, at the same time, goods and services can be purchased at low cost by the consumers.
4. *Syndicates* are not directly organs of the State, but rather private structures of workers and producers in all fields (agricultural, industrial, commercial, cultural, and professional) of human endeavor; they are self-contained branches of productive activity, organized along functional lines on the different levels of the country.
5. Work is considered to be a "social responsibility" for all able-bodied persons, and the State maintains the apparatus (i.e., special courts) for the equitable adjust-

ment of all disputes that may arise within/between the syndical-corporative groups, on behalf "the continued progress and development" of the Nation's economy.

B. General Organization of the Syndicates

Jose Ruiz, Minister Secretary-General of the National Movement and National Delegate of the Syndicates: "We do not want the State to replace the employer, but, without killing private enterprise and initiative, it must direct the economic policy of the Nation. And the instrument we consider best qualified to serve the State and the economy in their mutual relations is the syndical organization. . . . The syndical organization thus constituted, and provided with the appropriate organs for carrying out its tasks, operates in three main fields: economic policy, social justice, and assistance. All three, however, are intimately connected. The social and economic activities of the syndicates cannot be separated, for every economic problem is also a social problem, and every social question or measure has repercussions on the economic situation. Nevertheless, among these primary functions, our social action and the organization of assistance should be stressed, because all the major syndical undertakings are inspired by the desire to raise the standard of living of Spanish workers. . . . The workers today, thanks to our system, not only share in the management and running of the syndicates, but are also fully and effectively represented in the public life of the Nation. The syndical liaison officers in the factories of Spain are genuine workers, as also are the members of the Social and Economic Committees, and all of them are freely elected."

1. A hierarchical structural organization, from the Ministry and National Council of Corporations to the Directors and Committees of regional and provincial syndical units, down to the Managers and Committees of the local branches of production.

2. The twenty-six vertical National Syndicates are classified according to the nature of the production process, the materials used in production, the facilities involved in the distribution of products, and the particular type of goods or services.

Chart 33. SPANISH SYNDICAL-CORPORATIVE ADMINISTRATIVE ORGANIZATION

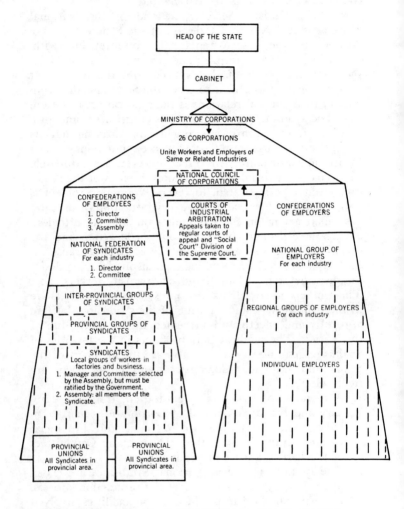

    a. Some of the important syndicates include textiles and clothing; transportation and communications; banking and insurance; the professions; and entertainment.

3. Important supervisorial and managerial positions are held by trusted Falangists and prominent supporters of the Franco regime.

4. Syndicates have a corporate or juridical status and are represented in the local and Provincial Councils and the National Congress *(Cortes).*

5. Courts of Industrial Arbitration (labor courts), although not strictly a part of the syndical structures, are available to these associations for the settlement of disputes between themselves or between workers and employers.

    a. These arbitral bodies may refer a dispute to a regular court for a final settlement.

    b. Appeals may be taken from the decisions of the labor courts to the regular courts of appeal.

6. Industrial practices and labor relations stress the importance of cooperative effort among all personnel involved in production and services, "in the advancement and protection of the Nation's interests."

C. THE COOPERATIVE UNIONS

1. These are auxiliaries of the syndicates and are similarly organized on functional and hierarchical (local, provincial and national) principles.

2. The *Cooperative Societies Law,* January 2, 1942, as supplemented by Decree on November 11, 1943, provided the basis for the expansion of the Spanish cooperative movement and as an auxiliary to national syndicalism; the Law established the *Cooperative Section,* or governing body, of the cooperative movement within the national syndical organization.

3. Local cooperative unions support the regional unions which, in turn, support the National Cooperative Unions.

4. Cooperative unions are either for a single labor sector exclusively or else they group together various related labor sectors.

5. The cooperatives are controlled and governed by representatives of their own affiliates selected through the union organization in a proportion of three workers for every employer; these representatives play a role in the provincial and national meetings and in the committees (See Section 10 below) of the Government.
   a. They study and decide what investments of capital shall be made, in line with percentages established by the State to guarantee the future of the organization and to finance projects of great national and social interest.
6. The income of the Cooperatives comes from dues set by law and based on the amount of earned wages; the workers pay approximately one-third, and the Company two-thirds, of the dues.
7. There are also more than 200 cooperative credit banks and about 600 rural cooperative savings banks; the latter take a leading part in operating the *State Agricultural Credit Service,* which is largely responsible for advances made in the economic, social and technical aspects of Spanish agriculture.
8. *Benefits from Cooperatives:*
   a. *Legal benefits:* various types of pensions and subsidies, for retirement, widows and orphans, sickness or prolonged illness, health assistance, marriage, families, etc.
   b. *Optional benefits* (i.e., which the cooperative *may* award)*:* labor credits and educational scholarships to the individual petitioner.
   c. *"Labor Universities,"* in the larger cities of Spain, are financed through cooperative contributions in order to place cultural activities within the reach of workers as well as to equip them for attaining better jobs and positions.
9. Much of the work and activities of the cooperatives are encouraged and supported by the *Labor Cooperative Service* within the national *Ministry of Labor.*
10. Also involved in economic coordination are the *Office of Coordination and Economic Planning* and the special ministerial Committees for Economic Affairs, Cultural Affairs, Social Questions, etc.

a. The Special Committees are designed to coordinate the actions of the ministries forming their membership, for any final decisions by the Cabinet.

b. Emphasis on ministerial coordination, particularly in the economic field, is construed to mean a recognition that economic developments in Spain have reached a point where periodic evaluations are essential to achieve stability and also to adopt further improved methods to ensure the proper functioning of the Nation's economy.

11. In sum, the *"cooperative formula"* has been applied, with varying degrees of success, to such productive areas as agriculture, handicrafts, retail trades, and fishing; and the *"cooperative movement"* is asserted to be the largest privately-constituted association Spain has ever known.

VII. JUDICIAL SYSTEM

A. ORGANIZATION OF COURTS

1. *Supreme Court*, which is divided into five Divisions:
   a. Court of Cassation: has appellate jurisdiction in private actions, civil and commercial.
   b. Court of Criminal Appeal: has appellate jurisdiction in criminal cases.
   c. Administrative Court (1): hears appeals against ministerial orders.
   d. Administrative Court (2): hears appeals against the decisions of provincial administrative courts.
   e. Social Court: has jurisdiction in cases involving social legislation and hears appeals against the decisions of labor courts.

2. *Regional courts* exercise appellate jurisdiction over the decisions of lower courts.

3. *District (provincial) courts* have original jurisdiction in civil and criminal cases and can review the decisions of local courts.

4. *Municipal or community courts* settle cases involving petty offenses and minor civil disputes.
   a. Justices of the Peace.

5. *Other courts*
   a. Ecclesiastical courts have exclusive jurisdiction in matrimonial affairs in Dioceses and Archdioceses.
      (1) Tribunal of the Rota, established in 1947 by agreement between the Spanish Government and the Holy See, has final jurisdiction in religious matters.
   b. Provincial administrative courts: hear cases involving ordinary administrative personnel; their decisions may be reviewed by the Fourth Division of the Supreme Court or by the Council of Ministers or Council of State.
   c. Military courts: settle disputes involving military personnel; no trial by jury; decisions are seldom, if ever, appealed to higher State authority.
   d. Labor (industrial arbitration) courts.
   e. Commercial and fiscal courts.
   f. Water courts.

B. JUDICIAL PRINCIPLES AND PERSONNEL
   1. Judges are represented in the National Congress *(Cortes)* and may influence, or be influenced by, the actions of that body.
   2. Organization and proceedings of the judiciary are determined, not by specific constitutional provisions, but by statutory enactments and local customs.
   3. Judges are selected by competitive examinations and confirmed by the Ministry of Justice and the Chief of the State; they
      a. Must take an unconditional oath of loyalty and allegiance to *el Caudillo* and the National Movement; the "security of the regime" is superior to the rights and interests of individual citizens and groups;
      b. Maintain their own representative structures, according to their particular judicial function and responsibility;
      c. Apply codified law (civil, criminal, commercial, municipal, etc.) and local traditions in deciding cases.
      d. Present decisions may have "persuasive influence" in future cases.
      e. Upon request, judges may advise or assist the "Gov-

ernment" in the framing of legislation (as may the Council of State).

    f. Enjoy the normal perquisites and tenure in office, but may be removed, suspended, or transferred in accordance with law.

4. There has been a recent trend towards further unification and standardization of the Spanish law, but the reform of the judicial organization and procedures is very slow.

VIII. LOCAL GOVERNMENT

A. Spanish local administration is composed of two types of division: Provinces and Municipalities. A single Act, revised on June 24, 1955, establishes the system for both and serves as a "Code of Local Administration." Theoretically, the institutions of local administration are independent, which would imply an important consequence, namely, that acts of local corporations in matters over which they have jurisdiction are enforceable without higher authorization or approval. However, in fact, they are always subject to the direction or revision of the central authorities. Illegal acts of local administration are presumably the subject of complaint by citizens before the provincial Courts of Administrative Disputes.

B. PROVINCES

1. Approximately fifty in number, with each one consisting of a group of municipalities or local areas.

2. Headed by a Civil Governor *(Intendente)*, appointed by and responsible to, the Minister of the Interior; the Governor
   a. Exercises delegated State authority and functions;
   b. Maintains the public order;
   c. Supervises the actions of the Provincial government.

3. Governed through an appointive and elective Provincial Council *(Diputación provincial)*, composed of a president, *ex offico*, and elected members (the representatives of intellectual, professional, and economic bodies), a secretariat, various committees and commissions, and divers administrative and technical personnel; the Council exercises various powers delegated or permitted by national law, such as to

Chart 34. AGENCIES OF PROVINCIAL AND LOCAL GOVERNMENT IN SPAIN

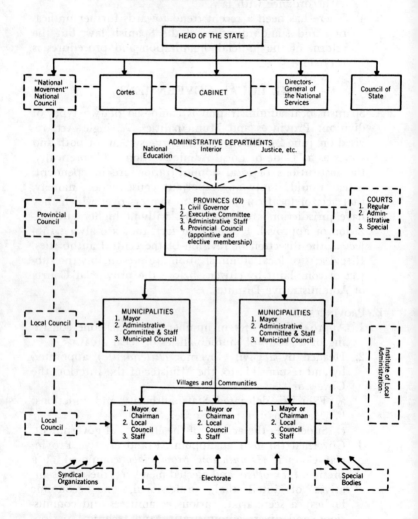

   a. Pass ordinary ordinances;
   b. Enact the provincial budget;
   c. Levy and collect taxes;
   d. Administer the public health;
   e. Help maintain the provincial public order;
   f. Represent (through part of its elective membership) and oversee the interests of local governments.
4. Provincial Councillors serve a six-year term, with one-half of their number changing every three years; they are frequently reelected to office.

C. MUNICIPALITIES
   1. Approximately 9300 in number, all of which are under provincial and/or national control.
   2. Headed by a Mayor *(Alcalde)*, who is both the agent of the provincial government and the local executive officer; he performs duties as prescribed by law.
   3. Governed through an elective Municipal Council *(Diputación)*, consisting of a chairman (the Mayor), elected members (the representatives of households, various syndical organizations, and economic, cultural, and professional bodies), a small secretariat, several committees, and administrative and staff personnel; the Council and its organs perform compulsory duties under the law, such as to
      a. Pass ordinances and enforce laws;
      b. Approve the local budget;
      c. Assess and collect taxes;
      d. Maintain the municipal properties.
   4. Municipal and town Councillors *(Concejales)* receive no regular pay and serve a two- or four-year term, with frequent reelection to office.
   5. An Institute of Local Administration, in Madrid, helps train local officials and also conducts studies on different aspects of municipal and town administration.

SELECTED READINGS

Altamire y Crevea, Rafael, *A History of Spain*. New York: D. Van Nostrand Company, Inc., 1949.
Buckley, P., *The Hispanic World*. New York: Holt, Rinehart & Winston, Inc., 1963.

Cleugh, James, *Spain in the Modern World*. New York: Alfred A. Knopf, Inc., 1953.

Coles, S. F., *Franco of Spain*. London: Burns and MacEachern, 1956.

Crow, J. A., *Spain: the Root and the Flower*. New York: Harper & Row, 1963.

Fairman, C., *Another Spain*. Toronto: Nelson and Sons, 1952.

Fernsworth, Lawrence, *Spain's Struggle for Freedom*. Boston: Beacon Press, 1957.

Hughes, Emmet John, *Report from Spain*. New York: Henry Holt and Company, 1957.

Hodgson, R. M., *Spain Resurgent*. Toronto: Macmillan Company, 1953.

La Souchere, E. de, *An Explanation of Spain*. New York: Random House, Inc., 1964.

Loder, D., *Land and People of Spain*. Toronto: Longmans, Green & Company, Inc., 1955.

de Madariaga, Salvador, *Spain, a Modern History*. New York: Frederick A. Praeger, Inc., 1959.

Manuel, Frank, *Politics of Modern Spain*. New York: McGraw-Hill Book Company, Inc., 1938.

Martin, R. C., *Spain*. New York: Macmillan Company, 1955.

Ogrizek, D., ed., *Spain*. New York: McGraw-Hill Book Company, Inc., 1955.

Oppenhejm, R., *Spain in the Looking Glass*. Toronto: Nelson and Sons, 1955.

Pattee, Richard, *This is Spain*. Milwaukee: Bruce Publishing Company, 1951.

Payne, Stanley G., *Falange*. Stanford: Stanford University Press, 1961.

Peers, Edgar Allison, *Spain*. London: Methuen, 1956.

Sanchez, J. M., *Reform and Reaction*. Durham: University of North Carolina Press, 1964.

Sitwell, S., *Spain*. New York: Frederick A. Praeger, Inc., 1953.

Spanish Information Service, *Spain*. Madrid: undated.

Chapter VII

SWEDEN

POPULATION: 8,000,000 (1965)
AREA: 173,665 sq. miles
CAPITAL: Stockholm

I. CHRONOLOGY

800—Beginning of the Viking Period of conquest and exploration.

1050–1250—Long and severe internal conflicts, chiefly between Christianity and paganism.

1350—Old provincial laws replaced by a National Law Code.

1397—Attempt made by a formal pact ("Union of Kalmar") to achieve a Scandinavian Union.

1435—Convening of the first Parliament *(Riksdag)* on the European continent.

1523—Birthdate of the modern Swedish monarchy with the coronation of Gustavus Vasa (Gustavus I).

1617—Promulgation of the first Organic Law of the *Riksdag.*

1697–1718—Reign of Charles XII ("the Lion of the North") and the collapse of the Swedish empire.

1719–1720—Preparation of the first comprehensive and systematic written constitution of the modern world.

1772—"Bloodless revolution" by Gustavus III ends the sovereignty of the Four Estates in the *Riksdag.*

1789—Acts of Union and Settlement begin the period of Gustavian absolutism (Gustavus III and IV).

1809—*Coup d'état* results in deposition of the king and the preparation of a new constitution ("Instrument of Government").

1818—Beginning of the Bernadotte dynasty under Jean Baptiste Jules Bernadotte (Charles XIV John) of Pontecorvo.

1866—"Four Estates" replaced by a bicameral *Riksdag*.

1905—End of the Union (since 1814) with Norway.

1920—First Labor Government assumes office.

1946–1949—Sweden joins the United Nations, the Marshall Plan, and the Council of Europe but does not join the Atlantic Community.

1950—Death of Gustavus V; his son, Gustavus VI Adolf, becomes King.

1953—Dag Hammarskjöld is elected Secretary-General of the United Nations.

1959—Sweden enters the European Free Trade Association (EFTA).

1964—Prime Minister Tage Erlander's Social Democrats retain majority in Lower House of *Riksdag* (Parliament) as result of General Elections.

II. SWEDISH CONSTITUTION

A. FUNDAMENTAL LAWS

1. *Instrument of Government*, 1809: this is the oldest written constitution in Europe still in force; it has been amended several times and work is now well-advanced on a major revision under a Royal Commission on Constitutional Reform to bring the whole constitution up to date.

2. *Act of Succession*, 1810: ". . . according to which the male heirs begotten by His Noble-Born Highness, the chosen Crown Prince of the realm of Sweden . . . shall have the right to the Royal Swedish throne and to accede to the government of Sweden." (*Preamble*)

3. *Organic Law of the Riksdag*, 1866: this law abolished the former "Four Estates" (i.e., nobility, clergy, burghers and peasants) and recreated the Parliament *(Riksdag)* in its present bicameral form; several electoral restrictions have since been removed to broaden the representative character of the Parliament.

4. *Freedom of the Press Act*, 1949: supplements the original law enacted in 1812, and guarantees complete freedom of the press.

B. FUNDAMENTAL PRINCIPLES OF GOVERNMENT

1. Sweden is governed by a King, a hereditary monarch, who "shall always belong to the pure Evangelical faith"

(Instrument of Government, Arts. 1–2); his authority and powers are "balanced" by constitutional and legal controls.

2. Popular sovereignty (although not mentioned *per se* in the Fundamental Laws) is expressed through free elections and representative legislative assemblies on each level of the State.

3. Multiparty Cabinet system, which operates without political instability, weakness, or frequent changes in the "Government."

4. Strong parliamentary authority, whose constitutional powers cannot be abrogated or encroached upon by the executive or judicial branches of government.

5. An independent judiciary, which serves as the guardian of the law and the legal rights of the citizenry.

6. Unitary system of a central and local governments.

7. Social and economic progress and development within the framework of private enterprise and democratic institutions and procedures.

C. Rights of the Citizen
1. Based upon the Fundamental Laws and subsequent statutory enactments; they include
   a. Rights and duties of citizenship.
   b. Freedom of speech, press, assembly, association, and petition.
   c. Freedom of individual conscience and religious beliefs.
   d. Protection of one's person, private property, and residence.
   e. Right to vote (at age 21) and to hold a seat in the *Riksdag* (at age 23), and to participate in referenda.
   f. Right to normal legal and judicial processes.
   g. Duty to perform individual services (e.g., military training and defense), as required by law.

D. Procedures for Constitutional Amendment
1. "Instrument of Government" and the other Constitutional Laws of the kingdom cannot be altered or replaced except by decision of the King and two ordinary sessions of the *Riksdag*" (Instrument of Government, Art. 81); this involves a

Chart 35. STRUCTURE OF THE SWEDISH GOVERNMENT

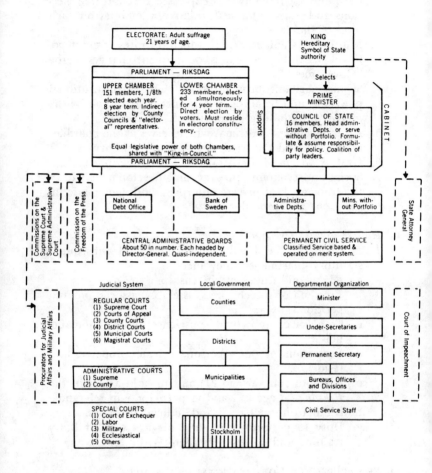

   a. Proposal to amend the Constitution passed by an ordinary majority vote in the two chambers of the *Riksdag* (Parliament).

   b. New general elections to the *Riksdag.*

   c. Ratification of the proposed amendment by an ordinary majority vote in the two chambers of the new *Riksdag.*

   d. Approval and public proclamation of the amendment of the King.

      (1) The King does not exercise his theoretical power to veto a proposed constitutional amendment.

      (2) Either the *Riksdag* or the "King-in-Council" (Council of State) can propose a constitutional amendment.

III. THE KING AND GOVERNMENT

A. THE KING

  1. *Succession to the Throne*

   a. Male line of the House of Bernadotte.

   b. *Riksdag* chooses a new Royal house should a Royal dynasty become extinct; the Council of State (cabinet) performs the powers of regency until the new King is elected.

   c. A Regent (or the Council of State when there is no Regent) conducts the affairs of State when the incumbent King is unable to function in Government.

   d. Princes of the Royal house marry only with the consent of the King, as recommended by the Council of State; to do otherwise would result in forfeiture of all hereditary rights to the Crown, for the particular Prince, his children, and his descendants.

  2. *Status and functions*

Although the King theoretically exercises the executive, legislative, and judicial powers of Government, he is, in actual practice, limited by constitutional interpretations and by the fact that virtually all his acts are recommended or approved by the Council of State, which body is responsible to the people's representatives in the national *Riksdag*. In this respect, plus the great personal prestige and symbolic importance he enjoys, the Swedish King is very similar to the British Monarch. The King formally

   a. "Governs the Realm" and represents the unity of the Swedish Nation.

   b. Nominates the Prime Minister and the Councillors of State.

   c. Presides over Council meetings and advises (and is advised by) its members.

   d. Appoints and receives diplomatic representatives and envoys.

   e. Enters into agreements with foreign States.

   f. Declares war and concludes peace in the name of the Swedish State.

   g. Serves as Commander in Chief of the Armed Forces.

   h. Proclaims emergency measures in times of stress and on behalf of the Nation's defense.

   i. Appoints the State Attorney General and other high State and Church officials.

   j. Grants awards and confers honors and titles of nobility.

   k. Confers naturalized citizenship on foreign-born men and women.

   l. Grants pardons in criminal cases, commutes death sentences, restores honors, and returns forfeited property.

   m. Convenes the *Riksdag* and addresses messages and proposals to it (on "that which has passeth in the realm" during the previous legislative session) and to the State Church Assembly and other public bodies.

   n. Shares the ordinance and lawmaking powers with the Council of State and *Riksdag*.

   o. Refers various matters to the State Law Council, consisting of three judges from the Supreme Court and one judge from the Supreme Administrative Court, for its legal opinion and advice.

   p. Participates in constitutional amendments.

   q. Heads, and must be a member of, the State Evangelical Church.

      (1) ". . . the King shall always profess the pure evangelical faith, as adopted . . . in the unaltered Augsburg Confession and in the Reso-

lution of the Uppsala Meeting of the year 1593 [and] princes of the Royal family shall be brought up in that same faith and within the realm. Any member of the Royal family not professing this faith shall be excluded from all rights of succession" (Art. 4, *Act of Succession*, 1810, as Amended).

r. Travels and represents the Swedish State abroad.

s. Approves the marriage of Royal Princes.

t. Performs significant social and ceremonial functions.

u. Enjoys personal inviolability and freedom from any prosecution for his actions.

v. Instrument of Government (Arts. 4 and 45) prohibits members and relatives of the Royal family from holding any incompatible "appanage or civil office."

B. Prime Minister and Council of State

1. *Selection, composition, organization, and tenure*

   a. Prime Minister and Councillors of State are nominated by the King and supported by the *Riksdag*; they are usually (but not always) Members of Parliament.

   b. Prime Minister is the leader of the strongest party in the *Riksdag* and the members of his Council (or "cabinet") represent the political parties roughly in proportion to their total party membership in the legislative body.

   c. Council of State includes eleven Councillors, each in charge of a Government Department, and three Councillors-without-Portfolio.

      (1) The eleven Departments (or Ministries) are: Foreign Affairs, Justice, Defense, Social Affairs, Communications, Finance, Education and Ecclesiastical Affairs, Agriculture, Commerce, Interior Affairs, and Civil Service.

      (2) Councillors-without-Portfolio sometimes serve as Deputy Ministers or perform other special duties, such as to direct the State's information activities and study various aspects of government reform.

(3) General organization of each Department includes the Minister, the Under-Secretary, the Permanent Secretary (who is always a ranking member of the civil service), and numerous bureaus, offices, and divisions.

    (a) Certain Departments, such as Foreign Affairs, Defense, and Interior and Health, have a special organizational setup for administration.

d. National Debt Office and the Bank of Sweden are completely independent of the Council of State.

e. Council of State remains in office until new parliamentary elections are held, or until it collectively resigns.

f. Councillors have the usual perquisites, privileges, and liabilities of their State office.

2. *Functions and powers*

a. Inform and advise the King on all State affairs.

b. Propose and countersign the Acts of the King (See Section A-2 above).

    (1) When a Minister countersigns a Royal Act, he assumes all legal and political responsibility for its constitutionality and also the faithful execution of its provisions.

c. Convene in Council meetings (with the King present and presiding) and in Cabinet meetings (in the absence of the King and with the Prime Minister presiding) to decide both the smaller and larger issues of State policy and interest.

d. Direct the various branches of State administration, largely through the Central Administrative Boards.

e. Issue and execute the King's Orders-in-Council.

f. Provide legislative initiative and direction in the *Riksdag*.

g. Assume full Cabinet responsibility to the *Riksdag* for governmental policy and actions.

h. Exercise the powers of a regency when the Royal house becomes extinct, or when an incumbent King is unable to perform his duties, and there is no Regent, until the *Riksdag* meets to determine the new Royal dynasty or otherwise provides for a regent.

i. Perform miscellaneous other functions stipulated by law.

C. CENTRAL ADMINISTRATIVE BOARDS

1. Approximately fifty quasi-independent central administrative boards, such as the Army Administration Board, the Board of Education, the Housing Board, the Medical Board, the Social Welfare Board, and the State Railways Board.

   a. Take orders only from the King-in-Council and not directly from an individual Minister who may be incidentally interested in their particular function or responsibility.

   b. Usually headed by some outstanding and high-ranking member of the Permanent Civil Service and have an organization that normally includes a Director-General, several assistants to this office, various Staff personnel, and a number of bureaus and divisions; some boards maintain County and District offices to supervise the County and local administration of their duties.

   c. Serve occasionally as administrative tribunals to examine citizen appeals against the rulings of local authorities or subordinate officials in the County governments.

2. Boards submit annual reports and budgetary estimates to the national government and, in general, function to "guard and promote" divers services of interest and benefit to Swedish citizens.

3. A *National Office of Public Accounts* is concerned with post-audits, and the agency or official authorizing payment of public monies is responsible for its being in accordance with the executive budget and with the rules and regulations issued with regard to its application.

D. CIVIL SERVICE

1. The large-scale District, County, and National bureaucracy is essentially a "classified service" based on the merit, rather than spoils, system.

2. Except for a few special "positions of confidence" (which lie outside the regular civil service regulations),

   security and permanence of employment is guaranteed.

    a. No arbitrary dismissals from the civil service, as an employee can be separated only for cause and after a fair hearing.

    b. Various representative employee organizations are concerned with conditions of work and other aspects of public personnel administration of interest to their members.

3. Strict supervision of the activities of civil servants is maintained and citizen complaints against either an unlawful action or the gross negligence of a civil servant are investigated by the State Attorney General's office.

    a. Procurator for Military Affairs and the Procurator for Judicial Affairs (who are responsible to the *Riksdag*) have similar responsibilities relating to the actions of military and civil courts.

    b. Freedom of the Press Act, 1949, requires the State to permit citizens to examine, freely, all public authority documents.

4. Continuous efforts are made to achieve greater efficiency and economy in the work of the civil service.

IV. POLITICAL PARTIES

A. GENERAL CHARACTERISTICS OF THE PARTY SYSTEM

1. Long-standing tradition of free and democratic political parties.

2. Multiparty system, with considerable unity and strength in party organization and membership and a sense of "responsibility" generally prevailing among the parties.

3. Individual voter has fairly wide choice of able party leaders and rather definitive party platforms and policies.

4. Close relationship between socio-economic interests and party patterns and activities.

5. Except for the Communist party (which also enjoys a legal existence), there is general agreement among the political parties on the basic forms and institutions of Government.

6. Parties originated in the *Riksdag* and later emerged also from the unrepresented sections of the populace.

7. Active membership in the local and national party organizations is very important to the individual politician who would be elected to public office.

B. LEADING PARTIES (in the order of their recent numerical representation in the bicameral *Riksdag*)

1. *Social Democratic Party:* a reformist, moderate, socialist party which supports social reform, the levelling of incomes, and various State controls; the political supremacy of this party seems to ensure the continuous development of "social welfare" (See Section VIII, below) in Sweden rather much in advance of that in the rest of western Europe as a whole.

2. *Liberal Party:* a "social-liberal" party which promotes various social welfare policies and individual initiative and freedom of enterprise.

3. *Center (Peasant) Party:* an extremely well-organized party which seeks important concessions to agricultural interests in return for its support of the welfare programs of the Social Democrats.

4. *Conservative Party:* "the party of the Right" which has in the past opposed electoral and social reforms and extensive anti-unemployment measures, and favors a strong national defense policy.

5. *Communist Party:* a party which reflects the Moscow-directed international Communist movement, and is largely a dissident labor group with only a small representation in the *Riksdag*.

C. PARTY ORGANIZATION

1. Includes the national chairman, the national committee, the national party congress (which is frequently supported by the auxiliary associations), the County constituency organizations, and the District and local political clubs.

2. Each party has its own method of nominating candidates to public office.

3. Sources and expenditure of party funds and the conduct of campaigns and elections are regulated by national law and established tradition.

4. Most of the parties represented in the *Riksdag* maintain a parliamentary party organization which has rather close ties with the extra-parliamentary (or national) party organization.

   a. The parliamentary party organization, or *Riksdag group (Riksdagsgruppen)*, consists of the members of a party in both houses who meet once a week to discuss questions in the present legislative session of interest to the party.

   b. The executive of the parliamentary party is called the *Council of Confidence (Förtroenderadet)*, consisting of 10–15 party leaders who are concerned chiefly with the nomination of party members for seats on parliamentary committees and the preparation of questions for discussion at the party meeting; frequently, the Council makes decisions at the meeting on behalf the entire parliamentary party.

   c. The leader of the national party organization is usually elected to the post of *Chairman* of the Parliamentary party.

   d. The parliamentary party *Office,* headed by a *Secretary* elected from among party members either within or outside the *Riksdag,* is of particular importance to the (non-Communist) "Opposition" parties who prepare most of the "private members' motions" and "questions" that are raised in the *Riksdag.*

   e. No less than in other parliamentary systems, party loyalty and discipline by the individual member is important and may determine one's obtaining a desired committee assignment, or position in the "Government" (if one's party holds office), or even reelection in the next General Election.

D. PARTY REPRESENTATION IN THE RIKSDAG
   1. *Upper Chamber* (1965)

Social Democrats	78	members
Liberals	26	"
Conservatives	26	"
Center (Peasant) Party	10	"
Communists	2	"
Total:	151	members

2. *Lower Chamber* (elected September, 1964)

Social Democrats	113	members
Liberals	43	"
Center (Peasant) Party	36	"
Conservatives	33	"
Communists	8	"

Total: 233 members

E. AUXILIARY ASSOCIATIONS

1. Special interest groups which have influence in the "Government" and/or representation in the *Riksdag.*
2. Approximately 147,000 organizations with a total membership of seven—eight million, including unions, cooperative societies, political groups, ideological associations, etc.
3. Two-thirds of Swedish men and a far smaller proportion of women belong to one or more organizations.
4. All of the auxiliary associations favor a better informed public and encourage their members to play a more active role in public affairs.
5. Important associations include the
   a. *National Confederation of Swedish Trade Unions* (LOS): the largest pressure group in Sweden; favors collective bargaining on behalf of manual workers and improvements in their working conditions; has forty-one member unions, with approximately one-and-a-half million members.
   b. *Swedish Employers Confederation* (SAF): represents more than 25,000 employers in collective bargaining with LOS on wages, working hours, and unemployment (under 2%), based on an agreement in 1938 setting the pattern for collective bargaining and for labor relations as a whole; "lockouts" (i.e., the closing of a business or wholesale dismissal of employees by the employer because the employees refuse to accept his terms or because the employer refuses to operate on terms set by a union) and strikes are infrequent.

NOTE: Sweden has an elaborate system for avoiding labor disputes. Over the past thirty years there have only been two serious conflicts. The law provides facilities for negotiations. If preliminary negotiations fail, employees are not allowed to strike until they have officially given a week's notice. This week is spent in efforts to avert conflict and, at this stage, the negotiations are led by a Government-appointed mediator or group of mediators. The right to resort to conflict measures is subject to certain limitations by law. Thus, while a labor agreement is still in force, no conflict measures may be taken in a dispute over the interpretation of the existing agreement. Actions taken in sympathy with illegal measures are not permitted. A special court—the Labor Court—has been set up to settle disputes over the interpretation of existing collective agreements. Of the court's seven members, two are proposed by the employers' organizations and two by the employees' organizations.

    c. *Swedish Central Organization of Salaried Employees* (TCO): organization for salaried employees and "white-collar" workers; rather politically-neutral; has thirty-three unions, with approximately 500,000 members.

    d. *Swedish Confederation of Professional Associations* (SACO): seceded from TCO; represents the legal, medical and other professions; has about 75,000 members.

    e. *Federation of Swedish Farmers' Association* (SLA) and *Swedish Farmers' Union* (RLF) represent various agricultural and cooperative interests.

    f. *Swedish Central Organization of Civil Servants* (SR): represents the interests of the public administrative bureaucracy, with about 20,000 members.

6. Various other non-conformist religious groups, sports clubs, women's organizations, adult education societies (some politically-affiliated, others not), temperance groups, charities, etc.

V. NATIONAL PARLIAMENT *(Riksdag)*

A. DESCRIPTIVE FEATURES OF THE RIKSDAG

    1. "The *Riksdag* represents the Swedish people" (The Instrument of Government, Art. 49).

2. Bicameral Parliament consists of an Upper Chamber and a Lower Chamber, both of which have approximately the same political composition and enjoy complete equality under the Constitution.

3. Members of both legislative Chambers are elected through a system of proportional representation, to secure a distribution of seats in strict proportion to the individual party's voting strength.

   a. The 151 Deputies in the Upper Chamber are elected indirectly by the County Councils and representatives of those cities which do not participate in the Council, for a term of eight years; one-eighth of their number is elected every year.

   b. The 233 Deputies in the Lower Chamber are elected directly by universal adult suffrage (the minimum voting age in Sweden is twenty-one years), for a term of four years; all of their number stand for election every fourth year.

   c. Members of the Lower Chamber must reside in the constituency they represent in the *Riksdag;* this is not a requirement for the members of the Upper Chamber.

   d. Civil servants may sit in the *Riksdag.*

   e. Vacant seats are not filled through by-elections, but by the candidate of the same political party who received the next largest number of votes in the last election.

4. Stability of the electorate and the proportional representation system both contribute to the constancy of relative party strength and membership in the *Riksdag.*

5. Deputies in the *Riksdag* share the legislative power with the King-in-Council (Council of State).

6. *Riksdag* convenes in regular spring and autumn sessions and in extraordinary sessions called either by the King or a fixed number of *Riksdagmen.*

7. King may dissolve either or both Chambers of the *Riksdag* and the members elected in the ensuing special election hold their seats only until the next regularly scheduled general election.

8. *Riksdagmen* receive an annual basic stipend, plus an

additional sum of money for travel and incidental expenses.

B. INTERNAL ORGANIZATION
1. *Speaker and two Deputy Speakers* in each Chamber (comparable with the Speaker in the British House of Commons).
2. *Speaker's Conference:* includes the Speaker, the Deputy Speakers, the chairmen of standing committees, and four members elected from each Chamber.
3. *Secretarial and clerical staff* in each Chamber: usually high-ranking civil servants selected from governmental agencies to perform special duties in each Chamber, as well as their regular responsibilities.
4. *Standing committees* (provided for in the Fundamental Laws, not in the Rules of the Parliament) include Agriculture, Banking, Constitution, Finance, Foreign Affairs, 1st, 2nd, and 3rd Judicial, Ways and Means, and Miscellaneous Affairs.
   a. Members are appointed in proportion to party representations in the *Riksdag.*
   b. Organization consists of the Chairman, a Vice-Chairman, the ordinary members, and a number of clerks chosen from the executive authority or the law courts.
   c. Procedures involve meetings in closed session, no formal minutes, no participation by Cabinet ministers (except those on the special Foreign Affairs Committee), use of various sources of information, no "burying of bills in committee," and usually, decisive recommendations to the Deputies in both Chambers of the *Riksdag.*
   d. Status and functions take on importance in that their small, expert membership (from both Chambers) represent the more important points of view, and they actually do most of the legislative work of the *Riksdag.*
5. *Special committees:* have a composition and organization similar to the standing committees and deal with important problems of interest to several of the latter.
6. *Ad hoc groups:* set up to perform designated adminis-

trative or technical duties in both Chambers of the *Riksdag.*

C. POWERS AND FUNCTIONS

1. Represent all the Swedish people.
2. Convene in ordinary and extraordinary meetings.
3. Pass resolutions and enact legislation.
4. Initiate and ratify constitutional amendments.
5. Call a national referendum.
6. Determine a new Royal house, or select a regent, when necessary.
7. Receive and consider messages and communications from the King and "Government."
8. Approve the Prime Minister and Council of State.
9. Receive special reports from the "Government" (particularly the Ministry for Foreign Affairs).
10. Raise questions and conduct interpellations.
11. Conduct legislative hearings and investigations (cabinet Ministers do not attend committee meetings).
12. Initiate impeachment proceedings against executive and judicial officers.
13. Approve the executive budget.
14. Levy taxes and appropriate monies.
15. Appoint State tax assessors.
16. Select special auditors to examine the state of public finance.
17. Control the Bank of Sweden *(Riksbank)* and the National Debt Office.
18. Approve important agreements with foreign States.
19. Adopt emergency measures for the national defense.
20. Advise the King to remove grossly negligent or incompetent Councillors of State and high court judges, etc.
21. Establish the organization of County and District governments.
22. Safeguard the "ancient privileges" of the realm.
23. Appoint, and receive reports from, special officers and agencies, such as the
    a. Procurator for Military Affairs.
    b. Procurator for Judicial Affairs.
    c. Commissions on the Supreme Court and the Supreme Administrative Court.
    d. Commission on the Freedom of the Press.

24. Perform other miscellaneous functions under the law.
25. Determine the date for adjournment of an ordinary session.

D. ENACTMENT OF LAW

Two unique features in the enactment of a law by the Swedish National Parliament are (1) the use of the Joint Standing Committee, in proposing the support of a bill in both legislative Chambers, and (2) the theory that the members of both Chambers shall simultaneously consider a bill. The Joint Standing Committee consists of Deputies from both Chambers of the *Riksdag*, roughly in proportion to total party strength in that body. Because of the impracticability of a Cabinet Minister defending his bill before both Chambers at the same time, and for certain other considerations, various techniques have been devised to circumvent the "constitutional theory" mentioned above. Theoretically, the King may veto a law enacted by the *Riksdag*, but, in practice, he does not exercise this power.

1. Pursuant to Rules of Procedure adopted jointly by both Chambers and also by each Chamber.
2. *Bills*
   a. "Government Propositions": introduced by Cabinet Ministers.
   b. "Private Member's Motions": introduced by an individual Deputy of a Chamber.
   c. Private members of the *Riksdag* may propose a motion that the "Government" fully investigate (by a Royal Commission and the State Law Council, consisting of three Supreme Court judges and one judge from the Supreme Administrative Court) some serious matter and then present the *Riksdag* with the legislative proposals necessary to deal effectively with the matter.
3. *Legislative procedure*
   a. Meeting called to order by the Speaker in each Chamber.
   b. Introduction of the Government Proposition or Private Member's Motion.

Chart 36. LAW-MAKING PROCESS IN SWEDEN

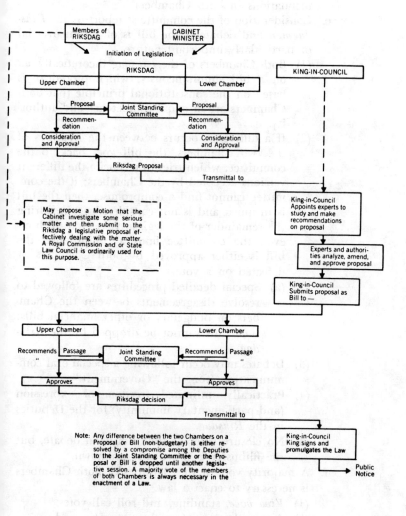

Members of RIKSDAG

CABINET MINISTER

Initiation of Legislation

RIKSDAG

KING-IN-COUNCIL

Upper Chamber

Lower Chamber

Proposal

Joint Standing Committee

Proposal

Recommendation

Recommendation

Consideration and Approval

Consideration and Approval

Riksdag Proposal

Transmittal to

King-in-Council Appoints experts to study and make recommendations on proposal

May propose a Motion that the Cabinet investigate some serious matter and then submit to the Riksdag a legislative proposal effectively dealing with the matter. A Royal Commission and or State Law Council is ordinarily used for this purpose.

Experts and authorities analyze, amend, and approve proposal

King-in-Council Submits proposal as Bill to —

Upper Chamber

Lower Chamber

Recommends Passage

Joint Standing Committee

Recommends Passage

Approves

Approves

Riksdag decision

Transmittal to

King-in-Council King signs and promulgates the Law

Note: Any difference between the two Chambers on a Proposal or Bill (non-budgetary) is either resolved by a compromise among the Deputies to the Joint Standing Committee or the Proposal or Bill is dropped until another legislative session. A majority vote of the members of both Chambers is always necessary in the enactment of a Law.

Public Notice

    c. Reference to the proper standing committee, without any preliminary debate, except in the case of budgetary propositions.

    d. Presentation of the committee's report and recommendations in both Chambers.

    e. Consideration of the committee's report by the *Riksdagmen* and debate if the bill is of a controversial or particularly important nature.

        (1) Both Chambers of the *Riksdag* theoretically act on a bill simultaneously, which procedure is based on the constitutional principle that both Chambers are of equal competence and authority.

        (2) If a difference occurs between the Deputies of the two Chambers, the bill goes back to the committee, which tries to reconcile the different versions accepted by the Chambers; if the committee cannot find a compromise, then the bill is dropped and is not considered again during the remainder of the legislative session; if, however, the committee finds a compromise, the bill is either approved by both Chambers or defeated on a vote.

            (a) Special detailed procedures are followed to resolve disagreements between the Chambers on budgetary or other financial bills; such bills cannot be dropped by the *Riksdag*.

        (3) Debates may occur following a special oral communication from the "Government."

        (4) Practically unlimited freedom of expression (and parliamentary immunity) for the Deputies in the *Riksdag*.

        (5) No closure rules or time limits on debate, but the filibuster is practically unknown.

    f. A majority vote of the Deputies of both Chambers is necessary to enact a law.

        (1) *Viva voce*, standing, and roll call votes.

        (2) A consultative referendum may be used.

    g. King confirms and promulgates the law.

VI. JUDICIAL SYSTEM

A. Theory and Practice of Law and Justice

1. Dual system of nationally integrated ordinary and administrative courts, with a number of additional investigative or adjudicative functionaries.
2. Judicial officials are appointed by the King-in-Council and cannot be removed from office except after full "inquiry and sentence," nor promoted or transferred to other posts except upon their own request.
3. Use of civil, criminal, ecclesiastical, military, and other codes of law.
4. No trial by jury except in press libel suits, but committees of laymen (panels) assist the regular judges in trying and deciding cases.
5. Operation of "procedural due process" in all the courts and fair treatment of prisoners and convicted persons.
6. Emphasis is given to "rehabilitative" rather than "retributive" justice in Swedish penology; corporal punishment is no longer administered, and the death penalty was abolished in 1921.
7. No judicial review of the constitutionality of legislation; the *Riksdag* periodically inquires into the actions of the judiciary, but the judiciary never adjudges the motives and enactments of the *Riksdagmen.*
8. Judicial decisions are issued in the King's name and bear his signature and/or seal.
9. Recent trend toward reform in judicial procedures, particularly in connection with the admissibility of evidence and the interrogation of witnesses.

B. Ordinary Courts

1. *Supreme Court*
   a. Consists of twelve or more Lords Justice appointed by the King in whom the judicial power is, theoretically, vested.
   b. Divided into two or more Sections, composed of three or more judges in each, to decide different types of cases.
   c. Maintains a secretariat to assist its conduct of judicial business.

      d. Exercises both original and appellate jurisdiction, serves as the final court of appeal, and interprets laws.

      e. Three of its members and one from the Supreme Administrative Court comprise the State Law Council, which advises the King, the Council of State, and Royal Commissions on legislative matters; the King may appoint an additional member to this body.

  2. *Courts of Appeal*

      a. Judges are appointed by the King-in-Council.

      b. Hear and decide cases on appeal from the lower courts.

  3. *County courts*

      a. Judges are appointed by the King-in-Council.

      b. Hear cases on appeal from the lower courts and exercise original jurisdiction in serious criminal and civil cases.

  4. *District and Municipal courts*

      a. Judges are appointed by the King-in-Council.

      b. Presided over by a single judge assisted by a committee of laymen who are popularly elected for a six-year term and are unpaid for their services.

      c. Courts in the larger cities may be divided into Sections, such as Police, Family Relations, and Children (juvenile problems).

  5. *Magistrat courts*

      a. King may appoint the local *Burgomaster* (Mayor) to preside over such a court, which normally includes at least two judges and sometimes laymen assistants.

      b. Try and decide small civil and criminal cases.

C. ADMINISTRATIVE COURTS

  1. *Supreme Administrative Court*

      a. Consists of seven or more Lords Justices of Administration appointed by the King and "who shall have held civil office and manifested insight, experience, and honesty" (Instrument of Government, Art. 18).

      b. Examines and decides appeals against the orders

CHART 37. ORGANIZATION OF THE SWEDISH COURT SYSTEM

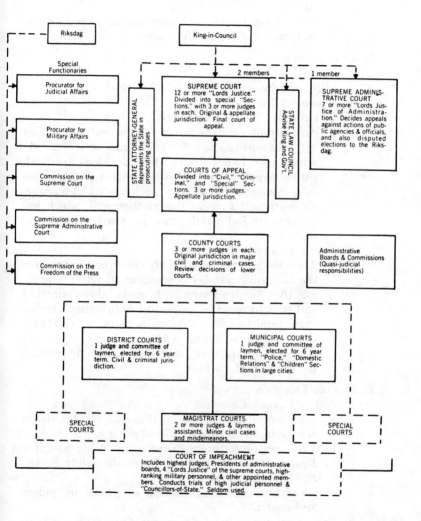

Riksdag

King-in-Council

Special Functionaries

Procurator for Judicial Affairs

Procurator for Military Affairs

Commission on the Supreme Court

Commission on the Supreme Administrative Court

Commission on the Freedom of the Press

STATE ATTORNEY-GENERAL
Represents the State in prosecuting cases

2 members

SUPREME COURT
12 or more "Lords Justice." Divided into special "Sections," with 3 or more judges in each. Original & appellate jurisdiction. Final court of appeal.

STATE LAW COUNCIL
Advise King and Gov't.

1 member

SUPREME ADMINIS-TRATIVE COURT
7 or more "Lords Justice of Administration." Decides appeals against actions of public agencies & officials, and also disputed elections to the Riksdag.

COURTS OF APPEAL
Divided into "Civil," "Criminal," and "Special" Sections. 3 or more judges. Appellate jurisdiction.

COUNTY COURTS
3 or more judges in each. Original jurisdiction in major civil and criminal cases. Review decisions of lower courts.

Administrative Boards & Commissions (Quasi-judicial responsibilities)

DISTRICT COURTS
1 judge and committee of laymen, elected for 6 year term. Civil & criminal jurisdiction.

MUNICIPAL COURTS
1 judge and committee of laymen, elected for 6 year term. "Police," "Domestic Relations" & "Children" Sections in large cities.

SPECIAL COURTS

MAGISTRAT COURTS
2 or more judges & laymen assistants. Minor civil cases and misdemeanors.

SPECIAL COURTS

COURT OF IMPEACHMENT
Includes highest judges, Presidents of administrative boards, 4 "Lords Justice" of the supreme courts, high-ranking military personnel, & other appointed members. Conducts trials of high judicial personnel & "Councillors-of-State." Seldom used.

and actions of the Departments (Ministries) of State and of other public offices.

c. Decides contested elections to the *Riksdag*.

d. Participates (one member) in the State Law Council.

2. Administrative boards and commissions sometimes exercise quasi-adjudicative functions.

D. OTHER COURTS

1. Ecclesiastical courts.

2. Military tribunals.

3. Courts of Exchequer.

4. Labor courts.

a. Any dispute over the interpretation and application of "labor-management" agreements must be submitted to a Labor Court whose decisions are final, without appeal, and which can impose penalties for infringement of labor laws. Both labor and management strongly support this arrangement, which has maintained industrial peace in Sweden for many years.

5. Youth welfare organizations.

a. The Government is especially concerned today with the increasing number of youthful offenders (a problem that Sweden shares with many other countries) and tries to provide "protective upbringing," rather than punishment, by placing them in carefully-selected and well-managed foster homes, boarding schools, and the like, and giving them individual treatment and therapy.

E. SPECIAL FUNCTIONARIES

1. *State Attorney General*

a. A person of considerable legal or judicial experience is appointed to this post by the King.

b. Institutes prosecutions in the name of the King (or Realm) in cases affecting the public safety or the rights of the Crown.

c. Supervises the administration of justice by judges and courts.

2. *Procurator for Judicial Affairs and Procurator for Military Affairs*

a. Appointed by, and responsible to, the *Riksdag*.

    b. Look into matters pertaining to the civil and military courts and their personnel and activities; the Procurators may initiate proceedings against this personnel for negligent or unlawful acts.

    c. May attend the deliberations of the various courts, boards, and tribunals, without a right to be heard by them, and then make reports with appropriate recommendations to the *Riksdag*.

    d. Procurators themselves may be dismissed by the *Riksdag* for cause.

3. *Court of Impeachment* (infrequently used)

    a. Composed of the President of the Svea Court of Appeal (presiding officer), the Presidents of all the administrative boards of the State, either the four senior "Lords Justices" of the Supreme Court or the Supreme Administrative Court, the Commander in Chief of the military establishments in Stockholm, high-ranking naval personnel, and other members of the Svea Court of Appeal and of the State's administrative boards, all of whom are appointed by the King.

    b. Conducts trials of members of the Supreme Court or the Supreme Administrative Court, as initiated either by the State Attorney General or the Procurator for Judicial Affairs, and pronounces sentences in public sessions without right of appeal; only the King may grant a pardon, without the reinstatement of the individual to the service of the realm.

        (1) Similar trials may be conducted involving Councillors of State.

4. *Commission on the Supreme Court and the Commission on the Supreme Administrative Court*

    a. Appointed every fourth year by the *Riksdag* to review and report on the actions of the members of these courts; although the judges can be "graciously discharged" from their offices by the King, the *Riksdag* cannot alter their court decisions.

5. *Commission on the Freedom of the Press*

    a. Appointed every fourth year by the *Riksdag* and consists of at least six prominent private citizens and the Procurator for Judicial Affairs.

    b. Reviews matters relative to the freedom of the press

and renders a report on them, with appropriate recommendations, to the *Riksdag*.

VII. LOCAL GOVERNMENT

A. Districts (Rural and Urban)
  1. *Legislature:* Town Meeting in rural areas and Council in the cities; members popularly elected for a four-year term in office; duties include the
     a. Determination of the local public policy;
     b. Examination and approval of the local executive budget;
     c. Appropriation of funds;
     d. Appointment of a Chairman and/or Mayor and executive and administrative officials;
     e. Enactment of local laws and ordinances;
     f. Miscellaneous other functions.
  2. *Executive authority:* Mayor, executive boards, and administrative staff, all of whom are appointed or approved by the Council.
     a. Mayor represents the District and sometimes has executive, legislative, and judicial responsibilities.
     b. Executive Board presents matters of local interest before the Council and executes its decisions, directs the local administrative services, manages the local properties, etc.
     c. Administrative staff are qualified civil service personnel chosen or approved by the Council to discharge the usual functions of local government.
  3. *Judiciary: Magistrat* courts; special divisions of the District courts
     a. County Boards approve local actions and review appeals against local orders which allegedly encroach upon the citizens' rights.

B. Counties (24)
  1. *Legislature:* County Council; members popularly elected, on the basis of proportional representation, for a four-year term in office; duties include the
     a. Determination of the County public policy;

Chart 38. AGENCIES OF LOCAL GOVERNMENT IN SWEDEN

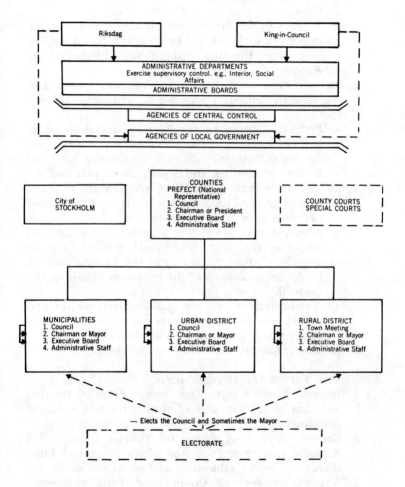

b. Enactment of the County budget and appropriation of funds for County expenditures;

c. Appointment of a Chairman and the members of administrative committees;

d. County ordinances;

e. General supervision of County affairs;

f. Reports to the Prefect, and through him to the national ministries of the Interior and Social Affairs;

g. Election of Deputies to the Upper Chamber of the *Riksdag.*

2. *Executive authority:* Prefect, Chairman or President of the Council, administrative boards, and administrative staff.

a. Prefect is chosen by the King-in-Council to represent the interests of the realm and supervise the execution of national policies in the County; local and County authorities are responsible to him and he, in turn, reports to the King and Council of State.

b. Chairman (or President) represents the County and performs various duties under law.

c. Administrative boards are branches of the national administration (e.g., health and medical care) or agencies ("interim bodies") of the County Council to discharge designated functions on behalf of the Council.

d. Administrative staff are qualified civil service personnel who discharge County functions and services under the general direction of the Council.

3. *Judiciary:* County courts and special courts.

C. RECENT TRENDS AND DEVELOPMENTS

1. Increase in the number and variety of local, District, and County services and administrative and technical personnel.

2. Greater cooperation among the District, County, and National Governments in the administration of functions (e.g., health, education, and social services).

3. National support of County and District interests through such activities as financial subsidies and the maintenance of professional schools of social work and public administration.

4. A plan has recently been introduced which will reduce the number of local governments from roughly 1000 to about 280 in the early 1970's and this, in turn, is expected to strengthen the average local government considerably.

VIII. SOCIAL WELFARE

Sweden is considerably ahead of most States in its social welfare program and provides almost complete protection and care for the citizen "from the cradle to the grave" (or, as one wag put it, "from the womb to the tomb"). Within a social system that encourages individual enterprise and self-reliance, Sweden pursues the "middle way" and administers aid on the basis of need rather than on ability to pay. The basic premise is that a State ultimately benefits from the care provided its citizenry and the social well-being of the individual is collated with the soundness and health of the State, and *vice versa*. Most, if not all, Swedish citizens favor a program of social welfare; the only differences relate to the pace at which it should be further developed. The following brief information is intended only to suggest the scope and contents of Sweden's social welfare program.

A. NORMAL BENEFITS
1. Children: family allowances; health supervision; free holiday transportation and holiday camps; nurseries and play centers; day care in private homes; special advice and assistance by expert child care officers.
2. Education: free public schools for all young people, at all levels; meals and supplies; grants for maintenance, travel, and scholarships; special funds for the training of professional and technical persons; use of public endowments, private funds, and "foundations."
3. Employment: free services by employment exchange offices; special employment services for youth, the disabled, persons in the arts and professions, and merchant seamen.
4. Marriage, maternity, and the home: home-furnishing loans to the newly-wed and for unmarried women with children; assistance and allowances before and after

childbirth; special free services; annual holiday benefits for housewives; rental allowances; public housing facilities.

5. Old age: national retirement pensions; special housing allowances; homes for old people who need permanent care.

B. EMERGENCY BENEFITS

1. Illness and accidents: medical treatment, hospitalization, and therapeutic services; special nursing homes, sanatoria, mental hospitals, summer health resorts, institutions for cripples and the disabled; care for chronic diseases and other disorders.

2. Disablement: public assistance and allowances in obtaining special employments; vocational training and training for work at home; aids (e.g., artificial limbs, hearing devices, seeing-eye dogs), care allowances; pensions and life annuities; public care for families suffering from the loss of the breadwinner.

3. Unemployment: arrangements for emergency or special work (as suggested above); unemployment benefits; travel allowances and allowances to pay for the cost of moving to the place of new employment.

4. Legal aid: free advice not in connection with judicial proceedings; free legal aid and counsel in litigative matters.

5. National service: pay for National Service men; special allowances for dependents of servicemen; life annuities for disabled servicemen or the widows and families of military personnel killed in service.

C. EXTRA ASSISTANCE AND BENEFITS, e.g., further home assistance and supplementary pensions, as provided by law.

SELECTED READINGS

Ames, J., *Co-operative Sweden Today*. Manchester: Co-operative Union, 1952.

Anderson, Ingvar, *A History of Sweden*. New York: Frederick A. Praeger, Inc., 1956.

Andren, Nils, *The Government of Sweden*. Stockholm: Swedish Institute, 1955.

Arneson, Ben A., *The Democratic Monarchies of Scandinavia*. New York: D. Van Nostrand Company, Inc., 1949.

Childs, Marquis William, *Sweden, the Middle Way*. New Haven: Yale University Press, 1948.

Cole, M., and C. Smith, eds., *Democratic Sweden*. London: G. Routledge & Sons, Ltd., 1938.

Fleisher, Wilfred, *Sweden, the Welfare State*. New York: John Day Company, Inc., 1956.

Foreign Ministries of Denmark, Finland, Iceland, Norway, and Sweden, *The Northern Countries*. Stockholm: 1951.

Gathorne-Hardy, G. M., and others, *The Scandinavian States and Finland; a Political and Economic Survey*. London: Royal Institute of International Affairs, 1951.

Harris, Thomas, *Sweden's Unorthodox Co-operatives*. Stockholm: KF, 1949.

Hästad, Elis, *The Parliament of Sweden*. London: Hansard Society, 1957.

Heckscher, Gunnar, *The Swedish Constitution, 1809–1959*. Stockholm: Swedish Institute, 1959.

Hedberg, Anders, *Co-operative Sweden*. Stockholm: KF, 1951.

Hesslen, Gunnar, *Public Administration in Sweden*. Stockholm: Swedish Institute, 1950.

Höjer, Karl J., *Social Welfare in Sweden*. Stockholm: Swedish Institute, 1949.

Kastrup, Allan, *The Making of Sweden*. New York: American-Swedish News Exchange, 1953.

Lundquist, G. (ed.) , *Sweden: Past and Present*. Stockholm: Bonnier, 1948.

Mare, Eric de, *Scandinavia: Sweden, Denmark and Norway*. London: B. T. Batsford, Ltd., 1952.

Ministry of Social Affairs (co-sponsor) , *Freedom and Welfare; Social Patterns in the Northern Countries of Europe*. Stockholm: Swedish Institute, 1953.

Nelson, George R., *Social Welfare in Scandinavia*. Copenhagen: Danish Ministry of Labour and Social Affairs, 1953.

Nilsson, Arne, *Sweden's Way to a Balanced Economy*. Stockholm: Swedish Institute, 1950.

Royal Institute of International Affairs, *The Scandinavian States and Finland*. London: 1951.

Rustow, D. A., *Politics of Compromise*. Princeton: Princeton University Press, 1956.

Social Benefits in Sweden. Stockholm: Swedish Institute, 1959.

Social Sweden. Stockholm: Swedish Institute, 1952.

Strode, Hudson, *Sweden; Model for a World*. New York: Harcourt, Brace & Company, 1949.

Tegner, Göran, *Social Security in Sweden*. Stockholm: Swedish Institute, 1956.

Toyne, S. M., *The Scandinavians in History*. New York: Longmans, Green & Company, Inc., 1949.

Chapter VIII

SWITZERLAND

POPULATION: 6,250,000 (1965)
AREA: 15,944 sq. miles
CAPITAL: Berne

I. CHRONOLOGY

1032—Holy Roman Empire extends its suzerainty over the Swiss people.

1291—Three Cantons of Uri, Schwyz, and Nidwalden unite in a defensive league (the "Eternal Alliance") against the royal House of Hapsburg.

1386–1389—Defeat of Austria at Sempach and Näfels and recognition by her of the "Eternal Alliance."

1499—After six costly battles the Swiss win complete independence from the Holy Roman Empire.

1519—Reformation leads to two-hundred years of religious and political dissensions in Switzerland.

1648—Peace of Westphalia accords international recognition to the emerging Swiss Confederation.

1712—Battle of Villmergen, won by the Protestants, ends the internal struggles.

1798—French forces enter Berne, proclaim the Helvetic Republic, and end the Cantonal system.

1803—Napoleon Bonaparte restores the Confederation under the "Act of Mediation."

1814—Neuchatel, Geneva, and Valais join the Confederation and increase the total number of Swiss Cantons to twenty-two.

1815—Congress of Vienna formally recognizes the Confederation of Switzerland and guarantees its independence and neutrality.

1848—New constitution is adopted after a short civil war between the Liberal Party and the seven Catholic Cantons.

1874—A revised Constitution is adopted by a majority vote in a free plebiscite.

1920—Switzerland joins the League of Nations.

1940—Communist Party is dissolved by a Federal edict.

1948—The Swiss participate in the Marshall Plan.

1960—The country continues to participate in aid to underdeveloped countries on a bilateral, as well as multilateral, basis; becomes a founding member of the European Free Trade Association (EFTA); and appoints parliamentary observers to the sessions of the Consultative Assembly of the Council of Europe.

1961—"Good offices" of Switzerland are accepted in various instances, e.g., American interests in Cuba are (at least temporarily) safeguarded by her, and she is able to assist in negotiations between France and the Provisional Government of Algeria.

1966—Switzerland maintains her traditional neutrality; does not enter the United Nations or the Economic Community of Europe as a full member; provides headquarters for numerous international organizations; and serves as a meeting place for peaceful negotiations by other States.

NOTE: *Committee for Coordination of Information on Switzerland in the United States* (New York): "Switzerland is the only country in the world to have adopted a foreign policy of permanent neutrality. This policy has two principal aspects: (1) keeping out of any 'foreign entanglements' which might lead to war and (2) remaining strong enough to discourage intervention by foreign Powers. At the same time Switzerland recognizes her responsibility towards the international community: she considers that, as a matter of enlightened self-interest and of moral obligation, her neutrality gives rise to the duty of international solidarity. This is why Switzerland has always endeavored to contribute to the peaceful settlement of the problems which arise between nations. She also eagerly participates in the work of international organizations, both humanitarian and otherwise, insofar as it is compatible with her neutrality. Hence today, though she has not joined the

United Nations, she is a member of most of their specialized agencies and she maintains a permanent observer at the U.N.'s seat in New York. . . . Swiss neutrality applies to the State; it does not mean moral neutrality for the individuals composing it. Both citizens and press remain free to express their views and judgment—and do so!"

II. SWISS CONSTITUTION

A. FEDERAL CONSTITUTION OF THE SWISS CONFEDERATION, 1874 (as amended and revised)
   1. Constitutional revisions are proposed by the Deputies in the Federal Assembly (Parliament) or on the initiative of 50,000 Swiss voters; the revisions enter into force when they have been accepted "by the majority of the Swiss citizens taking part in the vote thereon and by the majority of the States" (Art. 123); see IX-A-1 below.

B. FUNDAMENTAL PRINCIPLES OF GOVERNMENT
   1. Switzerland is a democratic State governed by "the rule of law."
   2. Federative Confederation, with a republican form of government.
   3. Will of the people is expressed through direct and universal elections, democratic political parties, representative legislative assemblies, and popular referenda on proposed laws and constitutional revisions.
   4. Bicameral National Parliament, which represents both the people and the States (Cantons), unicameral Cantonal Councils, and in certain Cantons, the town meeting or *Landsgemeinde*, i.e., direct democracy in action.
   5. A plural or collegial executive authority on all levels, but no true cabinet responsibility to the legislature.
   6. Independent judicial organizations, and impartial and democratic legal procedures.
   7. Division of powers between the central authority and the States, with emphasis placed upon cooperation and collaboration between them and among the citizenry in forming, implementing, and safeguarding the national will.

Chart 39. STRUCTURE OF THE SWISS GOVERNMENT

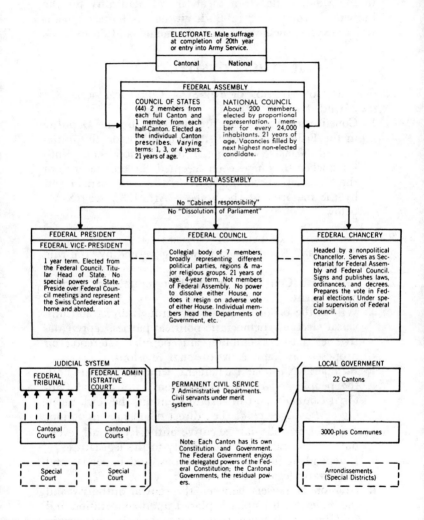

ELECTORATE: Male suffrage at completion of 20th year or entry into Army Service.

| Cantonal | National |

FEDERAL ASSEMBLY

COUNCIL OF STATES (44) 2 members from each full Canton and 1 member from each half-Canton. Elected as the individual Canton prescribes. Varying terms: 1, 3, or 4 years. 21 years of age.

NATIONAL COUNCIL About 200 members, elected by proportional representation. 1 member for every 24,000 inhabitants. 21 years of age. Vacancies filled by next highest non-elected candidate.

FEDERAL ASSEMBLY

No "Cabinet responsibility"
No "Dissolution of Parliament"

FEDERAL PRESIDENT
FEDERAL VICE-PRESIDENT

1 year term. Elected from the Federal Council. Titular Head of State. No special powers of State. Preside over Federal Council meetings and represent the Swiss Confederation at home and abroad.

FEDERAL COUNCIL

Collegial body of 7 members, broadly representing different political parties, regions & major religious groups. 21 years of age. 4-year term. Not members of Federal Assembly. No power to dissolve either House, nor does it resign on adverse vote of either House. Individual members head the Departments of Government, etc.

FEDERAL CHANCERY

Headed by a nonpolitical Chancellor. Serves as Secretariat for Federal Assembly and Federal Council. Signs and publishes laws, ordinances, and decrees. Prepares the vote in Federal elections. Under special supervision of Federal Council.

JUDICIAL SYSTEM

FEDERAL TRIBUNAL

FEDERAL ADMINISTRATIVE COURT

Cantonal Courts

Cantonal Courts

Special Court

Special Court

PERMANENT CIVIL SERVICE 7 Administrative Departments. Civil servants under merit system.

Note: Each Canton has its own Constitution and Government. The Federal Government enjoys the delegated powers of the Federal Constitution; the Cantonal Governments, the residual powers.

LOCAL GOVERNMENT

22 Cantons

3000-plus Communes

Arrondissements (Special Districts)

C. RIGHTS AND DUTIES OF CITIZENS

1. "All Swiss are equal before the law" (Art. 4); there are no privileged persons or groups.
2. Freedom of speech, press, assembly, religion, and the right of petition.
3. Inviolability of personal correspondence and communications.
4. Right of residence and freedom of movement.
5. Protection of the institution of marriage and the security of the home and family.
6. Protection of private property, but real property may be confiscated by the Confederation for the public use, provided just compensation is given to the owners.
7. Right to form associations (e.g., labor unions, business organizations, and professional groups) under law.
8. Freedom of trade and industry under reasonable restrictions.
9. Free and compulsory public primary education.
10. Right of Federal and Cantonal citizenship and to enjoy the rights, privileges, and protections of such citizenship.
11. Protection for *heimatlos* (homeless) persons, aliens, immigrants, and children born out of wedlock.
12. Right of political asylum under law.
13. Protection for the health, safety, morals, and social and economic welfare of the people and citizens (the Federal and Cantonal "police" power).
14. Right to ordinary legal processes and judicial procedures (e.g., legal counsel and trial by jury in criminal cases).
15. No extraordinary tribunals.
16. Prohibitions against both death sentences for political offenses and corporal punishments.
17. Constitutional and legal protections against the arbitrary actions of public officials.
18. Prohibitions against "the Order of Jesuits" or "other religious Orders whose activity is dangerous to the State . . ." (Art. 51); otherwise, the relations between Church and State varies among the Cantons, but there are no ecclesiastical jurisdictions.
19. Protection of the local languages: German, 73%;

French, 21%; Italian, 5%; and Romansch, 1%. Recent Swiss history records no rivalry, as in other continental European countries, among the linguistic minorities; they are not only respected, but their specific culture is protected and fostered with the help of State subsidies. The Swiss take pride in uniting three of the main languages of the world and a great many Swiss speak, read and write two or three languages fluently. The language does not serve to dominate, but is regarded as a means of better understanding.

20. Duty to observe the laws, pay taxes, etc., and "every male Swiss is liable to perform military service" (Art. 18).

21. Right of male citizens to vote and hold public office (see Section III, which follows).

III. SUFFRAGE AND DIRECT LEGISLATION

A. UNIVERSAL MALE SUFFRAGE

1. Normally, at age twenty (it may be higher in some Cantonal elections), when the Swiss male is called up for military training.

2. Nonresidents, the mentally unsound, delinquents, bankrupts, and a few others are disqualified from the franchise.

3. Voting is both a right and a duty, as the Federal Supreme Court will hear complaints from citizens regarding a denial of their right to vote or against irregular election procedures, and at least ten Cantons impose a fine for the male citizen's failure to vote under inexcusable circumstances.

4. There is no general female suffrage, although in some Cantons, such as Basle, Berne, Geneva, Neuchatel, and Vaud) women may participate in the election of local arbitration courts, vote on ecclesiastical matters, and also serve as joint guardians for designated persons and properties.

a. A proposed amendment to the Federal Constitution to give women the right to vote in Federal elections was rejected in a referendum (of men only!) held on February 1, 1959; the vote was 323,727 "for" and

654,939 "against" the proposition advocated by the Federal Assembly (Parliament).

   b. It has been the widespread opinion that a woman's place is in the home and participation in the suffrage should go only with the bearing of arms.

   c. Actually, even though women do not generally vote, they may exert considerable influence among their menfolk, particularly in regard to local and Cantonal affairs.

B. THE INITIATIVE

   1. This means, simply, the right of a designated number (50,000) of qualified male voters to propose the drafting of Federal constitutional legislation or some revision of the Federal Constitution and to secure a popular vote on the proposal; such proposals only take effect if the majority of the Cantons, as well as of the individual voters, decides in their favor.

   2. "Formulated" initiative is a special proposal, in final form, that has to be voted on by the qualified male electorate.

   3. "Unformulated" initiative is a general proposal with a suggestion to the Federal Assembly which, if it is approved by the male electorate, requires the Federal Assembly to draft a law embodying the suggestion; a second popular vote usually follows.

   4. Recent initiatives have included changes in the proportional system of electing Deputies to the National Council (lower house of the Federal Assembly) and a new referendum for treaties negotiated with foreign States.

C. THE REFERENDUM

   1. This means, broadly, with "the consultation of the people," or referral by the Federal Assembly to the male electorate, for its approval or rejection, the draft of a Federal constitutional law or some revision of the Federal Constitution; such drafts only become law if accepted by the majority, not only of all the voters, but also of the Cantons.

   2. "Compulsory" referendum requires that Acts of Gov-

ernment, such as a proposed constitutional revision, be presented to the voters in a popular election.

3. "Optional" referendum occurs when a popular vote is taken on an Act of Government, such as a treaty of lengthy or indefinite term with a foreign State, after a request by eight Cantons or a sufficient number (30,000) of signatures has been collected and produced within 90 days of the Act being passed by the Federal Assembly.

    a. A rather recent example was the petition submitted to a referendum on July 5, 1959, by the seven French-speaking districts in the Jura region of the Canton of Berne that they should be allowed to secede and form a separate Canton. This was rejected by the Canton of Berne as a whole and also by the seven districts concerned, although the majority for rejection in the districts was the smaller.

    b. The importance of this is obvious. There is no supremacy of power even in the Parliament and final authority rests on the general consent of the people. Nor is there "ministerial responsibility," because if one of the houses of the Federal Assembly votes against the Federal Council (the Executive), or if one of its measures is turned down by popular vote, the Federal Council does not resign but will adapt itself to the wishes of the Federal Assembly or the Nation. Referenda occur two or three times a year on the average.

D. GENERAL EVALUATION OF DIRECT LEGISLATION

    1. *Some alleged advantages*

        a. Popular vote keeps the people's representatives "on their toes" and makes them responsive to the expressed will of the people.

        b. Permanent domination (and possible selfish exploitation) of government by any single party or group is avoided by the exercise of direct legislation in the public interest.

        c. Individual citizen's interest is stimulated and he obtains further training and experience in government by this participation.

2. *Some alleged disadvantages*
   a. Popular vote too often reflects selfish individual or group interests and not a genuine expression of the general interest.
   b. Individual voters are not always the best judges of the requirements of public policy and its administration nor of the detailed legislation dealing with such complicated matters.
   c. Too-frequent elections, and the burden of having to be the ultimate legislator and judge, weary the voter of this "excessive" democracy.
3. Initiative and referendum are used in varying degrees by the Federal and Cantonal Governments in Switzerland.

IV. POLITICAL PARTIES

A. GENERAL CHARACTERISTICS OF THE PARTY SYSTEM
   1. Political parties are an integral part of the democratic national tradition, although they are not referred to *per se* in the Federal and Cantonal Constitutions.
   2. Multiparty system, without a one-party "Government" or a one-party "Opposition"; the "Government" is organized and conducted along the lines of peaceful collaboration among the leaders of several political parties and non-violent criticism by other party spokesmen in the Federal Assembly.
   3. All parties (non-Communist) support the basic tenets and practices of Western democracy and want to protect the present Constitution and federative form of Government.
   4. Party membership and principles reflect variegated social, economic, political, and religious interests, accounting for party differences on the objectives of the State and the methods to obtain them.
   5. Prevalence of loose-knit Cantonal (and sometimes National) party organizations, characterized by a general absence of career or professional politicians.
   6. Party system is complemented by popular participation in direct legislation and the new role and influence of special interest groups and associations.

B. LEADING PARTIES

1. *Social Democratic Party:* supports constitutional principles and trade-union socialism, with wider State control over big industries, the railways, the banks, and direct federal taxation; strongly anti-Communist.

2. *Radical Democratic Party:* advocates strong national unity and centralization, various reform and social welfare measures, and State control over railways.

3. *Catholic Conservative Party:* favors federalistic and conservative policies, some social welfare measures, and protection for the doctrines and institutions of the Catholic religion.

4. *Peasant Party:* advances strong national defense and the economic interests of the agrarian class, and, except for a protective customs policy in favor of its members, opposes the Socialists and State intervention in the economic life of the country.

5. *Landesring (Independent) Party:* usually supports the interests of middle-class economic groups, including defense of consumers' interests, the organization of large-scale cooperative societies, reduced living costs, antitrust legislation, and limited State intervention in economic life.

6. *Liberal Democratic Party:* advocates economic freedom for the individual, the representative political institutions of democracy, and a wide interpretation of Cantonal constitutions, but opposes any increase in the powers of the Confederation in relation to the Cantons.

7. *Democrats and Protestant Party:* defends basic Christian tenets and seeks to unite the liberal middle class in order to reconcile its interests with the achievement of social democracy.

8. *Popular Labor Party (Parti du Travail):* extreme Left-wing successor to the former Communist Party which was dissolved by Federal edict in 1940 (but decision revoked in 1945) and espouses the familiar Communist program.

9. Other political groups in the recent past have included a variety of both Left-wing and Right-wing "fronts," "movements," and "unions."

10. The relative importance of all these parties has de-

clined; none of them in the past several decades has held an absolute majority in the country, and while the members of the Federal Council have always been selected from among the largest parties, they have all the same lost their weight in the country. Power and responsibility are more evenly distributed today.

C. PARTY ORGANIZATION
  1. Each of the Swiss political parties has its own organization which normally includes the National Chairman and National Committee (or Staff), the National Party Conference and other meetings, and the various Cantonal and Communal party structures.
  2. Relationships among the Communal, Cantonal, and National party units vary among the political parties, but is considerably more close-knit among the Leftist and Rightist parties.
  3. Each party determines its own method and procedures for nominating candidates to public office, and the Swiss national government is more liberal in its attitude towards the sources and uses of party funds and the conduct of campaigns than governments in several other countries; withal, the federal law, established traditions, and a sense of political propriety ensure a free and honest "electoral process."
  4. Factors which tend to weaken party organization and lessen its importance:
     a. Limited number of nation-wide political issues and controversies.
     b. Federative system of government tends to create citizen interest in Cantonal and Communal affairs.
     c. Personal participation in government through the initiative and referendum.
     d. Increase in the number of representative economic organizations.
     e. Lack of the personality party, so characteristic of the western European and American political systems.
     f. General public indifference to responsible party membership.

D. Party Representation in the Federal Assembly
  1. *Council of States* (1963)

Catholic Conservatives	17	members
Radical Democrats	13	"
Peasant Party	4	"
Social Democrats	3	"
Liberal Democrats	3	"
Independents	2	"
Democrats and Protestant Party	2	"
Total:	44	members

  2. *National Council* (elected October 27, 1963)

Social Democrats	53	members
Radical Democrats	51	"
Catholic Conservatives	48	"
Peasant Party	22	"
Independents	10	"
Democrats and Protestant Party	6	"
Liberal Democrats	6	"
Popular Labor (Communists)	4	"
Total:	200	members

  3. *Hans Huber,* Federal Tribunal: [To summarize], "Neither the Confederation nor the Cantons have practiced the system by which two parties alternate in 'Government' and 'Opposition'. Moreover, it has very rarely happened that elections have caused a landslide in which the absolute majority passed to another party. If one party had or obtained an absolute majority, as a rule it soon handed over a few seats in the 'Government' to one or more minority parties. Switzerland has become the country of coalitions. This system meets the Swiss feeling for collaboration, the contempt of paper party programs and the distaste for violent party strife. On the other hand, the lack of useful criticism from an 'Opposition' recognized as a necessary factor in 'Government' has its drawbacks. Either the 'Opposition' parties in Switzerland are small, so that their criticism is disregarded, or they carry on a destructive or even revolutionary policy. In any case, the Swiss 'Opposition' can never be compared with the Eng-

lish . . . device of H. M. Opposition, the leader of which even receives an official salary."

V. FEDERAL ASSEMBLY

A. DESCRIPTIVE FEATURES OF THE FEDERAL ASSEMBLY
1. ". . . the supreme authority of the Confederation is exercised by the Federal Assembly . . ." (Art. 71).
2. Bicameral Federal Assembly is composed of representatives of varied occupations and interests; such as the farmers, trade unions, business and professional groups, Cantonal officials, etc.
3. There are no instructed Deputies (as in the *Bundesrat* in West Germany).
4. Both houses of the Federal Assembly have equal powers and duties in all legislative matters, and the consent of both is necessary in the enactment of law.
5. As there is no strict separation of powers, the members of the two houses sometimes come together in a joint meeting to perform quasi-executive and judicial functions (See Section "D" below).
6. Federal Assembly never takes a vote of confidence in the "Government" nor does the "Government" ever dissolve the Federal Assembly.

B. NATIONAL COUNCIL *(Nationalrat)*
1. *Membership*
    a. Consists of 200 members (one Councillor for every 24,000 inhabitants), elected directly by the qualified male electorate through a system of proportional representation, with each Canton or half-Canton forming a constituency or electoral college, for a term of four years.
        (1) Use of the secret ballot and no proxy voting.
        (2) Deputies must be lay citizens, at least twenty-one years of age, and not holders of any incompatible Federal office (i.e., membership in the Council of States, the Federal Council, and the Federal Tribunal).
        (3) Vacancies are filled by the non-elected candi-

dates from the same Canton next highest on the electoral list; by-elections are seldom used.

b. Enjoy personal inviolability and parliamentary immunity.

c. Receive a small *per diem* (65 francs) and travel allowances during the legislative session.

2. *Internal organization*

a. President and Vice-President: National Councillors elected by their fellow Deputies for a one-year term; the President is not immediately eligible for re-election, but the Vice-President is eligible for election to the presidency.

b. Regular, full-time, non-legislative staff: the secretaries, clerks, Sergeant-at-Arms, and Chaplain.

c. Standing and special committees.

d. Party structures: informal caucus, committees, leaders, and Swiss equivalent of "whips."

3. *Meetings*

a. Ordinary annual sessions and extraordinary sessions called by the Federal Council on the request of one-fourth of the National Councillors.

b. A quorum is necessary to conduct legislative business and consists of one-half the total number of Deputies plus one.

c. Meetings are public, and minutes and other written records are taken.

d. Rather full liberty is permitted the Deputies in the discharge of their duties, but the President or the house can issue orders or take whatever action is necessary to maintain order in the conduct of the legislative proceedings.

e. Decisions are taken by an absolute majority vote.

f. Extension of the legislative meetings and questions of adjournment are settled by common consent among the membership of the house.

g. Multilingual proceedings.

C. COUNCIL OF STATES (*Ständerat*)

1. *Membership*

a. Consist of forty-four members (two Councillors for every Canton and one Councillor for every half-

CHART 40. ORGANIZATION OF PARLIAMENT AND THE LAW-MAKING PROCESS IN SWITZERLAND

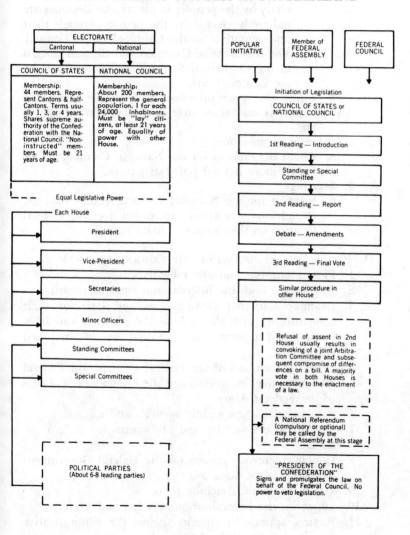

ELECTORATE
Cantonal | National

COUNCIL OF STATES
Membership: 44 members. Represent Cantons & half-Cantons. Terms usually 1, 3, or 4 years. Shares supreme authority of the Confederation with the National Council. "Non-instructed" members. Must be 21 years of age.

NATIONAL COUNCIL
Membership: About 200 members. Represent the general population. 1 for each 24,000 inhabitants. Must be "lay" citizens, at least 21 years of age. Equality of power with other House.

Equal Legislative Power

Each House

President

Vice-President

Secretaries

Minor Officers

Standing Committees

Special Committees

POLITICAL PARTIES
(About 6-8 leading parties)

POPULAR INITIATIVE | Member of FEDERAL ASSEMBLY | FEDERAL COUNCIL

Initiation of Legislation

COUNCIL OF STATES or NATIONAL COUNCIL

1st Reading — Introduction

Standing or Special Committee

2nd Reading — Report

Debate — Amendments

3rd Reading — Final Vote

Similar procedure in other House

Refusal of assent in 2nd House usually results in convoking of a joint Arbitration Committee and subsequent compromise of differences on a bill. A majority vote in both Houses is necessary to the enactment of a law.

A National Referendum (compulsory or optional) may be called by the Federal Assembly at this stage

"PRESIDENT OF THE CONFEDERATION"
Signs and promulgates the law on behalf of the Federal Council. No power to veto legislation.

Canton), selected according to procedures established by each Canton or half-Canton, for varied terms of office (usually one, three, or four years).

   (1) In some Cantons, the Deputies are elected directly by the people; in others, the Deputies are indirectly elected by the people through their representatives in the Cantonal Great Council.

   (2) The eligibility of Cantonal and Clerical officials to the Council of States is also determined by the Cantonal law.

b. Enjoy the same privileges and receive about the same pay and allowances as the National Councillors.

2. *Internal organization*

a. About the same as for the National Council, except for its more limited party structures.

3. *Meetings*

a. Same as for the National Council, except that the extraordinary sessions are called by the Federal Council on the request of five Cantons.

D. POWERS AND FUNCTIONS OF THE FEDERAL ASSEMBLY

1. Pass resolutions and enact legislation.
2. Provide for both the internal and external security.
3. Examine Cantonal Constitutions and laws for their compatibility with the Federal Constitution and laws.
4. Review and approve inter-Cantonal and international agreements.
5. Elect the members of the Federal Council, the Federal Tribunal, the Chancellor, and the Commander-in-Chief of the Federal Army.
6. Appoint other new public agencies and officials.
7. Determine the salaries and allowances for Federal officials.
8. Confer emergency powers on the Federal Government to maintain the State security.
9. Declare war and conclude peace.
10. Supervise the Federal administration and justice.
11. Review appeals by citizens against the administrative decisions of the Federal Council.

12. Approve State loans and expenditures, and audit State financial accounts.
13. Exercise the right of amnesty and issue pardons in cases involving violations of the Federal criminal law.
14. Perform other powers and functions as provided by the Federal Constitution and legislation (See Section VIII below).

E. ENACTMENT OF LAW
   1. *General steps*
      a. Introduction of a bill ("Government" or "Private Member's").
      b. Committee consideration and report.
      c. Discussion and debate.
      d. Voting.
      e. Consideration and approval by the other house.
         (1) An Arbitration Committee is sometimes used to compromise the differences between the two houses on a bill.
      f. Approval (no veto power) and promulgation by the Federal Council (through its President of the Swiss Confederation).
      g. Eight Cantons or 30,000 voters may sign a petition to put the referendum in motion against the Federal law.
   2. *Special legislative procedures*
      a. *Initiative:* the right of a Deputy (or a Canton in the Council of States) to make proposals and motions.
      b. *Postulate:* a resolution inviting the Federal Council to examine a question, without being formally bound by parliamentary instructions; this emanates from one house.
      c. *Motion:* a more detailed and imperative resolution, requesting the Federal Council to draft a legislative bill in accordance with parliamentary instructions; this emanates from both houses.
      d. *Interpellation:* the right of Deputies in the Federal Assembly to ask for explanations from the "Government" and then to debate the responses critically; it is noted again, however, that there is no vote of

confidence, dissolution of Parliament, or resignation of "Government" in Switzerland.

VI. THE GOVERNMENT

A. FEDERAL COUNCIL

1. "The supreme directing and executive authority of the Confederation is exercised by a Federal Council composed of seven members" (Art. 95); neither this collegial body nor the plural executive Council in a Canton are true Cabinets inasmuch as they do not provide political leadership in the legislative body nor can be forced to resign by it.

2. Federal Councillors represent different political parties (and also the linguistic and religious groups), yet they are rather independent of their party units in the Federal Assembly and stand united, as a governing group, on "Government" proposals and actions.

3. There can be only one Federal Councillor from a Canton and it is traditional for the Cantons of Berne, Vaud, and Zurich each to have a permanent seat in the Federal Council.

4. Federal Councillors are usually distinguished former members of the Federal Assembly, and frequently serve more than one term in office; upon their retirements from the Federal Council, they often return to responsible public duty in the Cantons or associate with the headquarters of some international organization in Switzerland.

5. *Membership and organization*

   a. Federal Councillors must be Swiss citizens, at least twenty-one years of age, and able to exercise all their civic rights; they cannot be members of the Federal Assembly nor can they simultaneously practice another profession or career.

   b. Federal Councillors are elected for a four-year term by a joint session of the Federal Assembly, following the elections to the National Council; they receive a regular annual salary (80,000 francs, or approximately $17,500) and travel and expense allowances.

   c. President and Vice-President of the Swiss Confederation (two members of the Federal Council) are elected each year by the Federal Assembly for a one-year term of office.

(1) President is not immediately re-eligible for election to either office, but the Vice-President is usually elected as the new President.

(2) President does not have greater powers than the other Federal Councillors, but he is given a slightly larger annual salary (90,000 francs) to serve as the chairman of Council meetings, represent the Swiss Confederation at home and abroad, and for entertainment purposes.

(3) Actually, the Swiss presidency is such an unprepossessing office that the Swiss jestingly boast of never knowing their President's name. The incumbent receives only $2.00 a day more than his Council salary and is permitted the use of a limousine only for official functions. A former President once said: "Don't call me the Head of the State; I'm only the President." Similar humor is noted in yet another story about the Federal Councillor who was asked why he traveled third-class on the railroad and said, "Because there is no fourth." Thus, a great blessing in Switzerland is that it has no "strong" man, no "indispensable" man, and cannot have under its Constitution (cf. De Gaulle in France, Brezhnev in the U.S.S.R., Franco in Spain and, perhaps, Sunday in Turkey). In short, the Swiss President has few powers and neither he nor the Federal Council as such can veto legislative bills.

d. Federal Councillors head the individual Departments (or ministries) of Government, as determined among themselves, including agriculture and industry; finance and customs; foreign affairs; interior; justice and police; military; and transport, communications and energy.

(1) Expert Directors supervise the various subdivisions and units in the Departments.

(2) Departments are staffed by a superior perma-

nent Civil Service, which is based on the merit
system and equitable personnel procedures.

e. Federal Councillors, as a group, are assisted by the
Federal Chancery, which serves as "the Secretariat of
the Federal Assembly and the Federal Council"
(Art. 105).

f. Recent proposals for the reorganization of the Federal Council have dealt with its size, the qualifications of members, staff assistance, its salaries and
allowances, its powers, and political leadership.

6. *Functions and powers*

a. Conduct Council meetings (a quorum of four Councillors is necessary).

b. Call in and utilize experts for special purposes.

c. Secure the observance of the Federal Constitution
and the laws of the Confederation.

d. Enforce the guarantee of the Cantonal Constitutions.

e. Propose laws, ordinances, and resolutions to the Federal Assembly (they may attend meetings of the
legislature, but they do not vote).

f. Apply Federal laws and ordinances, the judgments
of Federal adjudicative bodies, arbitration awards,
and agreements between Cantons.

g. Appoint designated public officials.

h. Examine and approve inter-Cantonal agreements
and international treaties.

i. Conduct the foreign affairs and international relations of the Confederation.

j. Safeguard the territorial integrity, political independence, and neutrality of the Swiss State.

k. Maintain the internal tranquillity, order, and security.

l. Undertake emergency measures, as permitted by
Federal law.

m. Supervise the various branches of the Federal administration and also those branches of Cantonal
administration placed under its care.

n. Examine and approve certain laws and ordinances
of the Cantons.

o. Prepare the executive budget, administer the finances, and render the accounts of the receipts and expenditures of the Confederation.

p. Submit, periodically, general reports on the domestic and foreign situations to the Federal Assembly.

q. Prepare and present special reports upon the request of one or both houses of the Federal Assembly.

r. Some of the foregoing powers (e.g., the enforcement of the rights of Swiss citizens under the Federal and Cantonal Constitutions, the applications of judicial and arbitral decisions, and the maintenance of the domestic tranquillity) are executed concurrently by the Federal Council and the executive councils in the Cantons.

s. Federal Councillors do not have the power to veto the actions of the Federal Assembly.

B. FEDERAL CHANCERY

1. *Organization and functions*

   a. Chancellor is appointed by the Federal Assembly, at the same time as the Federal Council; he heads the Chancery staff, signs all Federal laws and ordinances, and receives a regular annual salary.

   b. Chancery is organized under Federal law and is especially supervised by the Federal Council; some of the Chancery's duties are to

      (1) Provide the secretarial services for the Federal Assembly and Federal Council;

      (2) Prepare the votes in Federal elections;

      (3) Publish all Federal statutes, ordinances, and decrees.

VII. JUDICIAL SYSTEM

A. THEORY AND PRACTICE OF LAW AND JUSTICE

1. Twofold system of Federal (only one ordinary and one administrative court) and Cantonal courts.

2. Use of single judges, in a few Cantons, and the plural bench, which is the general practice, in all other Cantons.

3. Trials are conducted under the jurisdictions where disputes arise; "no person may be withdrawn from his natural judge" (Art. 58).

4. Equality of all citizens to judicial proceedings.
5. Prevalent use of trial by jury in Federal and Cantonal criminal cases, but not in civil cases.
6. Criminal justice (without capital punishment) is based largely on the Federal Penal Code (1942) which has been amended (1950) with respect to major crimes in order to reinforce the security of the State.
7. Administration of justice is "independent, impartial, informal, and inexpensive."
8. No judicial review of Federal legislation, but Cantonal Constitutions and laws may be examined for their constitutionality by the Federal judges.
9. Judges generally arrange and manage their own affairs and adopt their own rules and regulations.

B. FEDERAL TRIBUNAL *(Bundesgericht)*
   1. *Membership and organization*
      a. Any Swiss citizen who meets the requirements of membership in the National Council may be appointed to the Federal Tribunal; however, a Federal judge cannot hold any other position in the Federal or Cantonal Governments nor follow any other career or profession during his tenure on the Federal Tribunal.
      b. Both the regular judges (26–28) and supplementary judges (11–13) are appointed by the Federal Assembly for a six-year term and are immediately eligible for reappointment, but the President and Vice-President of the Tribunal serve in these capacities for two years and cannot be reelected; most judges serve for as long as they care to serve.
      c. Federal judges are paid a regular annual salary (53,000 francs) and, in due course, are entitled to pension rights under the law.
      d. Federal Tribunal consists of three Divisions, for the administration of criminal, civil, and public law in Federal matters; each Division is composed of from five to ten judges.
      e. Federal Tribunal organizes and directs its own secretariat and staff, and sits at Lausanne.

Chart 41. ORGANIZATION OF THE SWISS COURT SYSTEM

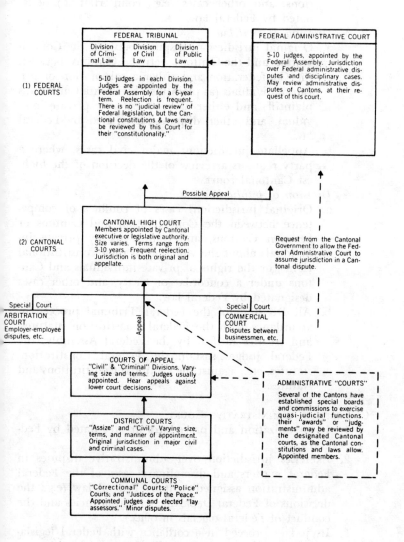

(1) FEDERAL COURTS

FEDERAL TRIBUNAL

Division of Criminal Law	Division of Civil Law	Division of Public Law

5-10 judges in each Division. Judges are appointed by the Federal Assembly for a 6-year term. Reelection is frequent. There is no "judicial review" of Federal legislation, but the Cantional constitutions & laws may be reviewed by this Court for their "constitutionality."

FEDERAL ADMINISTRATIVE COURT

5-10 judges, appointed by the Federal Assembly. Jurisdiction over Federal administrative disputes and disciplinary cases. May review administrative disputes of Cantons, at their request of this court.

Possible Appeal

(2) CANTONAL COURTS

CANTONAL HIGH COURT
Members appointed by Cantonal executive or legislative authority. Size varies. Terms range from 3-10 years. Frequent reelection. Jurisdiction is both original and appellate.

Request from the Cantonal Government to allow the Federal Administrative Court to assume jurisdiction in a Cantonal dispute.

Special Court

ARBITRATION COURT
Employer-employee disputes, etc.

Appeal

Special Court

COMMERCIAL COURT
Disputes between businessmen, etc.

COURTS OF APPEAL
"Civil" & "Criminal" Divisions. Varying size and terms. Judges usually appointed. Hear appeals against lower court decisions.

ADMINISTRATIVE "COURTS"

Several of the Cantons have established special boards and commissions to exercise quasi-judicial functions. their "awards" or "judgments" may be reviewed by the designated Cantonal courts, as the Cantonal constitutions and laws allow. Appointed members.

DISTRICT COURTS
"Assize" and "Civil." Varying size, terms, and manner of appointment. Original jurisdiction in major civil and criminal cases.

COMMUNAL COURTS
"Correctional" Courts; "Police" Courts; and "Justices of the Peace." Appointed judges and elected "lay assessors." Minor disputes.

2. *Division of criminal law*
   a. Original jurisdiction: cases of high treason against the Confederation, violence or revolt against a Federal authority, penal offenses against the law of nations, and other cases (e.g., counterfeiting) designated by Federal law.
3. *Division of civil law*
   a. Original jurisdiction: disputes between the Confederation and the Cantons, between Cantons, between the Confederation and either a corporation or private individuals (as plaintiffs), between a Canton (as plaintiff) and either a corporation or private individual, and other disputes designated by Federal law.
   b. Appellate jurisdiction: major civil cases, where a party requests a review of the decision of the highest Cantonal court.
4. *Division of public law*
   a. Original jurisdiction: cases of conflicts of competence between the Confederation and Cantons or between Cantons, and complaints by private individuals about the violation of their constitutional rights, or the rights of private individuals and Cantons under a concordat or treaty, and other cases designated by Federal law.
   b. All Divisions of the Federal Tribunal proceed in accordance with the Federal Constitution, statutes, and treaties ratified by the Federal Assembly; the Federal judges sustain the Federal Constitution, statutes, etc., against the Cantonal Constitutions and statutes.

C. FEDERAL ADMINISTRATIVE COURT
1. Its organization and procedures are regulated by Federal law.
2. Exercises jurisdiction over administrative disputes in Federal matters and disciplinary cases of the Federal administration assigned to it by Federal law (e.g., the decisions of Federal Departments and agencies and the conduct of Federal officials in office).
3. Its judges proceed in accordance with Federal legislation and treaties ratified by the Federal Assembly.

4. Cantons may request the Federal Administrative Court to assume jurisdiction in administrative disputes involving Cantonal affairs.

VIII. FEDERALISM: THE CONFEDERATION AND THE CANTONS

A. SIGNIFICANT FACTORS

1. Swiss Confederation consists of twenty-two sovereign Cantons.
2. Objectives of the Confederation are to maintain the independence of the country against foreigners and the peace and order at home, to safeguard the rights and liberties of the "Confederates," and to promote the common prosperity of the Nation.
3. Sovereignty of the Cantons is not limited, except by the provisions of the Federal Constitution and its laws.
4. A division of authority and responsibility between the Confederation and the Cantons; each one has certain powers within a prescribed area of competency and each one undertakes certain obligations to the other.
5. Confederation guarantees the sovereignty of the Cantons and the Cantons pledge themselves not to voluntarily renounce their sovereignty or entrust it to the Confederation.

B. THE CONFEDERATION

1. *Powers* (See Sections V-D, VI-A-6, VII-B, C, above).
2. *Classification of State functions*
   a. Functions administered solely by the Confederation: e.g., alcohol, coinage of money, customs, munitions, post offices, telegraphs, and telephones.
   b. Functions administered jointly by the Confederation and the Cantons: e.g., the aliens' police and military organization.
   c. Functions regulated by Federal law, but administered entirely by the Cantons: e.g., banks, fishing and wild life, forests, health, labor, the liberal professions, water resources.
   d. Functions within the Cantons' competence, but whose administration is controlled by the Confederation: e.g., bridges and roads.

C. The Cantons
   1. *Powers* (See Section IX below).
   2. *Some rights of the Cantons* (guaranteed by the Confederation)
      a. Protection of their territory, sovereignty, constitution, government, and the rights and liberties of their people.
      b. Protection of their general powers: legislative, executive, and judicial.
   3. *Some obligations of the Cantons* (guaranteed by the Cantons)
      a. Establish and maintain a constitutional and "republican" form of government, with the consent of their people, under law.
      b. Refrain from any prejudicial action with respect to the rights and privileges of their people (i.e., equal protection and rights of all Swiss before the law), the status of other Cantons (i.e., no separate alliances or treaties of a political nature between Cantons), and the internal security of the State (i.e., no violence or arming in the event of a disagreement with another Canton).
      c. Assist one another in the administration of justice and inter-Cantonal activities and contribute to the general interests and prosperity of the Nation.

D. Contemporary Patterns
   1. Cantons retain their primary position and importance in the affairs of the Swiss people.
   2. Cantons and the Confederation maintain a balance of power, with recurring counter-complementary tendencies of centralization and federalization in their relations.
   3. Concept and practice of cooperative or collaborative federalism continues to grow slowly, but steadily.

IX. LOCAL GOVERNMENT

A. Regular Cantons
   1. *Constitution*
      a. *Hans Huber*, Federal Tribunal: "The Swiss Cantons have to submit their Constitutions to the approval of the . . . Federal Assembly. A condition

of that approval is that the Cantons shall maintain a republican form of government, with direct or representative democracy. Further, every Cantonal Constitution must be subject to amendment if it is required by a majority of the electorate, and must have been passed by the majority before the [Federal Assembly] gives its approval. A counterpart of this provision may be seen in the fact that a majority of Cantons . . . is required for the adoption of the Federal Constitution. A new Federal Constitution, or a motion for partial revision of the existing one, can only be adopted and put into force if it has been passed by a majority of the electorate in addition to a majority of the Cantons. The Cantons, however, cannot vote separately as such; the majority of votes in the Cantonal polls is regarded as the vote of that Canton."

2. *Legislature* (unicameral Great Council)
   a. Members are elected through Cantonal electoral colleges according to election lists, either by an absolute majority of voters or by proportional representation, for a term of one to six years.
   b. Number of the Councillors varies (30 to 250), depending on constitutional provision and the size of the Canton; they receive no fixed salaries, but rather are granted *per diem* or half-day allowances.
   c. Convenes in both regular and special public meetings, as the Cantonal practice and prevailing circumstances allow.
   d. Functions and powers include: enact law, vote the annual budget, levy taxes, appropriate monies, audit financial accounts, appoint the Cantonal "Government" and oversee its administration, ratify inter-Cantonal agreements, provide for the legislative initiative and referendum (both compulsory and optional), grant Cantonal citizenship, decide questions of amnesty and pardon, issue emergency decrees, propose constitutional revisions, and perform other miscellaneous duties.

3. *Executive authority* (plural Council of State or Government Council)
   a. Members (5 to 11) may, in some instances, be di-

CHART 42. AGENCIES OF LOCAL GOVERNMENT IN SWITZERLAND

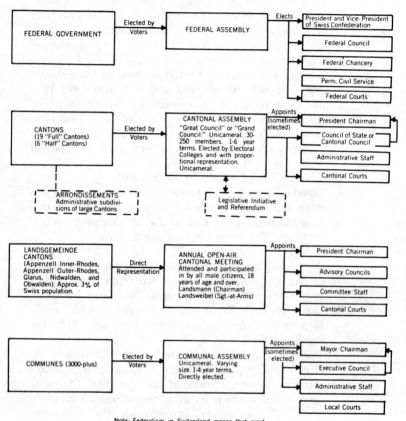

FEDERAL GOVERNMENT	Elected by Voters → FEDERAL ASSEMBLY	Elects → President and Vice-President of Swiss Confederation
		Federal Council
		Federal Chancery
		Perm. Civil Service
		Federal Courts

CANTONS (19 "Full" Cantons) (6 "Half" Cantons) — Elected by Voters → CANTONAL ASSEMBLY "Great Council" or "Grand Council." Unicameral. 30-250 members. 1-6 year terms. Elected by Electoral Colleges and with proportional representation. Unicameral. — Appoints (sometimes elected) → President Chairman; Council of State or Cantonal Council; Administrative Staff; Cantonal Courts

ARRONDISSEMENTS Administrative subdivisions of large Cantons

Legislative Initiative and Referendum

LANDSGEMEINDE CANTONS (Appenzell Inner-Rhodes, Appenzell Outer-Rhodes, Glarus, Nidwalden, and Obwalden). Approx. 3% of Swiss population. — Direct Representation → ANNUAL OPEN-AIR CANTONAL MEETING Attended and participated in by all male citizens, 18 years of age and over. Landsmann (Chairman) Landsweibel (Sgt.-at-Arms) — Appoints → President Chairman; Advisory Councils; Committee Staff; Cantonal Courts

COMMUNES (3000-plus) — Elected by Voters → COMMUNAL ASSEMBLY Unicameral. Varying size. 1-4 year terms. Directly elected. — Appoints (sometimes elected) → Mayor Chairman; Executive Council; Administrative Staff; Local Courts

Note: Federalism in Switzerland means that great emphasis is placed upon "Cantonal sovereignty," which is only limited by the Federal Constitution and its laws. The Confederation is obliged to guarantee the sovereignty of the Cantons while the latter, in turn, are pledged neither to renounce their sovereignty nor entrust it to the Confederation. Moreover, the individual Swiss is first a citizen of his Commune and Canton, and then of the Confederation.

rectly elected by the voters, but are usually appointed by the legislature, for a term of one to five years; they are immediately eligible for reelection and frequently serve many terms in office; they also receive regular salaries.

(1) They compose a coalition of representatives of varied political, economic, and religious interests.

(2) Some of them may also be members of the Cantonal legislature and the Federal Assembly.

(3) They can be dismissed by the legislature in all Cantons, and in four Cantons at the request of a stipulated number of people.

b. President (or Chairman) of the executive Council usually serves a one-year term in office and is not immediately eligible for reelection.

c. Conducts closed meetings, at a time and place determined by Cantonal law and practice.

d. Functions and powers include: head the individual Departments of government (e.g., Education, Finance, Justice, Police, Public Health, and Public Works), execute the Cantonal public policy, participate (sometimes) in the administration of Cantonal justice, appoint Cantonal officials, maintain relations with other Cantons and the Confederation (often through their memberships in the Federal Assembly), control the Canton's "Standing Force" (never more than 300 men, unless otherwise permitted by the Federal authority, or in the face of a Cantonal emergency), frame legislative measures and initiate them in the Cantonal legislature, confirm (no veto power) and promulgate laws enacted by the Cantonal legislature, and perform other miscellaneous duties.

4. *Judiciary* (as determined by each Cantonal Government)

a. There is tremendous variation among the Cantons in respect to the composition of courts, the manner of selecting judges, the judges' terms of office, and court jurisdictions and procedures.

b. Cantonal courts exercise original and appellate jurisdiction and apply both Cantonal and Federal law; they have no power of judicial review.

   c. Regular Cantonal judges are appointed either by the Cantonal executive authority or legislature, but the special lay judges (in some Cantons and in the Communes) are elected by the voters; the regular judges serve a term of three to ten years and all are immediately eligible for reelection; they also receive a regular salary or stipend.

   d. Hierarchy of Cantonal courts (from bottom to top) includes:

     (1) Justices of the Peace and Communal courts: small civil and criminal cases or misdemeanors.

     (2) District courts: more important civil and criminal cases and some appellate jurisdiction over the Communal courts.

     (3) Courts of Assize and Cassation: hear and review the most serious criminal cases.

     (4) Cantonal High Court: appellate jurisdiction over the decisions of the lower courts.

     (5) Special courts: such as the Arbitration Tribunal, which hears disputes between employers and workers, and the Commercial Tribunal, which settles disputes between businessmen, tradesmen, and consumers.

     (6) Federal Tribunal and Federal Administrative Court: hear appeals against the decisions of the Cantonal High Court or settle administrative disputes at the request of the Cantons.

   e. A public prosecutor represents the interests of the Canton in criminal cases.

  5. Large Cantons may be divided for administrative purposes into Districts *(Amtsbezirke)*, consisting of a number of Communes grouped together, each District with a Commissioner *(Regierungsstadthalter)* representing the Cantonal government.

B. *Landsgemeinde* CANTONS

  1. Small Cantons of Glarus, Nidwalden, Obwalden, and Inner and Outer Appenzell, with only about 3 per cent of the total Swiss population.

  2. *Landsgemeinde* is an annual meeting of all enfran-

chised males, on a Sunday morning in Spring, in a public square or at some historic open-meeting place; it is presided over by the *Landsmann* (Chairman of the Cantonal "Government") and order is maintained by the *Landsweibel* (roughly similar to a sergeant-at-arms); after opening prayers, hymns, and oaths, the participants, by show of hands

    a. Approve legislative measures presented before them;
    b. Confirm the Cantonal budget and all financial accounts;
    c. Provide for the performance of the public duties and services;
    d. Vote on drafted amendments to the Cantonal Constitution.

3. *Landsgemeinde* Cantons, in the interim between their annual "open-air" meetings, maintain a regular governmental organization, including designated legislative, executive, and judicial authorities, and special advisory councils.

C. COMMUNES

1. The 3000-plus Communes have varying degrees of local autonomy, depending on the provisions of the Cantonal Constitution and laws; some may administer their own affairs quite freely, while other Communes are more dependent upon the Cantonal authorities.

2. Communal structures usually include a popularly elected, unicameral legislative Council, a Mayor and an Executive Committee, and a local Justice of the Peace or Communal court; all these units perform duties characteristic of their offices on the local level.

3. Interest and participation in Communal affairs frequently provides the local citizens with the training and experience necessary for service, later on, in the Cantonal and Federal Governments.

SELECTED READINGS

Bonjour, *Swiss Neutrality: Its History and Meaning*. London: George Allen & Unwin, Ltd., 1946.

Codding, George A., Jr., *The Federal Government of Switzerland*. Boston: Houghton Mifflin Company, 1961.

De Beer, Gavin Rylands, *Speaking of Switzerland*. London: Eyre and Spottiswoode, 1952.

Gilliard, C., *A History of Switzerland*. New York: Macmillan Company, 1955.

Herold, J. Christopher, *The Swiss Without Halos*. New York: Columbia University Press, 1948.

Hofer, Walther, *Neutrality As the Principle of Swiss Foreign Policy*. Zurich: Schweizer Spiegel Verlag, 1957.

Huber, Hans, *How Switzerland Is Governed*. Zurich: Schweizer Spiegel Verlag, 1946.

Hughes, Christopher (trans.), *The Federal Constitution of Switzerland*. Oxford: Clarendon Press, 1954.

Kohn, Hans, *Nationalism and Liberty: the Swiss Example*. London: G. Allen & Unwin, 1956.

Lloyd, William B., Jr., *Waging Peace: the Swiss Experience*. Washington, D. C., Public Affairs Press, 1958.

Rappard, William E., *Collective Security in Swiss Experience*. London: George Allen & Unwin, Ltd., 1948.

————, *The Government of Switzerland*. New York: D. Van Nostrand Company, 1936.

Rice, William G., *Law Among States in Federacy*. Appleton, Wisconsin: C. C. Nelson Publishing Company, 1959.

Rougemont, Denis and Charlotte de Muret, *The Heart of Europe*. New York: Duell, Sloan and Pearce, 1941.

Sauser-Hall, Georges, *The Political Institutions of Switzerland*. New York: Swiss National Tourist Office Publishing Department, 1946.

Siegfried, André, *Switzerland: A Democratic Way of Life*. New York: Duell, Sloane and Pearce, 1950.

Soloveytchik, Georege, *Switzerland in Perspective*. Toronto: Oxford University Press, 1954.

Spiro, Herbert J., *Government by Constitution*. New York: Random House, Inc., 1959.

Swiss National Tourist Office, *All About Switzerland: a Short Survey*. Zürich: 1959.

Wheare, K. C., *Federal Government*. London: Oxford University Press, 1946.

————, *Modern Constitutions*. London: Oxford University Press, 1951.

Chapter IX

TURKEY

POPULATION: 30,500,000 (1964)
AREA: 296,503 sq. miles
CAPITAL: Ankara

I. CHRONOLOGY

1071—Defeat of Byzantine Emperor at Battle of Manzikert and inclusion of Asia Minor in emerging Turkish Empire.

1150—Anatolian Seljuks establish independent State.

1288–1326—Sultan Osman I extends territory of his Anatolian principality at expense of Byzantines.

1345–1541—Period of European expansion by Ottoman Turks.

1683–1699—Second Ottoman "siege of Vienna" climaxed by defeat of Turks and Treaty of Karlovitz with Russia, Poland, Austria, and Venice.

1774—Treaty of Kuchuk Kainarji gives Russia free navigation in Turkish waters, new ports in Crimea, right of intervention in Moldavia and Wallachia, and protectorate over Greek Orthodox Church in Istanbul.

1830—Greeks win independence, paving way for further dismemberment of Ottoman Empire.

1853–1856—Great Britain, France, and Sardinia support "the sick man of Europe" (Turkey) against advances of Russia in Crimea.

1908—"Young Turk Movement" dedicates itself to achievement of Western constitutionalism and other reforms in Turkey.

1918—Turkey suffers defeat in World War I as ally of "Central Powers."

1923–1938—Mustafa Kemal Atatürk ("Father of the Turks") creates First Turkish Republic and, under presidential policy of "benevolent dictatorship," achieves international peace and national reconstruction.

1945—Turkey declares war on Nazi Germany and later participates in San Francisco Conference to establish formal United Nations Organization.

1947—"Truman Doctrine" lays solid foundation for further cooperation between Turkey and the United States.

1950—Conduct of first democratic national elections in Turkey.

1960—*Coup d'etat* by "Committee on National Unity" results in new Constitution for Second Turkish Republic and promise of social, economic, and political reforms in Turkey.

1964—In spite of two parliamentary challenges, Prime Minister Ismet Inonu retains leadership over the coalition government; Turkey and Greece quarrel over the Cyprus issue and the former seems to establish a new friendship with the Soviet Union.

1965—Justice Party obtains a majority (240) of the seats (450) in the National Assembly in the Fall parliamentary elections; subsequently, Suleyman Demirel becomes Prime Minister.

1966—Moderate, pro-western General Cevdet Sunday is elected fifth President of the Turkish Republic by an overwhelming mandate of the Turkish Grand National Assembly.

II. TURKISH CONSTITUTION

A. TURKISH CONSTITUTION, 1961

1. Lays down the fundamental legal principles binding upon the various powers and organs of Government and individuals, and is superior to ordinary laws.

2. Presumably, no provision of the Constitution may be disregarded, nor its application suspended, for any reason or under any pretext.

3. Amendments to the Constitution are proposed in writing by at least a one-third majority of a plenary meeting of the Grand National Assembly (Parliament), and

are approved by at least a two-thirds majority of all the members in both houses.
   a. The form of the State as a Republic cannot be the subject of a constitutional amendment.

B. FUNDAMENTAL PRINCIPLES OF GOVERNMENT
   1. "The Turkish Republic is a nationalistic, democratic, secular, and social State" (Art. 2); these characteristics are explained, briefly, as follows:
      a. *Nationalistic:* the acceptance of all citizens as Turks, regardless of race or creed, and the rejection of all separatist tendencies.
      b. *Democratic:* there are no privileged persons or groups and the Government emphasizes the rights and interests of all the people.
      c. *Secular:* the separation of religion (or Church) from the State, but with a guarantee and protection of religious freedom.
      d. *Social:* the Government regulates some private enterprises and encourages new economic activities in order to raise the national standard of living and advance the public welfare; retrogressive traditions and institutions will be eliminated so that the Turkish nation can deal successfully with changing conditions and needs and make progress in all undertakings.
   2. Sovereignty belongs to all the people and is manifested through popular elections, party memberships, and representations in the Turkish Grand National Assembly (T.G.N.A.); the right to exercise sovereignty cannot be delegated to any one person, group, or class, nor may any person or agency exercise any State authority not legally derived from the Constitution.
   3. Bicameral National Parliament (Turkish Grand National Assembly: National Assembly and Senate of the Republic), exercises the legislative power which cannot be delegated.
   4. Cabinet-Parliamentary executive authority which functions according to constitutional principles and is selected (the President), approved and dismissed (the Prime Minister and Council of Ministers) by the Parliament.

Chart 43. STRUCTURE OF THE TURKISH GOVERNMENT

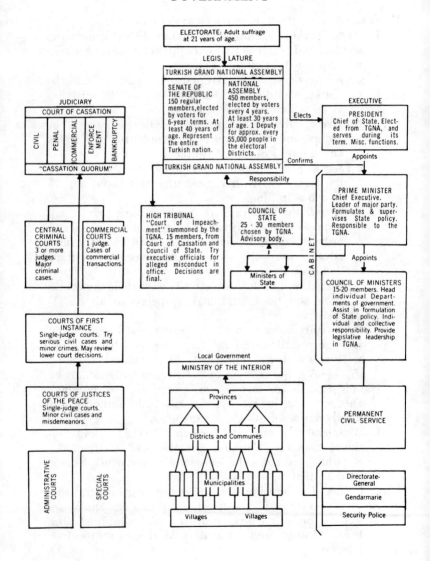

ELECTORATE: Adult suffrage at 21 years of age.

LEGISLATURE

TURKISH GRAND NATIONAL ASSEMBLY

SENATE OF THE REPUBLIC 150 regular members, elected by voters for 6-year terms. At least 40 years of age. Represent the entire Turkish nation.

NATIONAL ASSEMBLY 450 members, elected by voters every 4 years. At least 30 years of age. 1 Deputy for approx. every 55,000 people in the electoral Districts.

JUDICIARY

COURT OF CASSATION

CIVIL | PENAL | COMMERCIAL | ENFORCEMENT | BANKRUPTCY

"CASSATION QUORUM"

EXECUTIVE

PRESIDENT Chief of State. Elected from TGNA, and serves during its term. Misc. functions.

Elects

TURKISH GRAND NATIONAL ASSEMBLY

Confirms

Responsibility

Appoints

PRIME MINISTER Chief Executive. Leader of major party. Formulates & supervises State policy. Responsible to the TGNA.

HIGH TRIBUNAL "Court of Impeachment" summoned by the TGNA. 15 members, from Court of Cassation and Council of State. Try executive officials for alleged misconduct in office. Decisions are final.

COUNCIL OF STATE 25 - 30 members chosen by TGNA. Advisory body.

Ministers of State

CABINET

CENTRAL CRIMINAL COURTS 3 or more judges. Major criminal cases.

COMMERCIAL COURTS 1 judge. Cases of commercial transactions.

Appoints

COUNCIL OF MINISTERS 15-20 members. Head individual Departments of government. Assist in formulation of State policy. Individual and collective responsibility. Provide legislative leadership in TGNA.

COURTS OF FIRST INSTANCE Single-judge courts. Try serious civil cases and minor crimes. May review lower court decisions.

Local Government

MINISTRY OF THE INTERIOR

COURTS OF JUSTICES OF THE PEACE Single-judge courts. Minor civil cases and misdemeanors.

Provinces

Districts and Communes

PERMANENT CIVIL SERVICE

ADMINISTRATIVE COURTS

SPECIAL COURTS

Municipalities

Directorate-General

Gendarmarie

Security Police

Villages | Villages

5. Independent national judiciary, which is free from external controls other than the stipulated constitutional safeguards; neither the "Government" nor the Parliament can interfere with court proceedings nor vitiate the execution of court decisions; a new Constitutional Court seeks to protect the Constitution and ensure both individual rights and the legality of legislative and executive actions.

6. Unitary system of Government, with about the same highly-centralized control and direction over provincial and local authorities as existed under the First Republic (1924–1960).

7. In foreign affairs, Turkey assertedly supports the principles of the United Nations Charter and the "Declaration of Human Rights and Fundamental Freedoms," and is further desirous of maintaining her alliances with NATO and CENTO (Central Treaty) and "good neighbor" relations with all countries, particularly the United States; in the words of Mustafa Kemal Atatürk, this policy can be simply stated as "Peace at home, peace in the world."

C. GENERAL RIGHTS AND DUTIES OF CITIZENS

1. New Constitution affirms individual, social and economic, and political rights and duties according to the principles inherent in Western democracy.

2. Equality before the law and protection for the rights of all citizens irrespective of race, language, sex, political views and opinions, or religion.

3. Inviolability of one's person and domicile, of personal correspondence and private documents and papers, with no arbitrary deprivation or confiscation of one's personal properties.

4. Freedom of communication, movement, and travel; of conscience and thought; of speech and press; of association and assembly; of religion and worship; and to petition competent authorities and the Turkish Grand National Assembly.

5. No arbitrary personal seizures or arrests, or physical and mental mistreatments, or denial of access to law and a fair hearing before a competent court.

6. Status of citizenship and the rights and liberties of aliens are determined by law.

7. Right and duty to engage in an occupation, trade, or business of one's choice; to rest and leisure; and to social security and medical care.

8. Protection for "the home, the mother, and the child" (Art. 35).

9. Compulsory and free public primary education.

10. Right to form work associations, enter into contracts of employment, bargain collectively and strike, and to enjoy cooperative activities.

11. One may own and inherit real property, which can only be expropriated or nationalized on behalf the public interest and in accordance with law.

12. Citizens may enter the public service without any discrimination in hiring personnel other than job qualifications.

13. All men and women (other than those disqualified by law) over twenty-one years of age have the right to elect and be elected to public office.

14. Elections are free and secret and conducted on the basis of equality and impartiality.

    a. They are regulated in detail by special law and amendments subsequently passed by the Turkish Grand National Assembly. Only official ballots, containing the names and the emblems of the individual parties, are used. The votes in local, provincial, and national elections are tabulated by corresponding Electoral Boards (or Councils). In parliamentary elections, a Supreme Electoral Board decides, according to the latest census figures, the number of deputies to be elected to the National Assembly by each of the 67 Provinces and also the parties which are eligible to participate according to the provisions of law (which stipulates that they must be organized in at least 15 Provinces).

15. Citizens may establish, and join or withdraw from, political parties.

16. It is the right and duty of every Turk to take part in the defense of the homeland.

17. Every individual must pay taxes in proportion to his

financial capacity, and taxes, dues, charges, etc., are imposed only by law.

18. Government may proclaim a temporary state of partial or general martial law, with the approval of the Turkish Grand National Assembly.

III. POLITICAL PARTIES

A. GENERAL CHARACTERISTICS OF THE PARTY SYSTEM

1. Absence of a long-standing tradition of democratic political party life, but recent trend in direction of evolving such a system, with at least six parties represented in each house of the T.G.N.A.
2. A new role and purpose is given to opposition parties in the T.G.N.A. (cf. the limited conception of "party opposition" during the First Republic).
3. Geographic, economic, philosophic, and religious bases of party membership and policies.
4. Legal equality among the political parties (except the Communist Party, which is outlawed), in respect to their organizations, nomination of candidates, conduct of election campaigns, etc.
5. Some disagreement exists among the parties on the implementation of political and social principles, but general agreement among them on the need for basic reforms (e.g., new electoral procedures, further guarantees for the exercise of constitutional rights and freedoms, the reorganization of provincial and local governments, State action to encourage the growth and development of the economy and trade, etc.)
6. General similarity in party local, provincial, and national organizations.

B. LEADING PARTIES (because most of these are new parties, under the Constitution of 1961, it is a little early yet to state definitely what will become the sharp lines of demarcation among them in terms both of domestic and foreign affairs).

1. *Justice Party* (AP): believes in the fundamental rights of individuals and strives to achieve complete equality among all citizens throughout the country; espouses a

mixed economy within a context of planning and the attainment of social justice in keeping with this development.

2. *Republican People's Party* (CHP): believes in modern and progressive methods to attain rapid development in economic and social fields; would maintain a private sector in the economy.

3. *Nation Party* (MP) : opposes all Leftist tendencies and appeals to the middle-class.

4. *New Turkey Party* (YTP): believes that a true system of a mixed economy, somewhere between the extremes of private capitalism and public socialism is the only solution to Turkey's problems and guarantee of her future development.

5. *Turkish Labor Party* (TIP): believes that socialist methods is the only solution for the development of under-developed countries such as Turkey: land reform should be achieved immediately; industrialization, banking and insurance, and foreign trade should be conducted exclusively by the State; but probably a mixed economy will continue for many more years.

6. *Republican Peasants' Nation Party* (CKMP): believes that a mixed economy, based on social justice and scientific planning, is the proper basis for national development; private enterprise should be limited to fields of activity clearly designated by the economic plan.

C. PARTY ORGANIZATION

1. Each of the major parties has evolved a national party organization, consisting of the National Chairman; Secretary, or Secretary-General; the National Committee and staff; and the National Party Congress; other party structures are maintained on the *Vilayet* (Province) and local levels.

2. Parties largely determine their own methods and procedures for the nomination of candidates to public office.

3. Sources of party income and expenditures and the conduct of campaigns and elections are regulated by law, within the framework of constitutional guarantees for political association and free expression; however,

    a. "The statutes, programs, and activities of political parties shall conform to the principles of a democratic and secular Republic, based on human rights and liberties, and to the fundamental principle of the State's territorial and national integrity. Parties failing to conform to these provisions shall be permanently dissolved. . . . Actions in law involving the dissolution of political parties shall be heard at the Constitutional Court, and the verdict to dissolve them shall be rendered only by this Court" (Art. 57).

    b. Only the new Constitutional Court is empowered to render a verdict to dissolve a political party.

4. Six political parties also have new parliamentary party organizations (e.g., a chairman, caucus, and committees), with varying degrees of interdependency with the national party organizations.

5. Ancillary associations include agrarian, business and professional, labor, military and religious groups.

D. PARTY REPRESENTATION IN THE T.B.N.A. (composition of the Parliament in September, 1966)

PARTY	SENATE	NATIONAL ASSEMBLY	TOTAL
Justice Party	92	242	334
Republican People's Party	50	134	184
Nation Party	2	27	29
Life Senators	20	—	20
New Turkey Party	1	18	19
Turkish Labor Party	1	14	15
Republican Peasants' Nation Party	1	9	10
Independents	3	6	9
Senators appointed by the President of the Republic	15	—	15
TOTAL:	185	450	635

1. *Prime Minister Suleyman Demirel:* "The tendency, thought, and strength of . . . the Turkish nation are significant. Besides, we [the Justice Party] do not use our majority for the very erroneous and treacherous purpose of changing the regime and the institutions of

the regime. In our fundamental philosophy, a democratic regime and order are mandatory. Freedoms—and the protection of freedoms—are above all. The Constitution and the safeguarding and maintenance of constitutional order and institutions are the basis of our philosophy."

IV. TURKISH GRAND NATIONAL ASSEMBLY (T.G.N.A.)

A. DESCRIPTIVE FEATURES OF THE GRAND NATIONAL ASSEMBLY
1. Bicameral, representative, and democratic national Parliament, consisting of the National Assembly and the Senate of the Republic.
2. Popularly-elected as the legislative representative of the Nation, on whose behalf it exercises the rights of sovereignty.
3. Provides and controls the "Government" of the Turkish State.
4. Functions on the basis of multiparty politics, with leadership and direction primarily through the Justice Party and the Republican People's Party but with an evolving and loyal opposition of the lesser parties.
5. Composed of the representatives of diversified interest groups and geographical regions and organized along traditional parliamentary lines.
6. Individual Deputies represent neither their constituencies (Districts) nor constituents, but, theoretically, the entire Turkish people.

B. MEMBERSHIP AND ORGANIZATION
1. *National Assembly* consists of 450 Deputies elected according to a system of proportional representation for a term of four years; *Senate of the Republic* consists of 150 members elected under the majority system for a term of six years, with one-third of the Senators being elected every two years; an additional
   a. 20 members of the "Committee on National Unity" and former Presidents of the Republic are Senators *ex-officio*, and retain this position until such time as they join a political party.

    b. 15 presidential appointees are selected from among persons distinguished for their services in various fields and at least ten of them must not be members of any political party.

    c. One-third of the Senators elected by general ballot and appointed by the President of the Republic are rotated every two years.

2. Deputies must be at least thirty years of age; and Senators must be at least forty years of age; and also have a higher education and be eligible for election as a Deputy.

3. Civil servants may be candidates to the T.G.N.A. without having to resign from the public service, but judges and military personnel must resign their posts if they are parliamentary candidates.

4. Only citizens who are twenty-one years of age, and not among the categories disqualified by law (e.g., fraudulent bankrupts, criminals, those derelict in performing military service, the insane, persons under guardianship) may participate in elections to the T.G.N.A.

5. A Supreme Election Board (assisted by Provincial and local election boards) is primarily responsible for the procedures and conduct of the national elections, and helps decide disputed elections to the T.G.N.A.

    a. Composed of seven regular members and four alternates, six of whom are elected by the Court of Cassation and five by the Council of State from among their own memberships by secret ballot, and by an absolute majority of their plenary sessions.

6. No one may be simultaneously a member of both legislative chambers, nor while a member of the T.G.N.A. hold any incompatible office, such as membership in a court of law, the Armed Forces, the Council of State, or be employed by any governmental agency or other public corporate body or enterprise.

7. Vacancies among the elected members in a legislative chamber are filled in by-elections, which are held every two years at the same time as the Senatorial elections but not within one year prior to the general elections for the National Assembly.

Chart 44. ORGANIZATION OF PARLIAMENT AND THE LAW-MAKING PROCESS IN TURKEY

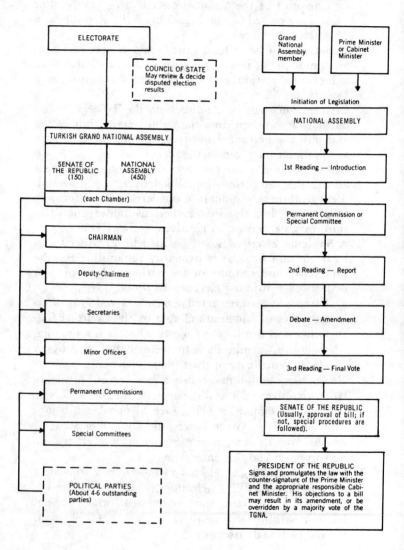

    a. Vacancies among the appointed Senators are filled by new presidential appointments within a period of thirty days after the vacancies occur.

8. Deputies and Senators take an oath of allegiance to the State and Nation, as follows:

   "I swear upon my honor that I will protect the independence of the State, and the integrity of the homeland and the Nation, that I will remain committed to the unqualified and unconditional sovereignty of the Nation, and to the principles of a democratic and secular Republic, and that I will make every effort to promote the happiness of the people" (Art. 77).

9. Members of Parliament also enjoy the familiar privileges (personal inviolability and parliamentary immunity) and perquisites (a regular salary and travel allowances) attending their office; disputes over the suspension of these attributes of membership are reviewed by the Constitutional Court.

10. Internal organization in each legislative chamber includes the

    a. Chairman and Deputy-Chairman, elected by the chamber from among its own membership by a two-thirds majority in a plenary session, and by a secret ballot for a term of two years;

    b. Chairmanship Council, so composed as to give proportionate representation to each political party represented in the chamber;

    c. Permanent and temporary Commissions (i.e., committees), with a similar basis of representation for their memberships.

    d. Various secretaries, clerks, etc.

    e. Chairman and Deputy Chairman are not permitted to participate in the activities of political parties, either within or outside their legislative chamber, nor can they participate in parliamentary debates except as required by their functions; nor do they vote.

    f. Chairman of the National Assembly presides over the joint sessions of the T.G.N.A.

11. Each chamber is governed by its own by-laws and disciplinary rules, and enforces them.

12. An absolute majority of its full membership is necessary for a quorum to conduct a meeting, and an absolute majority of the attending members to pass resolutions, in each legislative chamber.

13. Legislative debates in both chambers are public, except where the rules of procedure permit of closed sessions, and the debates are subsequently published *verbatim* in the official *Journal*.

14. National Assembly and Senate of the Republic convene in regular annual session and also in special or emergency meetings called by the President of the Republic on the request of the Prime Minister or the members of the T.G.N.A., as provided by the Constitution and laws.

C. FUNCTIONS AND POWERS

1. Pass resolutions and enact legislation.

2. Elect the President of the Republic and approve the selection of the Prime Minister and his cabinet Ministers from among its own membership or those qualified to be elected as a Deputy.

3. Approve the executive budget and audit the financial accounts of the State.

4. Conduct questions, general debates, parliamentary inquiries, and parliamentary investigations.

   a. Parliamentary investigations concerning the Prime Minister or other Ministers are decided at a plenary session of the T.G.N.A. and are carried out by a committee composed of an equal number of Deputies and Senators.

   b. Power of interpellation (i.e., to call upon a member of the Government to explain some official act or policy, which usually leads to a vote of confidence) is vested exclusively in the National Assembly.

5. Take "votes of confidence" and pass "motions of censure."

6. Exercise an impeachment power over executive officials.

   a. President of the Republic may be impeached for high treason upon the proposal of one-third of a plenary session of the T.G.N.A., and convicted by the vote of at least a two-thirds majority in a joint plenary session of both legislative chambers.

7. Reduce or modify sentences and see to the carrying out of death penalties pronounced by courts of law.
8. Proclaim pardons and partial or complete amnesties.
9. Approve executive agreements and treaties with foreign States.
10. Declare war and conclude peace.
11. Amend the Constitution.
12. Perform other miscellaneous duties as provided by the Constitution and laws.
13. President of the Senate of the Republic serves as the provisional President of the Republic, whenever this office is vacated, until a new President of the Republic is elected by the T.G.N.A.

D. GENERAL STEPS IN THE ENACTMENT OF LAW
1. Introduction of the bill in the National Assembly by the Prime Minister, a cabinet Minister, or a member of the T.G.N.A., with a right to defend the bill before the relevant committee in both legislative chambers.
2. Deliberation on the bill by the appropriate permanent or temporary Commission in the National Assembly.
3. Report and recommendations by the Commission in a plenary session.
4. Conduct of open discussion and debate.
5. Taking of the majority vote, usually by open ballot.
6. Transmittal of the bill to the Senate.
    a. If the bill is endorsed there by majority vote, it becomes law.
    b. If the bill is modified there, it must subsequently be endorsed by the National Assembly to become law.
    c. If the bill is not approved by the National Assembly in its modified form, a Mixed Committee (with equal representation from both legislative chambers) is established and the National Assembly must subsequently approve its modified bill, or the bill as modified by the Senate, or the bill as originally endorsed in the National Assembly.
    d. If the bill is rejected by the Senate by an absolute or two-thirds majority vote, it becomes law only if subsequently endorsed again by the National Assembly by the appropriate absolute or two-thirds majority vote.

e. If a bill rejected in the National Assembly is approved by the Senate, either with or without amendments, it only becomes law if subsequently endorsed by the National Assembly in the form in which it was approved in the Senate.

f. If a bill rejected in the National Assembly is not approved by the Senate, it is void.

g. If the Senate does not act on a bill transmitted by the National Assembly within the time limits specified in the Constitution, normally the bill becomes law at the end of the particular time limit.

h. Senate follows the same procedures as the National Assembly in its consideration and action on a bill.

7. Transmittal of the bill from the T.G.N.A. to the President of the Republic.

8. Promulgation of the law by the President.

a. A law is signed by the President and countersigned by the Prime Minister and the Minister whose Department (Ministry) is directly affected by the law.

b. President must sign a bill (and always an approved budgetary measure or constitutional amendment), or return it to the T.G.N.A. with his written objections, within a period of ten days; the T.G.N.A. may override the suspensory presidential veto by an absolute majority vote and the President must then sign and promulgate the law.

9. Special procedures are followed for the debate and adoption of the budget (involving a Mixed Committee of 35 Deputies and 15 Senators, with proportionate representation of the political parties in the T.G.N.A.) by the legislative chambers.

a. Members of the T.G.N.A. cannot increase proposed expenditures nor decrease specific incomes in approving the executive budget.

V. THE GOVERNMENT

A. PRESIDENT OF THE REPUBLIC

1. Elected for term of seven years from among those members of the T.G.N.A. who are at least forty years of age and have a higher education; election is by secret ballot,

and by a two-thirds majority on the first two ballots or an absolute majority thereafter of the plenary session.

a. President is not eligible for reelection.

b. He must dissociate himself from his party (usually the one that has been voted into office), and his status as a member of the T.G.N.A. ends.

2. Takes an oath of office to defend the Turkish State, etc., at his induction:

"As President of the Republic, I swear upon my honor that I will fight any threat directed against the independence of the Turkish State or against the integrity of the Fatherland and the Nation, that I will respect and defend the unqualified and unconditional sovereignty of the Nation, that I will not deviate from the principles of a democratic State based on the rule of law and human rights, that I will be free from all bias, and that I will do my utmost to protect and exalt the glory of the Turkish Republic and fulfill the task I have undertaken" (Art. 96).

3. Responsible for his actions to the T.G.N.A. and may be impeached (as previously described) for high treason by it; the Chairman of the Senate of the Republic refills his office whenever it is vacated.

4. Enjoys various immunities and perquisites as provided by law.

5. *Functions and powers*

a. Represents and defends the Turkish Republic and the integrity of the Turkish Nation at home and abroad.

b. Designates the Prime Minister who forms the Cabinet (Council of Ministers).

c. Presides over the T.G.N.A. on ceremonial occasions (he does not participate in the deliberations of either chamber nor cast his vote there as long as he is the President of the Republic) and also over meetings of the Council of Ministers.

d. Presents an Annual Address to the Turkish Grand National Assembly on the activities of the "Government" during the preceding year and the general legislative measures it recommends for the coming year.

e. Signs and promulgates laws, international conventions, and treaties approved by the "Government" and the T.G.N.A.

f. Countersigns executive decrees issued by the Prime Minister and the Council of Ministers.

g. Commutes or pardons on grounds of chronic physical disability or old age the sentences of convicted individuals.

h. Appoints diplomatic representatives to foreign States and receives their diplomatic representatives to Turkey.

i. Serves (nominally at least) as the Commander in Chief of the Armed Forces.

j. Presides over meetings of the National Security Council (composed of appropriate Ministers, the Chief of the General Staff, and representatives of the Armed Forces).

k. Appoints various executive and judicial officers, and serves in an *ex officio* capacity in designated agencies.

l. Performs other duties as required by the Constitution and laws.

B. PRIME MINISTER

1. Designated by the President of the Republic from among the members of the T.G.N.A.

2. He is usually the leader of the outstanding political party in the National Assembly.

3. Outlines his program and policy before each chamber of the T.G.N.A. and anticipates a vote of confidence by the National Assembly at the time of induction.

   a. However, in case the Prime Minister fails to receive a vote of confidence, the President of the Republic appoints a new Prime Minister. At the end of a third vote of no confidence, the President, in consultation with the chairmen in both legislative chambers, can decide to call for new General Elections which are then held immediately.

4. *Functions and powers*

   a. Serves as the Head of the Government and, as such, is primarily responsible for governmental policy and administration.

b. Nominates the Council of Ministers, usually from among members of his party who have been elected to Parliament, and other officials.

c. Supervises the implementation of the Government's general policy and the administration of the Council of Ministers.

d. Proposes legislation and participates in the deliberations of the T.G.N.A.

e. Countersigns laws and issues or countersigns executive degrees.

f. Presides over Cabinet and other meetings (e.g., National Security Council, in the absence of the President of the Republic).

g. Oversees the functions of the Chief of the General Staff, who is the real Commander in Chief of the Armed Forces appointed by the President of the Republic on the nomination of the Council of Ministers.

h. May ask for a vote of confidence from the National Assembly while in office.

i. *Exercises extraordinary powers in times of emergency:*

"In the event of war, or . . . in case of a revolt or . . . serious and active uprising against . . . the Republic, [the Prime Minister and] the Council of Ministers may proclaim martial law . . . for a length of time not exceeding one month, and shall immediately submit such proclamation to the approval of the Turkish Grand National Assembly. The Assembly . . . may curtail the period of martial law or abolish it altogether. If the legislative bodies are not in session, they shall be convened immediately. The extension of martial law, not exceeding two months each time, is subject to the decision of the Turkish Grand National Assembly. . . . In the event of martial law, or war in general, the specific provisions to be enforced, the manner in which government operations shall be conducted, and the manner in which freedoms shall be restricted shall be defined by law" (Art. 124).

(1) This section of the Constitution is quoted somewhat *in extenso* to point up the close relation-

ship on occasion of military leaders to active political forces and the importance of the Army, as "a factor in progress," in Turkey over the past one-hundred years. In fact, the late President, General Cemal Gursel, former Commander-in-Chief of the Army, led the *coup* against the corrupt political forces on May 27, 1960, and, as temporary Prime Minister, directed the drafting of the new Constitution. Suprisingly to many outside observers, perhaps, the Army is one of the really liberal forces in Turkey.

   j. Performs various other duties under the Constitution and laws.

C. COUNCIL OF MINISTERS (or Cabinet)

1. Ministers are nominated by the Prime Minister and appointed by the President of the Republic from among the members of the T.G.N.A. or from among those qualified for election as a Deputy.

2. Coalition Cabinet (of Republican and Justice parties) has recently included the Prime Minister, Deputy Prime Minister, four Ministers-of-State, and the following Ministers: Justice; National Defense; Interior; Foreign Affairs; Finance; Education; Public Works; Commerce; Health Customs and Monopolies; Agriculture; Industry; Labor; Press; Broadcasting and Tourism; and Reconstruction and Resettlement.

3. Each Minister is attached to one of the permanent Departments (Ministries); when he is absent from office, his duties are taken over by another Minister, instead of an under-secretary; a Cabinet Minister cannot take charge of more than one Department other than his own.

4. Ministers are individually and collectively responsible for their conduct and administration to the Prime Minister and the T.G.N.A.; they may be dismissed by the Prime Minister, or impeached by the T.G.N.A. and tried by the High Court (i.e., members of the Constitutional Court sitting in this capacity) and deprived of their ministerial status.

5. If the Council of Ministers is unseated twice by a vote

of no confidence by the National Assembly within a period of eighteen months, and if thereafter a third vote of no confidence is voted, the Prime Minister may request the President of the Republic to call new elections for the National Assembly.

a. Such a proclamation may be issued by the President, after consultation with the Chairmen of the T.G.N.A.

b. The Ministers resign and the Prime Minister then forms a new Provisional Council of Ministers consisting of members of the political parties in proportion to their representation in the National Assembly, but the new Ministers of Justice, Interior, and Communications must always come from the independent members in the T.G.N.A.; the Provisional Council functions only for the duration of the elections and until the new National Assembly convenes.

6. *Functions and powers*

a. Head the individual Departments and other agencies of government.

b. Participate in Cabinet meetings and in the deliberations of the T.G.N.A.

c. Propose laws directly to the National Assembly.

d. Issue orders and regulations in the enforcement of legislation.

e. Propose to the President of the Republic the appointment of various national and Provincial officials.

f. Oversee provincial and local government and administration.

g. Cooperate with the State Planning Organization and the T.G.N.A. in preparing and executing plans for the economic, social, and cultural development of the country.

h. Discharge other constitutional and legal duties and responsibilities.

i. Acts and procedures of the Administration may be reviewed by courts of law and the Administration held liable for damages resulting from unconstitutional, illegal, or negligent acts and operation.

j. A Court of Accounts audits all accounts of revenues,

expenditures, and properties of governmental agencies and enterprises, and reports on the same to the T.G.N.A.

7. *Administrative bureaucracy*
   a. Composed of employees who, generally-speaking, secure and hold their positions on the basis of open and competitive examinations.
   b. Present trend towards establishing a career public service, divorced from party politics, and also to reform and democratize the organization and procedures within the bureaucracy.
   c. Constitution contains general rules to govern the administrative bureaucracy; safeguards for government officials in disciplinary actions; limitations on the political activities of civil servants; statements of the liability of government employees for carrying out illegal orders; and provisions for emergency administration.
      (1) For example, with respect to illegal orders: "Persons employed in public services . . . shall not carry out an order of a superior if the person receiving the order considers it contrary to the provisions of . . . laws or the Constitution, and shall inform the person issuing the order of this contradiction. However, should the superior insist on the performance of his order, and reiterate it in writing, such order shall be carried out. In this case, the official enforcing the order shall not be held liable. An order which, by its very nature, constitutes a crime shall not be enforced in any manner whatsoever; any person carrying out such an order shall not be absolved from responsibility" (Art. 125). Similar provisions are found in the "Federal Officials Law" (1953) in the Federal Republic of Germany.

VI. JUDICIAL SYSTEM

A. Theory and Practice of Law and Justice
   1. Strict and equal application of the laws to all Turkish citizens.

2. Judicial review of the constitutionality of administrative acts and legislation.

3. All citizens have free recourse to regular legal and judicial processes in the defense of their general rights and interests.

4. Courts cannot refuse to hear cases which fall within their jurisdiction and competence.

5. Hearings are public, except where otherwise specifically provided by laws, and the individual is protected against having to testify alone in the absence of his legal counsel; there is no trial by jury.

6. Courts apply civil, criminal, commercial, and other codes of law.

7. Judicial decisions are made on behalf of the entire Turkish nation.

8. Right to make an appeal against a decision to a higher court (based on an alleged error in the application of law or procedure).

9. Organization, functions, and jurisdictions of courts, and the qualifications, manner of appointment, rights and duties, and compensation of judges, are regulated by law.

10. Judges are independent in the discharge of their duties, and they cannot be arbitrarily dismissed; retirement is compulsory at age sixty-five.

NOTE: In Turkey, crimes are either felonies or misdemeanors. Penalties for felonies include death by hanging, heavy jail sentence, heavy fines, and permanent or temporary deprivation of political rights and the right to hold public office. Penalties for misdemeanors include light jail sentence, light fines, and temporary prohibition to engage in a profession or trade. The Criminal Code (1961, as Amended) clearly defines felonies and misdemeanors, and their penalties. A death sentence must be affirmed by the Court of Cassation and the T.G.N.A. Ignorance of the law is no defense to a criminal charge. Criminal intent is usually necessary (with some exceptions) for punishment of felonies, but is not necessary for punishment of misdemeanors. Actions that might otherwise be criminal may be justified if they are performed in the enforcement of law, the prevention of crime, or the defense of person. There are no juvenile courts in Turkey and children, in the different age categories, may be adjudged in the regular courts as "capable" or "incapable" under the law; if the former, they are usually subject to institutional care or light sentence. Older persons, the deaf and the dumb, etc., are frequently given lighter sentences in criminal cases. Suspended sentences are not uncommon and, depending on circumstances, a complaint may be withdrawn, a trial discontinued, or a special pardon or general amnesty granted. There are also various "statutes of limitations" for the conduct of certain types of criminal cases.

B. LOWER COURTS
  1. *Courts of justices of the peace*
      a. Single-judge courts.
      b. Judge minor civil cases (e.g., collection of debts) and misdemeanors (e.g., disturbances of the peace); instituted by a private party or a public prosecutor.
  2. *Courts of first instance*
      a. Single-judge courts.
      b. Judge cases which are outside the jurisdiction of the Central Criminal Courts or the Commercial Courts (i.e., the more serious civil disputes and minor crimes); instituted by a private party or a public prosecutor.
  3. *Central Criminal Courts*
      a. Composed of at least three judges.
      b. Judge cases involving major crimes (i.e., punishable by more than five years' imprisonment, long-term imprisonment at hard labor, or by a heavier penalty); instituted by the public prosecutor.
  4. *Other courts*, with specialized membership, jurisdiction, organization, and functions, include the Commerce, Labor, "National Protection", and Collective Press Courts; their decisions can be appealed to the Court of Cassation. Also, a Court of Accounts audits all the revenues and disbursements of the State, in accordance with the laws and on behalf of the T.G.N.A.

C. HIGHER COURTS

1. *Court of Cassation*

a. Members elected by Supreme Council of Judges (See Section D below), with a Chairman and Deputy-Chairman elected from the membership in a plenary session by an absolute majority and by secret ballot.

b. Consists of Civil, Penal, Commercial, Enforcement, and Bankruptcy Chambers, each of which has a Chairman and member judges; all the Chambers together constitute the Court of Cassation Quorum, which has its own Chairman.

c. Reviews the decisions of lower courts and may remand a case to a lower court for retrial; if the original decision is sustained on retrial, the case may again be reviewed and finally disposed by the Court of Cassation in plenary session (Cassation Quorum).

d. Public prosecutor may, in the name of individuals or organizations, contest the legality of a decision by a lower court, or maintain that the disturbed social order was not restored.

2. *Council of State*

a. Chairman, members, and its Chief Attorney elected from among individuals qualified by law, by a committee from the Constitutional Court, by secret ballot and a two-thirds majority on the first two ballotings or an absolute majority thereafter.

b. Serves as both an administrative court of the first instance and an administrative court of the last instance in general.

c. Hears and settles administrative disputes and suits; expresses opinions on draft laws submitted by the Council of Ministers; examines draft regulations, specifications, and contracts of concessions; and discharges such other duties as prescribed by law.

d. In addition to the Council of State, there are other lower "administrative courts" (e.g., the District and Provincial Administrative Councils; the Tax Hearings Commissions and the Tax Appeals Commissions; and the District and Provincial Disciplinary Commissions), with limited and specific jurisdictions granted by various recent statutes. Their decisions can be appealed to the Council of State, unless otherwise provided by law.

3. *Military Court of Cassation*
   a. Members and its Chief Prosecutor appointed by President of the Republic from among individuals qualified by law, and who are at least forty years of age and have served for at least ten years as military judges or prosecutors; members elect the Chairman from among themselves.
   b. Serves as court of last instance in reviewing decisions and verdicts of lower military courts, and as court of first and last instance in special military cases as prescribed by law.

4. *Court of Jurisdictional Disputes*
   a. Membership and organization is to be determined by law, but the Chairman will be designated by the Constitutional Court from among its own regular or alternate members.
   b. Constitutionally empowered to settle disputes among civil, administrative, and military courts on jurisdictional matters and verdicts.

D. SUPREME COUNCIL OF JUDGES
   1. *Organization*
      a. Consists of 18 regular and 5 alternate members; 6 of the regular members are elected by the Court of Cassation and 6 by judges of the first rank from among themselves, and 3 each by the National Assembly and Senate of the Republic; the Court of Cassation elects 2 of the alternate members, while the judges of the first rank, the National Assembly, and Senate of the Republic each elect 1 alternate member.
      b. Supreme Council elects its Chairman from among its own members by a vote of absolute majority of its plenary session.
      c. Term of office of members is four years, with one-half the members elected every two years, and limitations on the right of re-election.
      d. Members cannot engage in any other duties or functions during their term in office.
      e. Further organization, methods of procedure, quorums for meetings and decisions, salaries, and

allowances of the Chairman and members, etc., are regulated by law.

    f. Minister of Justice may participate in meetings of the Supreme Council, but has no vote.

  2. *Functions and powers*

    a. Decides personnel matters about judges.

    b. May dismiss a judge, after a fair hearing, by absolute majority vote of its plenary session.

    c. Minister of Justice may request Supreme Council to initiate disciplinary action against a judge.

    d. Approves the abolition of a court or staff positions, and the changing of the area of jurisdiction of a court.

    e. Supervises the behavior of judges in the courts of law.

E. CONSTITUTIONAL COURT

  1. *Organization*

    a. Consists of 15 regular and 5 alternate members; 4 of the regular members are elected by the Court of Cassation, 3 by the Council of State from among its membership, 3 by the National Assembly and 2 by the Senate of the Republic, and 1 each by the Chief Prosecutor of the Republic, the Chief Attorney of the Council of State, and the Court of Accounts; the Court of Cassation elects 2 of the alternate members, while the Council of State and the legislative chambers of the T.G.N.A. each elect 1 alternate member.

    b. Constitutional Court elects its Chairman and a Deputy-Chairman for a term of four years, from among its own membership, by secret ballot and a two-thirds majority of its plenary session; reelection is permissible, and retirement is compulsory at age 65.

    c. Members cannot undertake any other public or private functions.

    d. Further organization, trial procedures, method of work, and the division of labor among its members are determined by its own self-drafted by-laws.

  2. *Functions and powers*

    a. Constitutional Court conducts its business on basis of written records, except when it acts as a High

Court and when it requires interested parties to present oral explanations.

b. The President of the Republic, the political parties represented in the T.G.N.A., one-sixth of the members of a legislative chamber, the Supreme Council of Judges, the Court of Cassation, the Council of State, the Military Court of Cassation, and the universities may initiate annulment suits based on unconstitutionality of laws or of by-laws of the T.G.N.A.

c. Rulings and annulments of the Court are final, non-retroactive, and binding throughout the Turkish Republic.

d. Sits as a High Court in impeachment proceedings: "The Constitutional Court shall try as a High Council [i.e., Court], the President of the Republic, the members of the Council of Ministers; the Chairman and members of the Court of Cassation; the Council of State; the Military Court of Cassation; the Supreme Council of Judges and the Court of Accounts, the Chief Prosecutor of the Republic, the Chief Attorney, the Chief Prosecutor of the Military Court of Cassation, as well as its own members for offenses connected with [the performance of] their duties. . . ." (Art. 147).

e. Discharges such other obligations as prescribed by the Constitution, but does NOT exercise appellate jurisdiction over the regular, administrative, and military court systems.

F. LAW-ENFORCEMENT OFFICERS AND AGENCIES

1. *Chief Prosecutor of the Republic,* elected by the plenary session of the Court of Cassation by an absolute majority and by secret ballot; represents the State and its interests in various cases in the courts of law; similar functions are performed by the *Chief Attorney of the Council of State* and the *Chief Prosecutor of the Military Court of Cassation* in matters that fall within their jurisdictions.

2. *Minister of the Interior,* who appoints, supervises, and is responsible for the

a. Regular police, centralized under the Directorate-General attached to the Ministry, with provincial, communal, and municipal subdivisions which collaborate in police matters with the corresponding executive authorities on each level of administration.

b. Administrative police, organized as the *Gendarmerie* within the Ministry, and divided into special Commands attached to the appropriate civil authorities on the provincial, communal, and municipal levels; the *Gendarmerie* consists of exceptional Army-trained men, who maintain order in the rural and outlying districts beyond the jurisdiction of the regular police.

c. Security police, under the central direction of the Ministry and also administered through territorial subdivisions, who are charged with the prevention of crimes and the maintenance of the State security; they have other special functions to perform under the laws.

3. *Minister of Justice*, who appoints and supervises the public prosecutors for each Province and its subdivisions.

4. *Council of Ministers* (Cabinet), which can proclaim a state of martial law not exceeding one month, with the approval of the T.G.N.A.; this can be extended two months each time.

VII. LOCAL GOVERNMENT

A. BASIC ELEMENTS OF LOCAL GOVERNMENT

1. Geographical and administrative subdivisions in Turkey include the Provinces, sub-Provinces or Districts, Communes, Municipalities, and Villages.

2. Provinces and their subdivisions have a full legal status as "corporate persons" and are administered on the basis of the decentralization and division of public functions.

3. Provincial and local administrators of national services are appointed by, and responsible to, the corresponding national ministry.

4. Ministry of the Interior (and through it, the Council of Ministers and the Turkish Grand National Assembly) controls the provincial and subordinate units in a number of ways, viz., basic legislation, financial assistance, review and audit of public expenditures, appointments, supervision of administrative services, inquiries and investigations, reports, etc.

5. Executive authority on one level is usually directly responsible to the executive authority on the next highest level of administration for the performance of governmental functions, except for Defense and Justice which are centrally administered throughout the country.

6. Qualifications, appointments or elections, rights, promotions, salaries, dismissals, etc., of all provincial and local officials are determined by laws; every public official or employee is personally responsible for his conduct and actions in his work.

7. Four years is the normal term in office for most elected local governmental personnel, although the term of appointed personnel may range from one to four years, and be renewable or not, depending on the particular office.

B. PROVINCES

1. *Executive authority:* Governor, appointed by the President of the Republic on the recommendation of the Minister of the Interior and the Cabinet; among other things, he

   a. Represents the central government (except for Defense and Justice).

   b. Supervises the general administration of the Province as conducted by his staff of administrative and technical experts.

   c. Presides, occasionally, over the meetings of the provincial General Assembly.

   d. Exercises a qualified executive veto power.

   e. Dissolves the Assembly, with the approval of the Ministry of the Interior; he must, however, call new provincial elections within three months.

2. *Legislature:* General Assembly, popularly elected by the voters for a four-year term; the Deputies hold periodic

meetings and are not paid a regular salary for their services; in-between legislative sessions, a special Interim Committee represents the interests of the people and, in varying degrees, checks the executive authority; the Deputies

a. Pass resolutions and enact provincial legislation.
b. Approve the budget and allot monies for public expenditures.
c. Review the provincial administration of national services.
d. Plan and provide the organization for various provincial functions.
e. Perform other legal responsibilities.

C. Districts and Communes

1. These are special administrative areas or administrative subdivisions of the central and provincial governments.
2. Executive authority in the District is the Lieutenant, appointed by and responsible to the Ministry of the Interior; the executive in the Commune is the Director, appointed by and responsible to the Governor of the Province.
3. There may, or may not, be popularly-elected Councils or other representations of the people residing in the Districts and Communes.

D. Municipalities

1. *Executive authority:* Mayor, appointed by the Municipal Assembly or elected by the voters; he represents the municipality, supervises the administration of its public services (with the help of the administrative staff), and performs other characteristic duties.
2. *Legislature:* Municipal Assembly, popularly-elected by the voters for a four-year term; the Deputies convene in legislative session three or more times a year and are not paid a regular salary for their services; they are concerned with such matters as the

   a. Enactment of budgets;
   b. Imposition of fines (but not taxes) and collection of fees and the profits from municipal enterprises;

Chart 45. AGENCIES OF LOCAL GOVERNMENT IN TURKEY

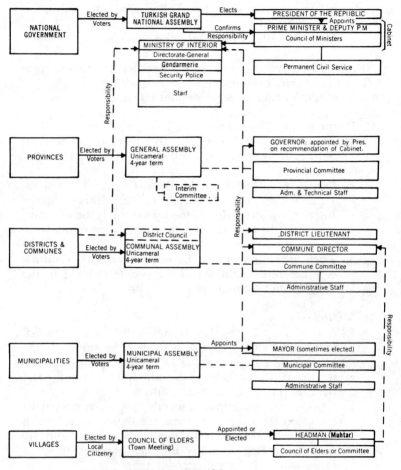

Note: The functions of Justice and National Defense
(security) are always administered throughout
the country under the direct authority and
supervision of the Ministry of Interior.

    c. Operation and regulation of public utilities and transportation;

    d. Administration and protection of the public welfare and safety;

    e. Observance of the public laws.

E. VILLAGES (the fundamental units of Turkish local government)

    1. *Executive authority:* Headman *(Muhtar)* and Council of Elders, elected by the local citizens; represent the village and perform duties as designated by the people.

    2. *Legislature:* Town Meeting (in the local Mosque), attended by the adult local citizens; collaborates with the executive authority in keeping the village public records, maintaining schools, providing the water supply, repairing public roads, and collecting local contributions.

SELECTED READINGS

Allen, Henry Elisha, *The Turkish Transformation.* Chicago: University of Chicago Press, 1935.

Armstrong, Harold Courteney, *Grey Wolf, Mustafa Kemal.* London: Arthur Barker, 1936.

Bisbee, Eleanor, *The New Turks: Pioneers of the Republic, 1920–1950.* Philadelphia: University of Pennsylvania Press, 1951.

Bonne, Alfred, *State and Economics in the Middle East; a Society in Transition.* London: Routledge and Paul, 1955.

Brock, R., *Ghost on Horseback.* New York: Duell and Company, 1954.

Cooke, Hedley V., *Challenge and Response in the Middle East.* New York: Harper & Brothers, Publishers, 1952.

Davis, Helen Miller, *Constitutions, Electoral Laws, Treaties of States in the Near and Middle East.* Durham: Duke University Press, 1953.

Ekrem, Selma, *Turkey, Old and New.* New York: Charles Scribner's Sons, 1947.

Jackh, Ernest, *The Rising Crescent; Turkey Yesterday, Today and Tomorrow.* New York: Rinehart & Company, Inc., 1944.

Karpat, Kemal H., *Turkey's Politics.* Princeton: Princeton University Press, 1959.

Kirk, George E., *Contemporary Arab Politics.* New York: Frederick A. Praeger, Inc., 1961.

Lengyel, Emil, *Turkey*. New York: Random House, Inc., 1941.

Lewis, Bernard, *The Emergence of Modern Turkey*. London: Oxford University Press, 1961.

Lewis, Geoffrey L., *Turkey*. New York: Frederick A. Praeger, Inc., 1955.

Luke, Harry Charles, *The Old Turkey and the New; from Byzantium to Ankara*. London: Bles, 1955.

Orga, Irfan, *Phoenix Ascendant; the Rise of Modern Turkey*. London: R. Hale, 1958.

Paneth, P., *Turkey—Decadence and Rebirth*. London: Alliance Press, 1945.

Price, M. Philips, *History of Turkey*. New York: Macmillan Company, 1956.

Tomlin, E. W., *Life in Modern Turkey*. Toronto: Nelson and Sons, 1946.

Ward, Barbara, *Turkey*. London: Oxford University Press, 1942.

Webster, Donald Everett, *The Turkey of Atatürk*. Philadelphia: American Academy of Political and Social Science, 1939.

APPENDIX

CONSTITUTION OF THE
GERMAN DEMOCRATIC REPUBLIC (1949)

Preamble

The German People, imbued with the desire to safeguard human liberty and rights, to reshape collective and economic life in accordance with the principles of social justice, to serve social progress, and to promote a secure peace and amity with all peoples, have adopted this Constitution.

A. FUNDAMENTALS OF STATE AUTHORITY

ARTICLE 1

Germany is an indivisible democratic republic, the foundations of which are the German Laender.

The (German Democratic) Republic decides on all issues which are essential to the existence and development of the German people as a whole, all other issues being decided upon by independent action of the Laender (states).

As a rule, decisions of the Republic are carried out by the Laender.

There is only one German nationality.

ARTICLE 2

The colors of the German Democratic Republic are black, red, and gold.

The capital of the Republic is Berlin.

ARTICLE 3

All state authority emanates from the people.

Every citizen has the right and the duty to take part in the formation of the political life of his Gemeinde (community), Kreis (county), Land (state) and of the German Democratic Republic.

This right of co-determination takes the form of:

    voting in popular initiatives and referendums;

    exercising the right to vote and standing for election;

entering upon public offices in general administration and in the administration of justice.

Every citizen has the right to submit petitions to the popular representative body.

State authority must serve the welfare of the people, liberty, peace, and the progress of democracy.

Those active in public service are servants of the community as a whole and not of any one party. Their activity is supervised by the popular representative body.

ARTICLE 4

All measures taken by state authority must be compatible with the principles which the Constitution has declared to be contained in state authority. Pursuant to Article 66 of this Constitution, the popular representative body is to decide on the constitutionality of such measures. Everyone has the right and the duty to resist measures contradicting enactments of the popular representative body.

Every citizen is in duty bound to act in accordance with the Constitution and to defend it against its enemies.

ARTICLE 5

The generally recognized rules of international law are binding upon state authority and every citizen.

It is the duty of state authority to maintain and cultivate amicable relations with all peoples.

No citizen may participate in belligerent actions designed to oppress any people.

B. CONTENTS AND LIMITS OF STATE AUTHORITY

I. Rights of the Citizen

ARTICLE 6

All citizens have equal rights before the law.

Incitement to boycott of democratic institutions or organizations, incitement to attempts on the life of democratic politicians, the manifestation of religious and racial hatred and of hatred against other peoples, militaristic propaganda and warmongering as well as any other discriminatory acts are felonious crimes within the meaning of the Penal Code. The exercise of democratic rights within the meaning of the Constitution is not an incitement to boycott.

Whoever has been convicted of such a crime is disqualified from holding public office or a leading position in economic or cultural life. He also loses the right to vote and to stand for election.

ARTICLE 7

Men and women have equal rights.

All laws and regulations which conflict with the equality of women are abolished.

ARTICLE 8

Personal liberty, inviolability of the home, secrecy of the mail, and the right to take up residence at any place are guaranteed. State authority may restrict or revoke these freedoms only on the basis of a law applicable to all citizens.

ARTICLE 9

All citizens have the right, within the limits of universally applicable laws, to express their opinion freely and publicly and to hold unarmed and peaceful assemblies for that purpose. This freedom shall not be restricted by any service or employment status, and no one may be discriminated against for exercising this right.

There is no press censorship.

ARTICLE 10

No citizen may be turned over to a foreign power by extradition.

Allies shall neither be extradited nor expelled, if, outside this country, they are subject to persecution because of their struggle in support of the principles embodied in this Constitution.

Every citizen has the right to emigrate. This right may be restricted only by a law of the Republic.

ARTICLE 11

Free ethnic development of foreign-language elements of the population of the Republic is to be promoted by legislative and administrative action. In particular, they must on no account be prevented from using their native language in matters of education, internal administration, and administration of justice.

ARTICLE 12

All citizens have the right to form associations or societies for purposes not conflicting with criminal law.

ARTICLE 13

Associations that, in accordance with their statutes, aim to bring about, on the basis of this Constitution, a democratic organization of public life and whose executive bodies are determined by their members, are entitled to submit nominations of candidates for election to membership in Gemeinde (community), Kreis (county), and Land (state) popular representative bodies.

Nominations for the People's Chamber may be made only by those associations which, pursuant to their statutes, aim to bring about the democratic organization of public and social life in the entire Republic and which maintain an organization throughout the territory of the Republic.

ARTICLE 14

Everyone is guaranteed the right to organize for the improvement of wages and working conditions. Any agreements and measures intended to restrict this right or impede it are unlawful and prohibited.

(Recognized) trade unions are vouchsafed the right to strike.

ARTICLE 15

(The individual's) capacity for work is protected by state authority.

The right to work is guaranteed. By means of economic control the state ensures to each citizen work and a living. Whenever suitable work cannot be found for him, he shall be provided necessary sustenance.

ARTICLE 16

Every worker is entitled to recreation, to an annual leave with pay and to being provided for in illness and old age.

Sundays, holidays, and the first of May are days of rest and are protected by law.

On the principle of autonomous administration by the insured, a unitary and comprehensive social insurance system serves to maintain the health and strength of the working population, to protect motherhood, and to provide against the economic consequences of old age, disability, unemployment, and other vicissitudes of life.

ARTICLE 17

Workers and employees shall play a decisive part in the regulation of industrial production, wages, and working conditions in enterprises.

Workers and employees shall exercise these rights through trade unions and Works Councils.

ARTICLE 18

The Republic shall establish uniform labor legislation, a uniform system of labor courts and uniform legislation for the protection of labor, in all of which the working population shall play a decisive part.

Working conditions must be such as to safeguard the health, cultural requirements, and family life of the workers.

Remuneration for work must correspond to performance and must provide a worthwhile existence for the worker and those dependents entitled to his support.

Men and women, adults and juveniles, are entitled to equal pay for equal work.

Women enjoy special protection in employment relations. The laws of the Republic shall provide for institutions enabling women to co-ordinate their tasks as citizens and workers with their duties as wives and mothers.

Juvenile workers shall be protected against exploitation and saved from falling into moral, physical, or mental neglect. Child labor is prohibited.

II. The Economic Order

ARTICLE 19

Organization of economic life must conform to the principles of social justice; it must guarantee to all an existence compatible with the dignity of man.

It is incumbent upon the economy to contribute to the benefit of the whole people and to the satisfaction of its wants and to insure that everybody will obtain, in accordance with his performance, a just share in the yield of production.

Freedom (of enterprise in the) economic (field) is guaranteed to the individual within the scope of the above tasks and aims.

ARTICLE 20

Farmers, traders, and craftsmen are to be given support in the development of their private initiative. Mutual aid through cooperatives is to be expanded.

ARTICLE 21

In order to secure the basic standard of living for its citizens and to promote their prosperity, the state, acting through its legislative bodies and with the direct participation of its citizens establishes a public economic plan. It is the task of the popular representative bodies to supervise the implementation of the plan.

ARTICLE 22

Private property is guaranteed by the Constitution. Its scope and its limitations are derived from law and from the obligations toward the welfare of the community at large.

The right of inheritance is guaranteed to the extent provided by civil law. The share of the Government in the estate is determined by law.

Intellectual work and the rights of authors, inventors, and artists enjoy protection, furtherance, and support by the Republic.

ARTICLE 23

Restrictions on private property and expropriations may be imposed only for the benefit of the general public and on a legal basis. They shall take place against reasonable compensation unless the law provides otherwise. If the amount of compensation is in dispute, recourse to the ordinary courts shall be open insofar as a law does not provide otherwise.

ARTICLE 24

Property commits to duties. Its use must not run counter to the public good.

Misuse of property with the intent of establishing an economic ascendancy to the detriment of the public good results in expropriation without compensation and transfer to the people's ownership.

Enterprises owned by war criminals and active National Socialists have been expropriated and will be transferred to the people's ownership (without compensation). The same shall apply to private enterprises offering their services to a warlike policy.

All private monopolistic formations such as cartels, syndicates, combines, trusts, and similar private organizations aiming at an increase of profits through the control of production, prices, and markets have been abolished and are prohibited.

Privately-owned large estates with an acreage of more than one hundred hectares are dissolved and shall be redistributed without compensation.

Following the accomplishment of the above agrarian reform, ownership of their land shall be guaranteed to the farmers.

ARTICLE 25

All mineral resources, all economically exploitable natural power sources, as well as the mining, iron and steel and electric power industries serving their exploitation, are to be transferred to the people's ownership.

Until such transfer, their use will be supervised by the Laender or by the Republic insofar as the interests of the whole of Germany are involved.

ARTICLE 26

Distribution and utilization of the land shall be supervised, and each abuse thereof shall be prevented. Incremental value of landed property which has accrued without expenditure of labor or capital is to be made of use to the collectivity.

Every citizen and every family shall be assured of a healthy dwelling befitting their needs. Herein special consideration shall be given to victims of fascism, to seriously disabled persons, to persons having incurred special war losses, and to resettlers.

Maintenance and furtherance of assured returns from agriculture will be safeguarded also by means of land planning and conservation.

ARTICLE 27

Private economic enterprises suitable for socialization may be transferred to collective ownership by law under the provisions dealing with expropriation.

The Republic, the Laender (states), the Kreise (counties) and Gemeinden (communities) may be given by law a decisive voice in the management, or otherwise, of enterprises and associations.

Economic enterprises and associations may, by legislation, be combined into autonomous organizations in order to ensure the collaboration of all working elements of the nation, to give workers and employers a share in the management, and to regulate production, manufacture, distribution, utilization, prices, as well as import and export of commodities along the principles of collective economic interests.

Consumer and buying co-operatives, profit-making co-operatives and agricultural co-operatives and their associations shall be integrated into the collective economy while preserving their statutes and characteristic features.

ARTICLE 28

Any alienation or encumbrance of landed property, productive plants or shares therein owned by the people must have the approval of the popular representative body exercising jurisdiction over the title-holding agency. Such approval requires at least a two-thirds majority of the statutory number of members.

ARTICLE 29

Property and income shall be taxed according to progressively increasing rates on the basis of social viewpoints and with particular consideration of family obligations.

Taxation must give special consideration to earned property and income.

III. Family and Motherhood

ARTICLE 30

Marriage and family are the foundations of collective life and are protected by the state.

All laws or statutory provisions by which the equal rights of men and women within the family are impaired are abrogated.

ARTICLE 31

Parents have the natural right to bring up their children in a democratic spirit which will enable them mentally and physically to become responsible individuals, and this is their supreme duty towards society.

ARTICLE 32

During maternity a woman has a rightful claim to particular protection and care by the state.

The Republic shall issue a law for the protection of mothers. Institutions are to be created to protect mother and child.

ARTICLE 33

Extra-marital birth is to be no ground for discrimination against either the child or the parents. Any laws and statutory provisions to be contrary are abrogated.

IV. Education

ARTICLE 34

Art, science, and their teaching, are free.

The state participates in their cultivation and grants them protection, especially against their abuse for purposes which are contrary to the provisions or the spirit of the Constitution.

ARTICLE 35

Every citizen has an equal right to education and to a free choice of his vocation.

Education of youth and adult education of the citizenry in intellectual or technical disciplines are provided by public institutions in all fields of national and social life.

ARTICLE 36

The Laender are responsible for the establishment of a public school system and for the practical operation of school instruction. To this effect the Republic shall issue uniform legislative provisions of a basic character. The Republic may itself establish public educational institutions.

The Republic shall issue uniform provisions for the training of teachers. Such training shall take place in the universities or institutions of equal status.

ARTICLE 37

The school educates the youth in the spirit of the Constitution to be independently thinking and responsibly acting individuals who will be able and willing to take their place in the life of the community at large.

As conveyor of culture, the school has the task of educating the youth to be truly humane in the spirit of peaceful and amicable co-operation in the life of nations and genuine democracy.

The parents shall participate in the school education of their children by councils of parents.

ARTICLE 38

Attendance at school is compulsory for all until completion of the eighteenth year of life. After completion of a primary school course compulsory for all children, training is pursued in a vocational or technical school, in high school, or in other public educational institutions. All juveniles under eighteen years of age must attend a vocational or training school unless they attend another (public) school. Private schools as substitutes for public schools (state or municipal) are inadmissible.

Vocational and technical schools afford general and vocational training.

High schools (Oberschule) pave the way for admission to a university. Such admission, however, does not require high school attendance; attendance at other public educational institutions, which shall be extended or created for that purpose, may take its place.

All citizens must be given the opportunity to prepare their admission to a university in special preparatory schools.

Members of all classes of the population shall be given an opportunity to acquire knowledge in colleges of the people without interruption of their occupational activities.

ARTICLE 39

Every child must be given the opportunity fully to develop its physical, mental, and moral capacities. The school career of youth must on no account depend on the social or economic position of the parents. Indeed, children who are at a disadvantage because of social conditions are to be given special care. Attendance at vocational school, high school, and university must be open to gifted pupils from all classes of the population.

Tuition is free. Textbooks and instructional material used in compulsory schools are furnished without cost: in case of need, attendance at vocational school, high school, and university will be promoted through scholarships and other measures.

ARTICLE 40

Religious instruction is a concern of the religious associations. The exercise of this right is guaranteed.

V. Religion and Religious Associations

ARTICLE 41

Every citizen enjoys complete freedom of faith and conscience. The practice of religion without interference enjoys the protection of the Republic.

Any abuse of establishments created by religious associations, of religious acts or religious instruction for purposes which are contrary to the principles of the Constitution or for purposes of party politics is prohibited. However, the right of religious associations to express an attitude in keeping with their own viewpoints issues vital for the people shall be uncontested.

ARTICLE 42

Civil or civic rights and duties are neither conditioned nor restricted by the practice of religion.

Exercise of civil or civic rights or the admission to public service is independent of a religious creed.

No one is required to disclose his religious belief. Administrative agencies have the right to make inquiries about a person's membership in a religious association only insofar as rights and duties are connected therewith, or a statistical survey directed by law requires it.

No one may be forced to attend religious rites or celebrations, or to participate in religious exercises, or to use a religious form of oath.

ARTICLE 43

There is no state church. Freedom of membership in religious association is guaranteed.

Every religious association regulates and administers its affairs autonomously and in accordance with the laws applicable to all.

Religious associations remain public law corporations insofar as they were such heretofore. Other religious associations are granted like rights upon their application, if through their organization and the number of their members they offer a guarantee of permanency. If several such public law religious associations join in a union, this union is also a corporation of public law.

Religious associations having public law status are entitled to levy taxes upon their members on the basis of the governmental tax list according to (the standards of) the general provisions.

Associations whose function is the common cultivation of a philosophy of life have the same status as religious associations.

ARTICLE 44

The right of the church to give religious instruction on school premises is guaranteed. Religious instruction is given by personnel selected by the church. No one may be forced to give, or be prevented from giving, religious instruction. Those entitled to bring up a child shall determine whether the latter shall receive religious instruction.

ARTICLE 45

Public contributions to religious associations, which rest upon law, contract, or special legal title, shall be abrogated by legislation.

Ownership and other rights of the religious associations and religious unions, in respect to their institutions, foundations, and other property devoted to purposes of worship, education, and charity, are guaranteed.

ARTICLE 46

Insofar as there exists a need for religious service and spiritual guidance in hospitals, penal institutions, or other public institutions, the religious associations are to be given an opportunity for religious exercises. No person may be forced to participate.

ARTICLE 47

Any person wishing to resign from a public-law religious association and to have such resignation become legally effective, shall declare his intention before a court, or submit it in form of a publicly attested individual declaration.

ARTICLE 48

Decisions as to whether children up to fourteen years of age shall belong to a religious association rests with the persons entitled to bring them up. Older children shall decide themselves whether or not they wish to be members of an association or organization professing a religious creed or a philosophy of life.

VI. Effectiveness of Basic Rights

ARTICLE 49

A basic right may not be violated in its essential content, not even where this Constitution authorizes its restriction by law or makes its further development subject to (specific) legislation.

C. ORGANIZATION OF STATE AUTHORITY

I. The Popular Representative Body of the Republic

ARTICLE 50

The supreme authority of the Republic is the People's Chamber.

ARTICLE 51

The People's Chamber is composed of the representatives of the German people.

Representatives are elected in universal, equal, direct, and secret ballot for a term of four years, according to the principles of proportional representation.

Representatives serve the people as a whole. They are bound only by their own conscience and are not bound by any instructions.

ARTICLE 52

All citizens who have passed their eighteenth birthday have the right to vote.

All citizens who have passed their twenty-first birthday may stand for election.

The People's Chamber consists of four hundred representatives.

Details are determined by an Electoral Law.

ARTICLE 53

Nominations for the People's Chamber may be submitted only by associations which satisfy the provisions of Article 13 paragraph 2.

Details are determined by a law of the Republic.

ARTICLE 54

Elections are held on a Sunday or legal holiday. Freedom and secrecy of the ballot are guaranteed.

ARTICLE 55

The People's Chamber convenes not later than thirty days after election, unless it is convoked by the previous Presidium for an earlier date.

The President must convoke the People's Chamber if the Government, or at least one-fifth of the representatives in the People's Chamber, so request.

ARTICLE 56

A new Chamber must be elected not later than sixty days after the end of a legislative term, or forty-five days after dissolution of the People's Chamber.

Before the completion of a legislative term, the People's Chamber may be dissolved only upon its own resolution or upon a referendum, except in the case described in Article 95, paragraph 6.

To dissolve the People's Chamber upon its own resolution, the consent of more than one-half of the statutory number of representatives is necessary.

ARTICLE 57

When first convening, the People's Chamber elects the Presidium and adopts Rules of Procedure.

Each parliamentary party is represented in the Presidium, provided that it has at least forty members.

The Presidium consists of the President, his deputies, and of associate members.

The President directs the business of the Presidium and presides over the deliberations of the People's Chamber. Maintenance of order on the premises of the Chamber is his prerogative.

ARTICLE 58

Resolutions of the Presidium are adopted by majority vote.

A quorum exists when at least half of the members of the Presidium are present.

Upon the resolution of the Presidium the acting President convokes the People's Chamber; he also fixes the date for new elections.

The Presidium continues in office until the convening of the new People's Chamber.

ARTICLE 59

The People's Chamber examines the accreditation of its members and decides on the validity of elections.

ARTICLE 60

For the periods when the People's Chamber is not in session, and after a legislative term has expired or the People's Chamber has been dissolved, the People's Chamber appoints three Standing Committees to carry on its functions, namely:

a Committee of General Affairs,
a Committee of Economic and Financial Affairs, and
a Committee of Foreign Affairs.

These Committees have the same rights as investigating committees.

ARTICLE 61

The People's Chamber adopts laws and resolutions by majority vote, unless this Constitution provides otherwise.

A quorum exists when more than half of the members of the Chamber are present.

ARTICLE 62
Deliberations of the People's Chamber and of its committees are open to the public. The public may be excluded from the People's Chamber if two-thirds of the representatives present so request, and from the committees on the demand of the majority of the members of such committees.

True records of public meetings of the People's Chamber or its committees do not entail any responsibility.

ARTICLE 63
The functions of the People's Chamber include:
    the determination of the principles of governmental policy, and of its implementation;
    the confirmation, supervision, and recall of the Government;
    the determination of administrative policies and supervision over all governmental agencies;
    the right to legislate, except when a (popular) referendum is held;
    decisions on the national budget, on the Economic Plan, on loans and credits of the Republic and the ratification of state treaties;
    the granting of amnesties;
    the election of the President of the Republic jointly with the Laender Chamber; and
    the election and recall of the members of the Supreme Court of the Republic and of the Prosecutor General of the Republic.

ARTICLE 64
For the purpose of obtaining information, the People's Chamber or any of its committees may request the presence of the Minister President or any other Minister, their permanent deputies, or the chiefs of administrative agencies of the Republic. The members of the Government and deputies designated by them are authorized to attend meetings of the People's Chamber and its committees at all times.

If they so request, members of the Government or their deputies must be given the floor during deliberations, regardless of the agenda.

They are subject to the disciplinary authority of the President.

ARTICLE 65

For the purpose of supervising the activities of governmental agencies, the People's Chamber has the right, or, if at least one-fifth of the statutory number of representatives so request, the duty, to appoint investigating committees. These committees takes such evidence as they, or the representatives having requested the investigation, deem necessary. They may for this purpose be represented by persons commissioned by them.

Courts and administrations must comply with the request of these committees, or persons acting on their instructions, for the taking of evidence and, upon demand, present their files for inspection.

In the taking of evidence by the investigating committees the provisions of the Criminal Procedure are applied correspondingly.

ARTICLE 66

For the duration of the legislative term the People's Chamber establishes a Constitutional Committee, in which all parliamentary parties are represented according to their (numerical) strength. To this Committee shall also belong three members of the Supreme Court of the Republic as well as three German professors of constitutional law who must on no account be members of the People's Chamber.

Members of the Constitutional Committee are elected by the People's Chamber.

(Only) the Constitutional Committee reviews laws of the Republic as to their constitutionality.

Constitutionality of laws of the Republic may be challenged by not less than one-third of the members of the People's Chamber, by its Presidium, by the President of the Republic, by the Government of the Republic, and by the Laender Chamber.

Disputes on constitutional questions between the Republic and the Laender, and the compatibility of Land legislation and legislation of the Republic, are reviewed by the Constitutional Committee, with the assistance of three elected delegates of the Laender Chamber.

Final decision with respect to the report of the Constitutional Committee is reserved to the People's Chamber; the latter's decision is binding on everyone.

The People's Chamber also determines the execution of its decision.

The People's Chamber is, in the exercise of the administrative supervision delegated to it, responsible for determining whether an administrative measure is unconstitutional.

ARTICLE 67

No proceedings, judicial or disciplinary, may at any time be instituted against any member of the People's Chamber for his vote or for any utterance made, in the exercise of his parliamentary functions, nor may he be otherwise called to account outside the Chamber. This does not apply to defamation in the meaning of the Penal Code, if it has been established to be such by an investigating committee of the People's Chamber.

Restraint of personal freedom, house searches, seizures, or criminal prosecution may not be instituted against representatives except with the consent of the People's Chamber.

Any criminal proceedings against a representative in the People's Chamber and any arrest or other restraint of his personal freedom, is suspended for the duration of the session upon demand of the Chamber of which the representative is a member.

Members of the People's Chamber have the right to refuse to give evidence concerning persons who confided facts to them in their capacity as representatives, or to whom they have entrusted facts in this capacity, as well as concerning those facts themselves. In respect to seizure of documents, they enjoy the same privileges as persons who have the legal right to refuse testimony.

No search or seizure may be conducted in the premises of the People's Chamber without the consent of the Presidium.

ARTICLE 68

Members of the People's Chamber do not require leave in order to perform their functions.

Persons standing as candidates for a seat in the People's Chamber must be granted such leave as is necessary to prepare for election.

Salaries and wages continue to be paid.

ARTICLE 69

Members in the People's Chamber receive an allowance for expenses, which is tax-exempt.

Renunciation of the allowance for expenses is inadmissible. The claim to the allowance for expenses cannot be transferred or garnisheed.

ARTICLE 70

Members of the People's Chamber are entitled to free travel in all public transport.

II. Representation of the Laender

ARTICLE 71

A Laender Chamber is established to represent the German Laender. In the Laender Chamber, each Land has one representative for every five hundred thousand inhabitants. Each Land has at least one representative.

ARTICLE 72

The representatives in the Laender Chamber are elected by the Landtage (Land legislatures) in proportion to the numerical strength of the parliamentary parties represented therein. Laender Chamber representatives will serve for the duration of the legislative term of the respective Landtag. As a rule, Laender Chamber representatives should be Landtag members.

Each Landtag ascertains the wishes of its Land on matters to be deliberated in the Laender Chamber. This does not affect the rights of the representatives, as laid down in the Land Constitutions, to follow freely the dictates of their conscience.

ARTICLE 73

The Laender Chamber elects its Presidium and adopts Rules of Procedure. The Presidium consists of the President, his deputies, and the associate members.

ARTICLE 74

The Laender Chamber is convoked by its President whenever it is necessary for the transaction of its business.

The Laender Chamber is also convoked upon the demand of one-fifth of its members.

ARTICLE 75

Meetings of the Laender Chamber are open to the public.

As far as provided in the Rules of Procedure, the public may be excluded if certain items of the agenda are discussed.

ARTICLE 76

The Laender Chamber makes its decisions by majority vote unless this Constitution provides otherwise.

ARTICLE 77

The Laender Chamber may set up all necessary committees as provided in the Rules of Procedure.

ARTICLE 78

The Laender Chamber has the right to introduce bills in the People's Chamber. It has the right to reject legislation as provided in Article 84 of this Constitution.

ARTICLE 79

Members of the Government of the Republic and of that of a Land have the right to, and, upon the demand of the Laender Chamber, are required to take part in the deliberation of the Laender Chamber and its committees. They must be given the floor on any matter under deliberation, if they so request.

The People's Chamber may, in special cases, delegate representatives from among their numbers to present the opinion of the People's Chamber to the Laender Chamber; the Laender Chamber has an equal right to present its opinion to the People's Chamber. The Laender Chamber may, if need be, instruct members of the Land Governments to present the attitude of the respective Governments to the People's Chamber.

ARTICLE 80

Article 67 and subsequent articles of this Constitution concerning the rights of the members of the People's Chamber apply correspondingly to the members of the Laender Chamber.

III. Legislation

ARTICLE 81

Laws are enacted by the People's Chamber, or directly by the people by means of a referendum.

ARTICLE 82

Bills are introduced by the Government, by the Laender Chamber, or by members of the People's Chamber. At least two readings will be held on any bill.

ARTICLE 83

The Constitution may be amended by legislation.

The People's Chamber may enact legislation to amend the Constitution only if at least two-thirds of the representatives are present, and such enactments require a two-thirds majority of those present.

If an amendment to the Constitution is to be adopted by means of a (popular) referendum, the approval of the majority of those entitled to vote is required.

ARTICLE 84

The Laender Chamber has the right to veto laws enacted by the People's Chamber. The veto must be lodged within two weeks after the final vote has been taken in the People's Chamber; reasons for the veto must be submitted within an additional two weeks. Otherwise it is understood that the Laender Chamber will not exercise its right of veto.

The People's Chamber may override this veto by upholding its decision after renewed deliberations.

If a two-thirds majority of the Laender Chamber representatives casting their votes upholds the measure.

For the Laender Chamber to veto legislation enacted by the People's Chamber to amend the Constitution, at least two-thirds of the members of the Laender Chamber must be present, and at least two-thirds thereof must vote for the veto.

The People's Chamber may override by upholding its amendment with the majority prescribed for amendments to the Constitution.

ARTICLE 85

The President of the People's Chamber shall engross all constitutionally enacted laws within the period of one month.

They are promulgated without delay by the President of the Republic in the Official Gazette of the Republic.

A law cannot be engrossed nor promulgated, if it has been declared unconstitutional within one month, as provided for in Article 66.

Unless otherwise provided, laws come into force on the fourteenth day after their promulgation.

ARTICLE 86

Engrossment and promulgation of a law are to be suspended for two months, if one-third of the representatives in the People's Chamber so request.

Upon expiration of this period, the law is to be engrossed and promulgated unless a popular initiative calls for a (popular) referendum against the enactment of the law.

Laws declared urgent by the majority of the representatives in the People's Chamber must be engrossed and promulgated despite such (public) demand.

ARTICLE 87

If the promulgation of a law has been suspended at the instance of at least one-third of the representatives in the People's Chamber, such law is to be submitted to a (popular) referendum upon the demand of one-twentieth of those entitled to vote.

A (popular) referendum shall furthermore be held, if requested by one-tenth of those entitled to vote or by recognized political parties or organized groups which can demonstrate satisfactorily that they represent one-fifth of those entitled to vote (constituting popular initiative).

A popular initiative must be based on a draft law, which law is to be submitted to the People's Chamber by the Government with a statement of the Government's position with respect to this law.

A (popular) referendum will take place only if the desired law has not been adopted by the People's Chamber in a version with which the petitioners or their representatives are in agreement.

A (popular) referendum shall not be held on the budget, on tax legislation, or on salary schedules.

A law submitted to a (popular) referendum is considered as adopted if it has received the consent of a majority of the votes cast.

A specific law shall regulate the procedures for popular initiative and (popular) referendum.

ARTICLE 88

The budget and the economic plan are adopted by law.

Amnesties require a (specific) law.

State treaties concerning matters of legislation are to be promulgated as laws.

ARTICLE 89

Laws which have been duly promulgated cannot be reconsidered by the judiciary with respect to their constitutionality.

After the review proceedings provided for in Article 66 have been instituted, all pending court proceedings shall be suspended until the review proceedings have been completed.

ARTICLE 90

General administrative regulations required for the implementation of the laws of the Republic will be issued by the Government of the Republic, unless the law provides otherwise.

IV. The Government of the Republic

ARTICLE 91

The Government of the Republic consists of the Minister President and the Ministers.

ARTICLE 92

The Minister President is appointed by the party with the greatest strength in the People's Chamber; he (the Minister President) forms the Government. All parties having at least forty representatives (in the People's Chamber) are represented by Ministers or State Secretaries in proportion to their strength. State Secretaries may attend meetings of the Government in an advisory capacity.

Should one parliamentary party refuse to be included, the Government will be formed without it.

Ministers should be members of the People's Chamber.

The People's Chamber approves the Government and the program submitted by it.

ARTICLE 93

On taking office, members of the Government shall be sworn in by the President of the Republic and pledged to perform their duties impartially for the welfare of the people and in faithful observance of the Constitution and the laws.

ARTICLE 94

The Government, and each of its members, require the confidence of the People's Chamber in order to perform their functions.

ARTICLE 95

The functions of the Cabinet are terminated if and when the People's Chamber passes a motion of no-confidence.

A motion of no-confidence will be voted on only if at the same time a new Minister President and his program are proposed. The notion of no-confidence and these proposals will be considered in one combined vote.

A vote of no-confidence shall not be effective unless the motion is carried by at least one-half (two hundred) of the statutory number of representatives.

A motion of no-confidence must be signed by at least one-fourth of the members of the People's Chamber. A vote on such a motion may not be taken prior to the second day after it has been debated, and not later than one week after its presentation.

Unless the new Government takes office within twenty-one days after the motion of no-confidence has been carried, that motion shall become void.

If the new Government receives a vote of no-confidence, the People's Chamber shall be considered dissolved.

The former Government continues its functions until a new Government has taken office.

ARTICLE 96

A member of the Government who receives a vote of no-confidence from the People's Chamber must resign. Unless decided otherwise by the People's Chamber, he is to continue his functions until his successor takes office.

The provision of Article 95, paragraph 3, is applicable correspondingly.

Any member of the Government may resign at any time. Unless decided otherwise by the People's Chamber, his official functions shall be performed by his deputy until a successor has been appointed.

ARTICLE 97

The Minister President presides over the Government and directs its business under Rules of Procedure to be decreed by the Government and communicated to the People's Chamber.

ARTICLE 98

The Minister President determines governmental policy in accordance with the guiding principles laid down by the People's Chamber. For this, he is responsible to the latter.

Within the framework of these guiding principles, each Minister directs independently the department entrusted to him and is personally responsible to the People's Chamber.

ARTICLE 99

Ministers shall refer to the Government, for deliberation and decision, all bills, any matters which must be referred to it under the Constitution or the law, as well as differences of opinion with respect to matters which fall within the competence of more than one Minister.

ARTICLE 100

The Government makes decisions by majority vote. In case of a tie, the Minister President shall cast the deciding vote.

V. The President of the Republic

ARTICLE 101

The President of the Republic is elected for a term of four years by the People's Chamber and the Laender Chamber, meeting in joint session, which is convoked and presided over by the President of the People's Chamber.

Any citizen who has reached the age of thirty-five years may stand for election.

ARTICLE 102

On assuming office, the President of the Republic takes the following oath before a joint session of the People's Chamber and the Laender Chamber:

"I swear that I will dedicate my strength to the welfare of the German people, that I will defend the Constitution and the laws of the Republic, that I will discharge my duties conscientiously and do justice to all."

ARTICLE 103

The President of the Republic may be recalled before the expiration of his term by a joint resolution of the People's Chamber and the Laender Chamber. Such a resolution requires a two-thirds majority of the statutory number of representatives.

ARTICLE 104

The President of the Republic promulgates the laws of the Republic.

He receives the oath of office from members of the Government upon their assumption of duties.

ARTICLE 105

The President of the Republic represents the Republic in international relations.

He concludes and signs treaties with foreign countries on behalf of the Republic.

He accredits and receives ambassadors and ministers.

ARTICLE 106

To become effective, all orders and decrees issued by the President of the Republic must be countersigned by the Minister President or the competent Minister.

ARTICLE 107

The President exercises the right of pardon on behalf of the Republic. In this function he is advised by a committee of the People's Chamber.

ARTICLE 108

Whenever the President of the Republic is unable to attend to his office, he is represented by the President of the People's Chamber. If such incapacity is expected to continue for a protracted period, a substitute will be appointed by (a specific) law.

Whenever the presidency is terminated prematurely, the same rule applies until the election of a new President.

VI. Republic and Laender

ARTICLE 109

Each Land must have a constitution which conforms to the principles of the Constitution of the Republic and under which the Landtag is the supreme and sole popular representative body in the Land.

The popular representative body must be elected, by all citizens entitled to do so, in universal, equal, direct, and secret ballot, held in accordance with the principles of proportional representation as laid down in the Electoral Law of the Republic.

ARTICLE 110

Any change in the territory of a Land and the formation of a new Land within the Republic requires a law of the Republic amending the Constitution.

Only an ordinary law (of the Republic) is required if the Laender immediately affected concur.

An ordinary law will likewise suffice, even if one of the Laender affected does not concur, provided, however, that the territorial change or the formation of a new Land is demanded by a plebiscite held in the territories concerned.

ARTICLE 111

The Republic may enact uniform legislation in any field. However, in so doing it should confine itself to laying down principles, provided this meets the need for uniform regulation.

To the extent that the Republic does not exercise its legislative power, the Laender shall have such power.

ARTICLE 112

The Republic has the exclusive right to legislate on:
   foreign relations;
   foreign trade;
   customs and the free movement of commodities within a unified customs and trade area;
   citizenship; freedom of movement; immigration and emigration; extradition; passport regulations and laws affecting the status of aliens;
   legislation on census and registry (marriage, divorce, and status of children);
   civil law; criminal law; the constitution of courts and their procedure;
   labor law;
   transport;
   the fields of postal, telecommunication, and radio broadcasting services;
   the fields of press and of film production, distribution, and display;
   currency and coinage, weights, measures, standards, and gauging;
   social insurance; and,
   war damages, occupation costs, and reparations.

ARTICLE 113

Legislation in the field of finance and taxation must be of such nature as not to infringe upon the existence of the Laender, the Kreise (counties) and Gemeinden (communities).

ARTICLE 114

Law of the whole of Germany overrides Land law.

ARTICLE 115

As a rule, the laws of the Republic are carried out by the executive agencies of the Laender, unless otherwise provided for in this Constitution or by a law. The Republic, insofar as there is a necessity, establishes its own administrative agencies by law.

ARTICLE 116

The Government of the Republic exercises supervision in those matters with respect to which the Republic has the right to legislate.

The Government of the Republic may issue general instructions where the laws of the Republic are not executed by its (own) administrative authorities. For the supervision of the execution of these laws and instructions, it is authorized to delegate commissioners to the implementing agencies. As for the powers of these commissioners, Article 65 is correspondingly applicable.

Upon the request of the Republic, the Laender governments are bound to remedy deficiencies discovered in the execution of the laws of the Republic.

Any controversies arising therefrom are to be examined and settled in accordance with the procedure specified in Article 66, paragraph 5.

VII. Administration of the Republic

ARTICLE 117

Maintenance of foreign relations is an exclusive concern of the Republic.

The Laender may conclude treaties with foreign states on matter within the competence of Land legislation; such treaties (before taking effect) are subject to the approval of the People's Chamber.

Treaties with foreign states concerning changes of national boundaries are concluded by the Republic, after the consent of the Land thereby affected has been obtained. Boundary changes may be effected only by a law of the Republic, unless a mere rectification of boundaries in uninhabited areas is involved.

ARTICLE 118

Germany forms a single customs and trade area, bounded by a common customs frontier.

Territories of foreign states or parts of such territories may be included in the German customs area by treaty or convention. Parts of the German customs area may be excluded therefrom by law.

Any goods enjoying internal free trade within the German customs area may, within the area, freely be introduced into, or carried in transit across the boundaries of, German Laender and across the boundaries of the territories of foreign states or parts of such territories included.

ARTICLE 119

Customs and such taxes as are regulated by laws of the Republic are administered by the Republic.

The power to levy taxes is, normally, vested in the Republic.

The Republic should levy taxes only to the extent required to cover its needs.

The Republic establishes its own agencies for the administration of taxes. In conjunction therewith, arrangements shall be made enabling the Laender to safeguard their special interests in the spheres of agriculture, commerce, handicrafts, trades or professions, manufacture and industry.

To the extent required for the uniform and equitable enforcement of its tax laws, the Republic shall enact legislation on the organization of tax administrations in the Laender, the organization and powers of the authorities entrusted with the enforcement of the tax laws of the Republic, the settlement of accounts with the Laender, and the reimbursement for the administrative costs incurred in the enforcement of the tax laws of the Republic.

ARTICLE 120

Taxes and other levies may be assessed only as provided by law.

Property, income, and excise tax legislation are to be kept in a suitable proportion to each other, and to be graduated according to social considerations.

Through sharply progressive tax rates on inheritance, the amassing of socially harmful fortunes should be prevented.

ARTICLE 121

Revenues and expenditures of the Republic must be estimated for each fiscal year and provided for in the budget. The budget is to be enacted by legislation before the beginning of the fiscal year.

ARTICLE 122

The Minister of Finance, in order to secure a discharge for the Government, gives an accounting to the People's Chamber of the revenues of the Republic and their use. The auditing of accounts is regulated by law of the Republic.

ARTICLE 123

Funds may be procured by borrowing only for extraordinary needs. Borrowing of such funds and the guaranteeing of loans as a charge of the Republic may be effected only on the basis of a law of the Republic.

ARTICLE 124

Postal, telecommunication, broadcasting, and railroad services are to be administered by the Republic.

The former Reich Autobahnen (auto-highways) and Reich highways as well as all roads for long-distance traffic are under the control of the Republic. The same provisions apply to waterways.

ARTICLE 125

Control of merchant shipping and the administration of maritime shipping, and of aids to navigation, are duties of the Republic.

VIII. Administration of Justice

ARTICLE 126

The ordinary administration of justice is exercised by the Supreme Court of the Republic and by courts of the Laender.

ARTICLE 127

In the exercise of their judicial function, the judges are independent and are bound only by the Constitution and the Law.

ARTICLE 128

Judges must be persons who, by their qualification and activity, offer the guarantee that they will exercise their office in accordance with the principles laid down in the Constitution.

ARTICLE 129

Through the development of law schools, the Republic provides an opportunity for members of all classes of the population to become qualified for the profession of judge, attorney, and public prosecutor.

ARTICLE 130

Laymen are, as much as possible, to be used as judges.

Laymen are elected, on the proposal of democratic parties and organizations, by the competent popular representative bodies.

ARTICLE 131

Judges of the Supreme Court of the Republic, and the Prosecutor General of the Laender, are elected by the Landtage upon their nomination by the Government of the Republic.

Judges of the High Courts of the Laender, and the Prosecutors General of the Laender, are elected by the Landtage upon their nomination by the Land governments.

All other judges are appointed by the Land governments.

ARTICLE 132

Judges of the Supreme Court, and the Prosecutor General of the Republic, may be recalled by the People's Chamber if they violate the Constitution, or the laws, or commit a serious breach of their duties as judge or public prosecutor.

This recall is effected after hearing the report of a Committee on Justice to be established in the People's Chamber.

The Committee on Justice is composed of the Chairman of the Legal Committee of the People's Chamber, three members of the People's Chamber, two members of the Supreme Court and one member of the Prosecutor General's office. It is presided over by the Chairman of the Legal Committee. The other Committee members are elected by the People's Chamber for the legislative term. The members of the Suprme Court and the Prosecutor General's office serving on the Committee of Justice cannot be members of the People's Chamber.

Judges elected by a Landtag, or appointed by a Land government, may be recalled by the respective Landtag. Their recall will be effected after hearing the report of a Committee on Justice to be set up with the respective Landtag. The Committee on Justice is composed of the Chairman of the Legal Committee of the Landtag, three members of the Landtag, two members of the Land High Court and one member of the Prosecutor General's office of the respective Land. It is presided over by the Chairman of the Legal Committee. The other Committee members are elected by the respective Landtag for the duration of the legislative term. The members of the (Land) High Court and of the Prosecutor General's office, and participating in the Committee on Justice, cannot be members of the Landtag.

Judges appointed by Land governments may, under the same conditions, be recalled by the respective Land government, provided that the consent of the Landtag Committee on Justice has been obtained.

ARTICLE 133

All court proceedings are open to the public.

In all matters involving a threat to public safety and order, or to public morals, the court may order the public to be excluded.

ARTICLE 134

No citizen should be deprived of his right to be tried before the judge having lawful jurisdiction in the matter. Extraordinary courts are inadmissible. The legislative authorities may set up courts for special matters only if their competence is to comprise categories of persons or issues defined beforehand and in a general way.

ARTICLE 135

Only such penalties may be imposed as have been provided for by law at the time the punishable act was committed.

No penal law has retroactive force.

Exceptions to this rule are measures and the application of provisions which are adopted for the overcoming of Nazism, Fascism, and militarism, or which are necessary for the prosecution of crimes against humanity.

ARTICLE 136

In cases of temporary arrest, house searches and seizures effected in the course of a preliminary investigation, the approval of a judge must be obtained without (undue) delay.

It rests with the judge alone to decide on the admissibility and continuance of an arrest. Persons arrested must be brought before a judge at the latest on the day after their apprehension. If pretrial confinement is ordered by the judge, he must make a periodic review as to whether continued detention is justified.

The reason for the detention is to be communicated to the arrested person at his first examination by a judge and, if he so desires, within an additional twenty-four hours to a person to be named by him.

ARTICLE 137

Execution of sentences is founded on the concept of reforming persons capable of rehabilitation through common productive work.

ARTICLE 138

Citizens are protected against unlawful administrative measures by the supervision exercised by the legislature and through recourse to administrative courts.

The structure and jurisdiction of administrative courts are regulated by law.

Principles applying to the election and recall of judges of ordinary courts apply correspondingly to the members of administrative courts.

IX. Administrative Autonomy

ARTICLE 139

Gemeinden and Gemeindeverbaende (communities and associated communities) enjoy administrative autonomy subject to the provisions of the laws of the Republic and the Laender.

Autonomy functions include determination and implementation of all policies concerning the economic, social, and cultural life of the Gemeinde or Gemeindeverband. Each task is to be accomplished by the lowest (local) administrative unit qualified for this purpose.

ARTICLE 140

Gemeinden and Gemeindeverbaende have representative bodies organized on democratic principles.

To assist them, committees are formed in which delegates of the democratic parties and organizations participate responsibly.

The right to vote and the procedure to be followed in (local) elections are governed by the provisions applying to elections to the People's Chamber and to the Landtage.

The right to vote may, however, by Land legislation be predicated on the length of residence in the (respective) locality for a period not to exceed half a year.

ARTICLE 141

For the due exercise of their functions, the elected executive authorities of Gemeinden and Gemeindeverbaende require the confidence of the (local) representative bodies.

ARTICLE 142

Supervision of the administrative autonomy practiced by Gemeinden and Gemeindeverbaende is limited to a review of the statutory compliance of adminstrative measures and of the observance of democratic administrative principles.

ARTICLE 143

The Republic and the Laender may delegate functions, and the application of laws, to the Gemeinden and Gemeindeverbaende.

X. Transitional and Concluding Provisions

ARTICLE 144

All provisions of this Constitution have direct force of law. Any provisions of the contrary are repealed herewith. Provisions superseding them and required to implement the Constitution are to take effect simultaneously with the Constitution. Existing laws are to be interpreted in the meaning of this Constitution.

Constitutional liberties and rights may not be used as arguments against past or future measures adopted for the overcoming of National Socialism and militarism, or to redress wrongs caused by them.

The above Constitution of the German Democratic Republic, worked out with the participation of the entire German People by the German People's Council, passed by it on March 19, 1949, confirmed by the Third German People's Congress on May 30, 1949, and put into effect by a Law of the Provisional People's Chamber dated October 7, 1949, is hereby promulgated.

Berlin, October 7, 1949.

The President of the
Provisional People's Chamber
of the German Democratic Republic
Dieckmann

POLITICAL CONSTITUTION
OF THE
PORTUGUESE REPUBLIC

(1953)

PART I

OF FUNDAMENTAL GUARANTEES

Title I
Of the Portuguese Nation

Art. 1.   The territory of Portugal is that which at present belongs to it and comprises:

I) in Europe: the mainland and the archipelagos of Madeira and the Azores;

II) in West Africa: the Cape Verde archipelago, Guinea, S. Tomé and Principe and their dependencies, S. Joao Baptista de Ajudá, Cabinda, and Angola:

III) in East Africa: Mozambique;

IV) in Asia: the State of India and Macao and their respective dependencies;

V) in Oceania: Timor and its dependencies.

The nation does not renounce the rights which it has or may hereafter acquire over any other territory.

Art. 2.   The State shall not in any way alienate part of the national territory or the sovereign rights it exercises over it, except in so far as concerns the rectification of frontiers when approved by the National Assembly.

1. No part of national territory may be acquired by the Government or public legal entity of a foreign country, except for the installation of diplomatic or consular representation where there is reciprocity in favor of the Portuguese State.

2. In the Overseas Territories, the acquisition by a foreign Government of land or buildings for the installation of consular representation shall be subject to the approval of the choice of the site in question by the Minister of Overseas Portugal.

Art. 3. The nation consists of all Portuguese citizens resident within or outside its territory and they shall be considered as subject to the State and Portuguese laws, without prejudice to the rules of international law which may be applicable.

Foreigners sojourning or resident in Portugal are also subject to the State and Portuguese laws, without prejudice to the provisions of international law.

Art. 4. The Portuguese nation is an independent State. Its sovereignty recognizes in the internal sphere morality and law as the only limitations; in the international field it recognizes only those limitations which are derived from conventions or treaties freely entered into, or from customary law freely accepted. It is the duty of the nation to co-operate with other states in preparing and adopting measures making for peace among people and for the progress of mankind.

Portugal advocates arbitration as a means of settling international disputes.

Art. 5. The Portuguese State is a unitary and corporative republic founded upon the equality of all its citizens in the eyes of the law, upon the free access for all classes to the benefits of civilization, and upon the participation of all the constituent forces of the nation in its administrative life and in the making of laws.

Equality before the law implies the right to be employed in public service according to ability or services rendered; it also involves no recognition of privilege of birth, nobility, title, sex, or social position, save only the distinction due to women by reason of their nature and in the interests of the family; in regard to the obligations and benefits of citizens, it involves those differences imposed by diversity of circumstances or arising out of natural conditions.

Art. 6. It is the duty of the State:

1. To promote the unity and establish the juridical order of the nation by defining and enforcing respect for the rights and guarantees of morality, justice or the law, in the interest of the individual, of the families, and the local autonomous and the public or private bodies;

2. To co-ordinate, stimulate, and direct all social activities in order to promote a proper harmony of interests within the lawful subordination of private interests to the general good;

3. To strive to improve the conditions of the least favored social classes, endeavoring to secure for them a standard of living compatible with human dignity;

4. To protect public health.

TITLE II
OF CITIZENS

Art. 7. The civil law defines how Portuguese citizenship is acquired and lost. A Portuguese citizen enjoys the rights and guarantees provided by the Constitution; naturalized citizens, however, are subject to the restrictions prescribed by law.

Foreigners resident in Portugal enjoy the same rights and guarantees, unless the law determines otherwise. This does not apply to political rights or to public rights which involve a duty towards the State, although, as regards public rights, reciprocal privileges granted to Portuguese nationals by other states shall be observed.

Art. 8. Portuguese citizens shall enjoy the following rights, liberties, and individual guarantees.

I) The right to life and personal safety;

I-A) The right to work within the terms prescribed by law;

II) The right to good name and reputation;

III) Liberty and inviolability of religious beliefs and practices, on the ground of holding which nobody may be persecuted, deprived of a right, or exempted from any obligation or civic duty. Nobody shall be compelled to answer questions concerning the religion he professes, except in a legally conducted census;

IV) The free expression of thought in any form;

V) Freedom of teaching;

VI) The inviolability of residence and the privacy of correspondence as may be determined by law;

VII) Freedom of choice of profession or nature of work, art, or trade, subject to such legal restrictions as may be necessary in the interests of public welfare and to monopolies which, by law, can only be granted by the State and administrative bodies for reasons of recognized public utility;

VIII) Nobody shall be deprived of personal liberty or arrested without being charged, except for cases coming within paragraphs 3 and 4 hereof;

IX) Nobody shall be sentenced for a criminal offense unless there is an existing law which declares the act or omission to be punishable;

X) To prepare a case in defense, the accused being given the necessary guarantees to this end both before and after being formally charged;

XI) Nobody shall be punished by imprisonment for an unlimited term or by death, except however, as regards the latter, during a state of war with a foreign country, in which case the sentence must be carried out in the theatre of war;

XII) There shall be no confiscation of goods nor can any personal punishment be inflicted except upon the delinquent;

XIII) Nobody shall suffer imprisonment for failure to pay costs or stamp duties;

XIV) Freedom of meeting and association;

XV) The right of property and its transmission during life or death as provided by the civil law;

XVI) Freedom from the payment of taxes not decreed in accordance with the Constitution;

XVII) The right to reparation for all actual damage in accordance with the provisions of the law, which may prescribe pecuniary reparation for damages of a moral character;

XVIII) The right of making representation or petition, claim or complaint, to sovereign or other public authority, on matters affecting personal rights or the general good;

XIX) The right of resistance to any order which may infringe individual guarantees, unless legally suspended, and of repelling by force private aggression when recourse to public authority is impossible;

XX) Sentences for criminal offenses shall be open to revision, and the right to an indemnity from the State for loss and damage shall be assured to the convicted person or his heirs by measures to be defined by law.

1. The enumeration of the above rights and guarantees shall not exclude any others derived from the Constitution or the law, it being understood that citizens should always exercise them without injuring the rights of third parties, or damaging the interests of society or moral principles.

2. Special laws shall govern the exercise of the freedom of expression of opinion, education, meeting, and of association. As regards the first item, they shall prevent, by precautionary or restrictive measures, the perversion of public opinion in its function as a social force, and shall protect the character of citizens, who, when libelled or abused in a periodical publication, shall have the right to have a correction or reply inserted in the same, free of charge, without prejudice to any other right or to such proceedings as may be determined by law.

3. Imprisonment without formal charge is permitted in cases of *flagrante delictu* and in cases of the following actually committed, prevented, or attempted crimes: those against the safety of the State; the counterfeiting of money, bank-notes, and government bonds; willful homicide; burglary or robbery; larceny, fraud, or embezzlement, when perpetrated by an habitual criminal; fraudulent bankruptcy; arson; the manufacture, possession, or use of explosive bombs and other similar appliances.

4. Except in the cases specified in the preceding paragraph, imprisonment in a public jail, or detention in a private residence or institution for lunatics, is only permitted on a written order from the competent authorities, and shall not be continued on the accused offering proper bail or bond in regard to residence, when allowed by law.

The exceptional safeguard of *habeas corpus* may be used against an abuse of authority in the circumstances prescribed in a special law.

Art. 9.   No one shall be prejudiced in his situation or permanent employment by virtue of the obligation to undergo military service or in consequence of his service in the civil defense of the territory.

Art. 10.   The State shall bestow distinctions of honor or rewards on those citizens who distinguish themselves by reason of personal merit or civic or military deeds, and likewise on foreigners when there is an international interest; the law prescribing the orders, decorations, medals, and diplomas for this purpose.

Art. 11.   All authorities are jointly and severally precluded from suspending the Constitution or limiting the rights therein established except in the cases therein provided.

TITLE III
OF THE FAMILY

Art. 12. The State shall ensure the constitution and protection of the family as the source of preservation and development of the race, as the first basis of education, discipline, and social harmony, and, as the foundation of all political and administrative order through family grouping and representation in the parish and in the town councils.

Art. 13. The constitution of the family is based upon:

I) marriage and legitimate offspring;

II) equality of rights and duties of husband and wife in regard to the maintenance and education of their legitimate children;

III) the obligation to register the marriage and birth of children.

1. The civil law shall determine the rules governing the persons and goods of husband and wife, parental authority and its substitution, the rights of succession in direct or collateral line, and the right of maintenance.

2. Legitimate children shall be guaranteed those full rights necessary for the order and unity of the family, and rights corresponding to their position shall also be recognized in the case of illegitimate children who can be recognized as offspring, and likewise unborn children, particularly the right to maintenance, which shall be the liability of those upon whom, after investigation, the duty is found to fall.

Art. 14. With the object of protecting the family it is the duty of the State and local bodies:

I) to encourage the establishment of separate homes under healthy conditions, and the institution of the family household;

II) to protect maternity;

III) to adjust taxation to the legitimate obligations of the family, and to promote the adoption of a family wage;

IV) to assist parents in the discharge of their duty of instructing and educating their children, and to co-operate with them by means of public institutions for education and correction, or by encouraging private establishments having the same objects;

V) to take all measures necessary to prevent the corruption of morals.

Art. 15.   The registration of the civil status of citizens is a matter proper to the State.

Title IV
Of Corporate Bodies

Art. 16.   It is the duty of the State to authorize, unless otherwise provided by law to the contrary, all corporative, collective, intellectual, or economic bodies, and to promote and assist their formation.

Art. 17.   The principal aims of the corporative bodies, referred to in the preceding article, shall be scientific, literary, or physical training, relief, alms, or charity; technical improvement or solidarity of interests.

The constitution of these bodies and the way in which they function shall be governed by special regulations.

Art. 18.   Foreigners domiciled in Portugal may be members of the corporative organizations referred to, on such conditions as may be determined by law; they shall not be allowed to share in the exercise of the political rights granted to these bodies.

Title V
Of the Family, Corporative Organizations
and Autonomous Bodies as Political Units

Art. 19.   It is the particular privilege of families to elect the parish councils.

This right is exercised by the head of the family.

Art. 20.   In the corporate organization all branches of the nation's activities shall be represented through their association in the corporative organizations, and it shall be their duty to participate in the election of town councils and provincial boards and the constitution of the Corporative Chamber.

Art. 21.   Under the political organization of the State the parish councils shall elect the town councils, which in turn shall elect the provincial boards. Local autonomous bodies shall be represented in the Corporative Chamber.

Title VI
Of Public Opinion

Art. 22.   Public opinion is a fundamental part of the policy and administration of the country; it shall be the duty of the

State to protect it against all those influences which distort it from the truth, justice, good administration, and the common weal.

Art. 23. The function of the press is of a public nature and for that reason it may not refuse to insert any official notices of normal dimensions on matters of national importance sent to it by the government.

TITLE VII
OF THE ADMINISTRATIVE ORDER

Art. 24. Civil servants are for the service of the community and not for that of any party or association of private interests; it is their duty to respect the authority of the State and cause others to do so.

Art. 25. The employees and servants of local autonomous authorities, of the corporative bodies and organizations for economic co-ordination, of bodies engaged in administrative public utilities, and of firms which conduct services of public interest, are subject to the discipline prescribed in the previous article.

Art. 26. Planned interruption of public services or of those of interest to the community shall involve the dismissal of the offenders, without prejudice to any other liability at law.

Art. 27. Nobody shall be allowed to hold more than one office in the employment either of the State or local bodies, or of both, except on such conditions as may be laid down by law.

Rules as to incompatibility, whether in regard to public offices or to the exercise of other professions in conjunction with same, shall be determined by a special law.

Art. 28. All citizens are bound to lend their services and co-operation to the State and local bodies as established by law and to contribute towards public expenditure according to their means.

TITLE VIII
OF THE ECONOMIC AND SOCIAL ORDER

Art. 29. The economic organization of the nation must provide the maximum production and wealth for the benefit of society, and shall create a collective existence from which shall flow power to the State and justice to its citizens.

Art. 30. The State shall conduct its economic relations with other countries according to the principle of proper co-operation, without prejudice to the commercial advantages to be obtained from any particular country, or the necessity for protection against external threats or attacks.

Art. 31. It shall be the right and duty of the State to co-ordinate and control economic and social life with the following objects:

I) to establish a proper balance of the population, of professions, of occupations, of capital, and of labor;

II) to protect the national economic system from agricultural, industrial, and commercial ventures of a parasitic nature, or those incompatible with the higher interests of human life;

III) to secure the lowest price and the highest wage consistent with fair remuneration for other factors of production, by means of improving technical methods, services, and credit;

IV) to develop the settlement of the national territories, to protect emigrants, and to regulate emigration.

Art. 32. The State shall encourage those private economic activities which are the most profitable, relative costs being equal, but without detriment to the social benefit conferred and to the protection due to small home industries.

Art. 33. The State may only intervene directly in the management of private economic ventures when it has to finance them and for the purpose of securing a larger measure of social benefit than would otherwise be the case.

State undertakings carried on for profit, even if working on the basis of free competition, are likewise subject to the provisions laid down in the latter part of the present article.

Art. 34. The State shall promote the formation and development of the national corporative economic system, taking care to prevent any tendency among its constituent bodies to indulge in unrestricted competition with each other, contrary to their own proper aims and those of society, and shall encourage them to collaborate as members of the same community.

Art. 35. Property, capital, and labor have a social function in the field of economic co-operation and common interest, and the law may determine the conditions of their use or exploitation in accordance with the community aim in view.

Art. 36. Labor, whether unskilled, skilled, or technical, may be associated with an undertaking in any form that circumstances render advisable.

Art. 37. Only economic corporations which are recognized by the State may conclude collective labor contracts, in accordance with the law, and those made without their intervention shall be null and void.

Art. 38. Disputes arising out of labor contracts shall be the concern of special tribunals.

Art. 39. In their economic relations with each another, neither capital nor labor shall be allowed to suspend operations with the object of imposing their respective claims.

Art. 40. Obstacles will be placed in the way of the accumulation of posts in private enterprises, as being contrary to public economy and morality.

Art. 41. The State shall promote and encourage community concerns and provident, co-operative, and mutual benefit institutions.

TITLE IX
OF EDUCATION, INSTRUCTION, AND NATIONAL CULTURE

Art. 42. Education and instruction are obligatory and are the concern of the family and of public or private institutions in co-operation with the same.

Art. 43. The State shall officially maintain primary, complementary, middle and high schools, and institutions for advanced education.

1. Elementary primary instruction is obligatory and may be given at home, or in private or state schools.

2. The arts and sciences shall be encouraged and their development, teaching, and dissemination favored, provided that respect is maintained for the Constitution, the authorities, and the co-ordinating functions of the State.

3. The instruction provided by the State, in addition to aiming at physical fitness and the improvement of intellectual faculties, has its object the formation of character and of professional ability as well as the development of all moral and civic qualities, the former along the traditional principles of the country and of Christian doctrine and morality.

4. No permission shall be required for the teaching of religion in private schools.

Art. 44.   The establishment of private schools on the lines of the State schools shall be free, but subject to State inspection; schools may be subsidized by the State or authorized to grant diplomas, if their *curricula* and standard of their teaching staff are not inferior to those of the corresponding public institutions.

TITLE X
OF THE RELATIONS OF THE STATE WITH THE CATHOLIC CHURCH AND OF THE REGIME OF WORSHIP

Art. 45.   The Catholic religion may be freely practiced, in public or in private, as the religion of the Portuguese Nation. The Catholic Church shall enjoy juridical personality and may organize itself in conformity with the canon law and create thereunder associations or organizations whose juridical personality shall be equally recognized. The relationship between the State and the Catholic Church shall be one of separation, with diplomatic relations maintained between the Holy See and Portugal by means of reciprocal representation, and concordate or agreements entered into in the sphere of the Padroado and where other matters of common interest are or need to be regulated.

Art. 46.   The State shall also insure freedom of worship and organization for all other religious faiths practiced in Portuguese territory, their outward manifestations (*as suas manifestacoes exteriores*) being regulated by law, and it may grant juridical personality to associations constituted in conformity with the creeds in question.

These provisions shall not apply to creeds incompatible with the life and physical integrity of the human person and with good behavior, or to the dissemination of doctrines contrary to the established social order.

Art. 47.   The State may not assign to any other purpose any chapel, building, or article belonging to a religious body.

Art. 48.   Public cemeteries shall be secular in character and ministers of any religion may freely practise their respective rites therein.

TITLE XI
OF THE PUBLIC AND PRIVATE DOMAINS OF THE STATE

Art. 49.   The public domain of the State shall comprise the following:

I) mineral deposits, medicinal mineral springs, and other natural wealth below the surface;

II) maritime waters and their shores;

III) lakes, lagoons, and watercourses navigable to ships or rafts, their respective beds or channels, and also any others recognized by special decree to be of public utility as suitable for the production of electric power, national or regional, or for irrigation;

IV) dykes opened up by the State;

V) the air over the land beyond such limits as the law fixes in favor of the owner of the surface;

VI) railways of public interest of any kind, public highways and roads;

VII) territorial areas reserved for military defense;

VIII) any other property placed by law under the regime of public domain.

1. The authority of the State over the property of the public domain and the use of it by citizens shall be governed by law and by the international conventions concluded by Portugal, without prejudice to the prior rights of the State and the acquired private rights of individuals. The latter rights, however, shall be subject to expropriation as may be determined by the public interest and upon payment of reasonable in-indemnity.

2. Rocks and common earths, and materials commonly employed in building are expressly excepted from the natural riches specified in No. (1) above.

3. The State shall undertake the demarcation of those private lands which abut on any property of public domain.

Art. 50. The administration on the mainland and in the adjacent islands of property owned by the State in a private capacity pertains to the Ministry of Finance, except when it is expressly attributed to any other Ministry.

Art. 51. No State property or rights which affect its prestige or the more important national interests may be alienated.

Art. 52. Artistic, historical, and natural monuments, and artistic objects officially recognized as such, are under the protection of the State, and their alienation in favor of foreigners is prohibited.

TITLE XII
OF NATIONAL DEFENSE

Art. 53.   The State shall assure the existence and prestige of those military institutions on land and sea which are required by the supreme needs of national defense to maintain order and public tranquillity.

There shall be a single military organization for the entire territory.

Art. 54.   Military service shall be general and compulsory. The law shall determine the conditions of service.

Art. 55.   The law shall regulate the general organization of the nation in wartime in accordance with the principle of a nation in arms.

Art. 56.   The State shall promote, encourage, and assist civil institutions whose aim is to teach and discipline young persons in preparation for the fulfillment of their military and patriotic duties.

Art. 57.   No citizen may hold or obtain employment from the State or local autonomous bodies unless he has fulfilled the duties to which he is liable under military law.

Art. 58.   The State guarantees protection and pensions to persons who are incapacitated in military service in defense of the country or of order, and likewise to the families of individuals who lose their lives in such service.

TITLE XIII
OF THE ADMINISTRATION OF UNDERTAKINGS
OF COLLECTIVE INTEREST

Art. 59.   All undertakings the object of which is the utilization or exploitation of anything forming part of the State public domain, are regarded as being of collective interest and are subject to special State regime of administration, competition, supervision, or control, in accordance with the needs of public security, national defense, and economic and social relations.

Art. 60.   The following shall conform with uniform rules, without prejudice to special circumstances where necessary in matters of secondary importance:

I) the establishment or alteration of land, river, maritime, or air communications, whatever their nature or purpose;

II) the construction of works for the utilization of water or coal for the production of electric power; the construction of grid systems for its transmission, supply, or distribution, and also in general works for agricultural drainage and irrigation purposes;

III) the exploitation of public services in connection with above mentioned communications, works, and grid system.

Art. 61. The State will promote the development of the public improvements mentioned in the previous article, namely the development of the national merchant navy; having particularly in view connections with the overseas territories and with those countries where the Portuguese are numerous.

Art. 62. The tariffs for the exploitation of public services in respect of which concessions have been granted are subject to control and legal inspection by the State.

Title XIV
Of State Finances

Art. 63. There shall be a single general State budget for the mainland and adjacent islands, showing the sum total of public receipts and expenditure and likewise those of the autonomous services. Detailed explanations of these may be published separately.

Art. 64. The general State budget shall be drawn up annually and put into effect by the Government, in conformity with the legal provisions in force and particularly for law of authorization mentioned in Article 91 (IV).

Art. 65. Expenditure corresponding to the legal or contractural obligations of the State, or that which is permanent by reason of its nature or purpose, including interest charges and amortization of the Public Debt, shall be taken as the basis for fixing taxation and other State revenue.

Art. 66. The budget shall state the measures which are essential for meeting the total expenditure.

Art. 67. The State may only borrow for extraordinary expenditure for economic expansion, for amortization of other loans, and for essential increase of State patrimony, or vital requirements for the defense and preservation of the nation.

Essential supplementary revenue may, however, be obtained by means of floating debt, representing receipts of the current administrative period, at the end of which the amount must be liquidated, or the Treasury placed in a position to liquidate it through its funds.

Art. 68.   The State may not reduce the capital or interest of the funded public debt to the detriment of the bondholders, but may convert it on equitable terms.

Art. 69.   Sums due on account of deposits placed in State funds or its credit institutions may not be subject to compulsory consolidation.

Art. 70.   The law shall fix general principles in regard to the following matters:

I) taxation;

II) rates chargeable on public services;

III) administration and exploitation of State property and undertakings.

1. In the matter of taxation the law shall determine the liability, rate, exemptions where proper, and the claims and reliefs to be allowed to the taxpayer.

2. The collection of taxes established for an indefinite time, or for a fixed period exceeding a single administrative period, shall be subject to the authorization of the National Assembly.

PART II

OF THE POLITICAL ORGANIZATION OF THE STATE

TITLE I
OF SOVEREIGNTY

Art. 71.   Sovereignty is vested in the nation; its representatives are the Head of the State, the National Assembly, the Government, and the Courts of Justice.

TITLE II
OF THE HEAD OF THE STATE

Chapter I

OF THE ELECTION OF THE PRESIDENT OF THE REPUBLIC
AND OF HIS PREROGATIVES

Art. 72.   The Chief of the State is the President of the Republic elected by the Nation.

1. The President is elected for a term of seven years which

may not be extended save in the case of events which make it impossible to summon the electoral colleges. In this event the mandate shall terminate as soon as his successor assumes office.

2. The election shall take place on the Sunday nearest to the sixth day preceding the end of each Presidential term, by direct suffrage of the citizen electors.

3. The final scrutiny of votes shall be made by the Supreme Court of Justice, which shall proclaim President the citizen obtaining the largest number of votes.

Art. 73. Only a Portuguese citizen over thirty-five years of age, who has always possessed Portuguese nationality, and is in full enjoyment of his civil and political rights, may be elected President of the Republic.

1. No candidate may stand for election who does not offer guarantees of respect for and fidelity to the fundamental principles of the political and social order laid down in the Constitution.

2. If the candidate elected is a member of the National Assembly he shall forfeit his seat.

Art. 74. Relatives of the kings of Portugal, up to the sixth degree are ineligible for the office of President of the Republic.

Art. 75. The President-elect shall assume his duties on the day on which his predecessor's mandate expires, and shall take office before the National Assembly, using the following form of oath:

I swear to maintain and loyally and faithfully to carry out the Constitution of the Republic, to observe the laws, to promote the general welfare of the nation and to uphold and protect the integrity and independence of the Portuguese fatherland.

Art. 76. The President of the Republic may only go abroad with the assent of the National Assembly and the Government.

Failure to observe the provisions of this Article shall in the full meaning of the law involve loss of office.

Art. 77. The President of the Republic shall receive a salary, fixed before his election, and he may choose two State properties for use as the Presidential Secretariat and as a private residence for himself and the members of his family.

Art. 78. The President of the Republic shall be directly and exclusively responsible to the nation for actions performed in the exercise of his duties. Both the exercise of the latter and his office as magistrate shall be independent of any vote of the National Assembly.

For crimes unconnected with the exercise of his functions the President shall be answerable to ordinary courts of law but only after conclusion of his mandate.

Art. 79. The President of the Republic may resign his office in a message addressed to the nation and published in the *Diário do Governo*.

Art. 80. In the event of the Presidency of the Republic falling vacant owing to the death, resignation, or permanent physical disability of the President, or owing to his absence abroad without the assent of the National Assembly and the Government, the National Assembly shall meet of its own right on the sixtieth day after the vacancy occurs, to deliberate on the presidential election.

1. The President's permanent physical disability must be recognized by the Council of State summoned for the purpose by the President of the Council of Ministers who, if the disability is confirmed, shall publish in the *Diario do Governo* an announcement of the presidential vacancy.

2. Until the election provided for in this article takes place or when for any reason there is a temporary interruption in the exercise of the presidential function, the President of the Council shall be invested with the attributes of the Chief of State in addition to those of his office.

Chapter II
OF THE ATTRIBUTES OF THE PRESIDENT OF THE REPUBLIC

Art. 81. It shall be the business of the President of the Republic:

I) to appoint the President of the Council and the Ministers from among Portuguese citizens, and to dismiss them;

II) solemnly to open the first meeting of each legislative session and to address messages to the National Assembly, directing them to its Chairman, who shall read them at the first meeting to be held after their receipt;

III) to fix a day, in accordance with the electoral law, for a general election or by-election of deputies;

IV) to confer constituent powers upon the National Assembly and to submit to a National Plebiscite such alterations of the Constitution as may refer to the legislative functions or to public bodies charged therewith, in accordance with Art. 135 (I) and (II);

V) to convene the National Assembly in extraordinary session, in time of urgent public emergency, for the consideration of specified matters, and to adjourn its sessions, without prejudice to the duration fixed for the Legislative Session in each year;

VI) to dissolve the National Assembly when the supreme interests of the nation so require;

VII) to represent the nation and direct the foreign policy of the State; to conclude international conventions and negotiate treaties of peace, alliance, arbitration, and commerce, submitting them through the government to the National Assembly for approval;

VIII) to grant pardons and commute punishments. No pardon may be granted until half the sentence has been served;

IX) to promulgate and cause to be published, the law and resolutions of the National Assembly as well as the Decree laying down regulations, and to sign all individual decrees in default of which they shall be considered as non-existent.

Art. 82. The acts of the President of the Republic must be countersigned by the President of the Council and by the appropriate Minister or Ministers; in default they shall be non-existent.

Counter-signatures are not required for:

I) the appointment and dismissal of the Council;

II) messages addressed to the National Assembly;

III) the message of resignation from office.

Chapter III
OF THE COUNCIL OF STATE

Art. 83. The President of the Republic shall perform his functions in conjunction with the Council of State, composed of the following members:

I) the President of the Council of Ministers;

II) the President of the National Assembly;

III) the President of the Corporative Chamber;

IV) the President of the Supreme Court of Justice;

V) the Procurator General of the Republic;

VI) ten public men of outstanding ability, appointed for life by the Chief of State.

Art. 84.   The Council of State shall be obliged to discharge the following functions:

a) to decide on the suitability of candidates to the Presidency of the Republic, for the purpose of the provision in paragraph I of Article 73;

b) to assist the Chief of State when exercising certain of the functions assigned to him by paragraphs 4, 5, 6 of Article 81 and the second paragraph of Article 87;

c) to deliver its opinion, in the manner laid down by paragraph 1, of Article 80, in all emergencies threatening the life of the Nation and whenever the President of the Republic deems it necessary to summon it.

The Council shall meet in its own right to consider candidatures for the Presidency of the Republic, and at such meetings neither the Chief of State nor any Councillor who is a candidate shall be present.

TITLE III
OF THE NATIONAL ASSEMBLY AND THE CORPORATIVE CHAMBER

Chapter I
OF THE NATIONAL ASSEMBLY

Art. 85.   The National Assembly shall be composed of one hundred and twenty Deputies, elected by the direct vote of the citizen electors, and its mandate will continue for a period of four years, which may not be prolonged save in the case of events which make the convocation of the electoral colleges impossible.

1. The necessary qualification for deputies, and the organization of the electoral colleges and procedure, shall be governed by a special law.

2. Nobody may be a member of the National Assembly and of the Corporative Chamber at the same time.

3. Vacancies occurring in the National Assembly, provided they attain the number fixed by the electoral law and not exceeding one-fifth of the total number of deputies required by law, shall be filled by means of by-elections, the respective mandates expiring with the life of the legislature.

4. Deputies may resign their mandates, but such resignation shall not be effective unless accepted by the As-

sembly or its Chairman, according to whether it is presented during or in an interval between sessions.

Art. 86. It shall be the duty of the National Assembly to examine and recognize the powers of its members, to elect its board, to draw up its own internal rules, and to regulate its police.

Art. 87. If the National Assembly is dissolved, elections shall be held within sixty days, under the electoral law in force at the time of the dissolution. The new Chambers shall meet within the thirty days following the closing of the electoral proceedings. If the legislative session of that year has not been concluded, they shall continue for the full legislative period without reckoning the time during which they functioned in completion of the previous legislative session, and without prejudice to the right of dissolution.

If the supreme interests of the country render it advisable, the period of sixty days mentioned in this article may be extended to six months.

Art. 88. After the final ordinary legislative session of the four-year period, the National Assembly shall remain in being until the results of the new general election have been ascertained.

Chapter II
OF THE MEMBERS OF THE NATIONAL ASSEMBLY

Art. 89. The members of the National Assembly shall enjoy the following immunities and privileges:

a) they may not be attacked for the opinion and votes given in the exercise of their mandates, subject to the limitations laid down in paragraphs 1 and 2;

b) they may not be called upon to serve on juries, or as experts or witnesses, without the sanction of the Assembly;

c) they may not be detained or arrested without the consent of the Assembly, except in cases of crimes punishable by the maximum sentence or its equivalent in the penal scale, provided that in the latter case they are arrested *in flagrante delictu* or under a warrant of the Court;

d) if criminal proceedings are taken against any deputy and he is formally charged, the judge shall notify the Assembly of the fact; the Assembly (save in the case mentioned in the latter part of paragraph (c) of this article) shall then decide whether or not the deputy shall be suspended to enable the proceedings to take their course;

e) they shall have the right to be remunerated as may be determined by the electoral law.

1. Freedom from attack in respect of their opinions and votes does not exempt members of the National Assembly from civil and criminal liability for defamation, calumny, and abuse, outrage of public morals, or open incitement to crime.

2. The National Assembly may withdraw the mandates of those deputies who express opinions opposed to the existence of Portugal as an independent state, or who in anyway instigate the violent overthrow of social and political order.

3. The immunities and privileges set out in b), d), and e) shall only be effective during the actual exercise of legislative functions.

Art. 90. Members of the National Assembly shall forfeit their seats in the following circumstances:

I) if they should accept any remunerated employment or commission by way of subsidy from the Government or from any foreign government;

II) if, being civil or military officers, they should exercise these functions during the actual session of the National Assembly;

III) if they should occupy posts of an administrative, executive, or inspectional nature otherwise than by government appointment; or as legal or technical advisers in undertakings or companies formed under special State contract or concessions, or which enjoy a State privilege not conferred by general law, or which receive a subsidy or guarantee of revenue or interest;

IV) if they should enter into contracts with the government;

V) if they should act as concessionaires, contractors, or partners in firms contracting for public concessions, public adjudicated contracts, or contracts subject to public tender; and also if they should participate in State financial operations.

1. The following are excepted from the provision laid down in No. (1) above:

a) temporary diplomatic missions and military commissions or military commands which do not involve residence away from the mainland;

b) appointments by advancement, legal promotions, acts

which confirming temporary appointments as definitive and appointments to equivalent posts arising out of the reorganization of services;

c) competitive appointments made by the government in pursuance of regulations, or in the recommendation of bodies legally entitled to recommend or choose officials; as also the appointments to posts and commissions only open to a certain class or category of officials.

2. The recognition by the President of the facts referred to in I) and II) shall have the same effect as the acceptance of resignation.

3. The circumstances mentioned in IV) and V), further, render the contracts and acts in question null and void.

Chapter III
Of the Attributes of the National Assembly

Art. 91. The functions of the National Assembly are:

I) to make, interpret, suspend, and revoke laws;

II) to safeguard the observance of the Constitution and the laws and to examine the acts of the government or the administration;

III) to receive the accounts for each economic year, both for metropolitan Portugal and the overseas territories. These shall be laid before it with the report and resolution of the Court of Accounts, if the accounts have been examined by this Court, and such other information as may be necessary for their appreciation;

IV) to authorize the government up to the 15th December each year to collect State revenues and to meet public expenditure for the ensuing financial period; also to determine in the appropriate authorizing enactment, the principles which shall govern that part of the budget dealing with expenditure of sums not fixed by previously existing laws;

V) to authorize the government to float loans or other similar operations not included in the floating debt, and to fix the general conditions of the same;

VI) except in the case of actual or imminent aggression by foreign forces, to authorize the Head of the State to make war (should recourse to arbitration be impossible or of no avail) and to make peace;

VII) in accordance with the provisions of Article 81 (VII), to approve all international conventions and treaties;

VIII) to declare martial law with total or partial suspension of the constitutional guarantees, in one or more places in the national territory, in the case of actual or imminent aggression by foreign forces, or when public order and safety are seriously disturbed or threatened;

IX) to define the boundaries of national territories;

X) to grant amnesties;

XI) to receive addresses from the Head of the State;

XII to discuss the revision of the Constitution;

XIII) to bestow legislative authority on the government.

Art. 92. Laws voted by the National Assembly must be confined to the examination of the general legal principles of the enactments, but the constitutional legality of any provisions contained therein may not be impugned on the ground of violation of such principles.

Art. 93. The approval of the general principles of the following shall be the exclusive concern of the National Assembly:

   a) the organization of national defense;

   b) the weight, value, and denomination of coinage in currency;

   c) the standards of weights and measures;

   d) the creation of banks or issuing institutions;

   e) the organization of the law-courts.

Chapter IV

OF THE ACTIVITIES OF THE NATIONAL ASSEMBLY AND OF THE PROMULGATION OF LAWS AND ORDERS

Art. 94. The National Assembly shall be in session for a period of three months, beginning on 25th November of each year, without prejudice to the provisions of Articles 75, 76, and 81 (V).

The President of the National Assembly, if he considers it proper, may extend the session of the National Assembly for one month and interrupt it without prejudice to the period fixed in this article for the same, provided always that its closure shall not be later than 30th April.

Art. 95. The National Assembly shall meet in full session and its decisions shall be taken by absolute majority vote, provided there is a quorum; it may set up permanent committees of its members or form special committees for specific purposes.

1. Plenary sessions are public, unless otherwise resolved by the Assembly or by its President.

2. Committees shall only sit during the session of the Assembly; they may, however, continue to act if so demanded by the nature of their purpose or by the special object for which they were created.

3. Ministers and Under-Secretaries may take part in the sessions where amendments suggested by the Corporative Chamber are under consideration; one delegate of that Chamber may take part in the proceedings.

Art. 96. Members of the National Assembly individually may refer to, consult, or request information from any official corporation or department in regard to matters of public administration; official departments, however, may not reply without the previous permission of their Minister, who may only lawfully withhold his consent for reasons of State secrecy.

Art. 97. The right to introduce legislations is vested equally in the government, and in any members of the National Assembly; individual members, however, may not introduce bills nor propose amendments involving any increase in State expenditure, or any reductions of State revenue created by former laws.

During the discussion of proposals or bills, the Government may submit amendments for the consideration of the Assembly provided those amendments deal with matters on which a vote has not yet been taken.

Art. 98. Bills passed by the National Assembly shall be sent to the President of the Republic for promulgation as law within the fifteen days following.

Bills not so promulgated shall be returned to the National Assembly for reconsideration and, if they are then passed by a two-thirds majority of its existing members, the Head of the State may maintain his refusal to promulgate them.

Art. 99. Promulgation of laws shall be in the following form:

"In the name of the Nation, the National Assembly decrees and I promulgate the following Law (or Order)."

The following shall be promulgated as Orders:

    a) the ratification of decree-laws;

b) the decisions referred to in Articles 2, 80 and Nos. 3, 6, 7, and 12 of Article 91 and other like Articles.

Art. 100. Any motions or bills brought before the National Assembly but not discussed during that session shall be re-introduced during the next session of the Assembly; should they finally be rejected they may not be introduced again in the same Legislative session, except in the case of a motion for dissolution of the National Assembly.

Art. 101. The regulations of the Assembly shall contain:

a) a prohibition to alter the order of the day by introduction of fresh matter without at least twenty-four hours previous notice;

b) the conditions for introducing bills.

Chapter V
OF THE CORPORATIVE CHAMBER

Art. 102. There shall be a Corporative Chamber, equal in length of term with the National Assembly, composed of representatives of local autonomous bodies and social interests, the latter being those of an administrative, moral, cultural, and economic order; the law shall designate those bodies on which such representation falls, the manner of their selections, and the duration of their mandate.

1. When vacancies occur in offices whose holders as such have a seat in the Corporative Chamber, the representation of such offices devolves upon those who properly substitute them according to law or by statute. The same principle applies to cases of impediment.

2. Except in the case mentioned in the preceding paragraph, vacancies occurring in the Corporative Chamber shall be filled in the same manner as the original officer was appointed.

3. The provisions of Article 89 and its subsections shall apply to the members of this Chamber; but the action envisaged in b), c), and d) of that Article shall be taken on the authority, or by the decision, of the President. The amount of the remuneration mentioned in e) (of Article 89) and the conditions on which it is granted shall be regulated by law.

Art. 103. It is the duty of the Corporative Chamber to report and give its opinion on all proposals or draft bills and on all international conventions or treaties submitted to the National Assembly, before discussion thereof is commenced by the latter.

1. The report shall be given within thirty days or within such period as the Government or the Assembly shall fix, if the matter concerned is considered to be urgent.

2. Should the time limit referred to in the preceding subsection expire before the report has been sent to the National Assembly discussion may proceed immediately.

3. If the Corporative Chamber, while advising on general grounds the rejection of a bill, recommends that it be replaced by another, the Government or any Deputy may adopt the bill in question and it shall then be considered jointly with the original bill, independently of further reference to the Corporative Chamber. If the latter suggests alterations of detail in a proposal or bill, the National Assembly may decide that the voting be cast first on the text proposed by the Corporative Chamber and any Deputy may always move such amendments as his own.

Art. 104. The Corporative Chamber shall function in plenary sessions or in committees and sub-committees.

1. There will be committees for administrative, moral, cultural, and economic questions and sub-committees for specialized questions within each committee.

2. When the matter under discussion so requires, two or more committees or sub-committees may meet jointly.

3. The President of the Council, the Minister of Corporations, and the Ministers and Under-Secretaries of State concerned, or their representatives, may take part in the discussion of proposals or bills, as also may a Deputy in the case of a bill which he has originated.

4. Sessions of the committees and sub-committees of the Corporative Chamber shall not be held in public, but plenary sessions may be.

Art. 105. The Government may consult the Corporative Chamber on enactments to be published or on draft bills to be presented to the National Assembly; it may decide that the work of the committees or sub-committees shall continue or take place during adjournments, interruptions, or intervals between legislative sessions; and it may request the convocation of all or any of the committees or sub-committees in order to make a communication to them.

1. The discussion of draft bills in the National Assembly shall not be dependent on fresh reference to the Corporative Chamber if the latter has already been consulted by the Government.

2. During the legislative session of the National Assembly, the Corporative Chamber may suggest to the Government such measures as it considers advisable or necessary.

Art. 106. The provisions of Article 86 apply to the Corporative Chamber, except insofar as concerns the verification of powers. This duty shall be entrusted to a special commission elected by the Chamber, and in Article 101 a) and b) the respective Committees and Sub-Committees shall also enjoy the facilities conferred by Article 96 on the members of the National Assembly.

TITLE IV
OF THE GOVERNMENT

Art. 107. The Government consists of the President of the Council, who may conduct the affairs of one or more ministries, and the Ministers; the latter shall be substituted by the former, in any official business, whenever Ministers are absent from the mainland and temporary ministers have not been appointed to the respective portfolios.

1. The President of the Council shall be appointed and dismissed at will by the President of the Republic. The Ministers and Under-Secretaries of State, if any, shall be appointed by the President of the Republic upon the recommendation of the President of the Council, who shall countersign their appointments and likewise the resignations of retiring ministers.

2. The functions of the Under-Secretaries of State cease upon the removal of the respective ministers.

Art. 108. The President of the Council shall be responsible to the President of the Republic for the general policy of the government and shall co-ordinate and direct the activities of all the Ministers, who shall be responsible to him politically for their acts.

Art. 109. It shall be the duty of the Government:

I) to countersign the acts of the President of the Republic;

II) to draw up decree laws and, in cases of urgency, to approve international conventions and treaties;

III) to draw up decrees, regulations, and instructions for the proper carrying out of laws;

IV) to superintend public administration as a whole, ensuring that the laws and resolutions of the National Assembly are carried out, controlling the acts of administrative bodies and of corporate entities of public administrative utility, and doing whatever may be necessary in relation to the appointment, transfer, resignation, retirement, superannuation, dismissal, or reinstatement of civil or military officers, subject to the right of recourse of the parties concerned to the competent courts.

1. Any action by the President of the Republic and the Government which involves an increase or decrease of revenue or expenditure shall be countersigned by the Minister of Finance.

2. Legislative authorizations may not be utilized more than once, except those which by their nature are for repeated use. The Government may, however, utilize them in stages until they expire.

3. Decree-laws published by the Government while the National Assembly is sitting, if they fall outside the scope authorized by law, shall be subject to ratification. This will be held to have been granted if, during the first ten sessions, after publication, at least ten Deputies have not required that such decree-laws be submitted to the Assembly for its consideration.

Should ratification be refused, the decree-law will cease to have effect from the day on which the appropriate notice, issued by the President of the Assembly, is published in the Government Gazette.

The ratification may be granted subject to amendments; in this case the decree-law will be sent to the Corporative Chamber, if it has not already been consulted, but will continue in force unless the National Assembly, by a majority of two-thirds of the Deputies actually functioning, suspends its effect insofar as concerns the creation or reorganization of services involving an increase of personnel or alteration of their respective ranks in relation to the existing staffs.

4. If the law by itself is not capable of practical application, the Government will issue appropriate decrees within six months, unless the law itself establishes some other period.

5. The appointment of Governors of the overseas Provinces shall be made by the Council of Ministers.

6. The appointment, transfer, removal, retirement, pension-

ing, dismissal, or reinstatement of the President of the Supreme Court of Justice, of the Procurator-General of the Republic, of diplomatic and consular agents, and of Governors-General and Governors of the Overseas Provinces, shall be made by decree.

Art. 110. Ministers may not exercise any other public duties, or any private employment, in addition to their ministerial offices.

1. Ministers shall be subject to the other prohibitions and provisions contained in Art. 90.

2. Members of the National Assembly or of the corporative Chamber who accept the office of Minister or Under-Secretary of State shall not forfeit their mandates, but they may not sit in their respective chambers.

Art. 111. The Council of Ministers shall meet when its President or the Head of State considers it necessary. When the said President or the Head of the State shall think fit, the meeting shall take place under the presidency of the latter and it shall be obligatory for the Head of the State to preside, when he has to use the powers conferred upon him in Article 81 (II), (III), (IV), (V), (VI), and (VIII).

Art. 112. The Government depends exclusively upon possessing the confidence of the President of the Republic, and its continuance in office shall not depend upon the fate of its draft bills, or upon any vote of the National Assembly.

Art. 113. The President of the Council shall transmit to the President of the National Assembly the draft bills to be submitted to the latter, together with any explanations requested of the government or which the government may deem appropriate.

The President of the Council may appear in the National Assembly to give his attention to any matters affecting the higher interests of the nation.

Art. 114. Each Minister is responsible politically, civilly, and criminally for any acts which he may legalize or carry out; Ministers shall be tried in the ordinary courts for acts involving civil or criminal liability.

If any Minister be prosecuted for a criminal offense, the Supreme Court of Justice in full session, the Attorney General of the Republic being present, shall provided the proceedings have not gone beyond the stage of formally charging the offender, decide whether the Minister shall be tried immediately, in which case his suspension shall be decided on, or whether the trial shall be conducted on the completion of his tenure of office.

Art. 115. Criminal liability attaches to Ministers and Under-Secretaries of State and government agents in respect of any acts directed:

I) against the political existence of the nation;

II) against the Constitution and the established political system;

III) against the free exercise of their functions by the representatives of national sovereignty;

IV) against the enjoyment and exercise of political and individual rights;

V) against the internal security of the country;

VI) against the integrity of the administration;

VII) against the custody and constitutional employment of public monies;

VIII) against the law dealing with public accounts.

Conviction for any of these crimes involves loss of office and exclusion from holding public office.

TITLE V
OF THE COURTS

Art. 116. The exercise of judicial functions belongs to the ordinary courts and special tribunals.

The Supreme Court of Justice and the judicial courts of first and second instance are the ordinary courts, and they shall have such material and territorial jurisdiction as determined by law.

Art. 117. The establishment of special courts with exclusive jurisdiction to try a certain category of crime or certain categories of crimes, is forbidden, unless the crimes are fiscal or social by nature or are against the safety of the State.

Art. 118. The State shall be represented in the courts by the Public Attorney.

Art. 119. Judges of the ordinary courts are appointed for life and cannot be removed; the conditions of their appointment, promotion, dismissal, suspension, transfer, and nomination outside the cadre shall be fixed by law and they may not accept any other office of profit from the government; this shall not, however, prejudice their being requisitioned for permanent or temporary commissions.

Art. 120.   Judges shall not be held responsible for the judgments pronounced by them, except in cases specified by law.

Art. 121.   The sittings of the courts shall be public, except in special cases prescribed by law, and whenever publicity would be contrary to good order, the interests of the State, or morality.

Art. 122.   In the execution of their decisions and judgments, the courts shall have the right to the collaboration of other authorities whenever required.

Art. 123.   In cases submitted for judgment the courts may not apply laws, decrees, or any other ordinances which transgress the provisions of this Constitution or violate the principles herein contained.

The organic or formal constitutional illegality of ordinances promulgated by the President of the Republic may only be called into question by the National Assembly, either on its own initiative or on that of the Government, and the National Assembly shall determine the effects of such constitutional illegality, without prejudice, however, to situations created by *causae judicatae*.

Art. 124.   As a means of preventing and suppressing crimes, penalties and precautionary measures shall be introduced for the protection of society and as far as possible for the social rehabilitation of the offender.

Title VI
Of the Administrative Divisions and Local Autonomous Authorities in Metropolitan Portugal

Art. 125.   The territory of the mainland is divided into boroughs, consisting of parishes, and grouped into districts and provinces, the boundaries of all such areas being established by law.

1. The boroughs of Lisbon and Oporto are subdivided into wards, and the latter into parishes.

2. The territorial division of the adjacent islands and its administrative organization shall be the subject of a special law.

Art. 126. Administrative authorities are the Town Councils and the Parish and Provincial Boards.

Art. 127.   The administrative activities of local autonomous authorities are subject to scrutiny by government inspectors and the resolutions of their executive committees may be subject to the confirmation or require the approval of other bodies or authorities and be submitted to examination.

Art. 128.   In order to give effect to their resolutions, and for other purposes specified by law, administrative authorities shall appoint a President or special sub-committees in accordance with the said law.

Art. 129.   Resolutions of administrative authorities can only be amended or annulled in the cases and in the manner prescribed by administrative enactments.

Art. 130.   Administrative authorities enjoy financial autonomy under conditions to be determined by law but town councils are bound to divide among the parishes, for the purpose of rural improvements, such part of their revenues as are fixed by law.

Art. 131.   Systems of local taxation shall be organized in such a manner as to avoid interfering with the general tax or financial organization of the State, and the circulation of produce and merchandise between different districts of the country.

Art. 132.   Administrative authorities may only be dissolved in such cases and in such manner as prescribed by administrative enactments.

TITLE VII
OVERSEAS PORTUGAL

Chapter I
FUNDAMENTAL PRINCIPLES

Art. 133.   It is intrinsic in the Portuguese Nation to fulfill its historic mission of colonization in the lands of the Discoveries under their sovereignty and to diffuse among the populations inhabiting them the benefits of their civilization, as also to exercise the moral influence enjoined upon it by the Patronage of the East.

Art. 134.   The Overseas Territories of Portugal described in Article 1, II-V, shall be known as Provinces. Their politico-administrative organization shall be on lines best suited to their geographical situation and their social standards.

Art. 135. The Overseas Provinces, as an integral part of the Portuguese State, are united as between themselves and with Metropolitan Portugal.

Art. 136. This unity between the Overseas Provinces and Metropolitan Portugal involves in particular the obligation to contribute in an adequate manner to the preservation of the integrity and defense of the whole Nation and the aims of the national policy as defined in the common interest, by the bodies in which sovereignty resides.

Chapter II
General Guarantees

Art. 137. The rights, liberties, and individual guarantees enshrined in the Constitution, are assured to nationals and foreigners alike in the Overseas Provinces, within the terms of the law, but without prejudice to the right to refuse entry to both national and foreigners into any Overseas Province or to order their expulsion, in accordance with the regulations, if grave inconvenience of a domestic or international character should be caused by their presence. Appeals against such decisions may be made to the Government alone.

Art. 138. Regard shall be given in the Overseas Territories to the state of development of the native inhabitants. To this end and where necessary there shall be established, by special statutes, in the spirit of Portuguese public and private law, systems in keeping with native usage and customs, provided that these are not incompatible with morality, the dictates of humanity, or the free exercise of Portuguese sovereignty.

Art. 139. The State shall ensure, in its Overseas Territories, liberty of conscience and the free exercise of the various religions, subject only to such restrictions as may be required for the preservation of the rights and interests of Portuguese sovereignty, for the maintenance of public order, and in conformity with international treaties and conventions.

Art. 140. The Portuguese Catholic missions overseas and the establishments for training personnel for their services and for those of the Padroado shall, in conformity with the Concordata and other agreements concluded with the Holy See, enjoy juridical personality and shall be protected and assisted by the State, as being institutions of education and assistance and instruments of civilization.

Chapter III
SPECIAL GUARANTEES FOR NATIVES

Art. 141. The State guarantees, through special measures in the stage of transition, the protection and defense of the natives living in the Provinces, in accordance with the principles of humanity and sovereignty, the provisions of this chapter and international conventions.

The authorities and the law-courts shall prevent and punish in accordance with the law all abuses against the persons and property of the natives.

Art. 142. The State shall establish public Portuguese institutions and encourage the establishment of private Portuguese institutions to uphold the rights of the natives and to give them assistance.

Art. 143. The natives are guaranteed, in accordance with the law, in their property and in the possession of their lands and crops, and this principle shall be respected in all concessions made by the State.

Art. 144. Natives contracted for the service of the State or for administrative bodies shall be paid for their work.

Art. 145. The following are prohibited:

1. Systems whereby the State undertakes to provide native labor to any firms working for their own profit;

2. Systems whereby the natives in any territorial area are compelled to work for such firms, whatever the pretext.

Art. 146. The State may only compel the natives to work on public works of general interest to the community, on tasks of which the finished product will belong to them, in the execution of judicial sentences of a penal character, or for the discharge of fiscal liabilities.

Art. 147. The system of native contract labor shall be based on individual liberty and on the right to a fair wage and assistance, the public authorities intervening only for the purpose of regulation.

Chapter IV
THE POLITICAL AND ADMINISTRATIVE SYSTEM

Art. 148. The Overseas Provinces shall be guaranteed the right of administrative decentralization and financial autonomy in conformity with the Constitution and with their state of development and resources, without prejudice to the provisions of Article 175.

Political unity shall be maintained in each Overseas Province by the establishment of a single capital and government of the Province.

Art. 149.   The Overseas Provinces shall, as a rule, be governed by special legislation passed by the legislative bodies of metropolitan Portugal or, according to circumstances in each Province, by the provincial legislative bodies, within the legislative limits established by law.

Art. 150.   The following bodies in Metropolitan Portugal shall have the right to legislative for Overseas Portugal:

1. The National Assembly, at the instance of the Minister of Overseas Portugal, on matters in which of necessity legislation is required by the terms of Art. 93, and also in the following:

a) The general system of government of the Overseas Provinces;

b) The definition of the powers of the Metropolitan Government and of the Governments of the Overseas Provinces in matters relating to the area and duration of territorial concessions or to others which involve exclusive rights or special privileges;

c) Authorization for contracts, not being loans, when they require special security or guarantees.

2. The Government when, under the terms of the Constitution, it has by decree-law, to take action affecting the whole national territory; or when an executive measure provides for questions of common concern both to Metropolitan Portugal and one or more of the Overseas Provinces.

3. The Minister for Overseas Portgual, whose authoriey covers all matters involving the higher or general interests of national policy in Overseas Portugal or which are common to more than one Overseas Province, as specified in the legal system described in 1 a) of this article.

1. The legislative power of the Minister for Overseas Portugal shall be exercised after consultation with the Council for the Overseas, except in cases of urgency and others prescribed by law, as also in those cases where the Council delays for more than thirty days in delivering its opinion on the reference made to it by the Minister. The executive measures taken in the exercise of his legislative power shall be published in the form of decrees, promulgated and countersigned as provided for by the Constitu-

tion. The form of a ministerial legislative enactment shall be adopted when the Minister is exercising his functions in any of the Overseas Provinces and that of an order in the other cases provided for in the law.

2. All enactments to be enforced in the Overseas Provinces shall contain an instruction from the Minister of Overseas, to the effect that they must be published in the Official Bulletin of the Province or Provinces concerned.

3. The constitutional validity of the provisions contained in such enactments shall not be contested on the grounds that they violate this article, save as provided in Article 123, *sole* paragraph.

Art. 151. All matters of exclusive concern to an Overseas Province and outside the scope, as defined in the previous Article, of the National Assembly, the Government, or the Minister for Overseas Portugal shall be dealt with by the legislative bodies of the Overseas Provinces prescribed by law.

1. Agreements and conventions outside the terms of Articles 81 (VII) and 91 (VII) which the governments of the Overseas Provinces, duly authorized, negotiate with the governments of other provinces or territories, national or foreign, shall require the approval of the Overseas Minister.

2. The enactments of the Overseas Governments cannot revoke, suspend, or run contrary to the provisions of the Constitution or of any other enactments passed by the legislative bodies of Metropolitan Portugal.

Art. 152. The legislative functions of each of the Governments of the Overseas Provinces, within their jurisdiction, shall be exercised under the supervision of the bodies in which sovereignty resides and shall be, as a rule, in accordance with the vote of a council in which representation is suited to local social conditions.

Art. 153. The Government shall superintend and control the whole administration of the Overseas Provinces, according to the Constitution and the organic law or laws referred to in Article 150 (1) a) through the bodies prescribed by those laws.

Art. 154. In each of the Overseas Provinces there shall be, as the supreme authority, a Governor or Governor-General, with powers and prerogatives defined by law. They shall not be entrusted in any way with powers which, under the Constitution, belong to the National Assembly, to the Government, or to the Minister for Overseas Portugal, save such limited powers as may be granted by the proper authority, for specified matters and in exceptional circumstances.

No person connected with the direction or management of enterprises which have their head offices or sphere of activity in a Province may be appointed Governor of that Province.

Art. 155. The executive functions in each Overseas Province shall be discharged by the Governor, who, in the cases provided for by law, shall be assisted by a consultative body.

Art. 156. The administrative division of the Overseas Provinces and the conditions on which local autonomous bodies may be established shall be decided by law, having regard to the importance, the development, and the population of each area.

Without prejudice to the provision of the *sole* paragraph of Article 7, foreigners permanently resident in a territory for not less than five years and who are able to read and write Portuguese may be members of administrative bodies up to a maximum of one third of the total number of members.

Art. 157. It is the supreme duty and honor of the Governor, in each of the Overseas Provinces, to uphold the sovereign rights of the Nation and to promote the welfare of the Province, in accordance with the principles enshrined in the Constitution and in the laws.

Chapter V
THE ECONOMIC ORDER

Art. 158. The economic organization of Overseas Portugal shall form part of the general economic organization of the Portuguese Nation and shall thereby take its place in the world economy.

To attain the ends indicated in this Article the free circulation of products within the whole national territory shall be facilitated by suitable means, including the gradual reduction or suspension of customs duties. The same principle shall be applied as far as possible to the movement of persons and capital.

Art. 159. The economic systems of the Overseas Provinces shall be established in harmony with the needs of their development and the well-being of their population, with fair reciprocity between them and the neighboring countries, and with the rights and legitimate advantages of the Portuguese Nation, of which they are an integral part.

Art. 160. Without prejudice to the decentralization prescribed by Article 148, it is for Metropolitan Portugal to secure, through measures taken by the competent bodies, a proper balance in the interests which, under the previous Article, should be considered as a whole in the economic systems of the Overseas Territories.

Art. 161. The law shall specify those areas of land and other properties overseas, which, because they are used or intended for use as public property or involve the prestige of the State or are required for supreme national purposes, cannot be ceded or in any way alienated.

The law shall also regulate the use or occupation of such areas of land by public or private bodies when it is in the interests of the State and on a temporary basis.

Art. 162. The concessions granted by the State or by the local autonomous bodies in the sphere of their competence shall always be subject to conditions which insure the national interest and other requirements of the national economy even when they are to be effected with the aid of foreign capital.

To this end special measures will be passed to govern the situation.

Art. 163. The administration and operation of ports and airports in Overseas Portugal shall in future be reserved to the State. Exceptions to this allowed in each port or airport in connection with certain installations or services shall be regulated by special law.

Art. 164. Neither the State nor local autonomous bodies may, in Overseas Portugal, grant to private or collective enterprise:

1. The exercise of the prerogatives of public administration;

2. The right to levy or fix any charge or tax. This does not include the collection of public revenue whose sale by auction is allowed by law;

3. The possessions of land or the exclusive right of prospecting for minerals, with the right of sub-lease to other enterprises.

In Overseas Territories where concessions of the nature of those mentioned in this Article exist, the following will be observed:

a) They may not be renewed, in whole or in part;

b) The State will exercise its right of cancellation or redemption, in accordance with the relevant laws or contracts.

Chapter VI
THE FINANCIAL SYSTEM

Art. 165. The Overseas Provinces shall have collective personality in public law, with the right to acquire, contract, and take legal proceedings.

Art. 166. Each of the Overseas Provinces has its own assets and liabilities, with the right to dispose of its property and revenue and the responsibility for its expenditure and debts and its acts and contracts, in conformity with the law.

Art. 167. The following are state property in each of the Overseas Provinces within the limits of its territory: waste lands and those lands in respect of which neither public nor private title has been finally established; unclaimed inheritances and other real or personal property which do not belong to anybody; real or personal property which the Overseas Province acquires, or which belong to it legally, outside its territory, including shares of profits or of any other kind which may be due to it.

1. The administration of those properties of the Overseas Provinces which are situated in Metropolitan Portugal shall be carried out by the Ministry for Overseas Portugal.

2. The shares and bonds of concessionary companies belonging to an Overseas Province may be made over or mortgaged only to the Public Treasury or to such credit establishments as the Government may designate; and the proceeds derived therefrom as a result of any financial operation may likewise be made over to the said institutions alone.

Art. 168. Each Overseas Province shall have its own separate budget, drawn up in accordance with a uniform plan and in harmony with the principles contained in Article 63 and 66, and approved in the appropriate Provincial bodies in accordance with such terms as may be enjoined by the law.

1. The budget of each Overseas Province shall include only such revenue and expenditure as is authorized by legal enactments.

2. If the budget cannot be put into effect by the begin-

ning of the final year, the budget of the previous year and the credits sanctioned to meet new permanent charges shall continue in force provisionally, on a monthly basis, but only in respect of ordinary expenditure.

Art. 169. The general system described in Article 150 a) shall provide for:

1. The expenditure and revenue which belong to the Overseas Provinces, separately or in common, as well as those pertaining to Metropolitan Portugal;

2. The rules of control or superintendence to which the Governments of the Overseas Provinces shall be subject by way of safeguard for their finances.

Art. 170. The accounting of the Overseas Provinces shall be organized like that of continental Portugal with such modifications as may be necessitated by special circumstances.

Art. 171. The annual accounts of the Overseas Provinces shall be sent to the Ministry for the Overseas Provinces for submission, after audit and check, to the Court of Accounts for their examination in the manner and within the time limit fixed by law; and for consideration by the National Assembly in accordance with Article 91 (3).

Art. 172. Continental Portugal shall give financial assistance to the Overseas Provinces, against the necessary guarantees.

Art. 173. The Overseas Provinces may not contract loans in foreign countries.

When it is necessary to have recourse to foreign markets to obtain capital intended for the Government of any Overseas Province, the financial operation shall be made exclusively to the account of Metropolitan Portugal, without the Province assuming any responsibility towards those markets. The Province in question shall, however, assume full responsibility vis-à-vis Metropolitan Portugal.

Art. 174. The rights of the Public Treasury or of the credit establishments described in Article 167 (2) as regards the past or future debts of the Overseas Provinces shall not be subject to prescription.

Art. 175. The financial autonomy of the Overseas Provinces shall be subject to such temporary restrictions as may be inevitable should a serious situation arise in connection with their finances or should there be danger of their affecting the finances of Metropolitan Portugal.

SUPPLEMENTARY PROVISIONS
A) Revision of the Constitution

Art. 176.   The Constitution may be revised every ten years, counted from the date of the last law of revision; and the National Assembly whose life includes the last year of the decade or the National Assemblies which follow the tenth year, shall, for this purpose, enjoy constituent powers until the law of revision is published.

1. Constitutional revision may be anticipated by five years if, at the beginning of the legislative session corresponding to the last year of the five-year term, it is so decided by two-thirds of the Deputies in effective exercise of their mandate.

In this case the ten-year period shall likewise be counted from the date of the law of revision then voted.

2. Once a proposal or draft bill for constitutional revision has been presented, others may only be presented within twenty days from the date of the first presentation.

3. Proposals or draft bills for constitutional revision shall not be accepted for consideration unless the proposed amendments are clearly defined.

4. As soon as the law of revision has been published the constituent powers of the National Assembly shall cease.

Art. 177.   Notwithstanding the provisions of the preceding Article, should public interest urgently demand it the Head of the State, after consulting the Council of State, may by a decree signed by all the Ministers:

I) determine that the National Assembly to be elected shall assume constituent powers and revise the Constitution in such parts as specified in the relative decree;

II) submit to a national plebiscite the alterations of the Constitution referring to the legislature or its instruments; such approved alterations shall enter into effect as soon as the final results of the plebiscite are published in the *Diario do Governo*.

Art. 178.   A transitional regime shall be adopted for carrying into effect the sole paragraph of Art. 53, with such temporary restrictions as are deemed essential.

Art. 179.   Until such time as the corporative organization of the Nation is completed, temporary measures shall be adopted to give effect to the principle of organic representation laid down in Title V of Part I.

Art. 180. Laws, and decrees having the force of law, that have been or may be published not later than the first meeting of the National Assembly shall continue in operation and remain in force as laws insofar as they contain nothing explicitly or implicitly contrary to the principles contained in the present Constitution.

Art. 181. The laws and decree laws referred to in the preceding article may nevertheless be revoked by regulating decrees in all matters concerning internal service organization provided the juridical position of private individuals at law and the statute of Civil Servants are unaffected.

The restrictions laid down in this article do not include laws and decree laws defining what constitutes legislative matter, nor the exceptions under Paragraph 1 of Art. 70 and Art. 93.

Part I.

1. This Constitution Act shall apply to all parts of the Kingdom of Denmark.

2. The form of government shall be that of a constitutional monarchy. The Royal Power shall be inherited by men and women in accordance with the provisions of the Succession to the Throne Act, 27th March, 1953.

3. The legislative power shall be vested in the King and the Folketing conjointly. The executive power shall be vested in the King. The judicial power shall be vested in the courts of justice.

4. The Evangelical Lutheran Church shall be the Established Church of Denmark, and, as such, it shall be supported by the State.

Part II.

5. The King shall not reign in other countries except with the consent of the Folketing.

6. The King shall be a member of the Evangelical Lutheran Church.

7. The King shall be of age when he has completed his eighteenth year. The same provision shall apply to the Successor to the Throne.

8. The King, prior to his accession to the Throne, shall

make a solemn Declaration in writing before the Council of State that he will faithfully adhere to the Constitution Act. Two identical originals of the Declaration shall be executed, one of which shall be handed over to the Folketing to be preserved in its archives, and the other shall be filed in the Public Record Office. Where the King, owing to his absence or for other reasons, is unable to sign the aforesaid Declaration immediately on his accession to the Throne, the government shall, unless otherwise provided by Statute, be conducted by the Council of State until such Declaration has been signed. Where the King already as Successor to the Throne has signed the aforesaid Declaration, he shall accede to the Throne immediately on its vacancy.

9. Provisions relating to the exercising of sovereign power in the event of the minority, illness, or absence of the King shall be laid down by Statute. Where on the vacancy of the Throne there is no Successor to the Throne, the Folketing shall elect a King and establish the future order of succession to the Throne.

10. (1) The Civil List of the King shall be granted for the duration of his reign by Statute. Such Statute shall also provide for the castles, palaces, and other State property which shall be placed at the disposal of the King for his use.

(2) The Civil List shall not be chargeable with any debt.

11. Members of the Royal House may be granted annuities by Statute. Such annuities shall not be enjoyed outside the Realm except with the consent of the Folketing.

PART III.

12. Subject to the limitations laid down in this Constitution Act, the King shall have the supreme authority in all the affairs of the Realm, and he shall exercise such supreme authority through the Ministers.

13. The King shall not be answerable for his actions; his person shall be sacrosanct. The Ministers shall be responsible for the conduct of the government; their responsibility shall be determined by Statute.

14. The King shall appoint and dismiss the Prime Minister and the other Ministers. He shall decide upon the number of Ministers and upon the distribution of the duties of government among them. The signature of the King to resolu-

tions relating to legislation and government shall make such resolutions valid, provided that the signature of the King is accompanied by the signature or signatures of one or more Ministers. A Minister who has signed a resolution shall be responsible for the resolution.

15. (1) A Minister shall not remain in office after the Folketing has passed a vote of no confidence in him.

(2) Where the Folketing passes a vote of no confidence in the Prime Minister, he shall ask for the dismissal of the Ministry unless writs are to be issued for a general election. Where a vote of censure has been passed on a Ministry, or it has asked for its dismissal, it shall continue in office until a new Ministry has been appointed. Ministers who continue in office as aforesaid shall do only what is necessary for the purpose of the uninterrupted conduct of official business.

16. Ministers may be impeached by the King or the Folketing with maladministration of office. The High Court of the Realm shall try cases of impeachment brought against Ministers for maladministration of office.

17. (1) The body of Ministers shall form the Council of State, in which the Successor to the Throne shall have a seat when he is of age. The Council of State shall be presided over by the King except in the instance mentioned in section 8, and in the instances where the Legislature in pursuance of section 9 may have delegated the conduct of the government to the Council of State.

(2) All Bills and important government measures shall be discussed in the Council of State.

18. If the King should be prevented from holding a Council of State he may entrust the discussion of a matter to a Council of Ministers. Such Council of Ministers shall consist of all the Ministers, and it shall be presided over by the Prime Minister. The vote of each Minister shall be entered in a minute book, and any question shall be decided by a majority of votes. The Prime Minister shall submit the Minutes, signed by the Ministers present, to the King, who shall decide whether he will immediately consent to the recommendations of the Council of Ministers, or have the matter brought before him in a Council of State.

19. (1) The King shall act on behalf of the Realm in international affairs; provided that, without the consent of the Folketing, the King shall not undertake any act whereby the

territory of the Realm will be increased or decreased, nor shall he enter into any obligation which for fulfillment requires the concurrence of the Folketing, or which otherwise is of major importance; nor shall the King, except with the consent of the Folketing, terminate any international treaty entered into with the consent of the Folketing.

(2) Except for purposes of defense against an armed attack upon the Realm or Danish forces, the King shall not use military force against any foreign state without the consent of the Folketing. Any measure which the King may take in pursuance of this provision shall immediately be submitted to the Folketing. If the Folketing is not in session it shall be convoked immediately.

(3) The Folketing shall appoint from among its Members a Foreign Affairs Committee, which the Government shall consult prior to the making of any decision of major importance to foreign policy. Rules applying to the Foreign Affairs Committee shall be laid down by Statute.

20. (1) Powers vested in the authorities of the Realm under this Constitution Act may, to such extent as shall be provided by Statute, be delegated to international authorities set up by mutual agreement with other states for the promotion of international rules of law and co-operation.

(2) For the passing of a Bill dealing with the above a majority of five-sixths of the Members of the Folketing shall be required. If this majority is not obtained, whereas the majority required for the passing of ordinary Bills is obtained, and if the Government maintains it, the Bill shall be submitted to the Electorate for approval or rejection in accordance with the rules for Referenda laid down in section 42.

21. The King may cause Bills and other measures to be introduced in the Folketing.

22. A Bill passed by the Folketing shall become law if it receives the Royal Assent not later than thirty days after it was finally passed. The King shall order the promulgation of Statutes and shall see to it that they are carried into effect.

23. In an emergency the King may, when the Folketing cannot assemble, issue provisional laws, provided that they shall not be at variance with the Constitution Act, and that they shall always immediately on the assembling of the Folketing be submitted to it for approval or rejection.

24. The King shall have the prerogative of mercy and of

granting amnesty. The King may grant Ministers a pardon for sentences passed upon them by the High Court of the Realm only with the consent of the Folketing.

25. The King may either directly or through the relevant Government authorities make such grants and grant such exemptions from the Statutes as are either warranted under the rules existing before the 5th June, 1849, or have been warranted by a Statute passed since that date.

26. The King may cause money to be coined as provided by Statute.

27. (1) Rules governing the appointment of civil servants shall be laid down by Statute. No person shall be appointed a civil servant unless he is a Danish subject. Civil servants who are appointed by the King shall make a solemn declaration to the effect that they will adhere to the Constitution Act.

(2) Rules governing the dismissal, transfer, and pensioning of civil servants shall be laid down by Statute, confer section 64.

(3) Civil servants appointed by the King shall only be transferred without their consent if they do not suffer any loss in the income accruing from their post or offices, and if they have been offered the choice of such transfer or retirement on pension under the general rules and regulations.

PART IV.

28. The Folketing shall consist of one assembly of not more than one hundred and seventy-nine Members of whom two Members shall be elected on the Faeroe Islands, and two Members in Greenland.

29. (1) Any Danish subject whose permanent residence is in the Realm, and who has the age qualification for suffrage provided for in subsection (2) of this section shall have the right to vote at Folketing elections, provided that he has not been declared incapable of conducting his own affairs. It shall be laid down by Statute to what extent conviction and public assistance amounting to poor relief within the meaning of the law shall entail disfranchisement.

(2) The age qualification for suffrage shall be such as has resulted from the Referendum held under the Act dated the 25th March, 1953. Such age qualification for suffrage may be altered at any time by Statute. A Bill passed by the Folketing

for the purpose of such enactment shall receive the Royal Assent only when the provision on the alteration in the age qualification for suffrage has been put to a Referendum in accordance with subsection (5) of section 42, which has not resulted in the rejection of the provision.

30. (1) Any person who has a right to vote at Folketing elections shall be eligible for membership of the Folketing, unless he has been convicted of an act which in the eyes of the public makes him unworthy of being a Member of the Folketing.

(2) Civil servants who are elected Members of the Folketing shall not require permission from the Government to accept their election.

31. (1) The Members of the Folketing shall be elected by general and direct ballot.

(2) Rules for the exercise of the suffrage shall be laid down by the Elections Act, which, to secure equal representation of the various opinions of the Electorate, shall prescribe the manner of election and decide whether proportional representation shall be adopted with or without elections in single-member constituencies.

(3) In determining the number of seats to be allotted to each area regard shall be paid to the number of inhabitants, the number of electors, and the density of population.

(4) The Elections Act shall provide rules governing the election of substitutes and their admission to the Folketing, and also rules for the procedure to be adopted where a new election is required.

(5) Special rules for the representation of Greenland in the Folketing may be laid down by Statute.

32. (1) The members of the Folketing shall be elected for a period of four years.

(2) The King may at any time issue writs for a new election with the effect that the existing seats shall be vacated upon a new election. Provided that writs for an election shall not be issued after the appointment of a new Ministry until the Prime Minister has presented himself to the Folketing.

(3) The Prime Minister shall cause a general election to be held before the expiration of the period for which the Folketing has been elected.

(4) No seats shall be vacated until a new election has been held.

(5) Special rules may be provided by Statute for the commencement and determination of Faeroe Islands and Greenland representation in the Folketing.

(6) If a Member of the Folketing becomes ineligible his seat in the Folketing shall become vacant.

(7) On approval of his election each new Member shall make a solemn declaration that he will adhere to the Constitution Act.

33. The Folketing itself shall determine the validity of the election of any Member and decide whether a Member has lost his eligibility or not.

34. The Folketing shall be inviolable. Any person who attacks its security or freedom, or any person who issues or obeys any command aiming thereat shall be deemed guilty of high treason.

PART V.

35. (1) A newly elected Folketing shall assemble at twelve o'clock noon on the twelfth week-day after the day of election, unless the King has previously convoked a meeting of its Members.

(2) Immediately after the proving of the mandates the Folketing shall constitute itself by the election of a President and Vice-Presidents.

36. (1) The sessional year of the Folketing shall commence on the first Tuesday of October, and shall continue until the first Tuesday of October of the following year.

(2) On the first day of the sessional year at twelve o'clock noon the Members shall assemble for a new session of the Folketing.

37. The Folketing shall meet in the place where the Government has its seat. Provided that in extraordinary circumstances the Folketing may assemble elsewhere in the Realm.

38. (1) At the first meeting in the sessional year the Prime Minister shall render an account of the general state of the country and of the measures proposed by the Government.

(2) Such account shall be made the subject of a general debate.

39. The President of the Folketing shall convene the meetings of the Folketing, stating the Order of the Day. The President shall convene a meeting of the Folketing upon a requisition being made in writing by at least two-fifths of the

Members of the Folketing or the Prime Minister, stating the Order of the Day.

40. The Ministers shall ex officio be entitled to attend the sittings of the Folketing and to address the Folketing during the debates as often as they may desire, provided that they abide by the Rules of Procedure of the Folketing. They shall be entitled to vote only when they are Members of the Folketing.

41. (1) Any Member of the Folketing shall be entitled to introduce Bills and other measures.

(2) No Bill shall be finally passed until it has been read three times in the Folketing.

(3) Two-fifths of the Members of the Folketing may request of the President that the third reading of a Bill shall not take place until twelve week-days after its passing the second reading. The request shall be made in writing and signed by the Members making it. Provided that there shall be no such postponement in connection with Finance Bills, Supplementary Appropriation Bills, Provisional Appropriation Bills, Government Loan Bills, Naturalization Bills, Expropriation Bills, Indirect Taxation Bills, and, in emergencies, Bills the enactment of which cannot be postponed owing to the intent of the Act.

(4) In the case of a new election and at the end of the sessional year all Bills and other measures which have not been finally passed, shall be dropped.

42. (1) Where a Bill has been passed by the Folketing, one-third of the Members of the Folketing may within three week-days from the final passing of the Bill request of the President that the Bill be subjected to a Referendum. Such request shall be made in writing and signed by the Members making the request.

(2) Except in the instance mentioned in subsection 7, no Bill which may be subjected to a Referendum, confer subsection (6), shall receive the Royal Assent before the expiration of the time limit mentioned in subsection (1), or before a Referendum requested as aforesaid has taken place.

(3) Where a Referendum on a Bill has been requested the Folketing may within a period of five week-days from the final passing of the Bill resolve that the Bill shall be withdrawn.

(4) Where the Folketing has made no resolution in ac-

cordance with subsection (3), notice to the effect that the Bill will be put to a Referendum shall without delay be given to the Prime Minister, who shall then cause the Bill to be published together with a statement that a Referendum will be held. The Referendum shall be held in accordance with the decision of the Prime Minister not less than twelve and not more than eighteen week-days after the publication of the Bill.

(5) At the Referendum votes shall be case for or against the Bill. For the Bill to be rejected a majority of the electors taking part in the voting, however, not less than thirty per centum of all persons entitled to vote, shall have voted against the Bill.

(6) Finance Bills, Supplementary Appropriation Bills, Provisional Appropriation Bills, Government Loan Bills, Civil Servants (Amendment) Bills, Salaries and Pensions Bills, Naturalization Bills, Expropriation Bills, Taxation (Direct and Indirect) Bills, as well as Bills introduced for the purpose of discharging existing treaty obligations shall not be subject to a decision by Referendum. This provision shall also apply to the Bills referred to in sections 8, 9, 10, and 11, and to such resolutions as are provided for in section 19, if existing in the form of a law, unless it has been provided by a special Act that such resolutions shall be put to a Referendum. Amendments of the Constitution Act shall be governed by the rules laid down in section 88.

(7) In an emergency a Bill that may be subjected to a Referendum may receive the Royal Assent immediately after it has been passed, provided that the Bill contains a provision to that effect. Where under the rules of subsection (1) one-third of the Members of the Folketing request a Referendum on the Bill or on the Act to which the Royal Assent has been given, such Referendum shall be held in accordance with the above rules. Where the Act is rejected by the Referendum, an announcement to that effect shall be made by the Prime Minister without undue delay and not later than fourteen days after the Referendum was held. From the date of such announcement the Act shall become ineffective.

(8) Rules for Referenda, including the extent to which Referenda shall be held on the Faeroe Islands and in Greenland, shall be laid down by Statute.

43. No taxes shall be imposed, altered, or repealed except by Statute; nor shall any man be conscripted or any public

loan be raised except by Statute.

44. (1) No alien shall be naturalized except by Statute.

(2) The extent of the right of aliens to become owners of real property shall be laid down by Statute.

45. (1) A Finance Bill for the next financial year shall be laid before the Folketing not later than four months before the beginning of such financial year.

(2) Where it is expected that the reading of the Finance Bill for the next financial year will not be completed before the commencement of that financial year, a Provisional Appropriation Bill shall be laid before the Folketing.

46. (1) Taxes shall not be levied before the Finance Act or a Provisional Appropriation Act has been passed by the Folketing.

(2) No expenditure shall be defrayed unless provided for by the Finance Act passed by the Folketing, or by a Supplementary Appropriation Act, or by a Provisional Appropriation Act passed by the Folketing.

47. (1) The ·Public Accounts shall be submitted to the Folketing not later than six months after the expiration of the financial year.

(2) The Folketing shall elect a number of Auditors. Such Auditors shall examine the annual Public Accounts and see that all the revenues of the State have been duly entered therein, and that no expenditure has been defrayed unless provided for by the Finance Act or some other Appropriation Act. The Auditors shall be entitled to demand all necessary information, and shall have a right of access to all necessary documents. Rules providing for the number of Auditors and their duties shall be laid down by Statute.

(3) The Public Accounts together with the Auditors' Report shall be submitted to the Folketing for its decision.

48. The Folketing shall lay down its own Rules of Porcedure, including the rules governing its conduct of business and the maintenance of order.

49. The sittings of the Folketing shall be public. Provided that the President, or such number of Members as may be provided for by the Rules of Procedure, or a Minister shall be entitled to demand the removal of all unauthorized persons, whereupon it shall be decided without a debate whether the matter shall be debated at a public or a secret sitting.

50. In order to make a decision more than one-half of the

Members of the Folketing shall be present and take part in the voting.

51. The Folketing may appoint committees from among its Members to investigate matters of general importance. Such committees shall be entitled to demand written or oral information both from private citizens and from public authorities.

52. The election by the Folketing of Members to sit on committees and of Members to perform special duties shall be according to proportional representation.

53. With the consent of the Folketing any Member thereof may submit for discussion any matter of public interest and request a statement thereon from the Ministers.

54. Petitions may be submitted to the Folketing only through one of its Members.

55. By Statute shall be provided for the appointment by the Folketing of one or two persons, who shall not be Members of the Folketing, to control the civil and military administration of the State.

56. The Members of the Folketing shall be bound solely by their own consciences and not by any directions given by their electors.

57. No Member of the Folketing shall be prosecuted or imprisoned in any manner whatsoever without the consent of the Folketing, unless he is caught in flagrante delicto. Outside the Folketing no Member shall be held liable for his utterances in the Folketing save by the consent of the Folketing.

58. The Members of the Folketing shall be paid such remuneration as may be provided for in the Elections Act.

Part VI.

59. (1) The High Court of the Realm shall consist of up to fifteen of the eldest—according to seniority of office—ordinary members of the highest court of justice of the Realm, and an equal number of members elected for six years by the Folketing according to proportional representation. One or more substitutes shall be elected for each elected member. No Member of the Folketing shall be elected a member of the High Court of the Realm, nor shall a Member of the Folketing act as a member of the High Court of the Realm. Where in a particular instance some of the members of the highest court of justice of the Realm are prevented from taking part

in the trial of a case, an equal number of the members of the High Court of the Realm last elected by the Folketing shall retire from their seats.

(2) The High Court of the Realm shall elect a president from among its members.

(3) Where a case has been brought before the High Court of the Realm, the members elected by the Folketing shall retain their seats in the High Court of the Realm for the duration of such case, even if the period for which they were elected has expired.

(4) Rules for the High Court of the Realm shall be provided by Statute.

60. (1) The High Court of the Realm shall try such actions as may be brought by the King or the Folketing against Ministers.

(2) With the consent of the Folketing the King may cause to be tried before the High Court of the Realm also other persons for crimes which he may deem to be particularly dangerous to the State.

61. The exercise of the judiciary power shall be governed only by Statute. Extraordinary courts of justice with judicial power shall not be established.

62. The administration of justice shall always remain independent of the executive power. Rules to this effect shall be laid down by Statute.

63. (1) The courts of justice shall be entitled to decide any question bearing upon the scope of the authority of the executive power. However, a person who wants to query such authority shall not, by bringing the case before the courts of justice, avoid temporary compliance with orders given by the executive power.

(2) Questions bearing upon the scope of the authority of the executive power may be referred by Statute for decision to one or more administrative courts. Provided that an appeal from the decision of the administrative courts shall lie to the highest court of the Realm. Rules governing this procedure shall be laid down by Statute.

64. In the performance of their duties the judges shall be directed solely by the law. Judges shall not be dismissed except by judgment, nor shall they be transferred against their will, except in instances where a rearrangement of the courts of justice is made. However, a judge who has completed his

sixty-fifth year may be retired, but without loss of income up to the time he is due for retirement on account of age.

65. (1) In the administration of justice all proceedings shall be public and oral to the widest possible extent.

(2) Laymen shall take part in criminal procedure. The cases and the form in which such participation shall take place, including what cases are to be tried by jury, shall be provided for by Statute.

Part VII.

66. The constitution of the Established Church shall be laid down by Statute.

67. The citizens shall be entitled to form congregations for the worship of God in a manner consistent with their convictions, provided that nothing at variance with good morals or public order shall be taught or done.

68. No one shall be liable to make personal contributions to any denomination other than the one to which he adheres.

69. Rules for religious bodies dissenting from the Established Church shall be laid down by Statute.

70. No person shall for reasons of his creed or descent be deprived of access to complete enjoyment of his civic and political rights, nor shall he for such reasons evade compliance with any common civic duty.

Part VIII.

71. (1) Personal liberty shall be inviolable. No Danish subject shall in any manner whatever be deprived of his liberty because of his political or religious convictions or because of his descent.

(2) A person shall be deprived of his liberty only where this is warranted by law.

(3) Any person who is taken into custody shall be brought before a judge within twenty-four hours. Where the person taken into custody cannot be released immediately, the judge shall decide, stating the grounds in an order to be given as soon as possible and at the latest within three days, whether the person taken into custody shall be committed to prison, and in cases where he can be released on bail, the judge shall determine the nature and amount of such bail. This provi-

sion may be departed from by Statute as far as Greenland is concerned, if for local considerations such departure may be deemed necessary.

(4) The finding given by the judge may at once be separately appealed against by the person concerned to a higher court of justice.

(5) No person shall be remanded for an offense that can involve only punishment consisting of a fine or mitigated imprisonment (haefte).

(6) Outside criminal procedure the legality of deprivation of liberty which is not by order of a judicial authority, and which is not warranted by the legislation dealing with aliens, shall at the request of the person who has been deprived of his liberty, or at the request of any person acting on his behalf, be brought before the ordinary courts of justice or other judicial authority for decision. Rules governing this procedure shall be provided by Statute.

(7) The persons mentioned in subsection (6) shall be under supervision by a board set up by the Folketing, to which board the persons concerned shall be permitted to apply.

72. The dwelling shall be inviolable. House searching, seizure, and examination of letters and other papers as well as any breach of the secrecy to be observed in postal telegraph, and telephone matters shall take place only under a judicial order unless particular exception is warranted by Statute.

73. (1) The right of property shall be inviolable. No person shall be ordered to cede his property except where required by the public weal. It can be done only as provided by Statute and against full compensation.

(2) Where a Bill relating to the expropriation of property has been passed, one-third of the Members of the Folketing may within three week-days from the final passing of such Bill, demand that it shall not be presented for the Royal Assent until new elections to the Folketing have been held and the Bill has again been passed by the Folketing assembling thereupon.

(3) Any question of the legality of an act of expropriation and the amount of compensation may be brought before the courts of justice. The hearing of issues relating to the amount of the compensation may by Statute be referred to courts of justice established for such purpose.

74. Any restraint of the free and equal access to trade which

is not based on the public weal, shall be abolished by Statute.

75. (1) In order to advance the public weal efforts shall be made to afford work to every able-bodied citizen on terms that will secure his existence.

(2) Any person unable to support himself or his dependents shall, where no other person is responsible for his or their maintenance, be entitled to receive public assistance, provided that he shall comply with the obligations imposed by Statute in such respect.

76. All children of school age shall be entitled to free instruction in the elementary schools. Parents or guardians who themselves arrange for their children or wards receiving instruction equal to the general elementary school standard, shall not be obliged to have their children or wards taught in an elementary school.

77. Any person shall be entitled to publish his thoughts in printing, in writing, and in speech, provided that he may be held answerable in a court of justice. Censorship and other preventive measures shall never again be introduced.

78. (1) The citizens shall be entitled without previous permission to form associations for any lawful purpose.

(2) Associations employing violence, or aiming at attaining their object by violence, by instigation to violence, or by similar punishable influence on people of other views, shall be dissolved by judgment.

(3) No association shall be dissolved by any government measure. However, an association may be temporarily prohibited, provided that proceedings be immediately taken against it for its dissolution.

(4) Cases relating to the dissolution of political associations may without special permission be brought before the highest court of justice of the Realm.

(5) The legal effects of the dissolution shall be determined by Statute.

79. The citizens shall without previous permission be entitled to assemble unarmed. The police shall be entitled to be present at public meetings. Open-air meetings may be prohibited when it is feared that they may constitute a danger to the public peace.

80. In case of riots the armed forces, unless attacked, may take action only after the crowd in the name of the King and the Law has three times been called upon to disperse, and such

warning has been unheeded.

81. Every male person able to carry arms shall be liable with his person to contribute to the defense of his country under such rules as are laid down by Statute.

82. The right of the municipalities to manage their own affairs independently under the supervision of the State shall be laid down by Statute.

83. All privileges by legislation attached to nobility, title, and rank shall be abolished.

84. In future no fiefs, estates tail in land or estates tail in personal property shall be created.

85. The provisions of sections 71, 78, and 79 shall only by applicable to the defense forces subject to such limitations as are consequential to the provisions of military laws.

Part IX.

86. The age qualification for local government electors and congregational council electors shall be that applying at any time to Folketing electors. With reference to the Faeroe Islands and Greenland the age qualification for local government electors and congregational council electors shall be such as may be provided for by Statute or fixed in accordance with Statute.

87. Citizens of Iceland who enjoy equal rights with citizens of Denmark under the Danish-Icelandic Union (Abolition), etc. Act, shall continue to enjoy the rights attached to Danish citizenship under the provisions of the Constitution Act.

Part X.

88. When the Folketing passes a Bill for the purposes of a new constitutional provision, and the Government wishes to proceed with the matter, writs shall be issued for the election of Members of a new Folketing. If the Bill is passed unamended by the Folketing assembling after the election, the Bill shall within six months after its final passing be submitted to the Electors for approval or rejection by direct voting. Rules for this voting shall be laid down by Statute. If a majority of the persons taking part in the voting, and at least 40 per centum of the Electorate has voted in favor of the Bill as passed by the Folketing, and if the Bill receives the Royal Assent it shall form an integral part of the Constitution Act.

Part XI.

89. This Constitution Act shall come into operation at once. Provided that the *Rigsdag* last elected under the Constitution of the Kingdom of Denmark Act, 5th June, 1915, as amended on the 10th September, 1920, shall continue to exist until a general election has been held in accordance with the rules laid down in Part IV. Until a general election has been held the provisions laid down for the *Rigsdag* in the Constitution of the Kingdom of Denmark Act, 5th June, 1915, as amended on the 10th September, 1920, shall remain in force.

THE SUCCESSION TO THE THRONE ACT

1. The Throne shall be inherited by the descendants of King Christian X and Queen Alexandrine.

2. On the demise of a King the Throne shall pass to his son or daughter so that a son shall take precedence of a daughter, and where there are several children of the same sex the eldest child shall take precedence of a younger child.

Where one of the King's children has died the issue of the deceased shall take his place in accordance with the lineal descent and the rules laid down in subsection I.

3. On the demise of a King who has left no issue entitled to succeed to the Throne, the Throne shall pass to his brother or sister with preference for the brother. Where the King has one or more brothers or one or more sisters, or where any of his brothers or sisters have died, the rules of section 2 shall apply correspondingly.

4. Where there is no person entitled to succeed to the Throne under the rules of sections 2 and 3, the Throne shall pass to the then nearest collateral line of the descendants of King Christian X and Queen Alexandrine in accordance with the lineal descent, and with preference correspondingly for men over women, and for the elder over the younger as laid down in sections 2 and 3.

5. Only children born of lawful marriage shall be entitled to succeed to the Throne.

The King shall not enter into marriage without the consent of the *Rigsdag*.

Where a person entitled to succeed to the Throne enters

into marriage without the consent of the King given in the Council of State, the person in question shall forfeit his right of succession to the Throne for himself and the children born of the marriage and for their issue.

6. The provisions of sections 2-5 shall apply correspondingly in the case of the abdication of a King.

7. This Act shall come into operation at the same time as the Constitution of the Kingdom of Denmark Act, 5th June, 1953.

INDEX*

A

B

202777